Flowers of the West Wales Coast

ABOUT THE BOOK

This book is an absolute delight, and a timely reminder of what a brilliant naturalist, writer and photographer Mike Alexander was.

– Iolo Williams, naturalist and TV presenter

What a wonderful production! Here is a book that can be an expert companion in the real world, or a delightful friend if you are an armchair botanist. It is a real pleasure to relive the excitement of plant-hunting in these wonderful parts of Wales.

– Goronwy Wynne, author of *Blodau Cymru*

This book is a delightful invitation to share the company of the author along the coastline of west Wales... and to enjoy with him the wildflowers of its clifftops, dunes and shorelines and the islands that lie beguilingly offshore. This is Mike Alexander's *cynefin* (or place he belongs), and it is a tribute to his photographic skills and the charm of his writing that we too can feel we have seen the sights he wishes to share with us.

– John Rodwell, Editor of *British Plant Communities*

Flowers of the West Wales Coast

Mike Alexander

y lolfa

First impression: 2026

The publishers wish to acknowledge the support of the Books Council of Wales.

Cover design: Mike Alexander
Cover images and all other images: Mike Alexander (© Rosanne Alexander)
Front cover: Red campion on Skomer (looking across South Haven)
Back cover: Thrift and sea campion on Skomer
(looking across South Haven towards the warden's house), 1980s.
Design: Richard Huw Pritchard

ISBN: 978-1-80099-720-2

Y Lolfa Cyf., Talybont, Ceredigion SY24 5HE

e-mail ylolfa@ylolfa.com
website www.ylolfa.com
tel 01970 832 304

Contents

Y BLODAU
HEDD WYN

Mae blodau'r maes yn codi
Yn wyn ac aur i'r nen,
A pheraroglau'r awel
Yn siglo trwy'r gwenith gwyn.
Mae'r rhosyn yn y dyffryn
Yn agor yn ei fri,
A glaw man haf yn pefrio
Fel deigryn ar ei lli.

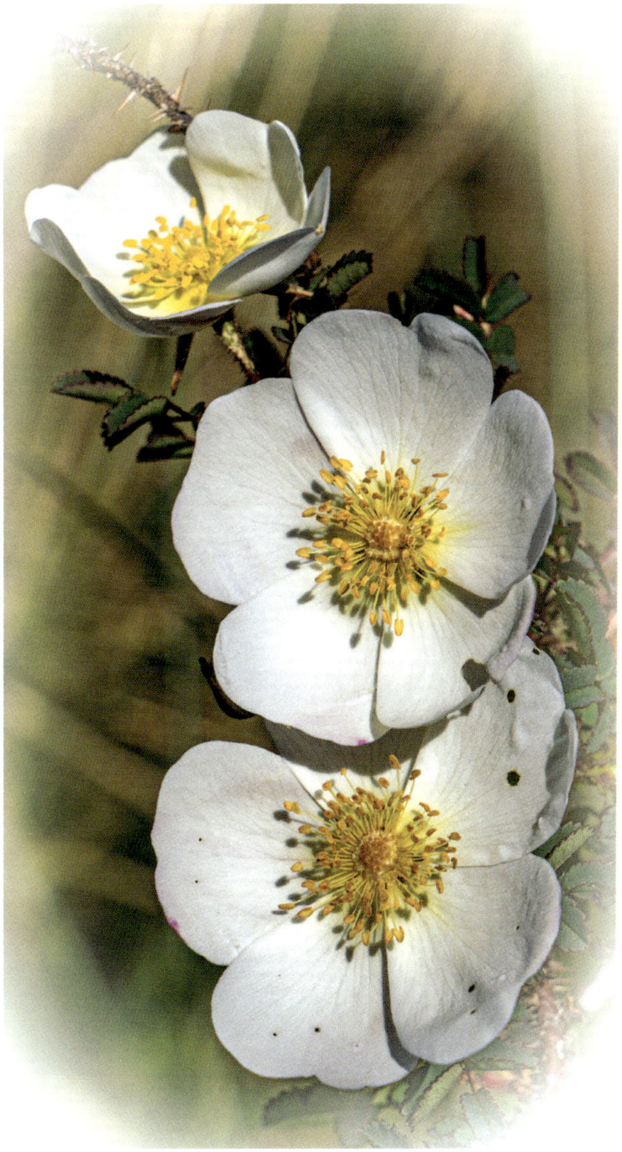

THE FLOWERS
HEDD WYN

The flowers of the field rise,
In white and gold to the sky,
And the fragrance of the breeze
Sways through the golden wheat.
The rose in the valley
Unfolds in its pride,
And the fine summer rain glistens
Like a tear upon its hue.

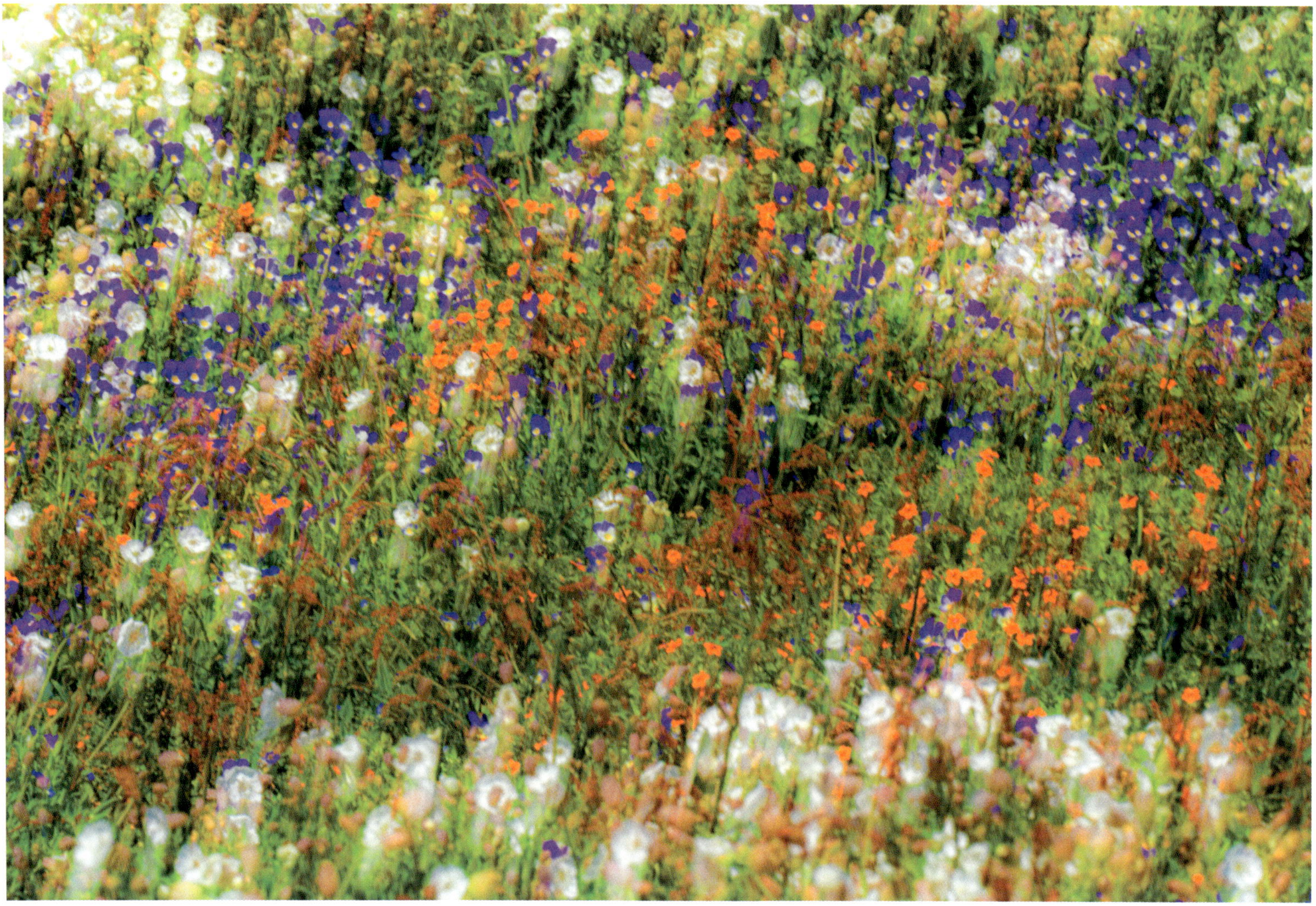

Foreword

by Professor John Rodwell, Editor of *British Plant Communities*

This book is a delightful invitation to share the company of the author along the coastline of west Wales, and to enjoy with him the wildflowers of its clifftops, dunes and shorelines and the islands that lie beguilingly offshore. This is Mike Alexander's *cynefin*, or place he belongs, and it is a tribute to his photographic skills and the charm of his writing that we too can feel we have seen the sights he wishes to share with us. The generosity of his experience from early childhood, through his wardenship of Skomer and his long career caring for the landscape and nature of Wales left him with a deep love of the distinctive flora of the coast and the stories the plants have to tell. And here those stories can be ours.

The language of this book is not scientific and the author is not concerned first and foremost with the fine detail of plant names and classification: sometimes he tells us the best approach is to enjoy the spectacle of their flowering, their fruiting or their colourful foliage. This is a book for the casual or inexperienced observer, not just for the knowledgeable enthusiast. It is sure to nourish in anyone a love of plants and the places where they can be found. It is an invitation to celebrate their diversity and the contribution that they go on making to landscapes that we know are changing, not always for the best.

His selection of plants is a personal one – those whose flowers went on delighting him in the beauty of their colour and form, their peculiarities close up, or the drama they present when growing en masse. We see them in landscapes that are sometimes spectacular coastal panoramas, in other cases intimate lane-sides. Quite often he has a tale of childhood to tell, when his walks to school, games with friends, moments of family or farming life have left with him – and now with us – indelible memories that can go on delighting. Sights from the past, smells brought to mind, sweet or bitter tastes remembered on the tongue; all these give depth to what he has to say.

The accounts of the plants and the wonderful photographs tell us where we should look for them and give key features we can watch out for. The text is also frequently enriched with details of mythology, folklore and ways in which the plants have been used for food or medicines. Or they give us warnings about irritable prickles and even deadly poisonous potency. Look out, then! And just look: stop awhile, look down as well as up and around, and see what the west Wales coast continues to show us, to enlighten us and make us happy.

There are some environmental professionals who have little hinterland behind their workaday front. Mike Alexander was not one of them and here we see something of the inner passion that nourished his life and the many ways in which he helped sustain the Welsh landscape and its nature. In the words of one of the many writers and poets he quotes, he shares with us here a pageant which unfolds itself in scene-pictures that succeed each other in a stately procession.

Bluebells and red campion on Skomer

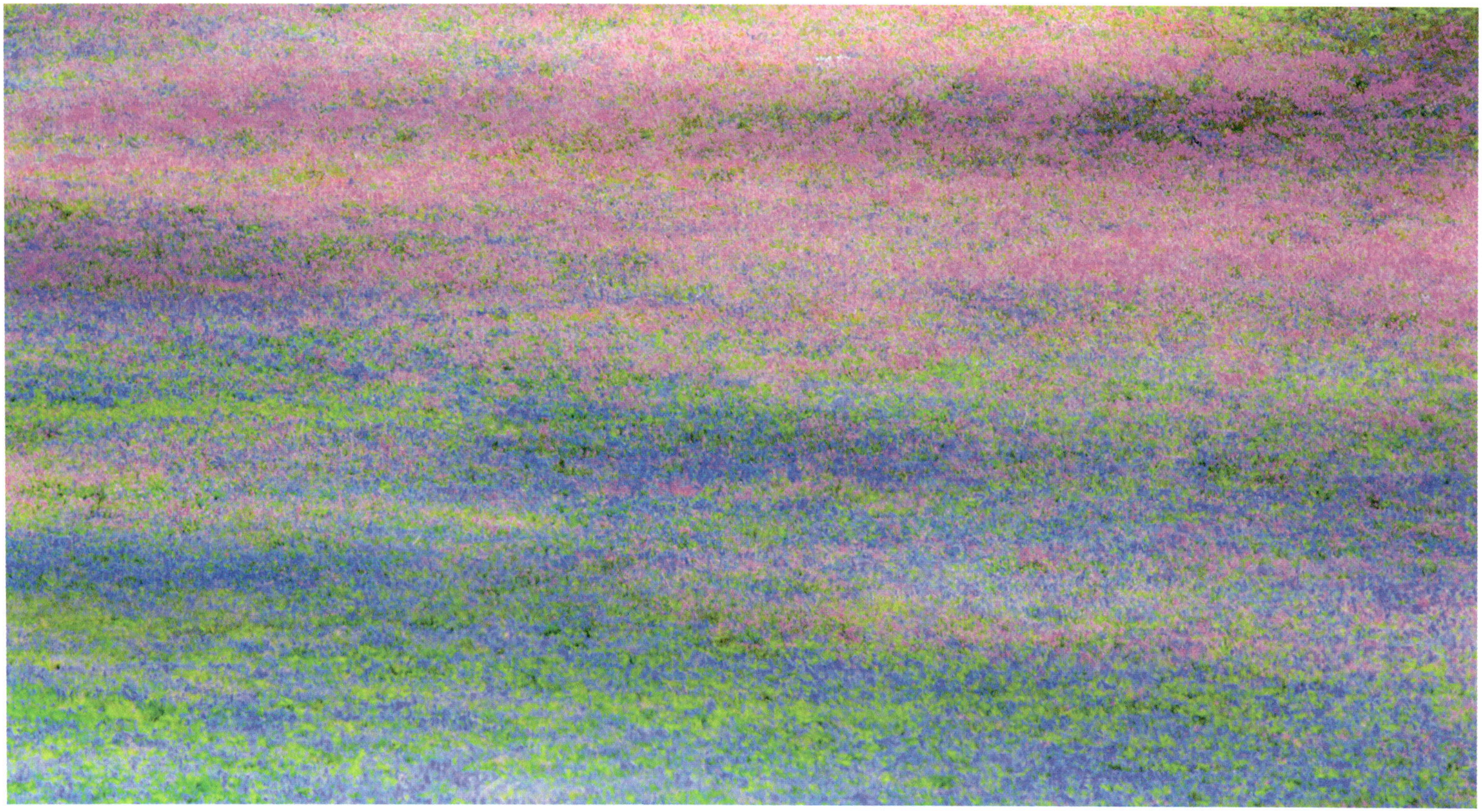

Introduction

'Earth laughs in flowers.' Ralph Waldo Emerson wrote this simple but profound line in his poem of 1846, 'Hamatreya: Earth Song'. It captures the spirit of nature's beauty and reminds us of the joy and happiness that flowers can bring to our lives. My earliest memories of this experience are from the 1950s, deep in the Ceredigion countryside, where we lived at Trawscoed and then Abermagwr, in the Ystwyth Valley. I started school a couple of months before my fourth birthday, because my friend next door was two months older, and our parents decided that we should start school together. It seems impossible today, but the school was a two-mile walk away, with the 'big' children (10-year-olds) responsible for the infants on a journey along country lanes that took us through woodlands and fields. Three things dominate my memory. The first was the fear of y *bwci bo*. My friend Rhiannon was insistent that, whatever they might be, they definitely lurked in the woods, waiting for us. The second, happier, memory is of the gorgeous flowering rhododendrons that lined our route, and the third is of the delicate blue harebells which were so common in the hedges. I don't remember much about my days in the infant class, other than the warmth of an open coal fire and the writing slates, with their squeaky pencils, which we used to learn the alphabet. Above all, though, I remember the frequent nature walks, and the time our teacher drew a *lili wen fach* (snowdrop) on the blackboard, using green and white chalk.

As I grew older, I took every possible opportunity to spend time on my Uncle Jeff's farm. He delighted in nature and always shared the names of natural things and their stories. It was my uncle who nurtured that seed first sown in infant school, but it was a teenage experience that confirmed my passion. I was

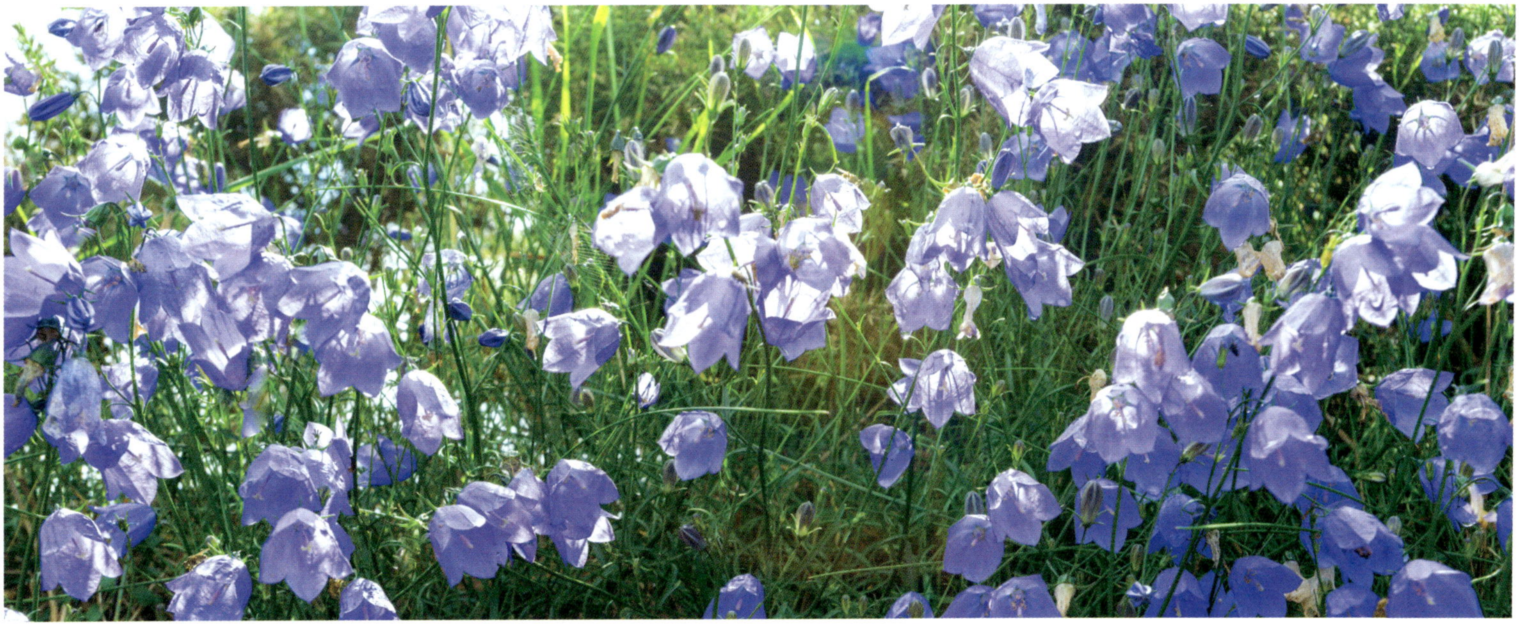

Harebell Clychau'r Eos *Campanula rotundifolia*

a very unwilling pupil at Gwendraeth Grammar School when, in the spring of 1962, five school friends and I were taken on a Saturday school trip to Skomer Island by two teachers: Mr Leslie Jones, who taught zoology, and Mr Allan Griffiths, who taught us chemistry. It is a day that is clearly and indelibly marked in my memory, because it provided the direction for my entire life. I had decided, even before we left Skomer that day, that eventually I was going to become the warden. It took a while, but in 1976 I returned as island warden, with my wife, Rosanne, and spent the best ten years of my life on Skomer.

I am not a botanist, but that has done nothing to diminish my obsession with wildflowers. They have enriched my life and brought so much pleasure that I hope this book may be a way of inspiring others. Through my photographs, I would like to share something of what wildflowers have meant to me. Over the many decades I have spent walking coastal footpaths, I have always noticed how few people glance downwards at the amazing spectacle beneath their feet. Many may look up towards the birds, but most would be unaware of anything more than a few of the commonest plants. The ability to see and understand how the flowers all around us are completely part of a place and its history can make any experience of the countryside more meaningful and rewarding. I am convinced that we will only conserve the things that we value, and if this book can bring people just a little closer to the magnificent wild landscapes around our coasts, it may make some contribution towards protecting them for the future.

In his famous, but melancholy, poem, 'The Flower That Smiles To-day', Shelley wrote about the brevity of all things. It is faintly echoed by the line in the Revd Eli Jenkins' prayer from Dylan Thomas' *Under Milk Wood*, reflecting on 'all poor creatures born to die'. Both focus on an element of the natural life cycle which may seem quite grim, until we remember that at the heart of the cycle is regeneration or renewal. The wonder of flowers is that they renew. Yes, they are 'born to die', and some have the briefest of lives, but many plants will live well beyond our lifetimes, flowering year after year for decades or more. While annual flowers have a short life, the purpose of the flower is to produce seed for the next generation. This, really, is the miracle of flowers: that, in response to the seasons and nature's cycle, they deliver a wonderful, ever-changing kaleidoscope of colour and form. It is these fleeting glimpses, along with the thrill of anticipating the next flowering season, that enhance our experience. Would a field of buttercups be so special if it was there forever? Some of these sentiments are captured in this brief excerpt from Shelley's poem:

> The flower that smiles to-day
> To-morrow dies;
> All that we wish to stay
> Tempts and then flies.
> What is this world's delight?
> Lightning that mocks the night,
> Brief even as bright.

This is not an identification book, but a celebration of wildflowers: a picture book with just enough text to encourage you to go and explore further. There are already many outstanding wildflower guides available, which highlight the defining features of each plant and provide enough detailed information to give you confidence in your identification. There are also some extremely clever plant-identification apps, which will be able to identify everything in this book and more. They are an excellent aid to your initial identification, and certainly speed up the learning process, but they can never be a substitute for a good flower guide, which will give a much better understanding of the plants you are looking at. I will just add one note of caution about using photographs for plant identification: make sure that the crucial identification features, like leaf form and flower structure, are visible. I have failed to do this sometimes, and arrived home to find that I have simply added to my collection of images that will remain forever anonymous.

The most difficult part of compiling this book was deciding which plants to include, and, in the end, I decided that it would have to be a completely personal selection. I began by making lists of the important coastal species, but soon realised that I didn't know what 'important' might mean. I have therefore tried to include the species which typify or define the coastal vegetation, the colourful and spectacular species, and those with an interesting story to tell. There are a few species that I would like to have included, but which didn't prove to be quite photogenic enough.

I have deliberately avoided the scientific or botanical language which would be more relevant to an identification guide. This book is for the casual or inexperienced observer, as well as the committed plant lover, and I want the text to be as widely accessible as possible. I have had to include some words that may not be familiar to readers with absolutely no gardening or botanical experience, but there is a short glossary at the end of the book.

Snowdrops in the rain

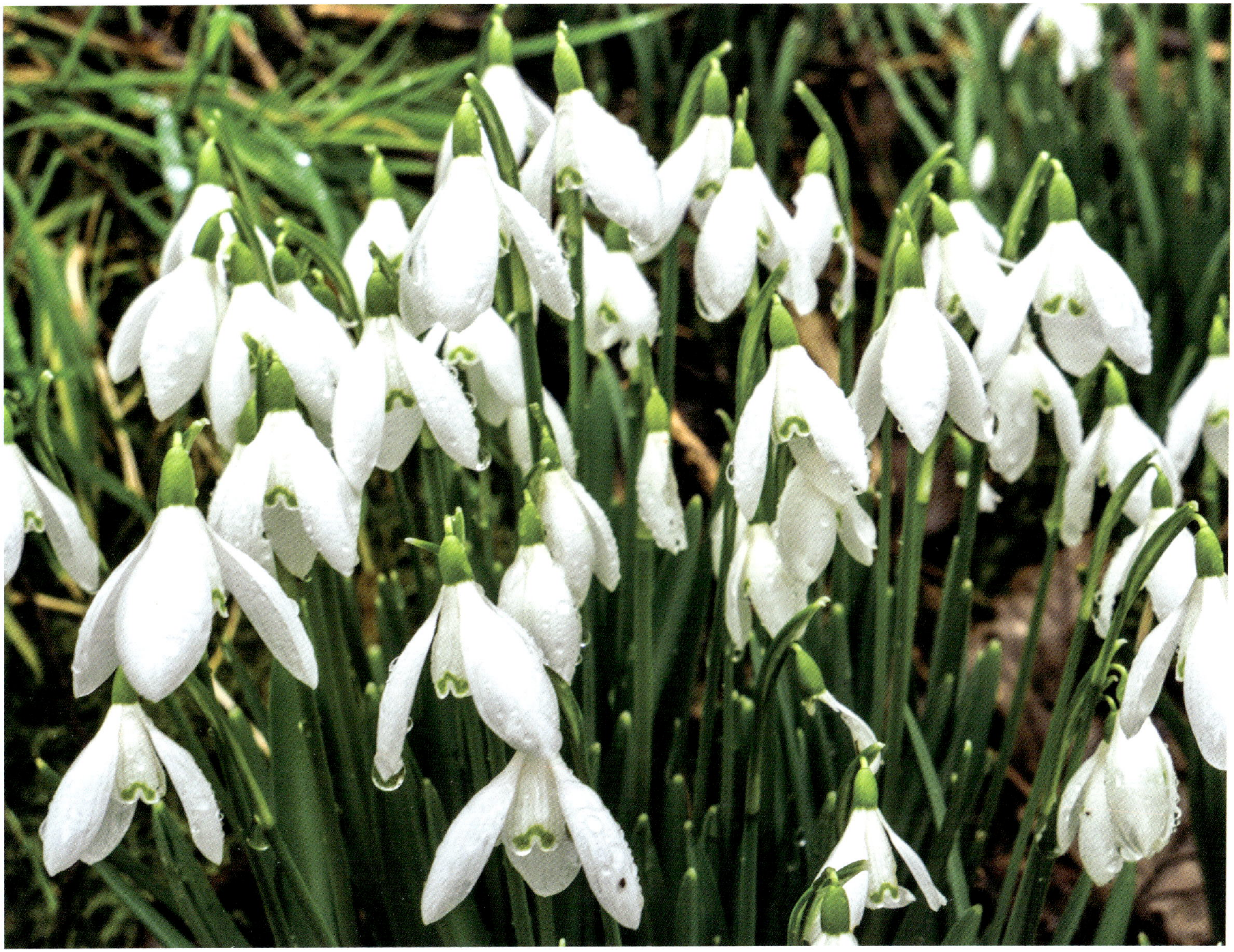

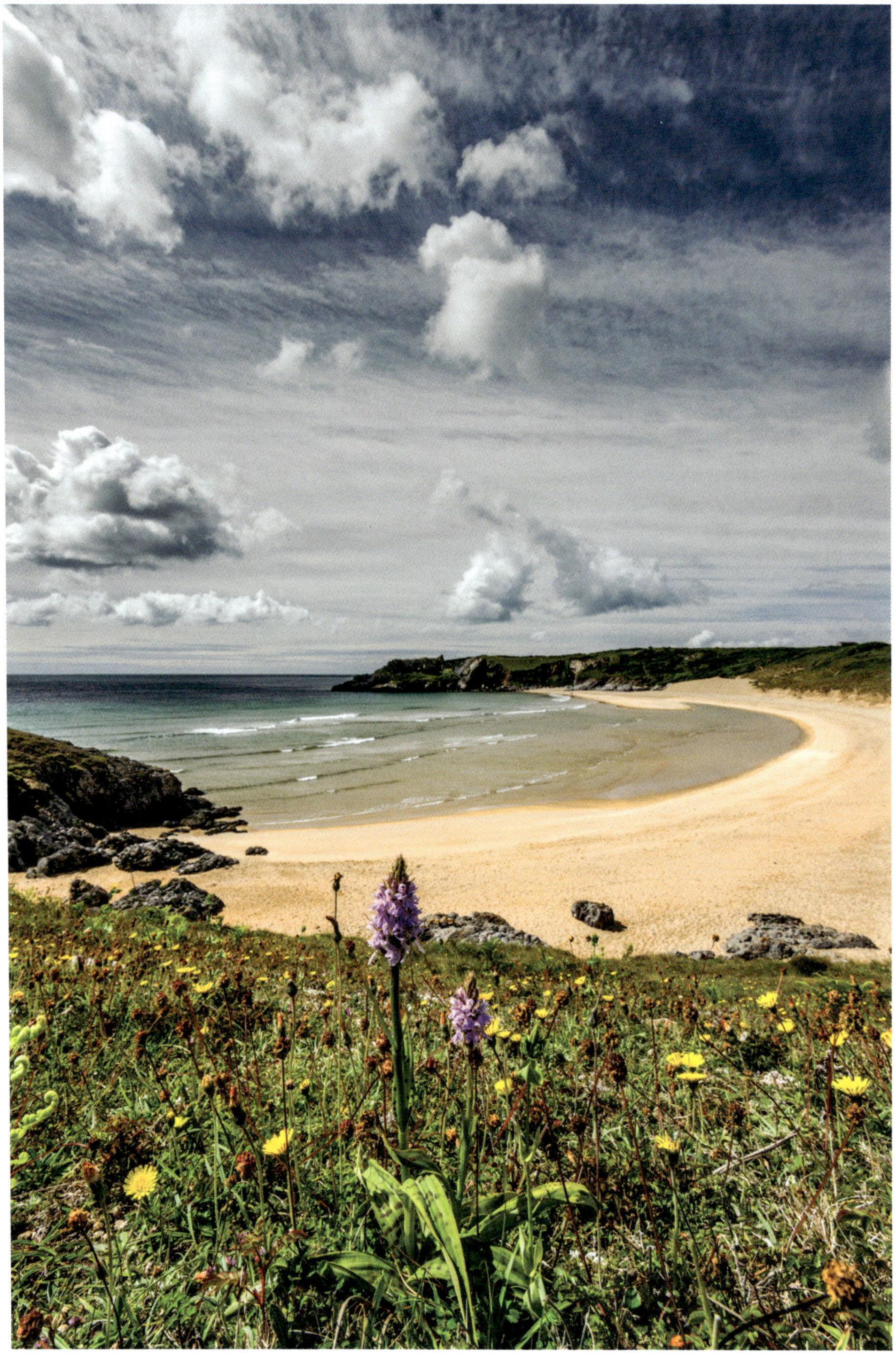

Common Spotted-orchid Tegeirian Brych *Dactylorhiza fuchsii*

The West Wales Coast

The west Wales coast is a glorious panorama of rugged cliffs, extensive sand-dune systems, shingle banks, salt marshes and estuaries: places where, although the human footprint is clearly discernible, nature maintains a powerful influence. Our greatest impact has been the effect of centuries of coastal engineering and land reclamation, offshore dredging, and the construction of breakwaters and other structures. We have also, over the years, introduced a variety of non-native, invasive species, which could easily displace the natural vegetation if left unchecked. Rivers continue to discharge grossly polluted water into the estuaries, seawater temperature is increasing and sea levels are rising. Our very presence is a significant problem, and much of the natural coast must be included among the most threatened habitats in Europe. Despite all this, the coast continues to provide opportunities where some of the most robustly natural habitats can survive. Many have been modified, and the natural plant composition and distribution will have changed, but the surviving species are mostly locally native.

My definition of the west Wales coast includes the coastlines of Pembrokeshire and Cardigan Bay. Ynys Enlli (Bardsey), off the western tip of the Llŷn Peninsula, marks the northern extreme of Cardigan Bay. The low-lying cliffs and sandy beaches of the southern Llŷn Peninsula lead to the stunning Glaslyn and Dwyryd estuaries, through which the vast Eryri (Snowdonia) glaciers once flowed. The coast immediately to the south is dominated by the extensive sand-dune systems of Morfa Harlech and Morfa Dyffryn, with their sweeping views of Eryri and Yr Wyddfa (Snowdon). Further south, the Mawddach, described by William Wordsworth as 'the sublime estuary', is, without doubt, the most beautiful of all Welsh estuaries. It is soon followed to the south by the next great Cardigan Bay estuary, the Dyfi, which includes yet another fine sand-dune system at Ynyslas. The diverse Cardigan Bay sand-dune systems are extremely rich wildflower sites, providing some of the best locations to see coastal flowers, and are wonderful for orchids. Cardigan Bay, with its high cliffs and often secluded beaches and river estuaries, curves gently southward, through Aberystwyth, Aberaeron, New Quay and Llangrannog, to Cardigan Island, where the Teifi Estuary marks the boundary between the Ceredigion and north Pembrokeshire coasts.

The south-western section of Cardigan Bay terminates at St David's Head, with the islands of Ynys Dewi (Ramsey) and the Bishops and Clerks. From Ramsey, the entire sweep of St Brides Bay, south to Skomer Island, is evident. The bay has a mix of rocky cliffs and sandy beaches, with a magnificent shingle ridge at Newgale. The footpaths to the north, flanking Ramsey Sound, and the route south, along the red sandstone cliffs, include some of the best places to enjoy a dazzling display of spring flowers. The hard, volcanic rocks of Skomer Island and the tip of the Marloes Peninsula define the southern extreme of St Brides Bay. From this point, the relatively sheltered St Brides Bay gives way to some of the most extremely exposed Atlantic cliffs and beaches. Skokholm Island lies two miles offshore, sharing the same beautiful old red sandstone as the nearby mainland cliffs. The golden beach at Marloes Sands dominates this section of coast, which eventually leads on to St Ann's Head and the western entrance to the great ria (drowned valley) of Milford Haven. The old red sandstone continues around the eastern mouth of the Haven until it meets the wildest of the Pembrokeshire beaches: Freshwater West and Frainslake Sands. The Castlemartin Peninsula, to the south and east, is a coastline of towering grey limestone cliffs with majestic stacks and arches, and some of the richest coastal grasslands in Wales. This is followed by alternating bands of red sandstone and outcrops of limestone, until they reach the exposed coal measures around Amroth in the east.

Ynys Enlli (Bardsey) from Mynydd Mawr

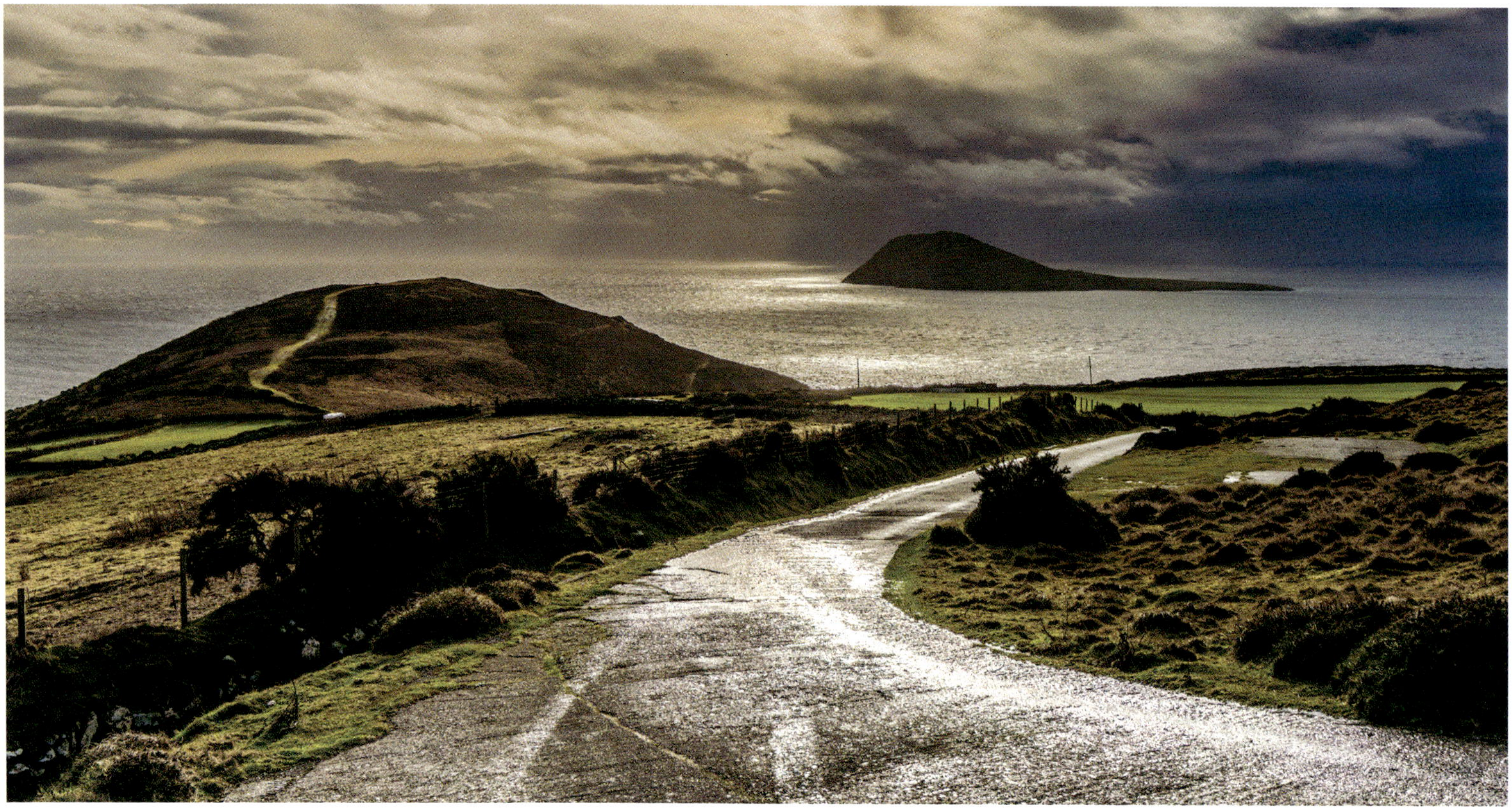

Aberdaron

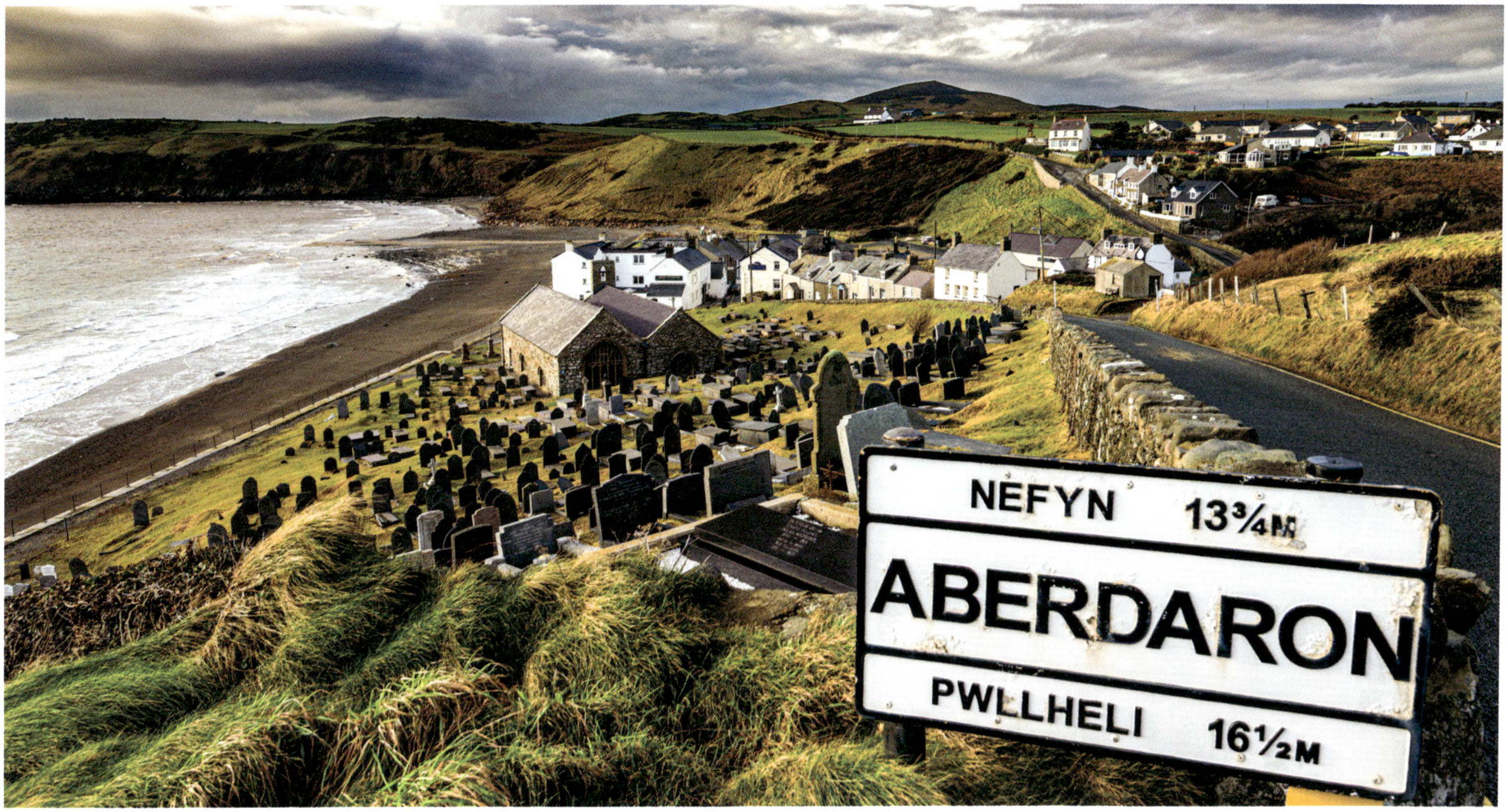

Morfa Harlech

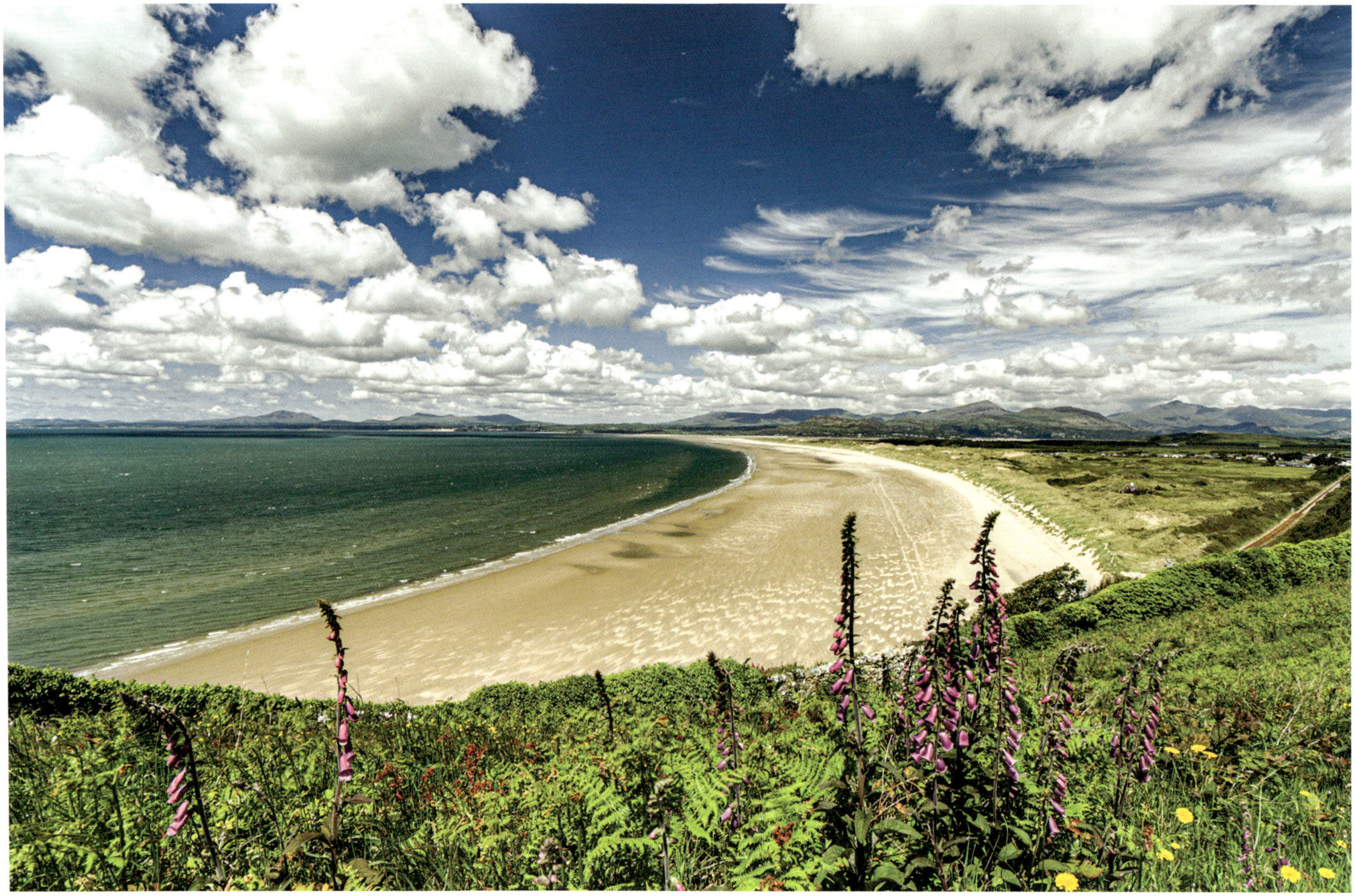

Morfa Mawddach

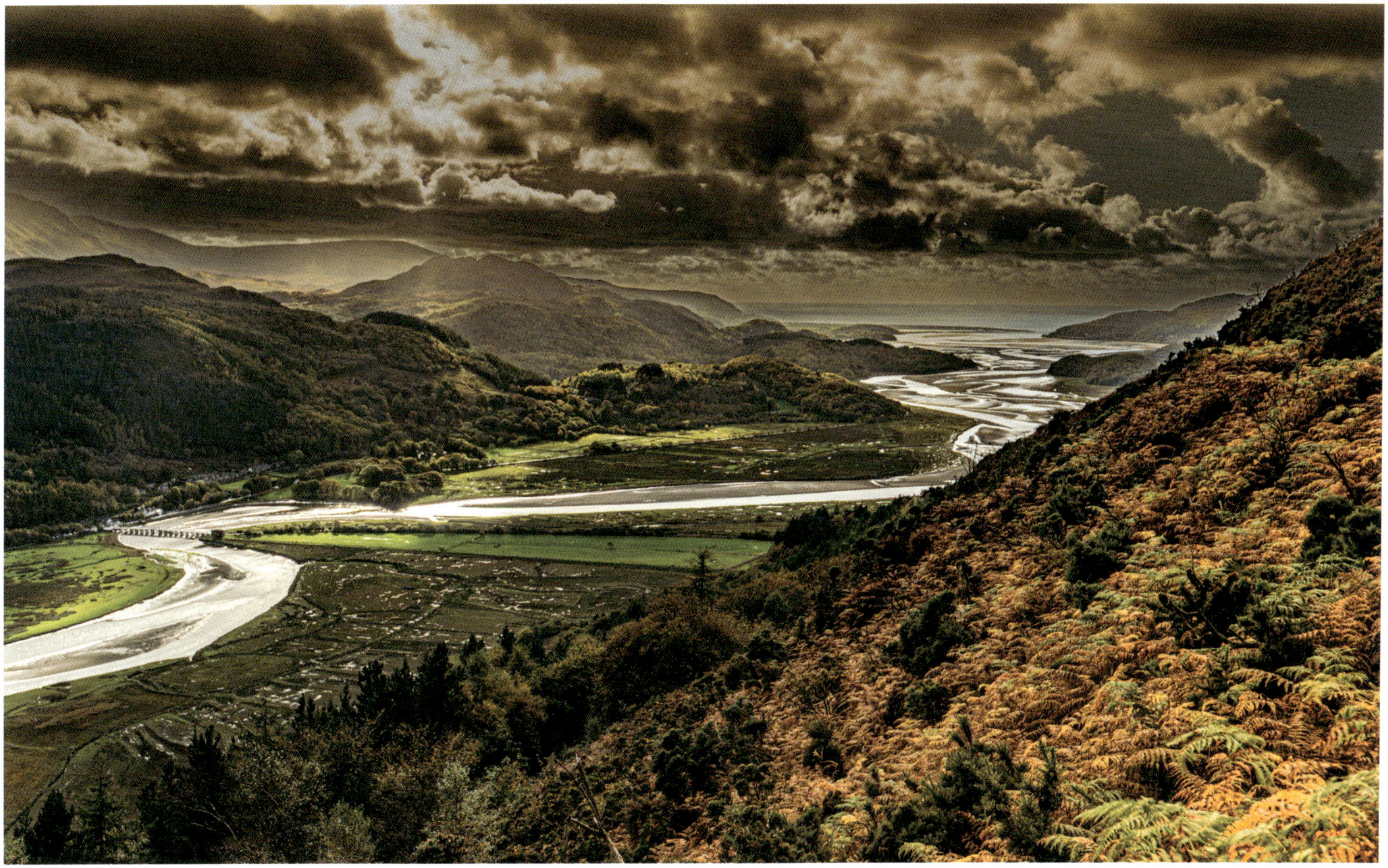

Ynys-las

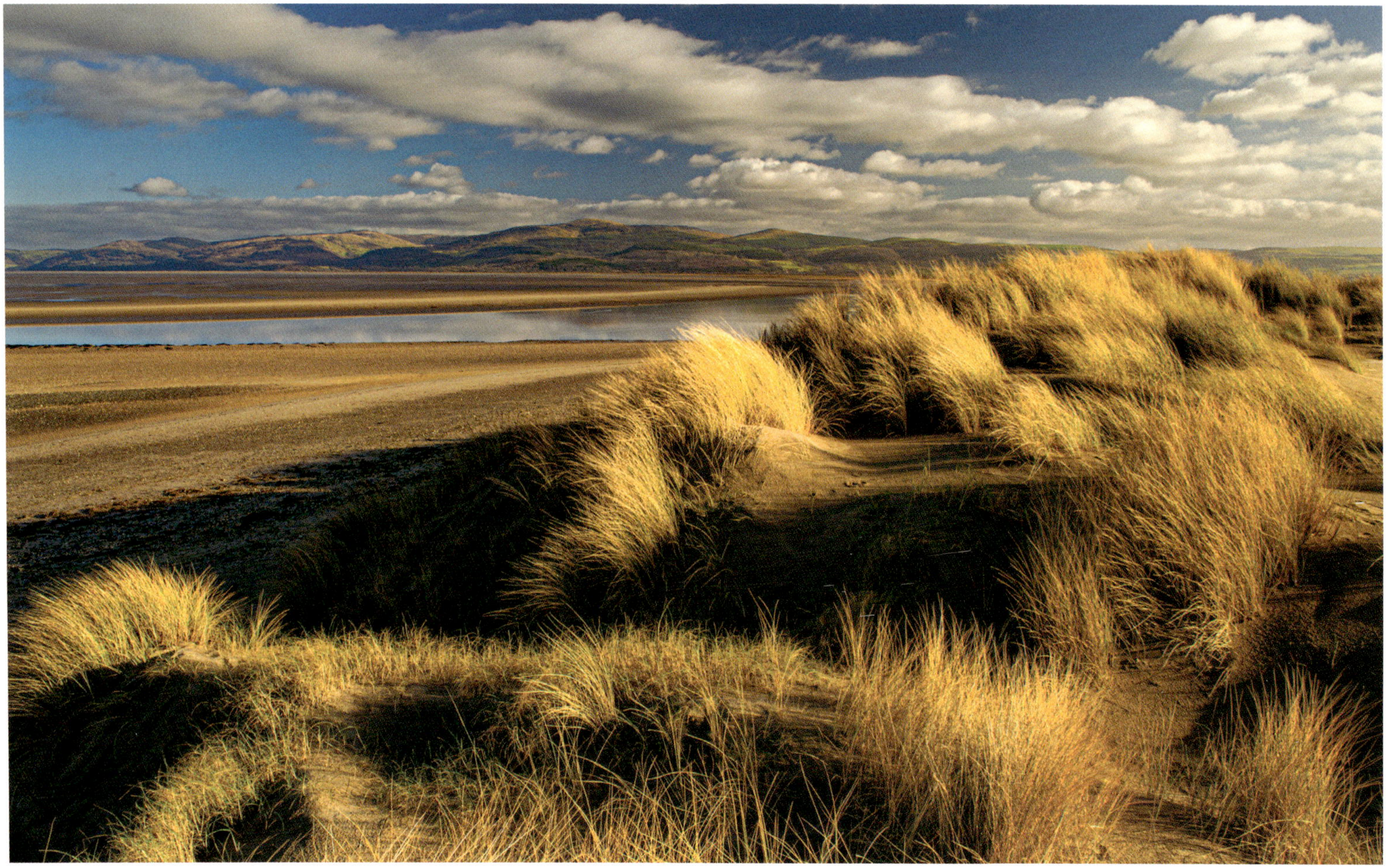

Cribinau, Porthgain

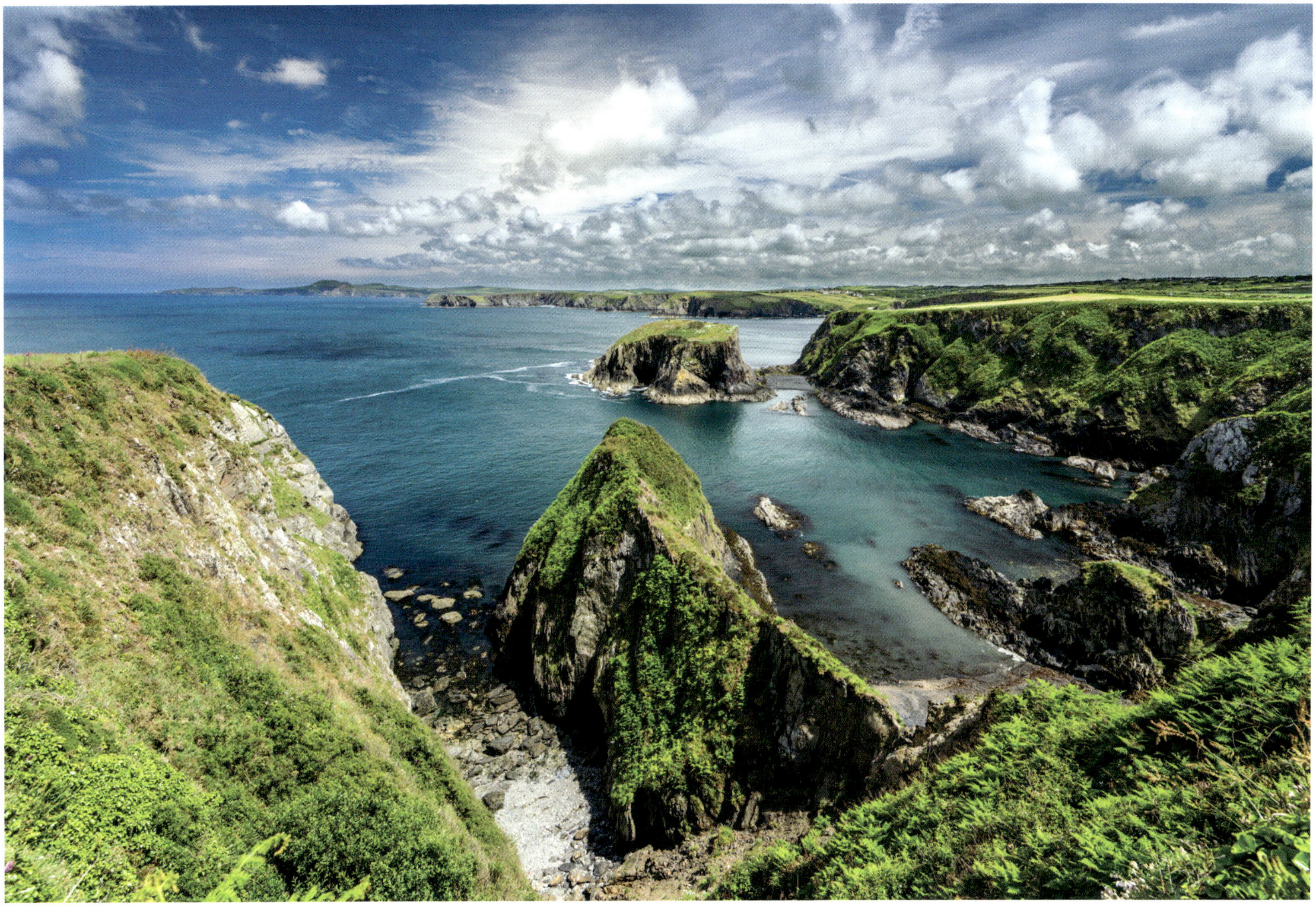

Musselwick

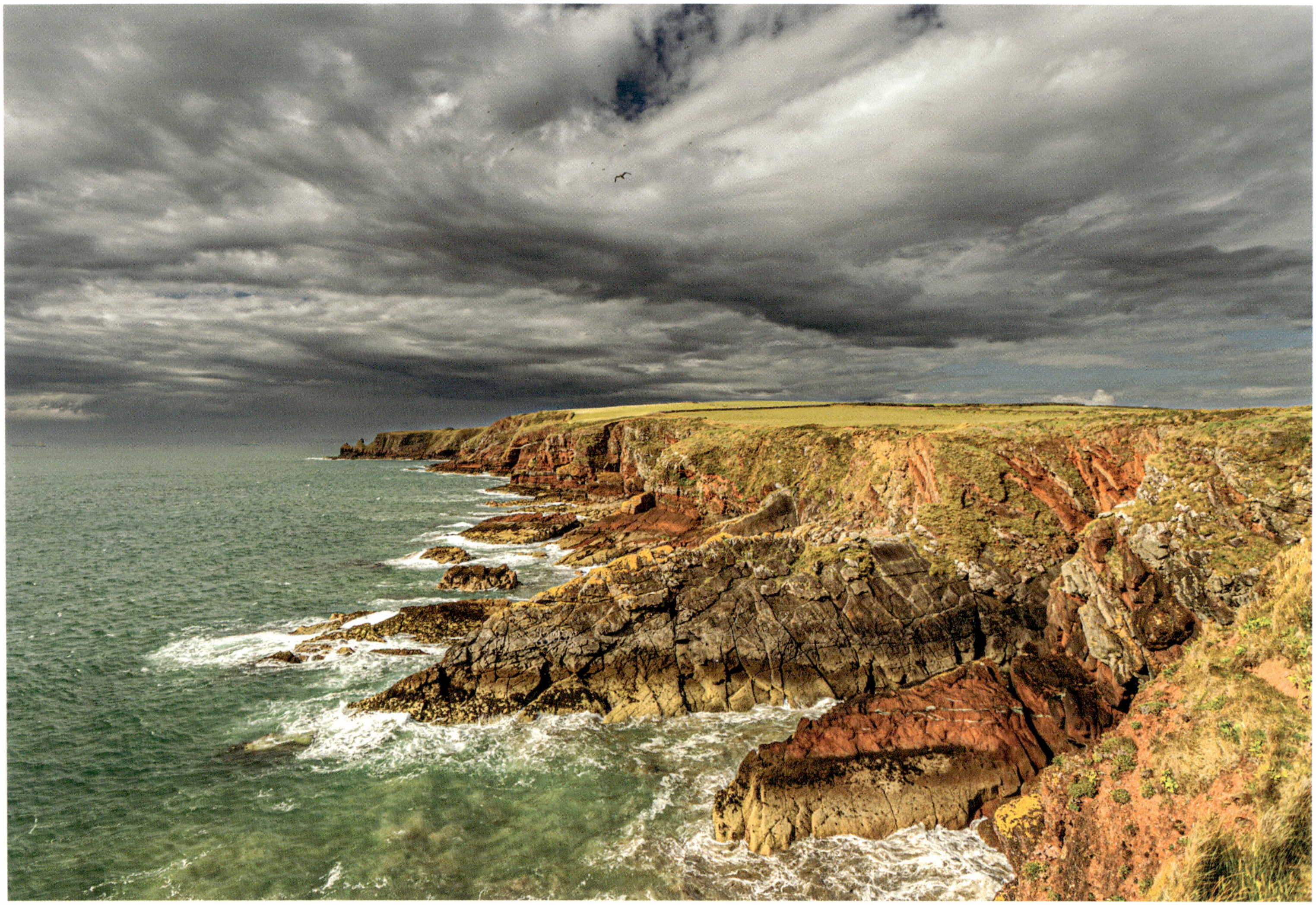

Skomer

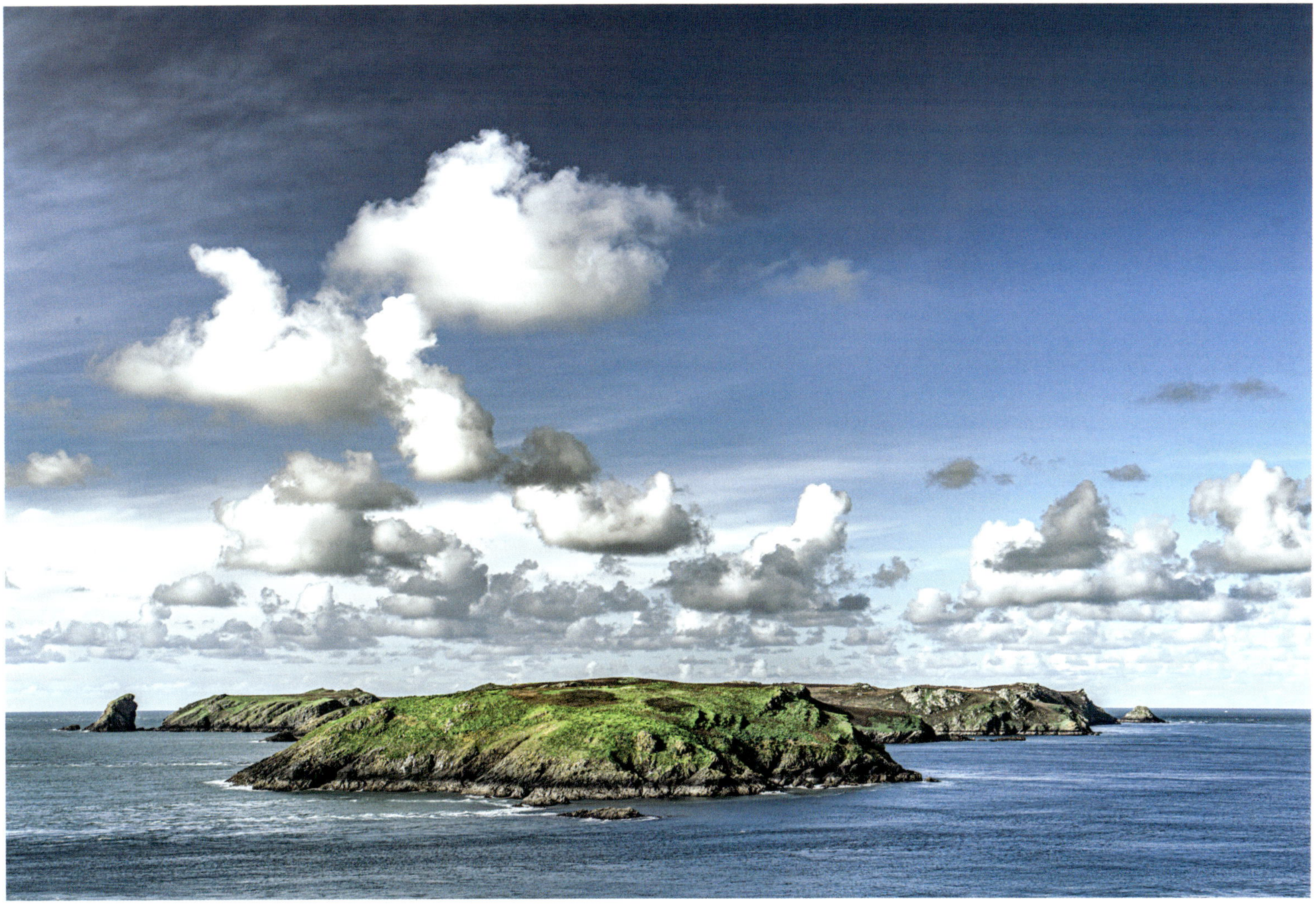

The Wick, Skomer

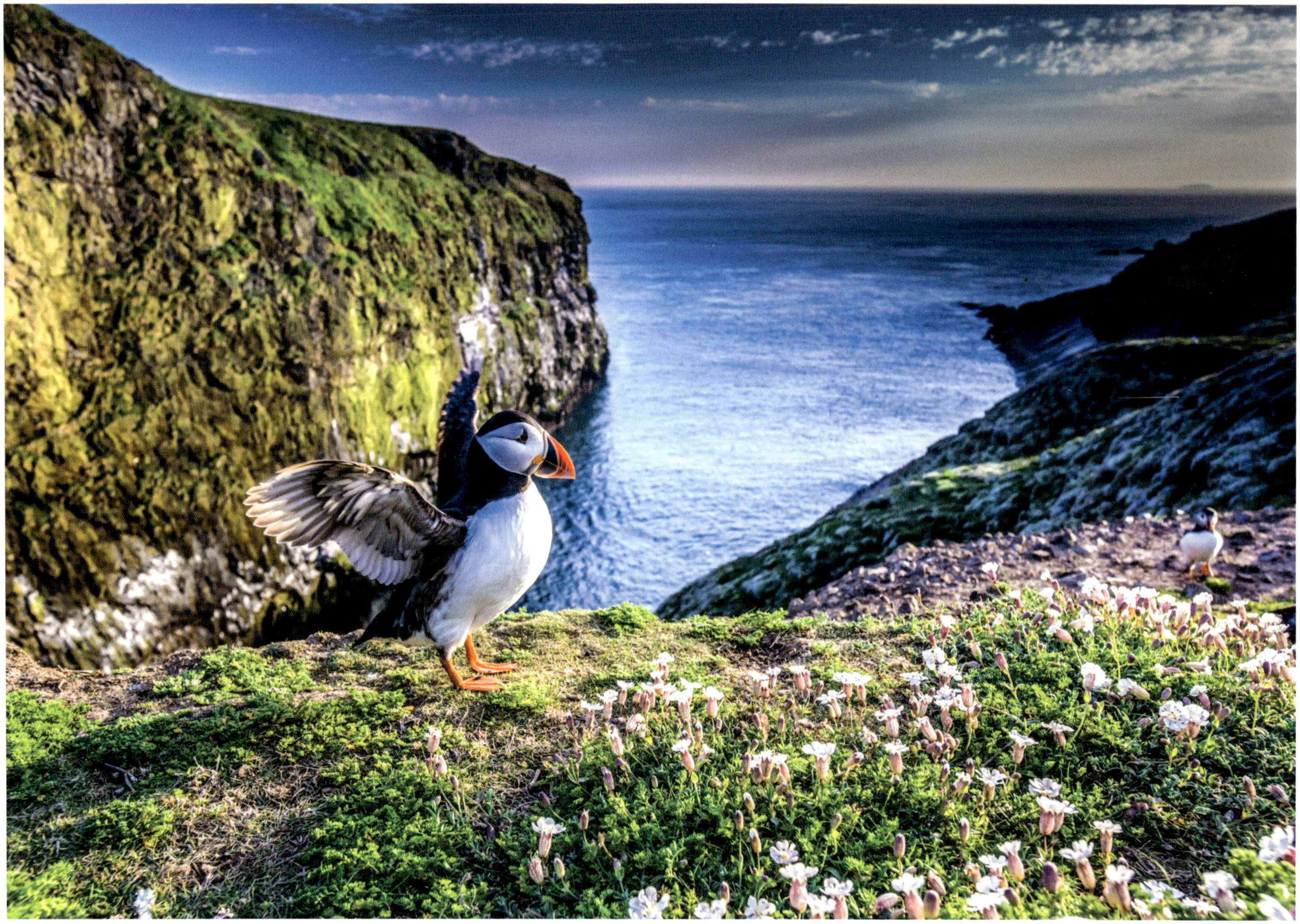

The Green Bridge of Wales, Stack Rocks, Pembrokeshire

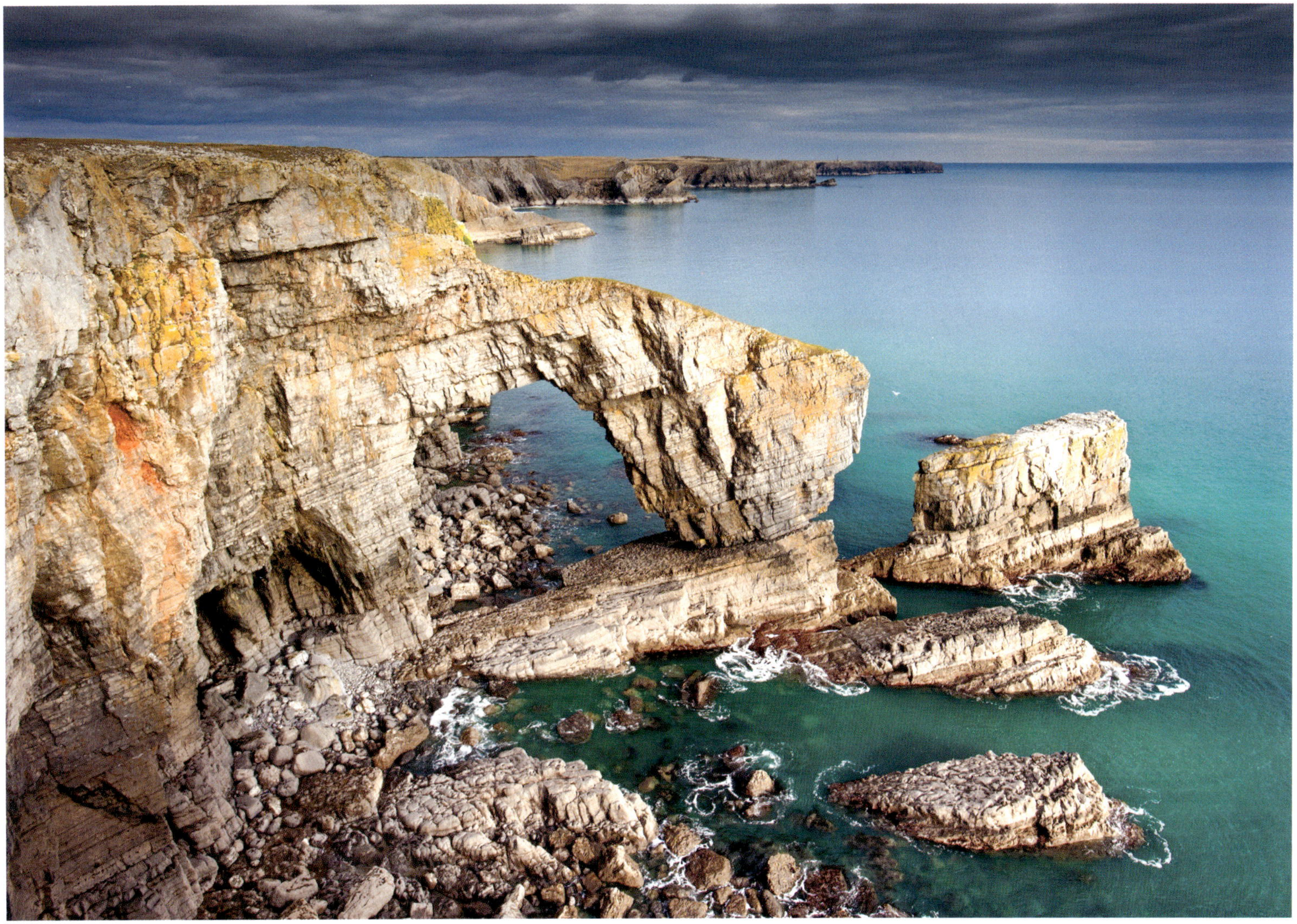

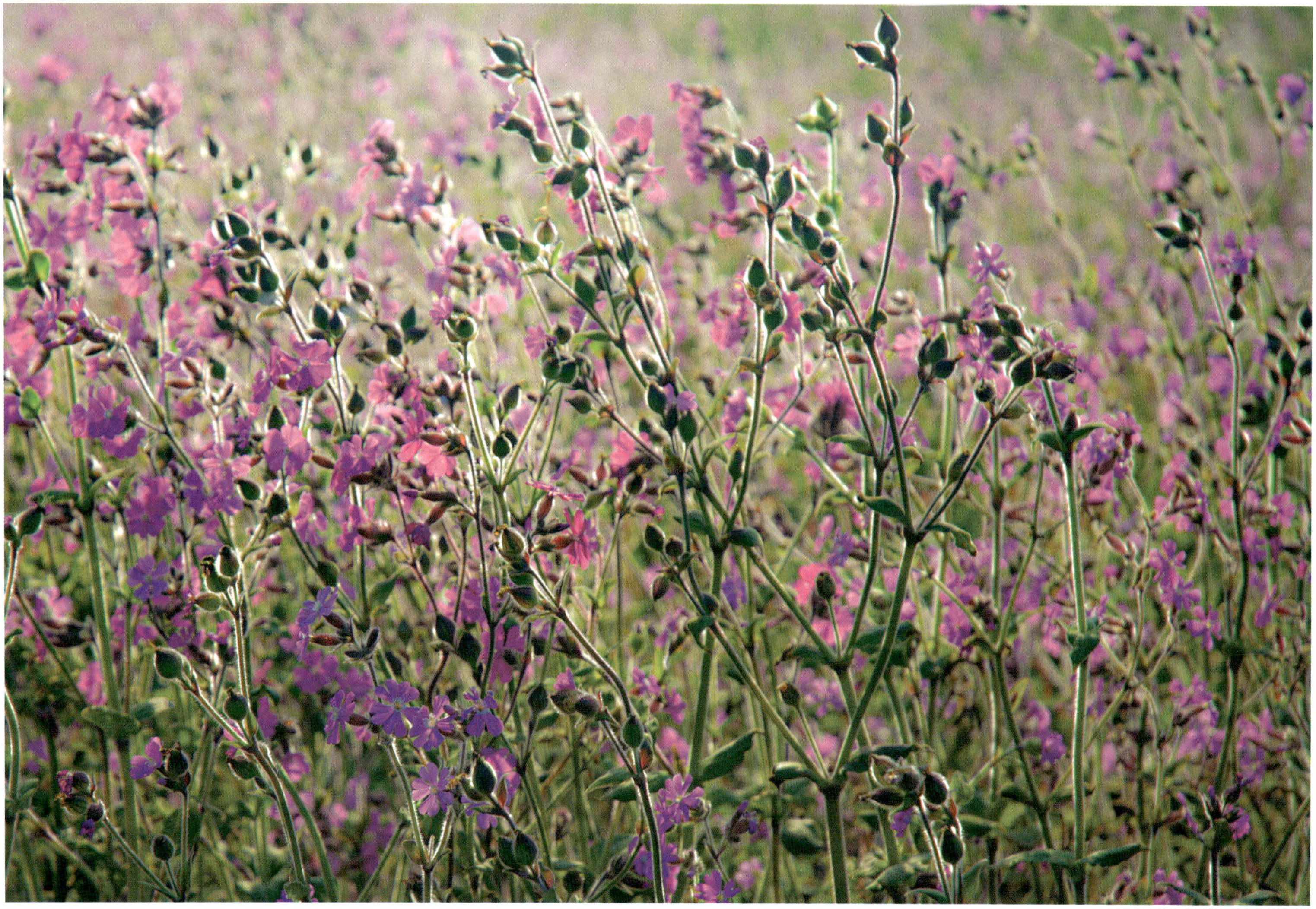

Red Campion Blodyn Neidr *Silene dioica*

The Flowers

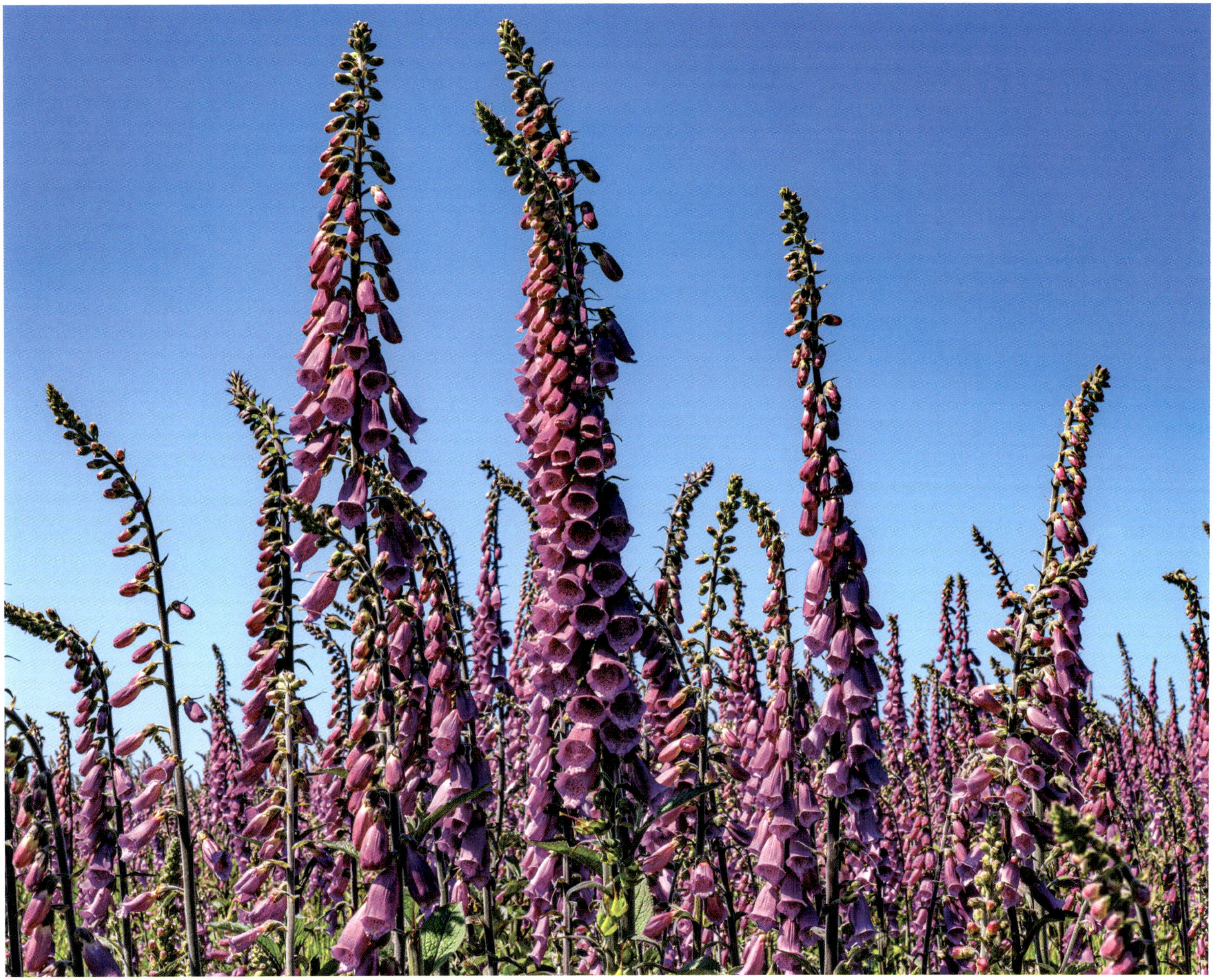

Foxglove Bysedd y Cŵn *Digitalis purpurea*

Buttercup Family Teulu'r Blodyn Ymenyn

I am sure that buttercups need no introduction, as they are such familiar spring and early summer flowers, common in most swards, including parkland, roadside verges and, of course, coastal grassland. The buttercup's family name, *ranunculus*, comes from the Latin word *rana*, meaning frog. This is because many members of the buttercup family grow in wet places, which they share with frogs.

Buttercups are a flower laden with our childhood memories. As children, we would hold a buttercup under a friend's chin and ask, 'Do you like butter?' If there was a yellow reflection on the skin, the answer was 'yes' – although, of course, it was always 'yes' on a sunny day.

For good reasons, buttercups are not popular among farmers. During the first part of the last century, before the advent of excessive agricultural mechanisation, grasslands were often full of buttercups. This was, and continues to be, a problem in grazing pastures, where animals will avoid buttercups because of their strong, bitter taste. The meadow buttercup's specific scientific name is *acris*, which means 'bitter'. This explains why Culpeper, the seventeenth-century English botanist and herbalist, wrote, 'many are the names this furious biting herb hath obtained, almost enough to make up a Welchman's pedigree'.

All parts of the plant are poisonous to people and animals. Fortunately, this is not an issue in hay meadows, as buttercups lose their toxicity when dried in a hay crop. Buttercups also have a damaging impact on soils because they reduce potassium, which inhibits the growth of nutritious and valuable clovers.

There are many species of buttercup on the coasts, but I will focus just on two: one of the more common buttercups and the lesser celandine.

Creeping Buttercup
Blodyn Ymenyn Ymlusgol
Ranunculus repens

Creeping buttercups are the most common of all. They grow almost everywhere in coastal pastures. The photograph was taken alongside the coast footpath a little to the east of St Brides, with Stack Rocks in the distance.

Lesser Celandine
Llygad Ebrill
Ranunculus ficaria

Lesser celandine has shiny-yellow, starlike flowers with eight to twelve petals, which only open in sunshine. In common with other members of the buttercup family, their petals are highly reflective and contrast intensely with the heart-shaped, glossy dark-green leaves. Lesser celandines prefer shady, damp situations, so try looking out for them in sheltered places; hedge-banks are ideal.

They are always one of the first flowers to appear in late winter, and I have often seen them blooming in January, but the flowering season is usually February to May. They really are a cheerful sight on bleak, cold February days. The Welsh name, *llygad Ebrill*, translates as 'April's eye'.

The following lines by William Wordsworth, which give the sense that he really knew and understood these flowers, are taken from his poem, 'The Lesser Celandine':

> There is a Flower, the Lesser Celandine,
> That shrinks, like many more, from cold and rain;
> And, the first moment that the sun may shine,
> Bright as the sun himself, 'tis out again!

Warey Haven, St Brides

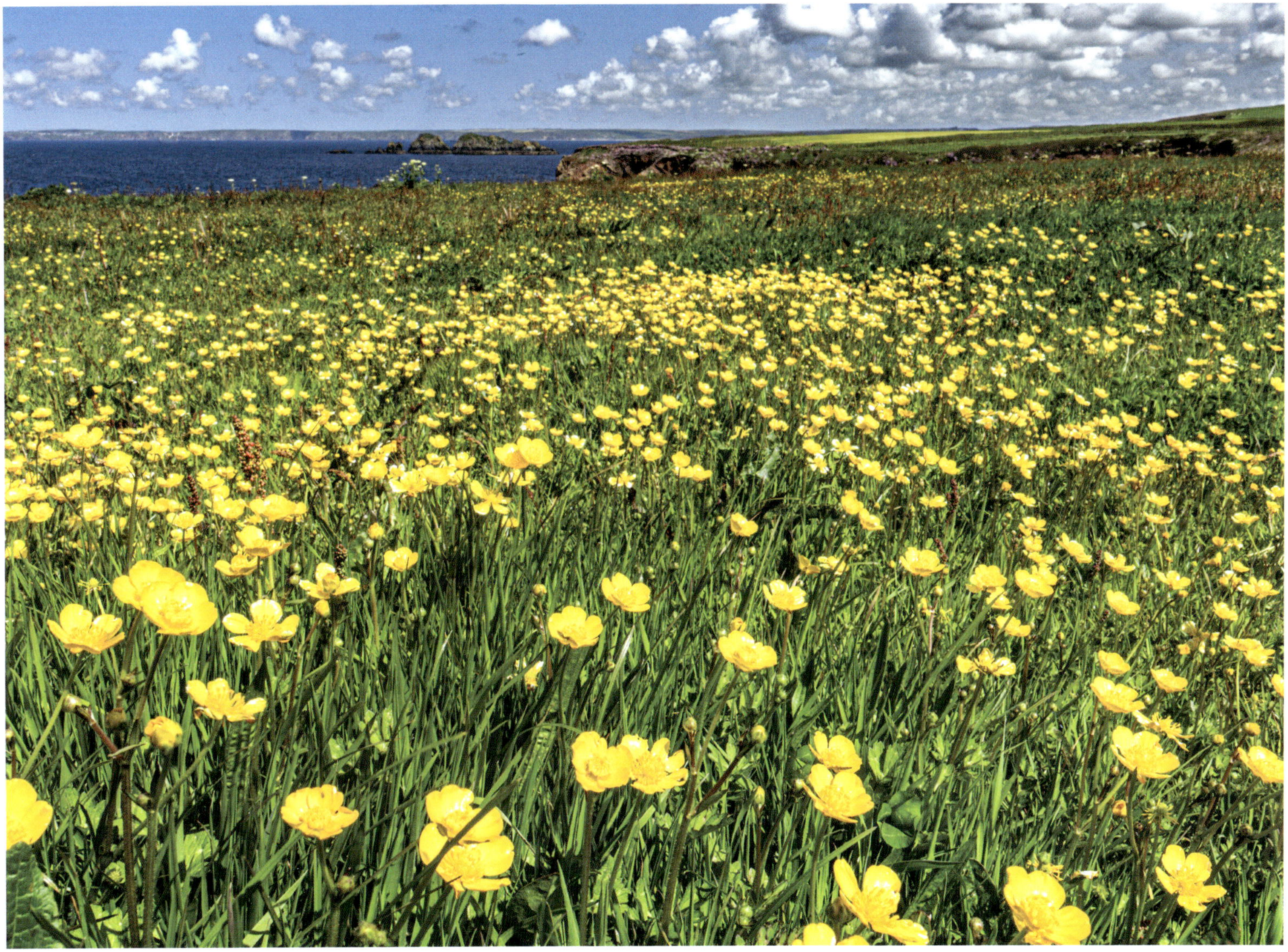

Creeping Buttercup Blodyn Ymenyn Ymlusgol *Ranunculus repens*

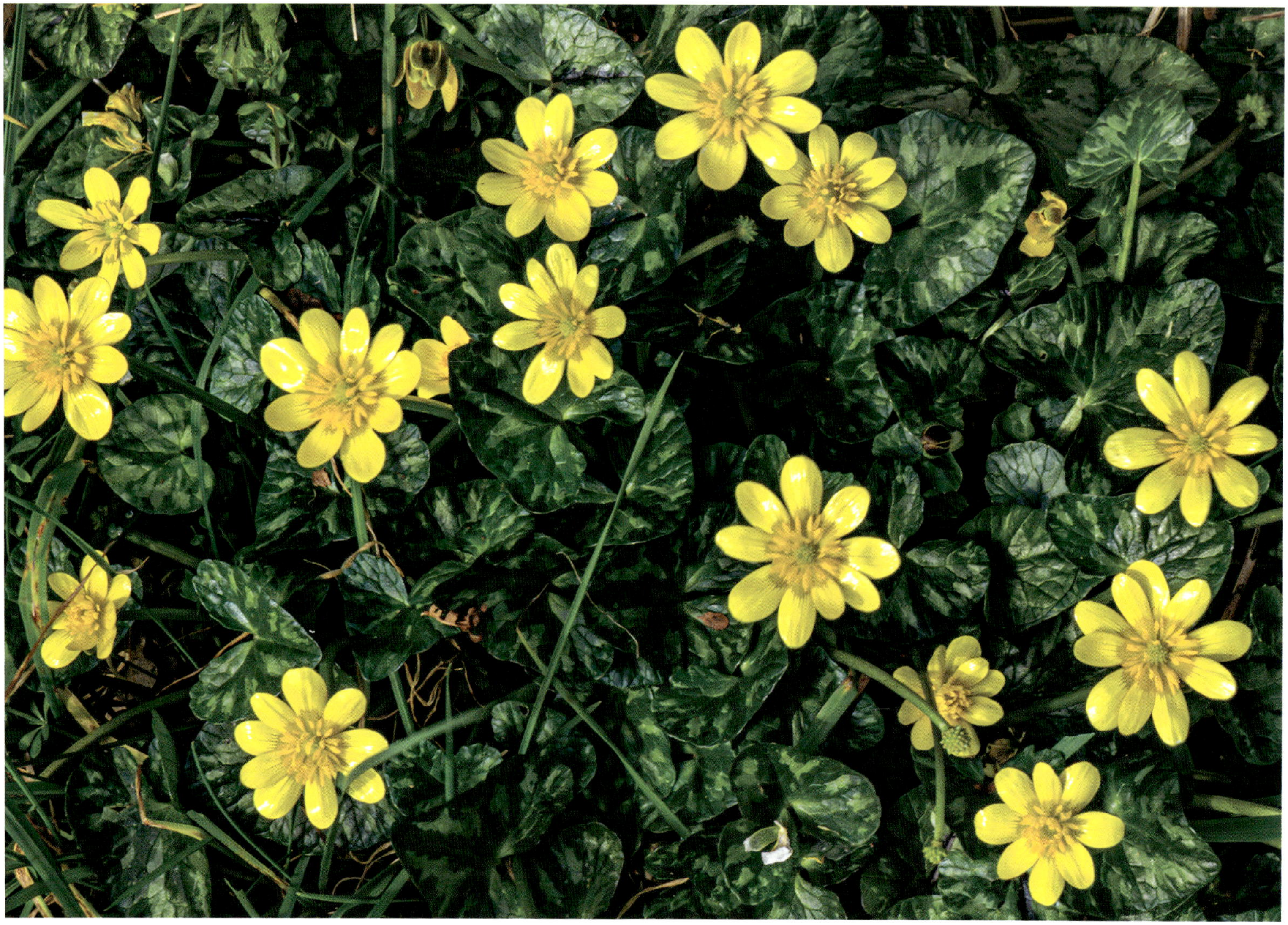

Lesser Celandine Llygad Ebrill *Ranunculus ficaria*

Poppy Family **Teulu'r Pabi**

Yellow Horned-poppy
Pabi Corniog Melyn
Glaucium flavum

Yellow horned-poppies, sometimes known as sea poppies, are easily recognised: they have poppy-like, golden-yellow flowers and long, curved seed capsules. These are the 'horns' which give the plant its name. They can be up to 30 cm in length and are claimed to be the longest seed pod of any British plant. The fleshy, deeply segmented leaves are blue-grey, or glaucous, and covered in white hairs. It is described in many books as a common coastal species, but this is misleading. They are very localised on the Welsh coast and are almost entirely restricted to shingle shores, but they are also content growing on the track ballast of the Cambrian Coast Railway. All parts of the plant are very poisonous and, in common with most toxic species, it has a long history of use as a medicine. It is closely related to the opium poppy but is nowhere near as potent. It does, however, have pain-relieving properties and is used as a remedy for insomnia. In Ancient Greece, it was associated with Morpheus, the god of sleep and dreams. The Greeks believed that the poppy would induce prophetic dreams.

The following poem from 1864 perfectly captures the spirit of this delightful flower.

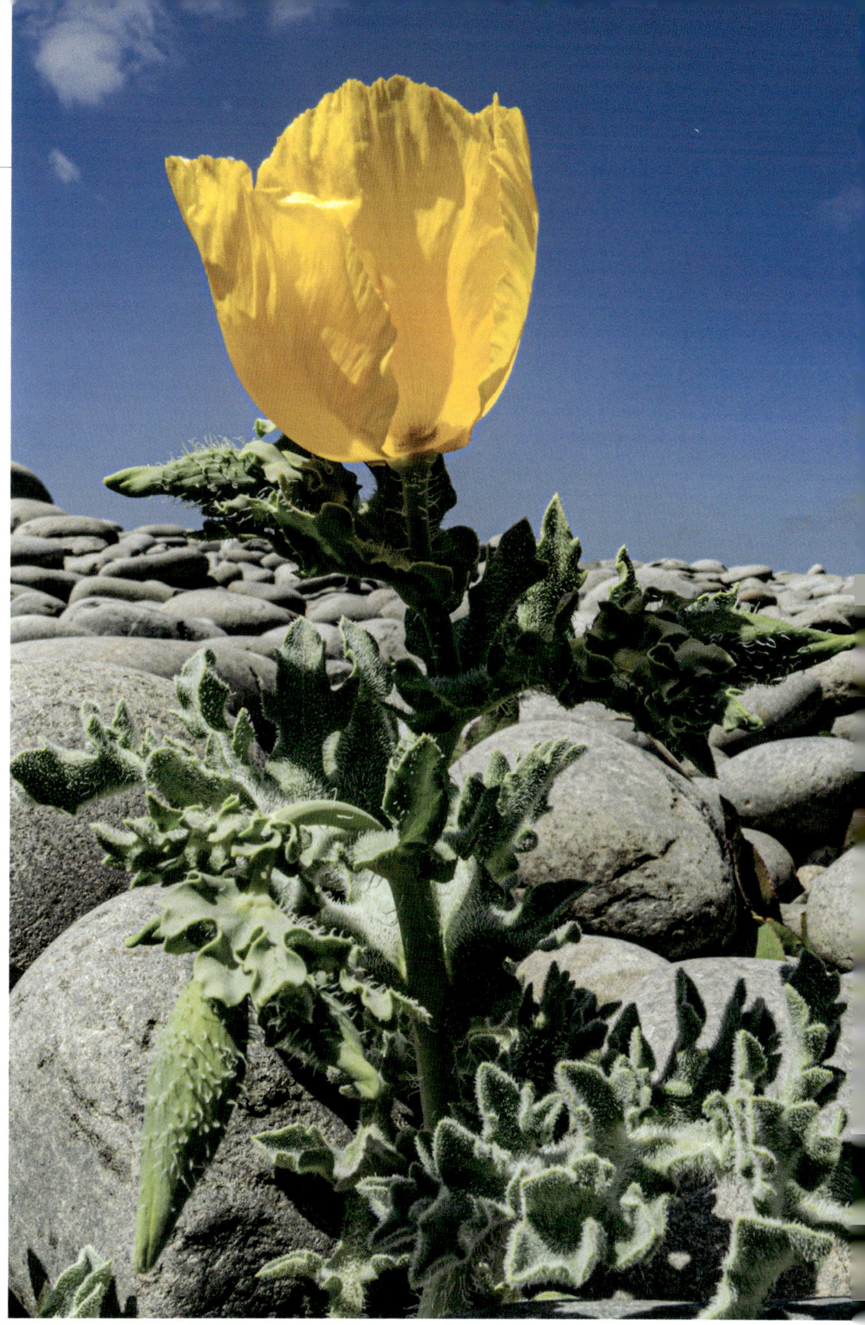

Yellow Horned-poppy
Pabi Corniog Melyn
Glaucium flavum

A Poppy Grows Upon the Shore
Robert Bridges

A poppy grows upon the shore,
Bursts her twin cup in summer late:
Her leaves are glaucous-green and hoar,
Her petals yellow, delicate.

Oft to her cousins turns her thought,
In wonder if they care that she
Is fed with spray for dew, and caught
By every gale that sweeps the sea.

She has no lovers like the red,
That dances with the noble corn:
Her blossoms on the waves are shed,
Where she stands shivering and forlorn.

Fumitory Family Teulu Mwg y Ddaear

Common Fumitory
Mwg-y-ddaear Cyffredin
Fumaria officinalis

Fumitory's English name comes from the Latin *fumus terrae*, meaning 'smoke of the earth', and it also has the same meaning in Welsh. The sprawling grey-green, much-divided foliage, with dark-tipped pink flowers, can appear smoky or misty, but the reason for its name is more likely that when the roots are freshly pulled from the soil, they have a smoky smell.

It is not a plant that is frequently encountered around the cliffs, but the hedge-banks along the section of coast running north from St Justinian are one of the best places.

It has been an important medicinal plant since ancient times. Dioscorides, the Greek physician and 'father of pharmacology', claimed that the juice cleared the eyesight. Later, in medieval times, it was used to treat intestinal disorders and as a purifier of blood. Herbalists use it to treat conjunctivitis and skin diseases, but, beware, it is a poisonous species.

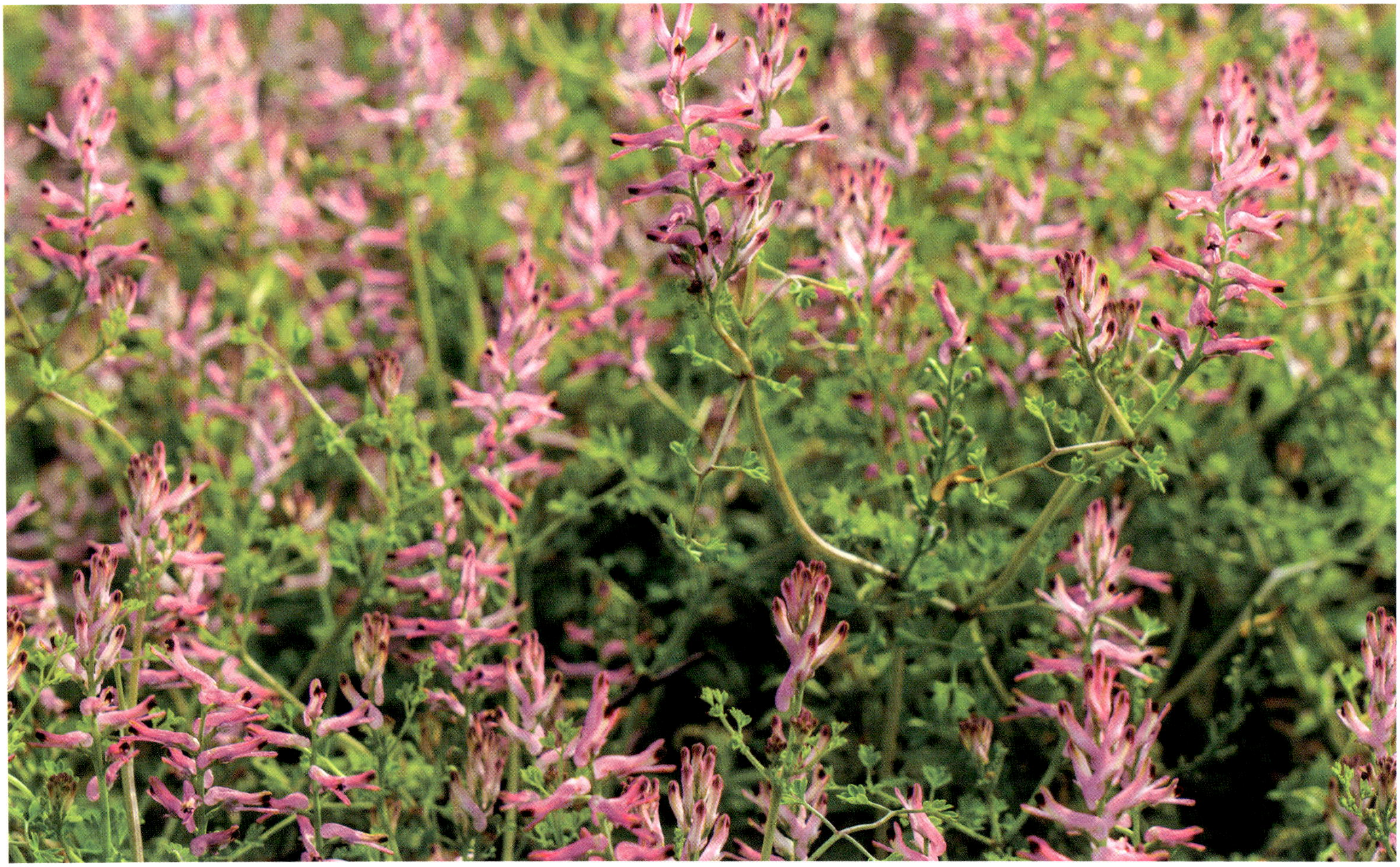

Common Fumitory Mwg-y-ddaear Cyffredin *Fumaria officinalis*

Goosefoot Troed yr Ŵydd

This is a large genus of plants belonging to the amaranth family. These often rank-smelling, salt-tolerant plants are not spectacular and are usually overlooked, despite being common around the coast. I have only included two species. The name goosefoot is because the leaves of many species resemble a goose's foot.

Spear-leaved Orache
Llygwyn Tryfal
Atriplex prostrata

Spear-leaved orache is common and widespread. It is a spreading, often prostrate, plant, which is green when young, but usually reddens as it gets older. It can be abundant in the enriched soils near seabird colonies.

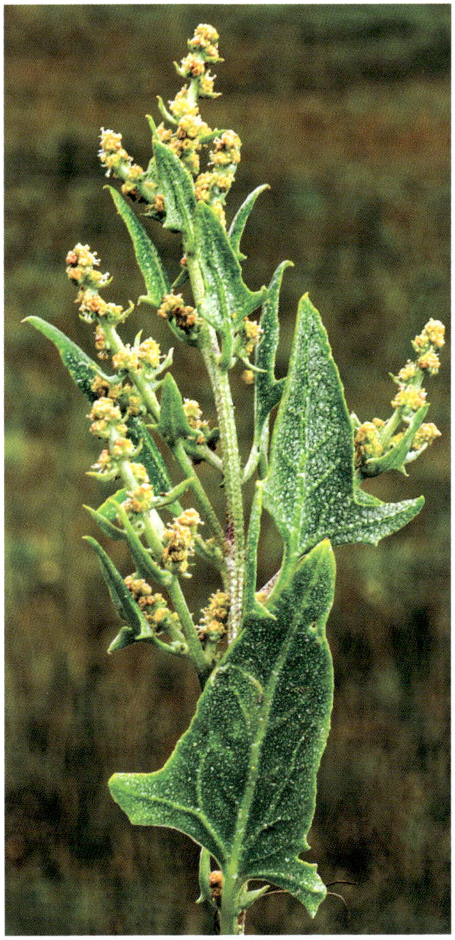

Spear-leaved Orache
Llygwyn Tryfal
Atriplex prostrata

Sea Beet
Betysen Arfor
Beta vulgaris ssp. maritima

Sea beet is possibly the most easily identified member of the goosefoot family. It is an erect and sprawling perennial, with large, succulent oval, glossy dark-green leaves. Individual plants can be up to a metre high. It is widespread and frequent on coastal clifftops, sand dunes and salt marshes.Prized by wild-food foragers, it tastes good either raw or cooked, and is often likened to spinach. It is the wild ancestor of many important domestic vegetables, including beetroot and Swiss chard. Sea beet has long been used in traditional medicine. It is believed to have diuretic, anti-inflammatory and antioxidant effects. It is worth a taste when you find it, but perhaps not when it is growing close to dog-frequented footpaths.

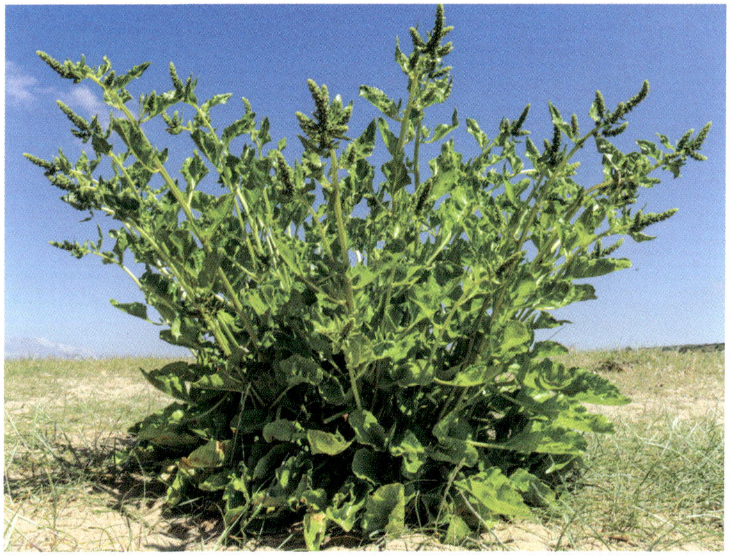

Sea Beet
Betysen Arfor
Beta vulgaris ssp. maritima

St Justinian

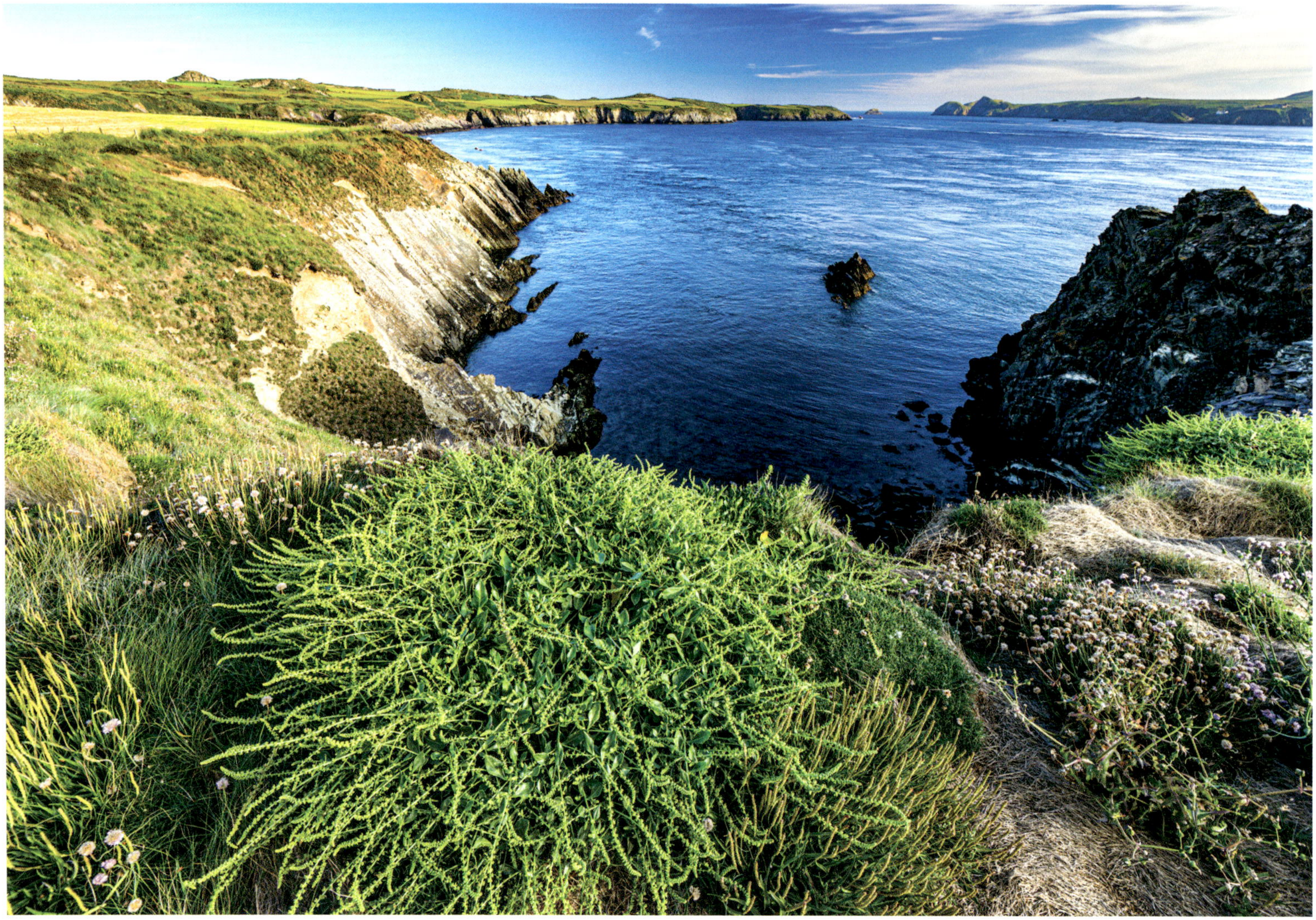

Sea Beet Betysen Arfor *Beta vulgaris ssp. maritima*

Pink Family Teulu Penigan

Red Campion
Blodyn Neidr
Silene dioica

Red campion is most often encountered as individual plants or in small clumps, scattered in hedgerows and among other rank vegetation, but occasionally – for example, on the offshore islands – it can dominate the late-spring landscape in swathes of glorious pinks and reds. The scientific name begins with *Silene*, the feminine form of *Silenus*, the Greek god of drunkenness and wine, who is usually depicted as a fat, jovial and drunken old man, often covered in sticky foam. Female red campion flowers produce a froth or foam that helps to catch pollen from visiting insects. Campions have roots that contain a compound called saponin, which can be used as a soap substitute. The mildly toxic soap is extracted by simmering the root in hot water; among other purposes, it was used for washing hair and clothes. Red campion has a few English common names, including adder's flower. The Welsh name is *blodyn neidr*, which translates as 'snake flower'. Both are good names for a plant traditionally regarded as a cure for snake bites.

Sea Campion
Gludlys Arfor
Silene uniflora

Sea campion is a very typical coastal flower, and one that I have grown to love. There are stretches of the Pembrokeshire coast path so dominated by sea campion that, on a still, warm day, the honey scent is almost intoxicating. Although mainly known as a coastal plant, it can also be found inland, favouring river shingle and the shores of upland lakes. It can tolerate high levels of lead and is not uncommon on the spoil heaps of old Mid Wales lead mines. It has a high tolerance of the nutrient-enriched soils around seabird colonies, and this is one factor which helps to explain its abundance on parts of the coast. Sadly, for a flower that is an important part of the coastal landscape, the folklore is scant. Apparently, it should never be picked and taken indoors for fear of inviting death. Given that it grows mainly on steep cliffs, the story is a good way of dissuading children who might otherwise be tempted to gather the flowers.

Rock Sea-spurrey
Troellig Arfor y Clogwyn
Spergularia rupicola

Rock sea-spurrey is aptly named for a flower that literally grows out of the coastal rocks. It can make use of the smallest dry crevice, where it can out-compete other, more demanding, species. It is a low, spreading plant, with succulent leaves, typical of plants which grow in challenging cliff-edge conditions. The delicate pale-violet, five-petalled flowers are quite distinctive, and, occasionally, if conditions are favourable, plants can produce large, dense clusters of blooms.

Greater Sea-spurrey
Troellig Arfor Mawr
Spergularia media

Greater sea-spurrey can almost be regarded as the salt-marsh version of rock sea-spurrey. In common with that species, its most notable feature is its ability to survive in harsh, maritime conditions. The fleshy stem and leaves help to conserve water, and deep roots anchor the plants in soft, sandy salt-marsh soils. Sea-spurreys had several traditional medicinal uses: the leaves and stems have been used to treat conditions such as inflammation, fever and urinary tract infections.

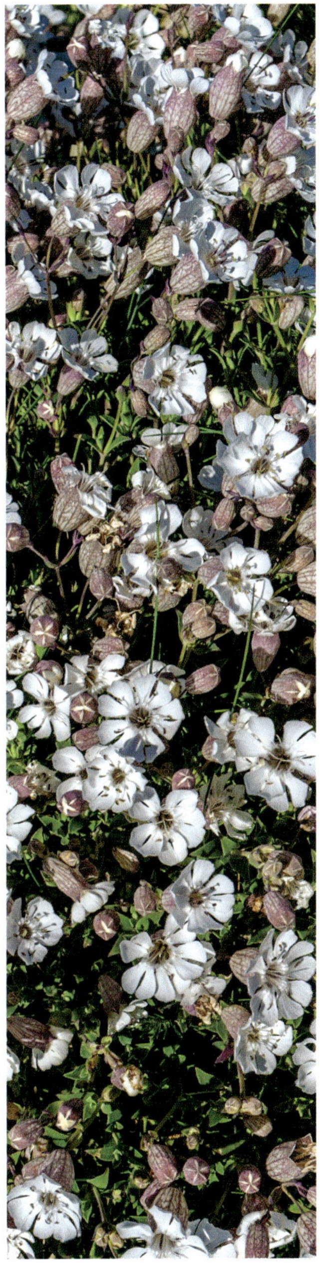

Sea campion
Gludlys arfor
Silene uniflora

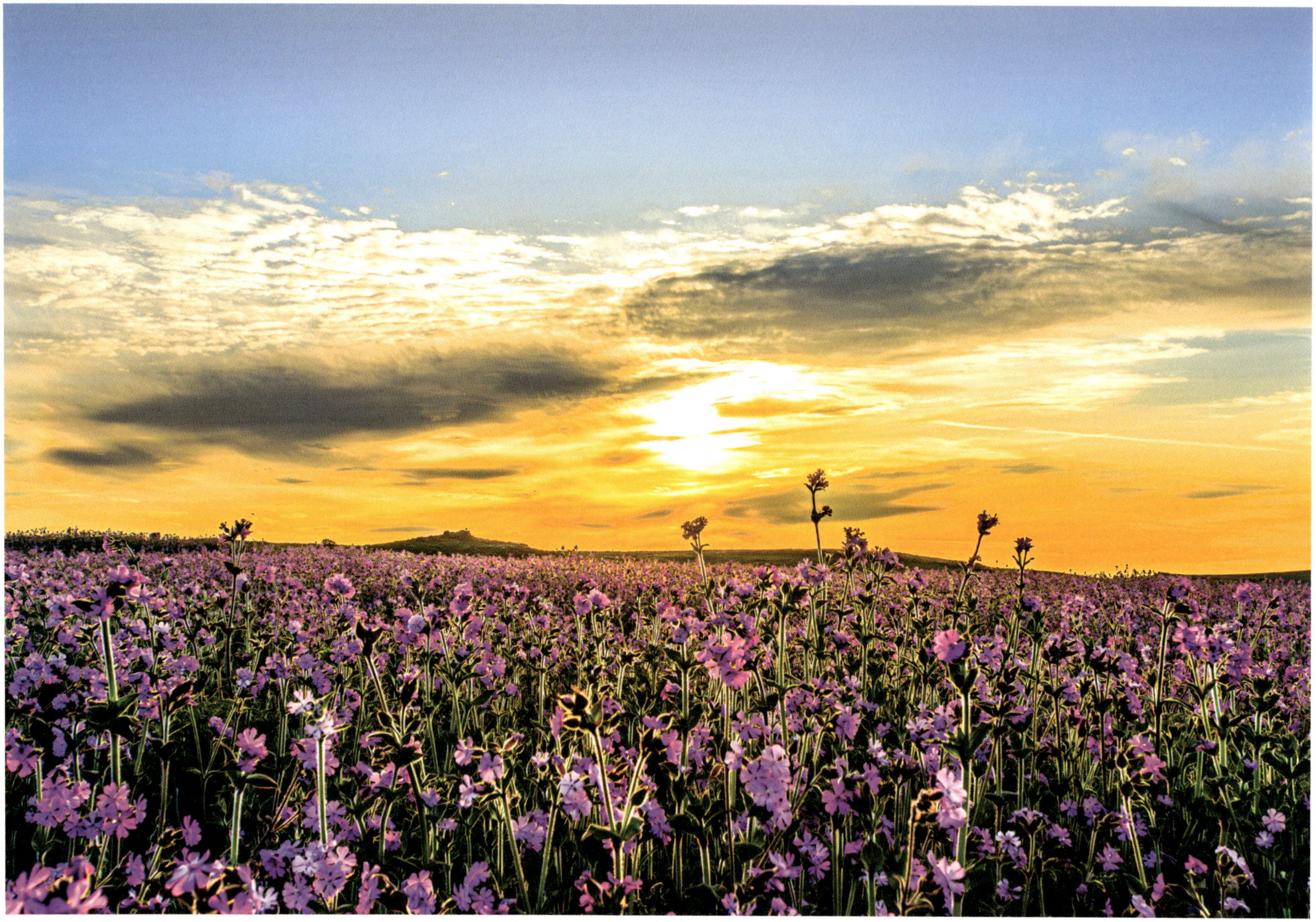

Red Campion Blodyn Neidr *Silene dioica*

Skokholm

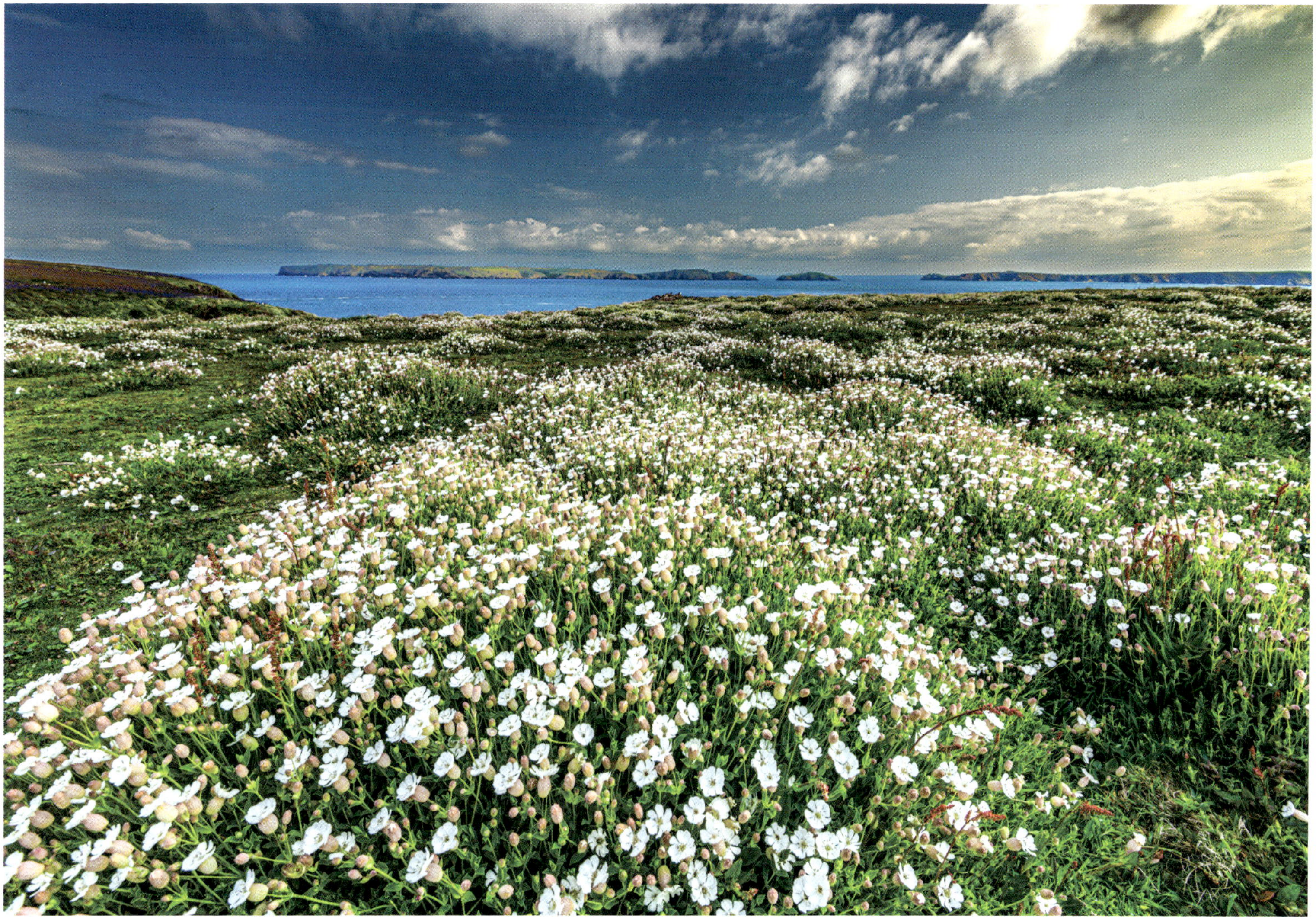

Sea Campion Gludlys Arfor *Silene uniflora*

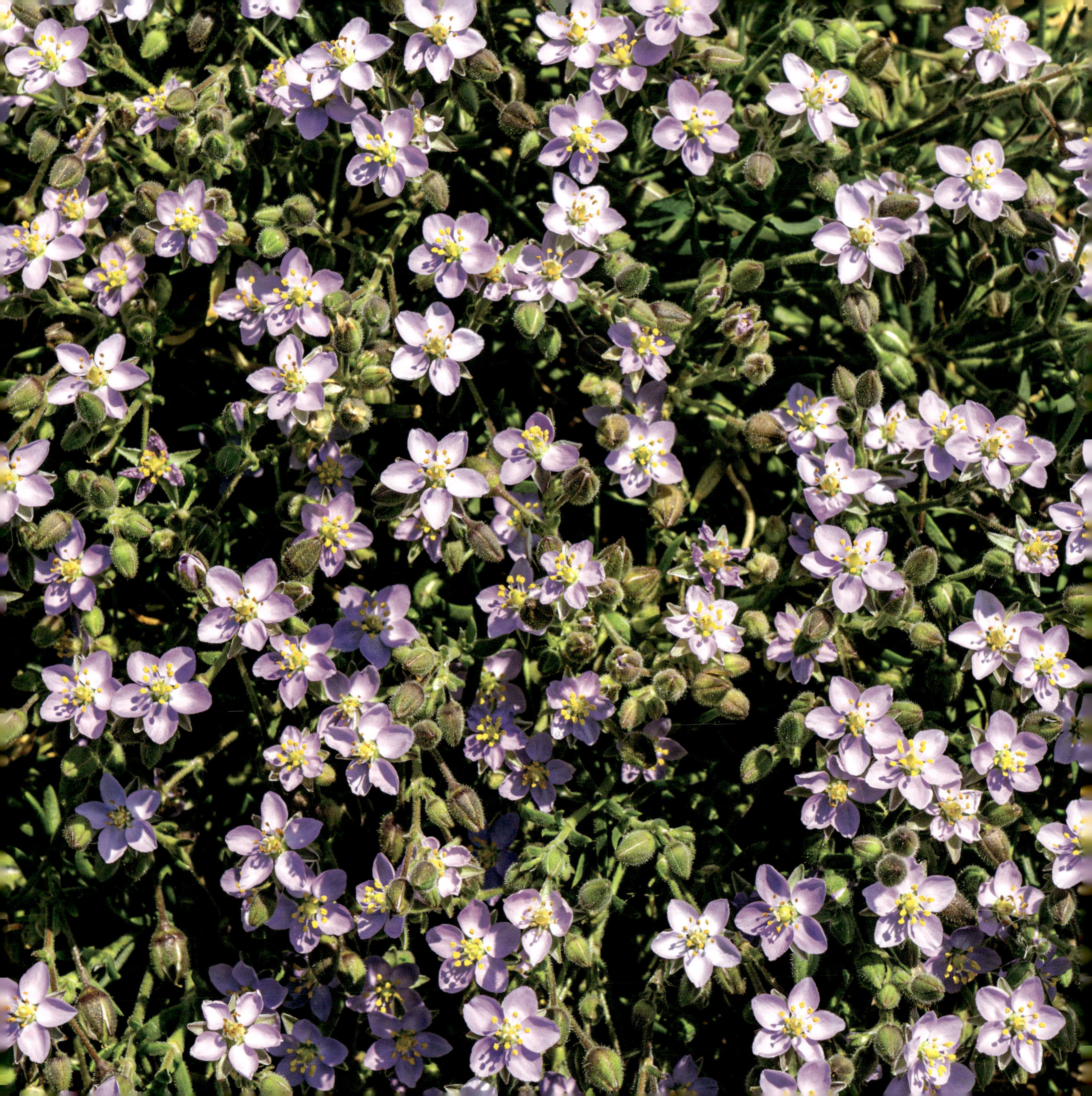

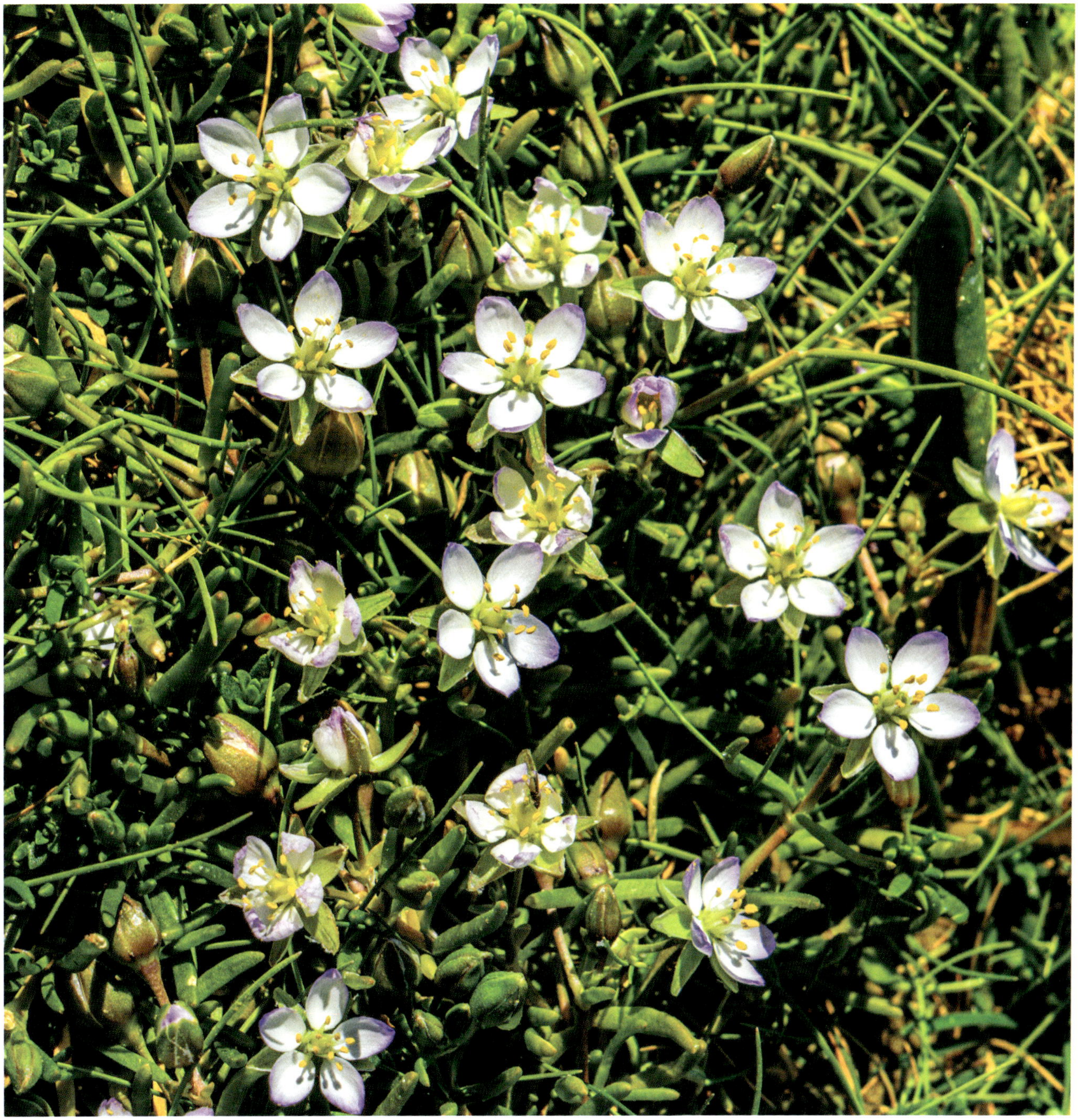

Above: Greater Sea-spurrey Troellig Arfor Mawr *Spergularia media*

Previous page: Rock Sea-spurrey Troellig Arfor y Clogwyn *Spergularia rupicola*

Thrift Family Teulu Clustog Fair

Two members of this family frequent the rocky coasts of west Wales, while a third species, the lax-flowered lavender (not included here), is restricted to salt marshes.

Thrift
Clustog Fair
Armeria maritima

Thrift, or sea pink, is the county flower of Pembrokeshire. The compact, dark green cushions of slender, linear leaves are covered with beautiful pink inflorescences, with the colour varying from cushion to cushion. Some have deep pink flowers, while others are barely more than white, with a full range of delicate shades in between. If you look closely, you will see that the inflorescences are clusters of tiny flowers, each with five petals. The main flowering season is from late April through to the end of June, but May is the best month.

The origin of the common name, thrift, is uncertain. The most frequent suggestion is that it is derived from the tufts of tightly packed leaves, which help conserve fresh water in salty, exposed conditions. Anyone old enough to remember pre-decimal British coinage might recall the large nickel-brass threepenny bit which was minted between 1937 and 1952 – a coin with so much character that I always found it intriguing. The tails side of the coin was decorated with a tuft of thrift: a pun from a time when saving, making, mending and general thrift were part of everyday life. The Welsh name for thrift is *clustog Fair* (Mary's pillow), but my favourite name is the Irish Gaelic *tonna chladaich*, which translates as 'beach wave'. Thrift is a member of the *Plumbaginaceae*, the plumbago or leadwort family. The Latin name for lead is *plumbum*, and the family name comes from the ancient belief that these plants could cure lead poisoning.

Thrift is not commonly used by herbalists. John Gerard's 1597 herbal does not make any claim to medicinal properties: 'neither doth any seeke into the nature thereof, but esteem them only for their beautie and pleasure in gardens'. Thrift was a popular garden plant in the sixteenth century and is still valued today.

Rock Sea-lavender
Lafant Môr y Creigiau
Limonium binervosum

Rock sea-lavenders comprise a complex group of different species and subspecies which have evolved in quite distinct geographical locations. There are six species in Pembrokeshire alone. The identification of individual species is probably best left to experts, but, regardless of our botanical skills, we can all enjoy these wonderfully robust and colourful flowers. The purple or violet blooms appear in high summer, mainly July and August, and will nearly always be found on the edge of rocky cliffs.

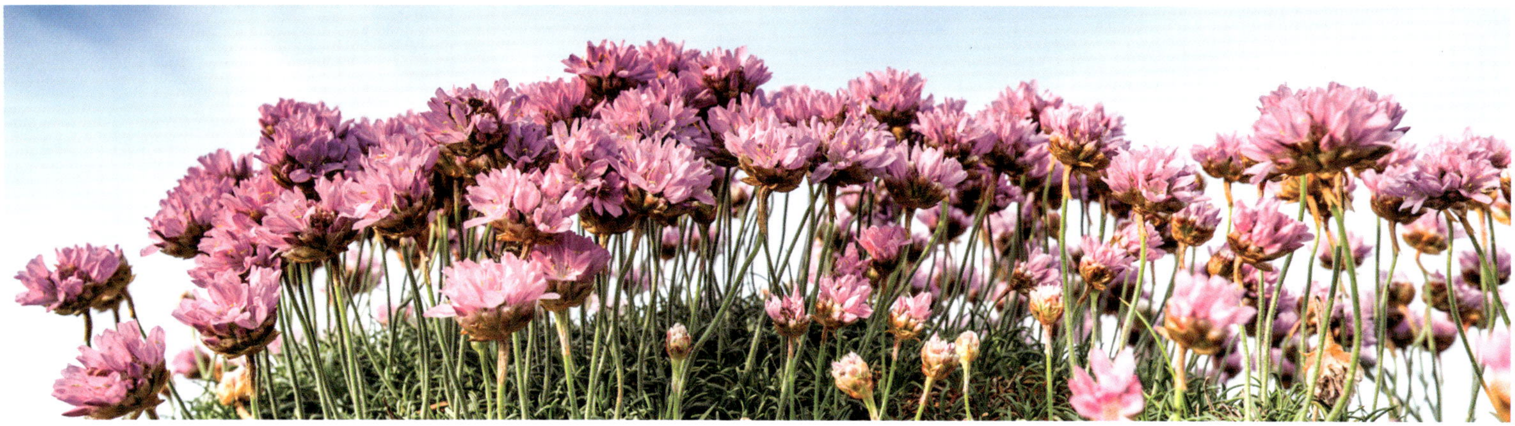

Mill Haven, St Brides

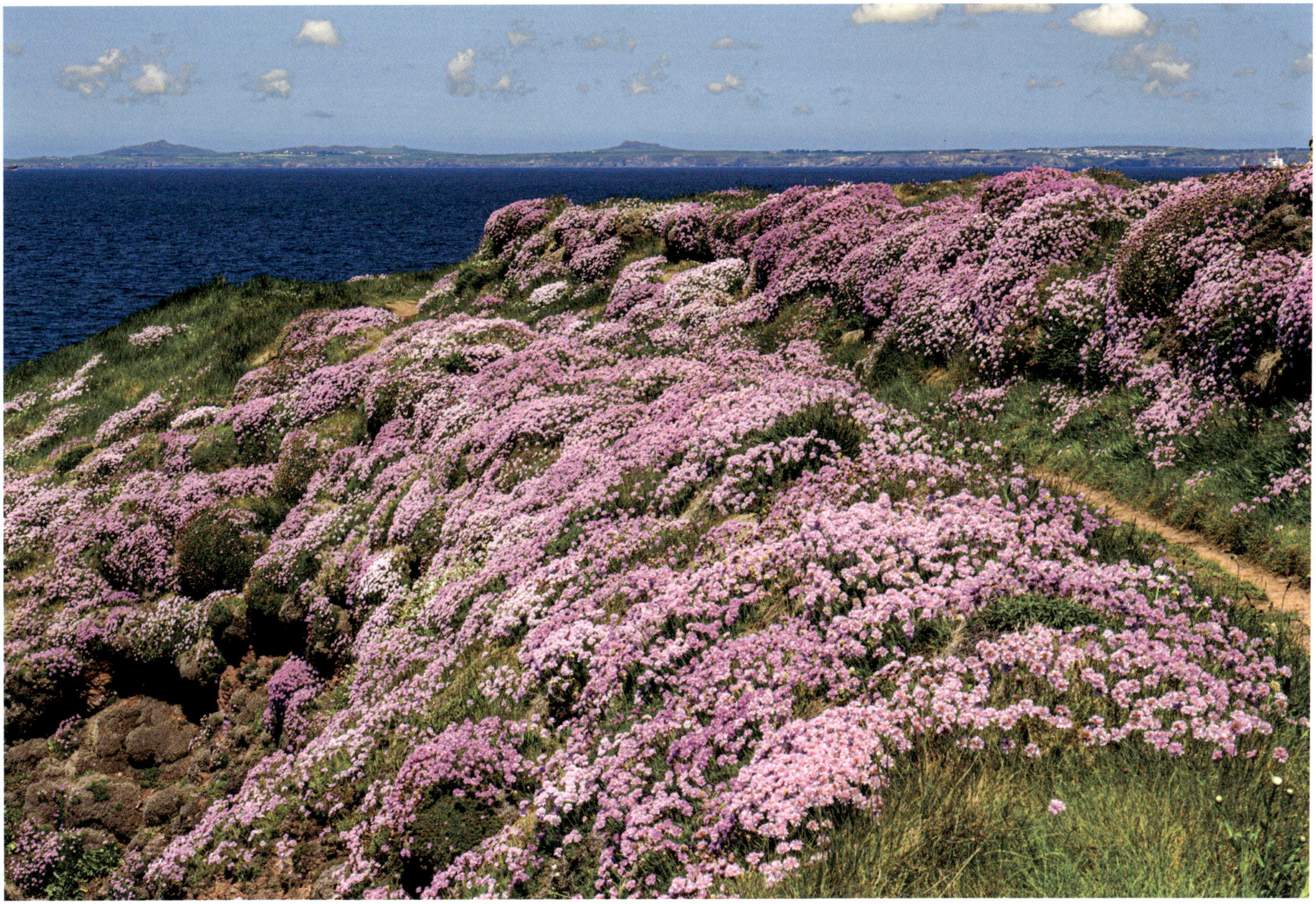

Above and left: Thrift Clustog Fair *Armeria maritima*

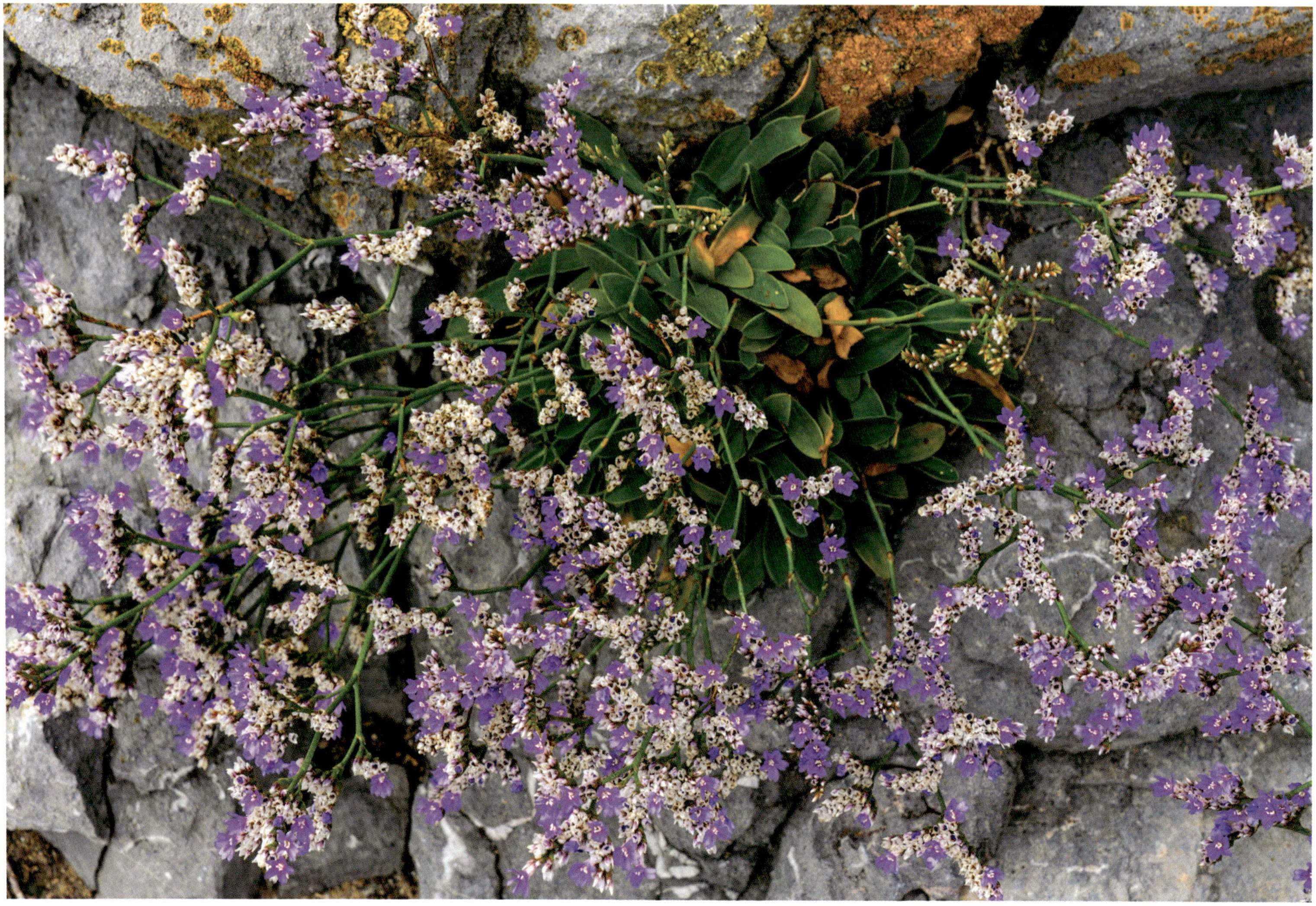

Rock Sea-lavender Lafant Môr y Creigiau *Limonium binervosum*

St John's-wort Family Teulu'r Eurinllys

St John's-wort is a well-known and popular herbal medicine, used to treat depression and other mental health problems. The family of plants is thought to get its common name from the Order of Saint John, which used it to treat wounds during the crusades. Another possibility is that it was associated with the feast of St John the Baptist on 24 June, which replaced earlier pagan midsummer festivals.

Perforate St John's-wort
Eurinllys Trydwll
Hypericum perforatum

Perforate St John's-wort is the most common member of this family. It is a relatively tall plant, growing up to 1.5 m in height, though perhaps just 80 cm in exposed coastal settings, and is easily identified by its yellow, star-shaped flowers with black dots, or glands, around the edges. On close inspection, the leaves appear to be full of tiny holes, but these are actually colourless glands. There is a similar, but less common, plant called imperforate St John's-wort, but, as the name implies, the 'holes' are missing from its leaves.

Tutsan
Dail y Beiblau
Hypericum androsaemum

Tutsan has strikingly attractive foliage. This shrubby plant has broad, oval leaves, arranged in opposite pairs. The flowers are gold, with a haze of yellow stamens. Each flower produces a single berry, which begins yellow-green and ripens through a red, or cherry, stage before ending up almost black. Look out for them in more sheltered or shady places. The older leaves have a resinous or fruity smell and, because of this, they were often used as bookmarks, particularly in the Bible. The Welsh name, *dail y Beiblau*, translates as 'Bible leaves'.

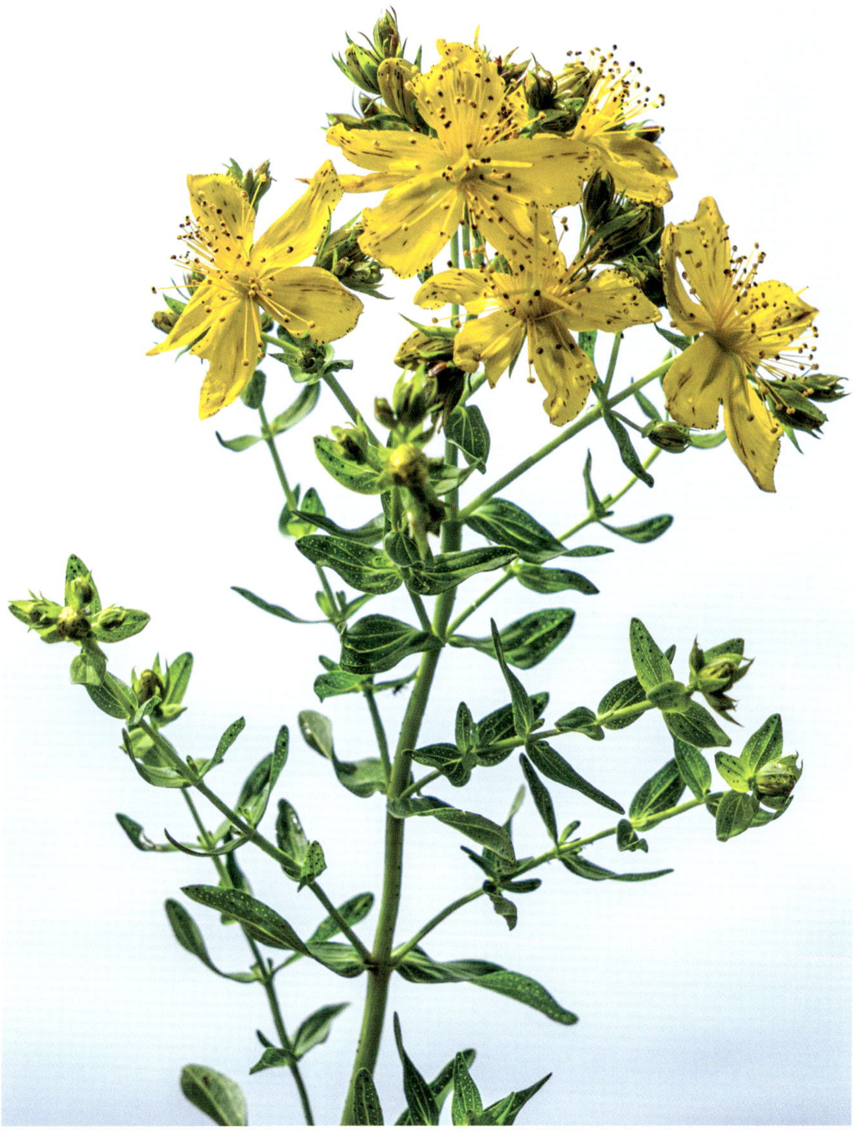

Perforate St John's-wort Eurinllys Trydwll *Hypericum perforatum*

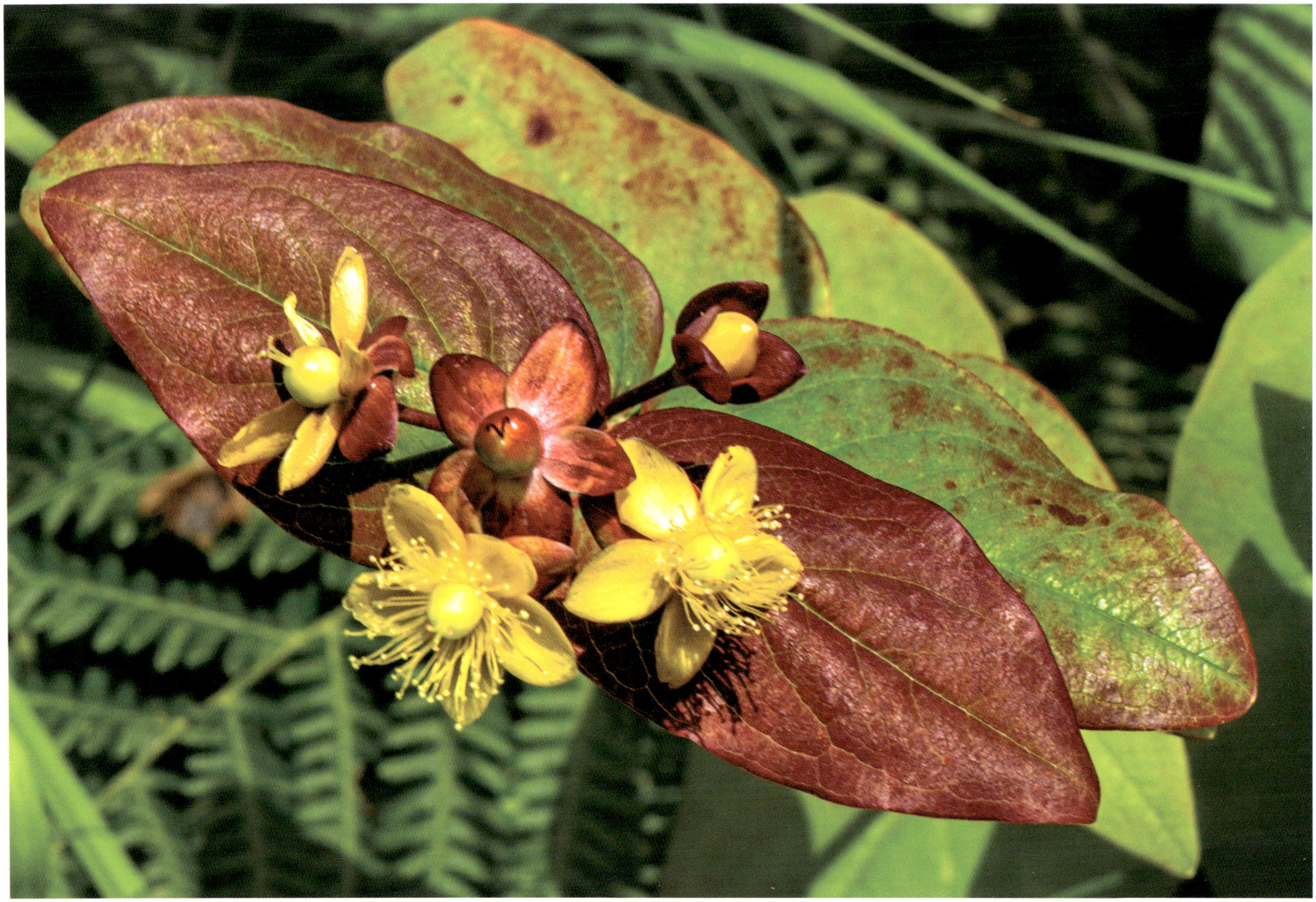

Tutsan Dail y Beiblau *Hypericum androsaemum*

Mallow Family Teulu'r Hocysen

Mallows are a beautiful family of plants, with many of its members more closely resembling cultivated garden flowers than anything that might be expected to grow in the wild. There are two species which are reasonably common on the coast, and both of the photographs included here were taken on the coast path near St Justinian, in north Pembrokeshire – a good location for these species.

Common Mallow
Hocysen
Malva sylvestris

Common mallow is a large, bushy plant. It has a profusion of splendid, funnel-like pink flowers, with each of the five petals having purple stripes. It is a relatively widespread species, often found on waste ground and road verges. It is especially common in Wales, and favours clifftops.

Tree-mallow
Hocyswydden
Malva arborea

Tree-mallow can grow to 2.5 metres tall. It is a robust species which can certainly rival the dramatic beauty of its relatives. While the flowers are sparser than those of the common mallow, they are even more spectacular. With deep pink, red-veined petals, the centre of each bloom is dark, almost black, contrasting strongly with the paler tips of the petals. It is tree-like, with large lobed, velvety leaves, which have the ability to withstand salt. This salt tolerance is clearly why tree-mallows are found mainly in coastal locations. They have become common on waste ground and around semi-derelict buildings in some coastal towns and cities. Look for them on the exposed edges of cliffs and close to nesting seabirds. Tree-mallows are popular with gardeners, so be aware that there may be cultivated varieties. In Greek mythology, tree-mallow was created by Aphrodite, the goddess of love, beauty and fertility. It was said that when the leaves were placed under a pillow, the sleeping person would dream of their future lover.

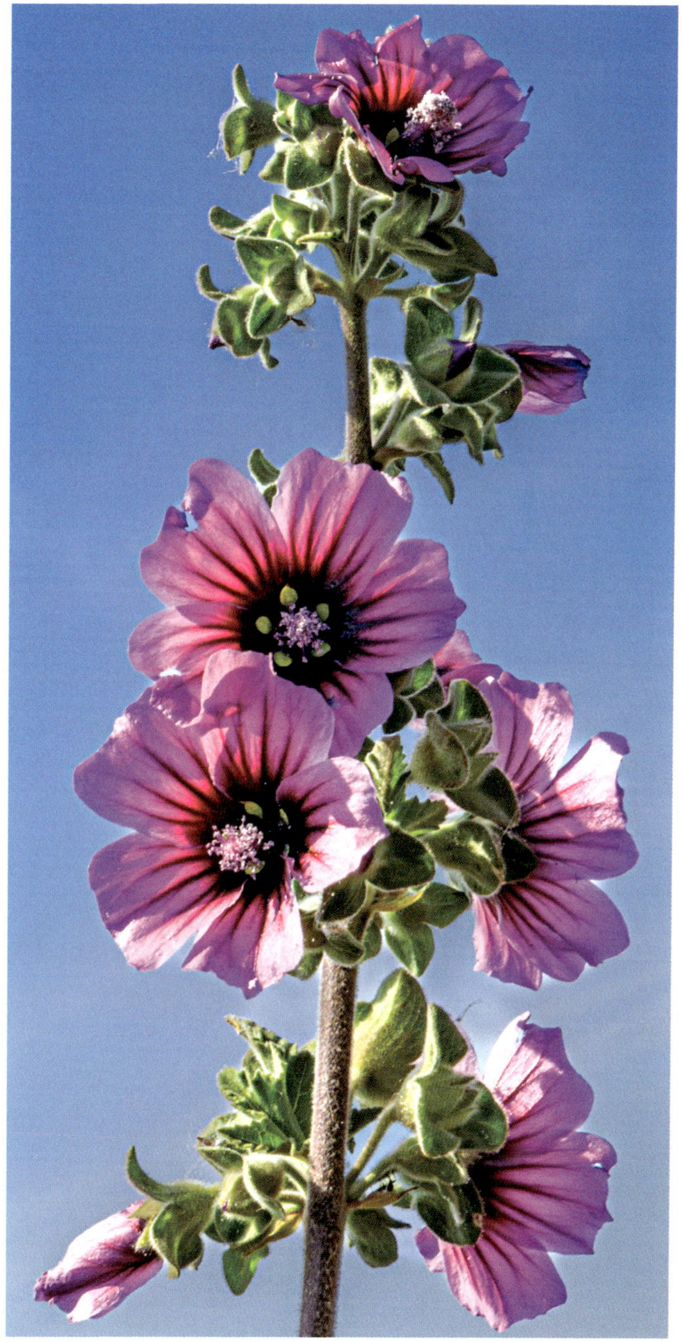

Tree-mallow Hocyswydden *Malva arborea*

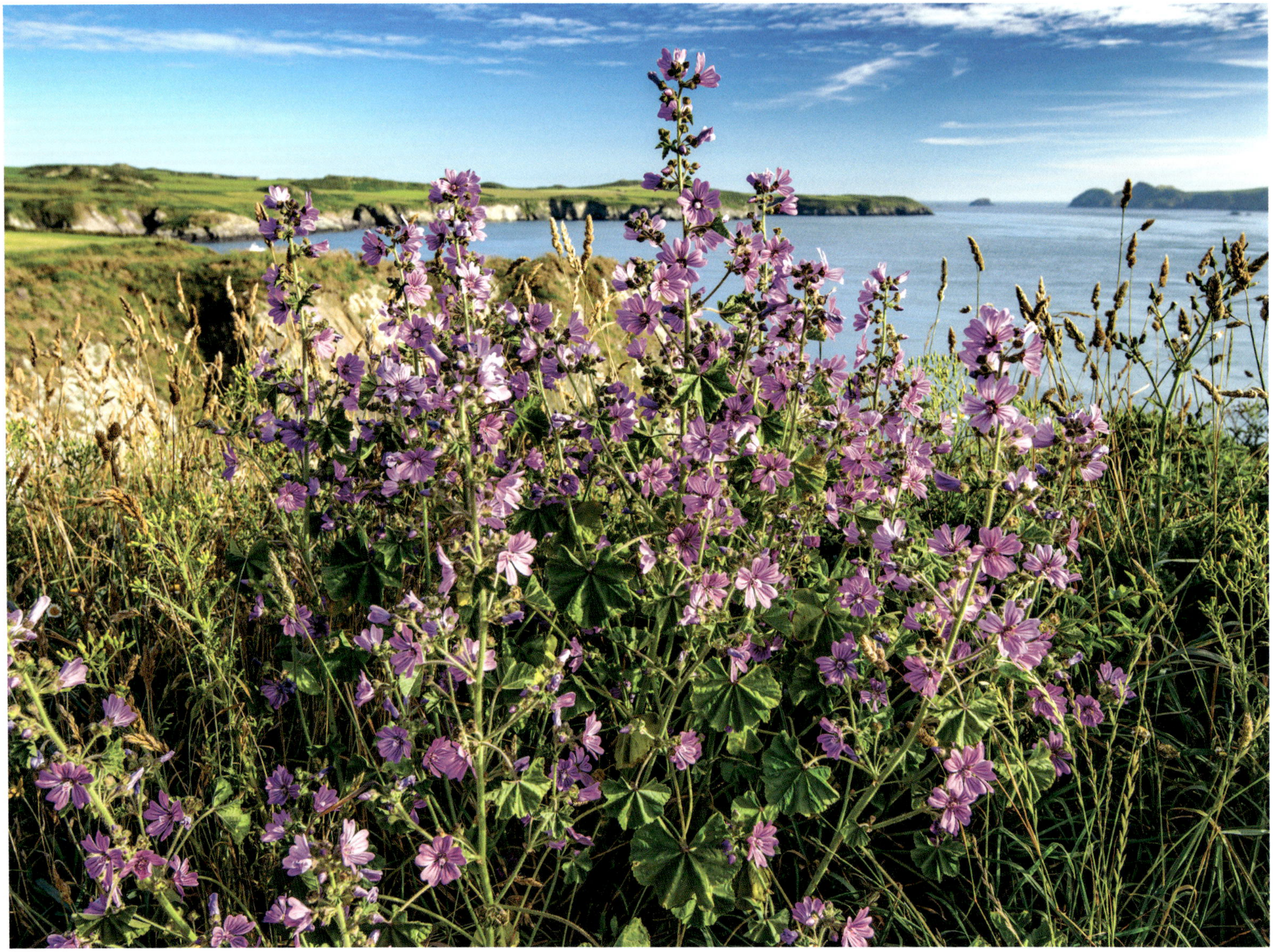

Common Mallow Hocysen *Malva sylvestris*

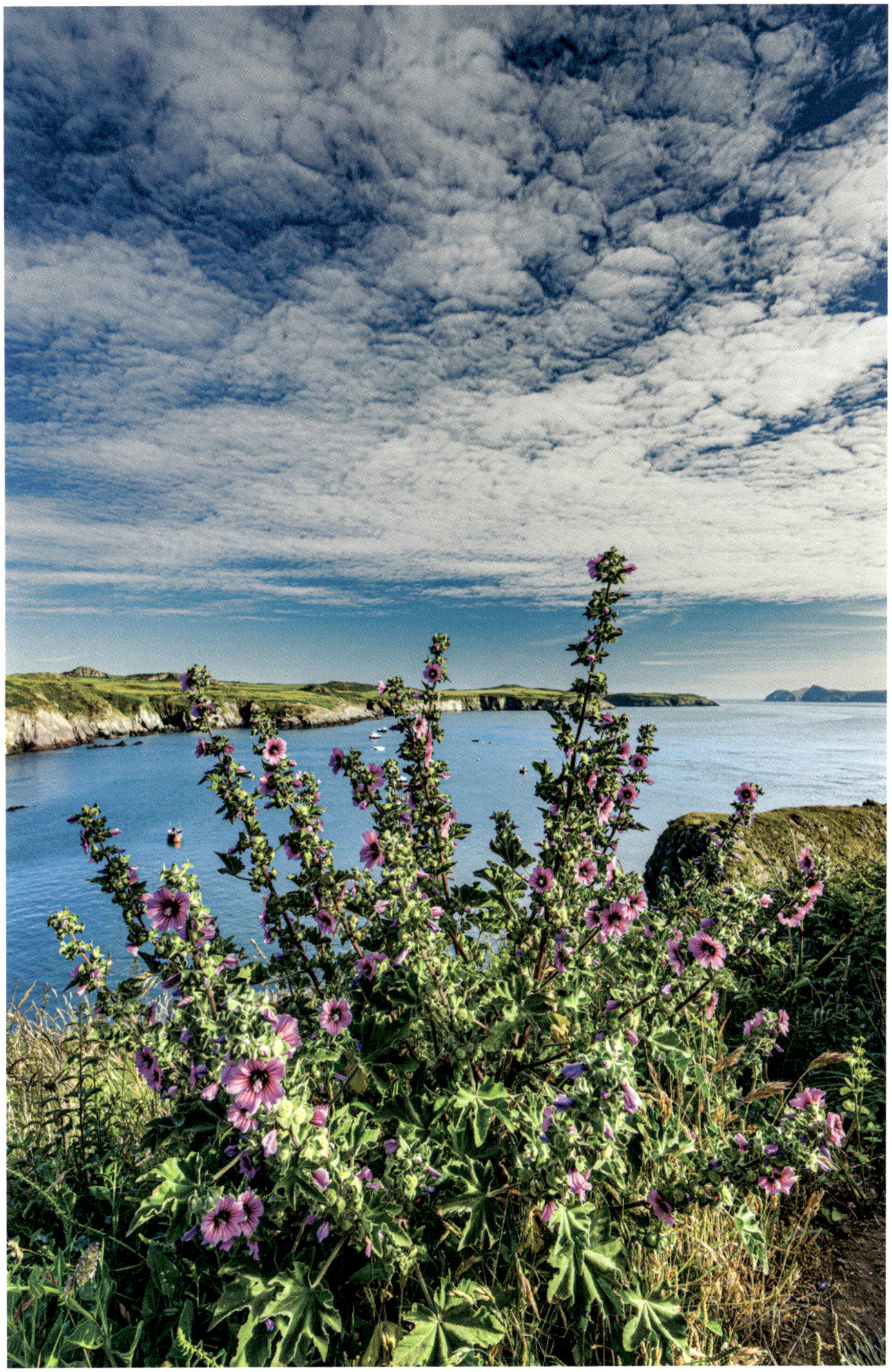

Tree-mallow Hocyswydden *Malva arborea*

Violet Family Teulu'r Fioled

I have included two members of this family: the wild pansy and common dog-violet. The violets are reasonably common and widespread, but the pansies have a restricted distribution in west Wales, where they are found mainly on coastal sand dunes. If you can picture a garden pansy, it will be easy to recognise the much smaller wild version.

Wild Pansy
Trilliw
Viola tricolor

Wild pansy has several different English names, most now archaic. These include love-in-idleness, heart's ease and heart's delight. In Shakespeare's *A Midsummer Night's Dream*, Oberon talks about a little western flower that maidens call love-in-idleness being imbued with some of Cupid's powers when accidentally shot with one of his arrows. Oberon sends Puck to find some. When dripped on someone's eyes, the magic love potion made from the flowers causes the individual to fall madly in love with the next live creature that they see. You will need to read Shakespeare for the full story, but here is a snippet:

> Yet mark'd I where the bolt of Cupid fell:
> It fell upon a little western flower,
> Before milk-white, now purple with love's wound,
> And maidens call it love-in-idleness.
> Fetch me that flower; the herb I shew'd thee once:
> The juice of it on sleeping eye-lids laid
> Will make or man or woman madly dote
> Upon the next live creature that it sees.

This is a big tale for a small, but charming, flower. I have included two photographs of the pansies to illustrate their exceptional beauty. The first is a wonderful patch of almost uniform purple-blue petals, with white and yellow centres. The second illustrates the wide variety of colours and patterns that can be seen in the wild. The lower pair of matching flowers is very different to the top yellow-white example. The photographs were taken on Skokholm, where there is an unusual population. In some parts of the island, there are extensive areas where all the pansies are yellow-white, and others where the purple-blue flowers dominate.

Wild pansies have been cultivated since the Middle Ages and bred in Britain since 1810. They were valued for their health benefits, and used in folk medicine for the treatment of epilepsy, eczema, asthma, bronchitis and common colds.

Common Dog-violet
Fioled Gyffredin
Viola riviniana

The common dog-violet was given the name 'dog' because of its lack of scent, which distinguishes it from the scented sweet violet. They might not be quite as exquisite as their sweet relative, but they are still one of the most attractive spring flowers. Dog-violets are shade-tolerant and will avoid direct sunlight. They are found frequently around coasts, mainly in slightly sheltered grassy places.

Dog-violets have a similar range of medicinal uses to pansies, including for respiratory problems and headaches, and are sometimes used in traditional medicine to treat arthritis and rheumatism. The following lines, which really catch the character of this flower, are from 'The Violet', by Jane Taylor, who lived from 1783 to 1824:

> Down in a green and shady bed
> A modest violet grew;
> Its stalk was bent, it hung its head,
> As if to hide from view.
>
> And yet it was a lovely flower,
> Its colours bright and fair;
> It might have graced a rosy bower,
> Instead of hiding there.

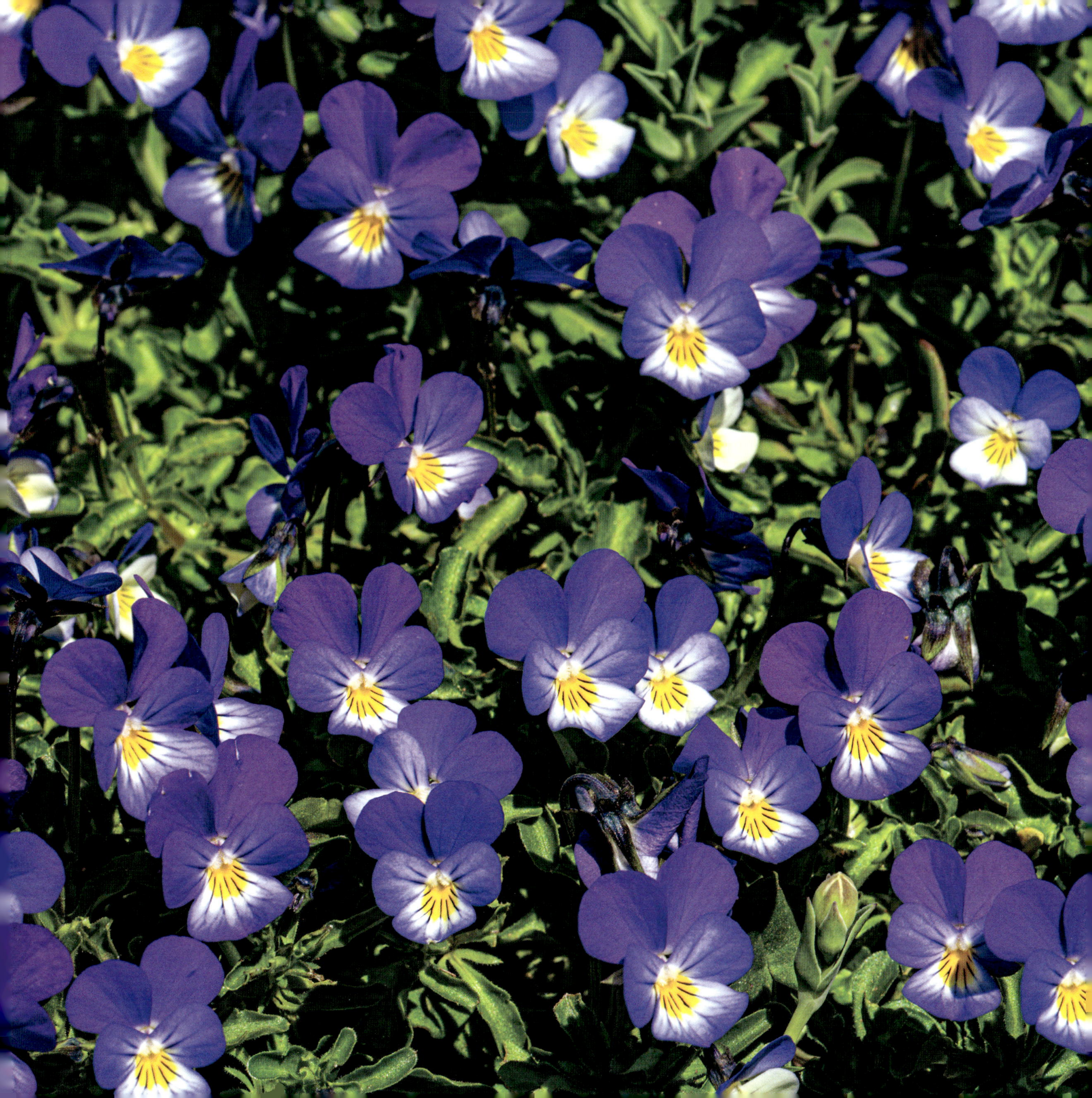

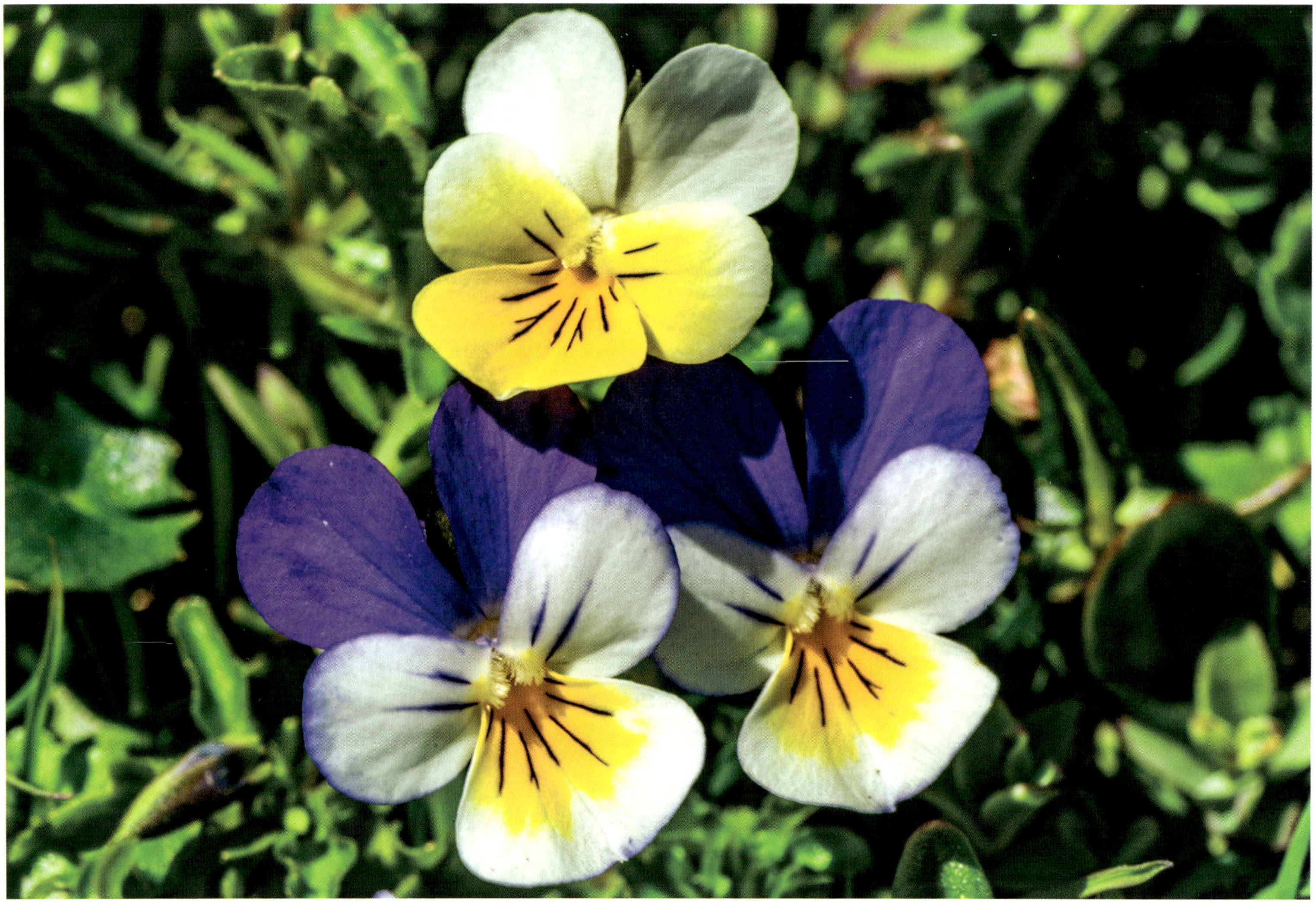

Above and previous page: Wild Pansy Trilliw *Viola tricolor*

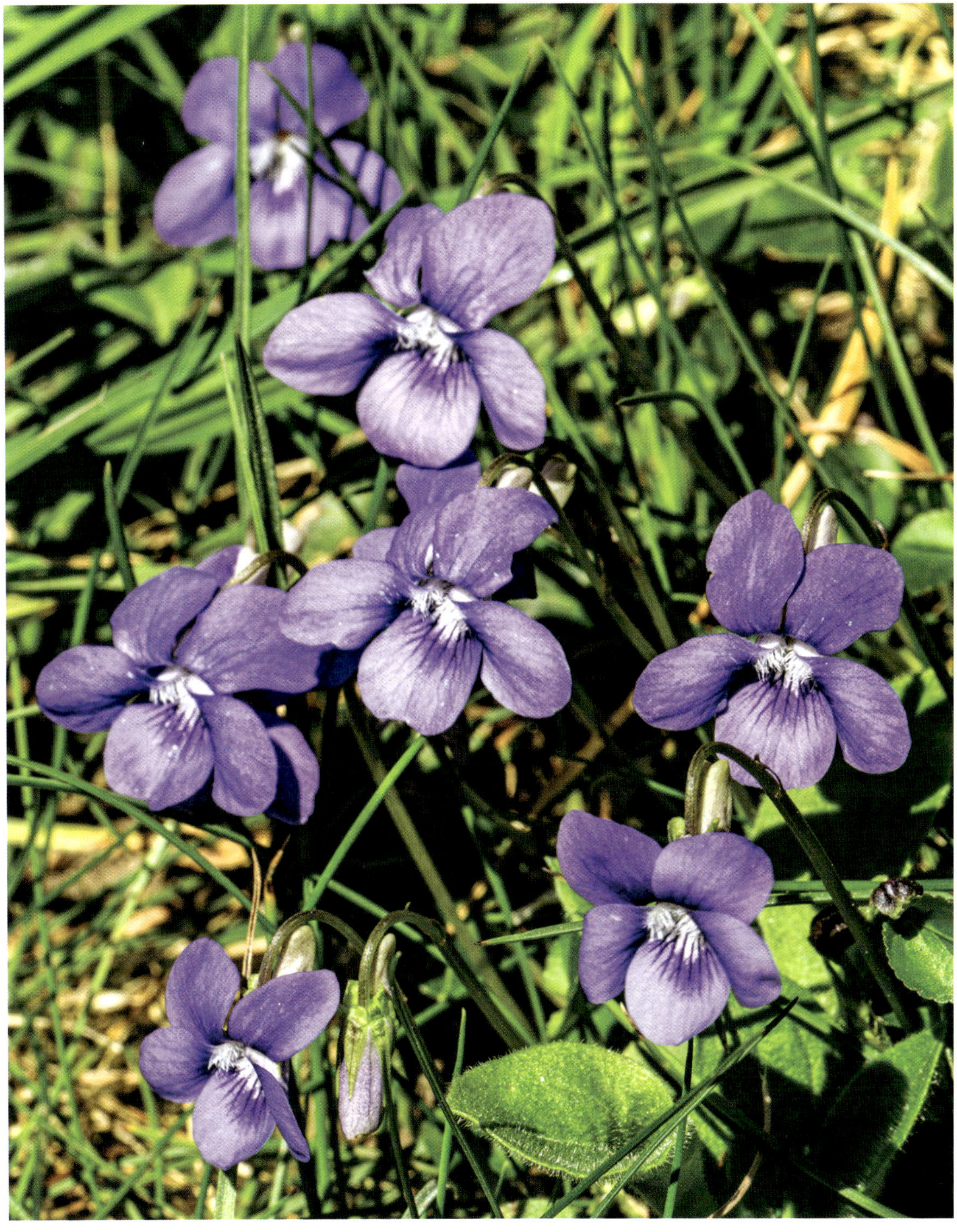

Common Dog-violet Fioled Gyffredin *Viola riviniana*

Cabbage Family Teulu'r Fresychen

This is a relatively large family, which is well represented along the coasts. Most are fairly nondescript, so I decided to limit my choice to sea rocket and two species of scurvygrass, as they are such typical spring coastal flowers, with the glossy, succulent leaves which are a clear characteristic of a salt-tolerant species. They are coastal species, but are increasing as a consequence of winter road salting, and now sometimes follow the road verges inland. Some of the best displays in Pembrokeshire are on roadsides. The leaves are rich in vitamin C, which has long been recognised as a cure for scurvy, a serious deficiency disease common in sailors on long sea voyages.

Common Scurvygrass
Llwylys Cyffredin
Cochlearia officinalis

Common scurvygrass is noticeably the larger of the two species. The best distinguishing feature is the rounded, kidney-shaped basal leaves, which become arrow-shaped further up the stem. It is common in most coastal habitats, thriving on salt marshes, sea cliffs and most places in between. It makes an early appearance in April, but is at its best in May, when the clusters of white flowers can be dazzling. Although it may flower into October, the later season blooms are often disappointing.

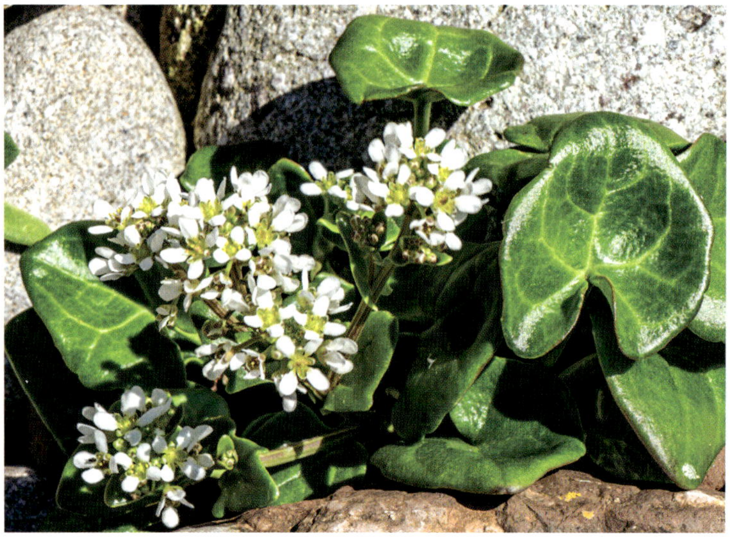

Common Scurvygrass Llwylys Cyffredin *Cochlearia officinalis*

Danish Scurvygrass
Llwylys Denmarc
Cochlearia danica

Danish scurvygrass is similar to common scurvygrass, but smaller and less robust, with a prostrate, or sprawling, form. The basal leaves are heart-shaped, but the ivy-shaped stem leaves are the most distinctive. Its location preferences are also similar to common scurvygrass.

Sea Rocket
Hegydd Arfor
Cakile maritima

Sea rocket is the only lilac-coloured flower that you will find at the edge of the tide. This member of the cabbage family can sometimes appear in great profusion along a sandy shore. I have vivid memories of the strandline at Morfa Harlech, in Meirionnydd, adorned with a wide band of sea rocket and clouded with dancing white butterflies. The floating seeds are dispersed by tides and wind, often ending their journey along the upper strandline, where they can thrive in these most adverse conditions. The strandline flora is an ephemeral community, often absent for many years, and only reappearing when several different influences coincide: one of these must be a deposit of seeds which have survived the winter storms. Sea rocket is a key species in the stabilisation of embryo dunes and initiating the dune-building process.

Warey Haven, St Brides

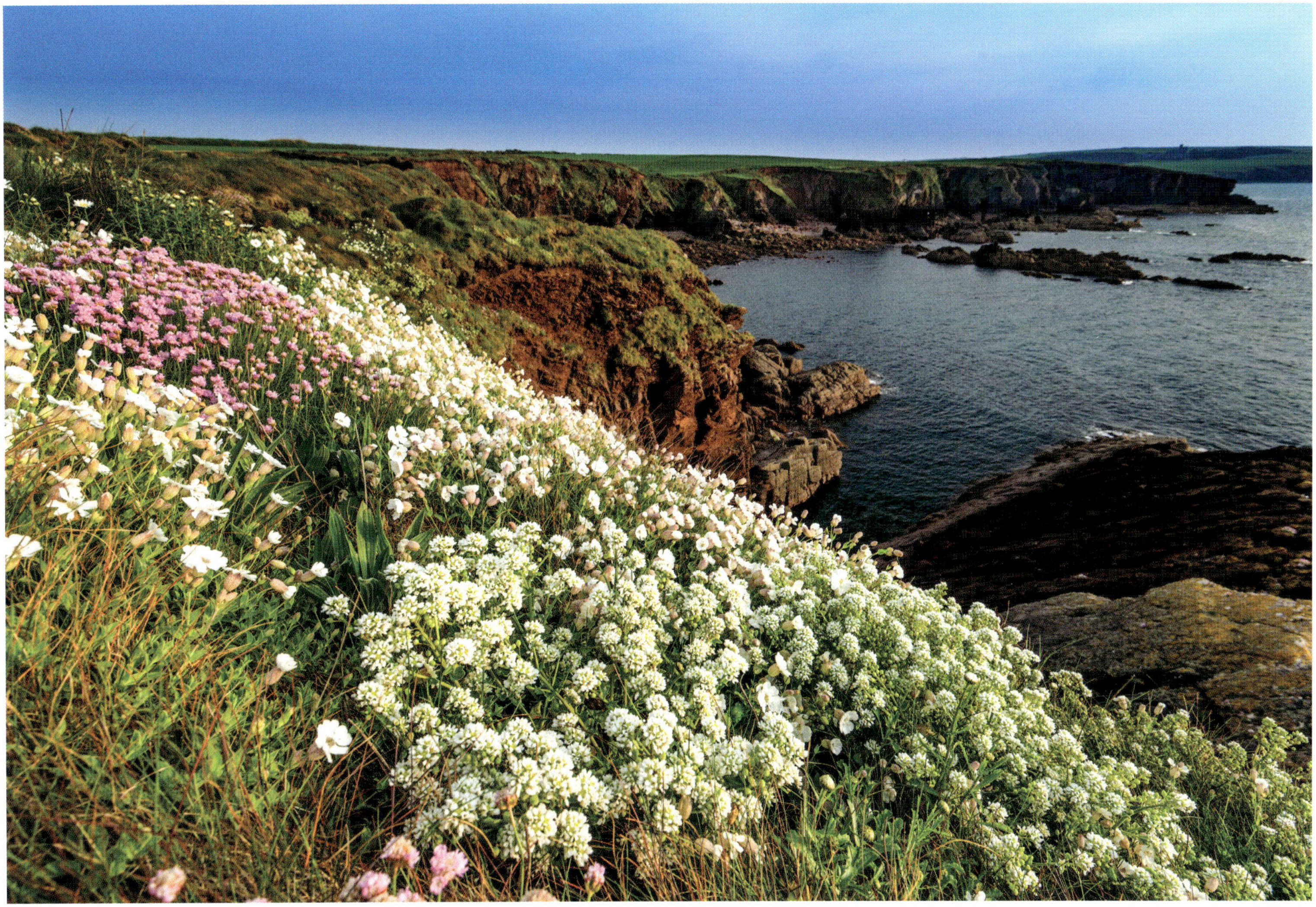

Danish Scurvygrass Llwylys Denmarc *Cochlearia danica*

St Brides Haven

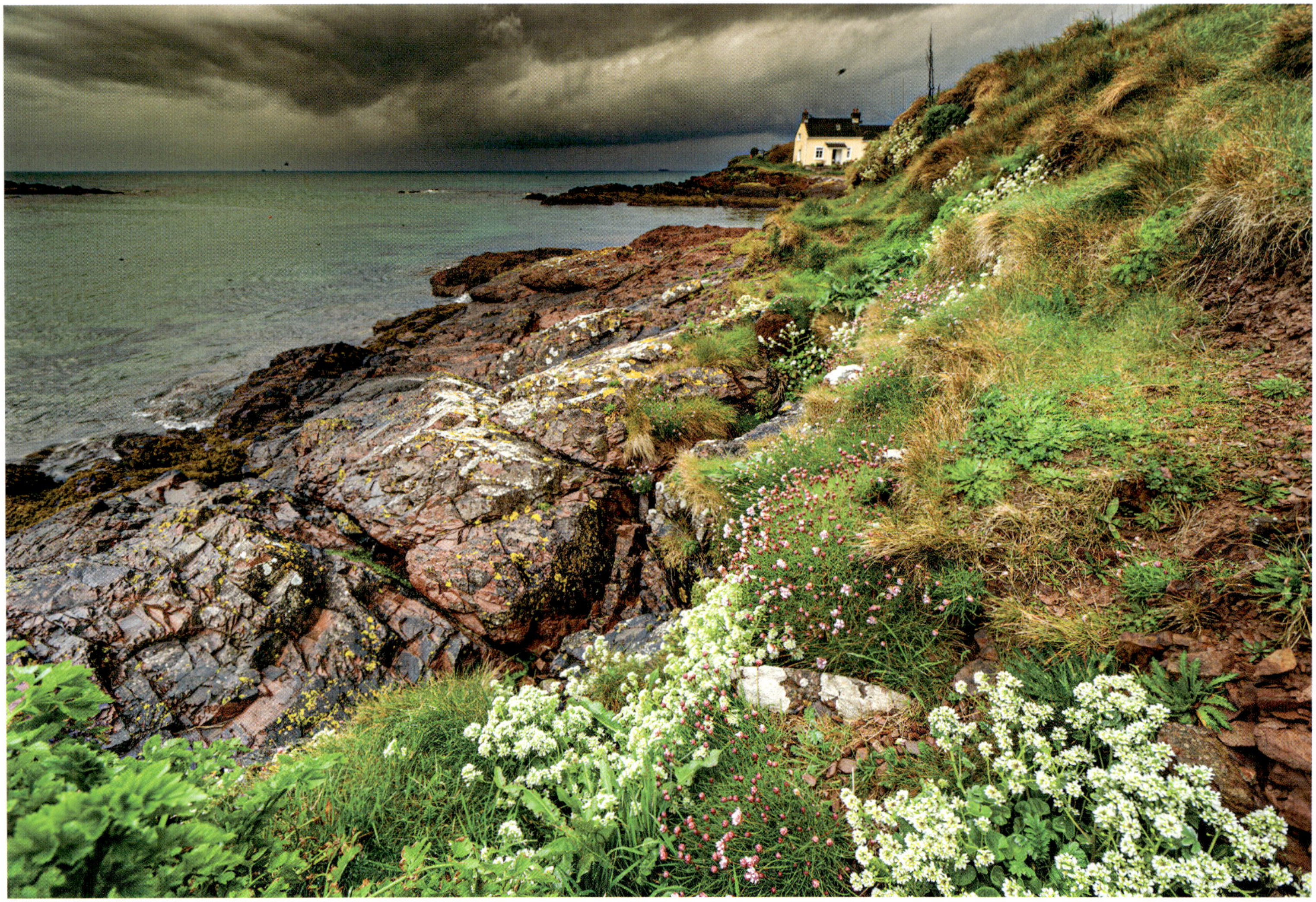

Common Scurvygrass Llwylys Cyffredin *Cochlearia officinalis*

Morfa Harlech

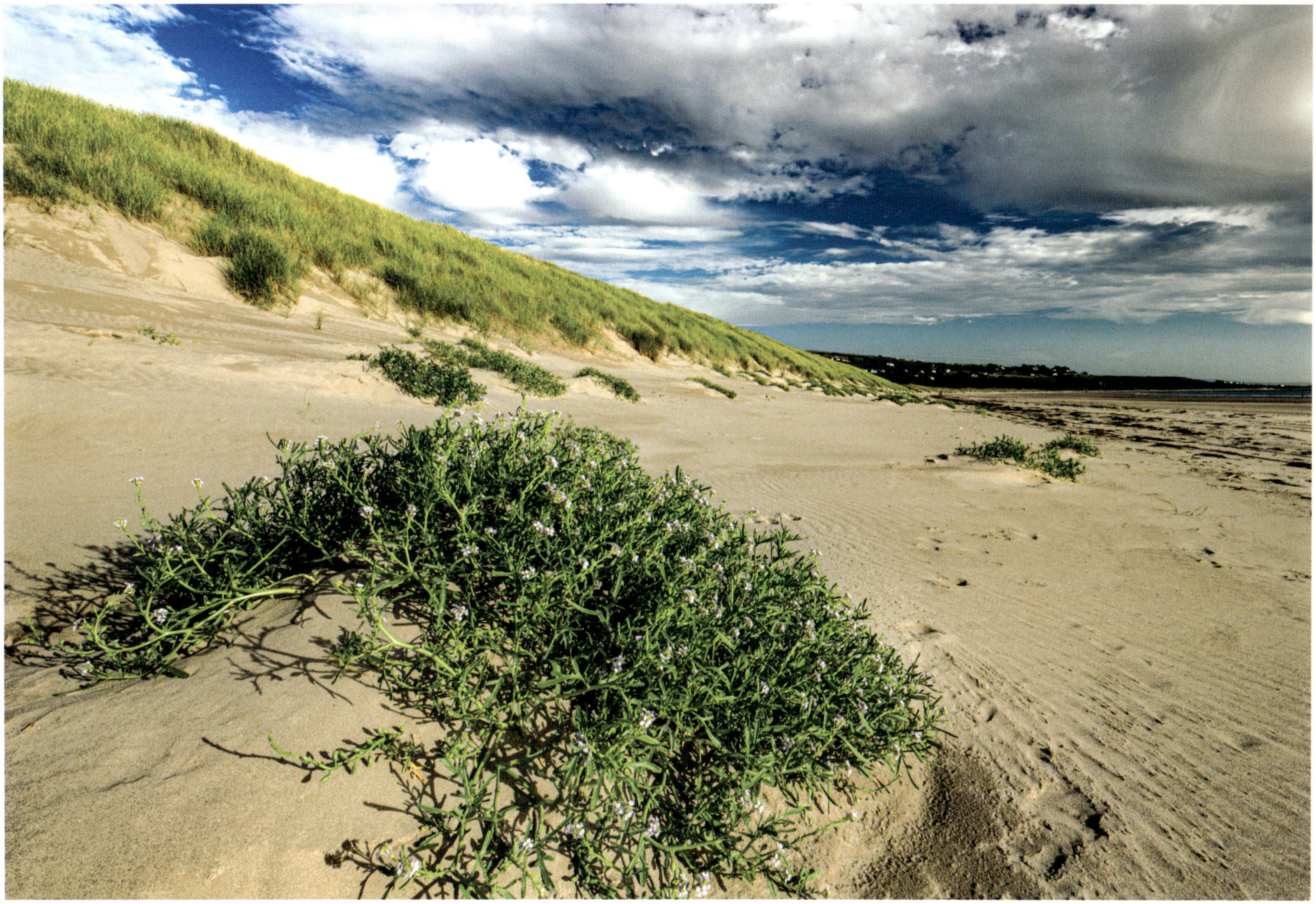

Sea Rocket Hegydd Arfor *Cakile maritima*

Mignonette Family Teulu'r Felengu

Wild Mignonette
Melengu Wyllt Ddi-sawr
Reseda lutea

Wild mignonette is a widespread species with an intriguing name, which I could never pronounce and consequently struggled to remember. The name is reputedly from the French *mignon*, meaning 'dainty'. There is a type of fine French bobbin lace called mignonette, and I wonder if the flowers' light, delicate and lacy appearance contributed to its name. The best place to see mignonette is the limestone grassland and fixed dunes between Broad Haven and Stackpole Head. This was where I took the photograph – on a June evening, when the low sun was streaming through the sward, highlighting the mignonette. The pale-yellow, sweet-smelling flowers have been used since the first millennium BC to make a yellow dye called weld, although a closely related plant, known as dyer's weed or weld, was more widely used. The flowers are also used for perfumery and some traditional medicine.

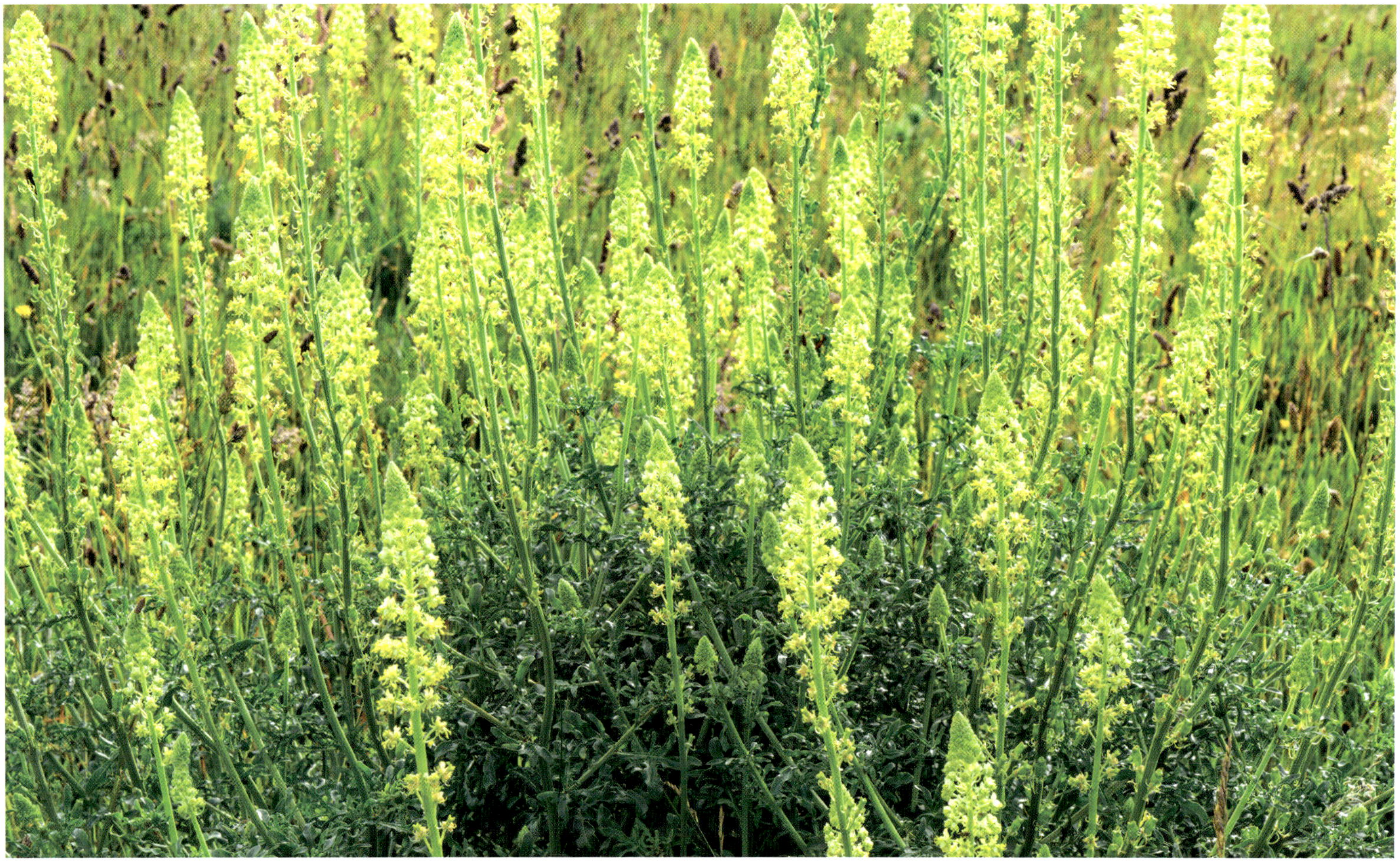

Wild Mignonette Melengu Wyllt Ddi-sawr *Reseda lutea*

Heath Family Teulu'r Grug

Coastal heaths were once common and widespread plant communities. They would have been a familiar sight to Victorian, and earlier, farmers. Heaths were mainly an expression of a long relationship between people and nature. All the species in the heath communities were native, but the specific mix of plants within those communities was influenced by human intervention. This was mainly through the introduction of grazing, but also burning and, occasionally, cutting.

It is worth taking a short diversion at this point to consider the concept of a plant community. Habitats are easily explained. They are the major divisions in the landscape: woodland, grassland, coastal dune systems, etc. Plant communities are the more subtle subdivisions within a habitat: assemblages of plants with a distinct and unique composition and structure. The species that comprise a community come together and associate in a particular place and time; they are species which share a dependence on, or a tolerance for, a variety of influences. The influences can be natural or the consequence of human intervention, or (as is the case with most heaths) a combination of the two. Unfortunately, heaths are no longer abundant, having declined mainly because of agricultural changes or abandonment. Today, most farmers and graziers are reluctant to graze their livestock on the cliffs. In the absence of animals, the heaths have, in some places, become completely overgrown with scrubby species. In others, they have been lost to over-grazing and the application of artificial fertilisers.

There are – or used to be – a variety of different heath communities, the most natural occurring in the more extreme, exposed and saltwater-drenched locations, where the hardy heath species were easily able to out-compete those less tolerant of exposure. Most communities existed in the slightly more sheltered areas, where grazing and other farming activities suppressed the more palatable grasses and other competing species. The heath communities provide opportunities for a surprising variety of species, many of which are included in this book under their own families, including blackthorn, brambles, gorse, broom, honeysuckle and spring squill. The squill heath community is one of the rarest, lighting the landscape with a splash of brilliance. It is dominated by heather, with a good sprinkling of bright blue, starry squill. The Deer Park, on the headland opposite Skomer Island, has some of the best squill heath. My favourite of all heath communities is the glorious mix of deep yellow western gorse and the vivid purple bell heather, which paints the coast in a striking mix of complementary colours. Sadly, it is now found in only a few places. One of the best is St Davids Head and, as with all heaths, it reaches its peak in late July and August, providing a late-summer spectacle that can easily compete with the best that spring has to offer.

Heather
Grug
Calluna vulgaris

Heather is the most common and familiar of the heath species, and is widespread on coast, moor and mountain. Heather has a long history of human use, including for fodder, thatch and rope-making. It was traditionally used to make brooms, which is why it was given its scientific name, *Calluna*, derived from the Ancient Greek word *kalluno*, 'to sweep clean'. Heather is an important source of nectar and habitat to a wide range of butterflies and moths, including the magnificent emperor moth. I am never sure which is the most impressive: the large, day-flying adult moths with peacock-like eyespots on all four wings, or the caterpillars with their garish electric-green bodies decorated with black hoops and raised lemon-yellow spots.

The poem on the next page, in the Welsh *englyn* form, is one of a set of twelve that earned Eifion Wyn a prize at the 1906 National Eisteddfod in Caernarfon. It beautifully captures the essence of heather, thriving in the thinnest, rockiest soils and exuding that heady, honeyed scent of high summer.

Blodau'r Grug
Eifion Wyn

Tlws eu tw', liaws tawel – gemau teg
gwmwd haul ac awel;
crog glychau'r creigle uchel
fflur y main, ffiolau'r mêl.

Heather Flowers
Eifion Wyn

Pretty in their growth, a quiet host – fine gems
a plot in sun and breeze;
hanging bells of the high rock
mass of flowers, vialled honey.

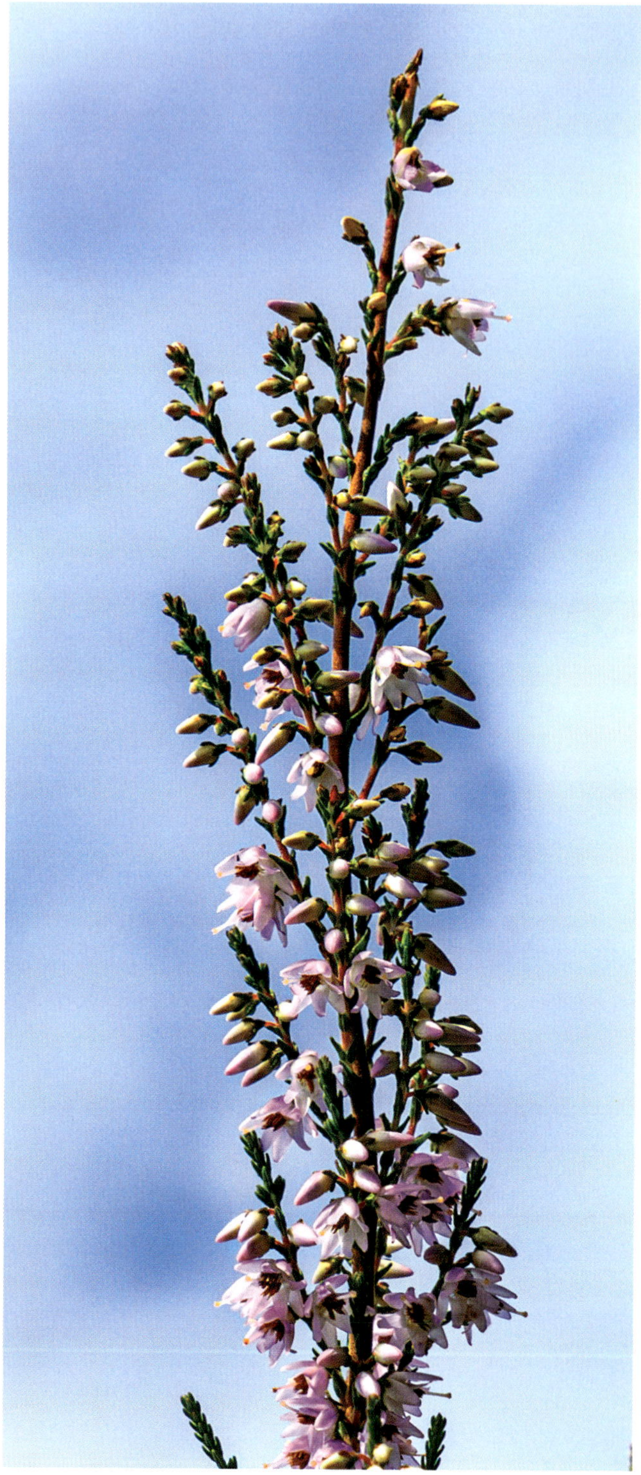

Heather
Grug
Calluna vulgaris

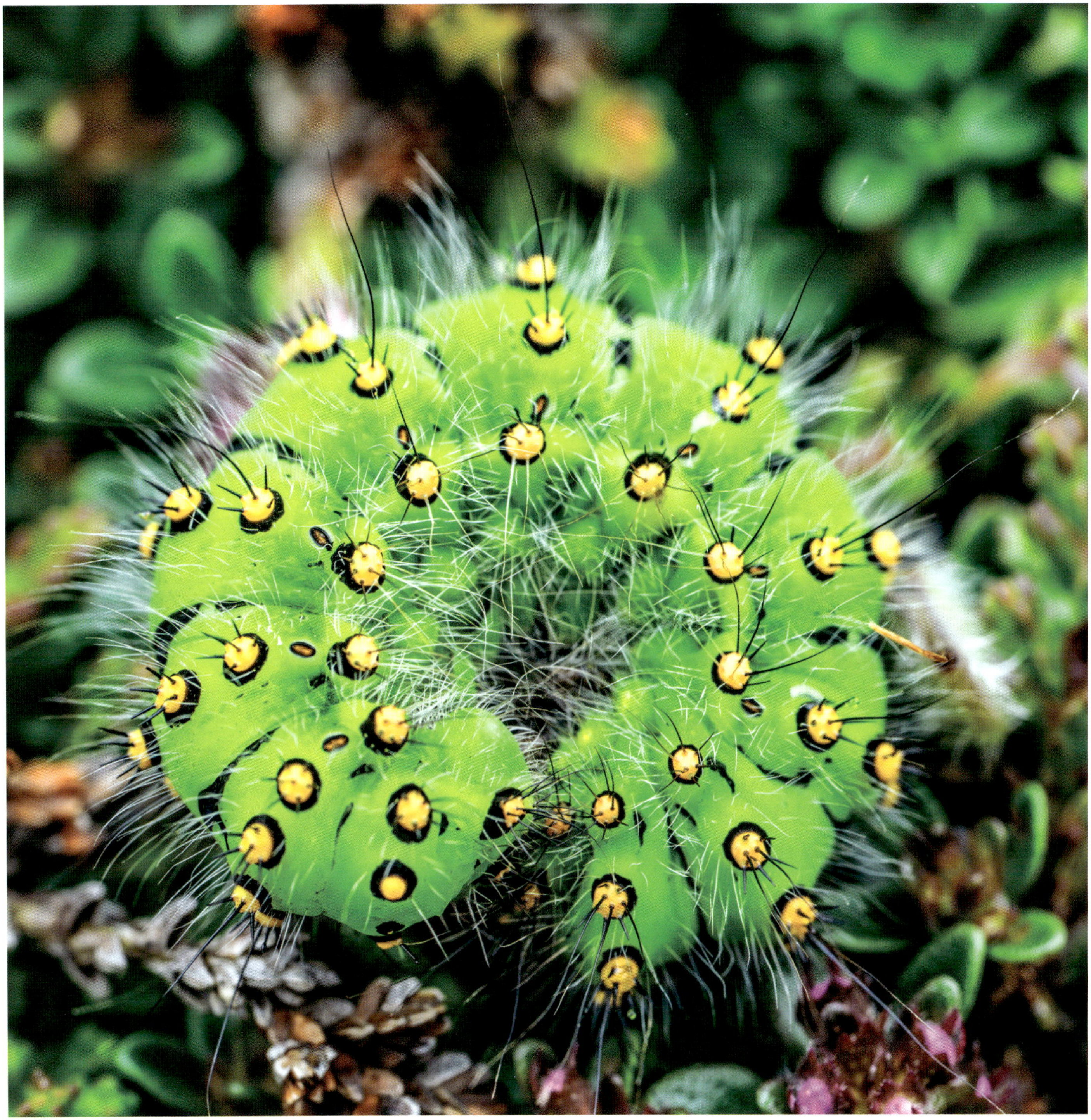

Emperor moth caterpillar lindysen yr Ymerawdwr *larva Saturnia pavonia*

Ynys Dewi (Ramsey Island)

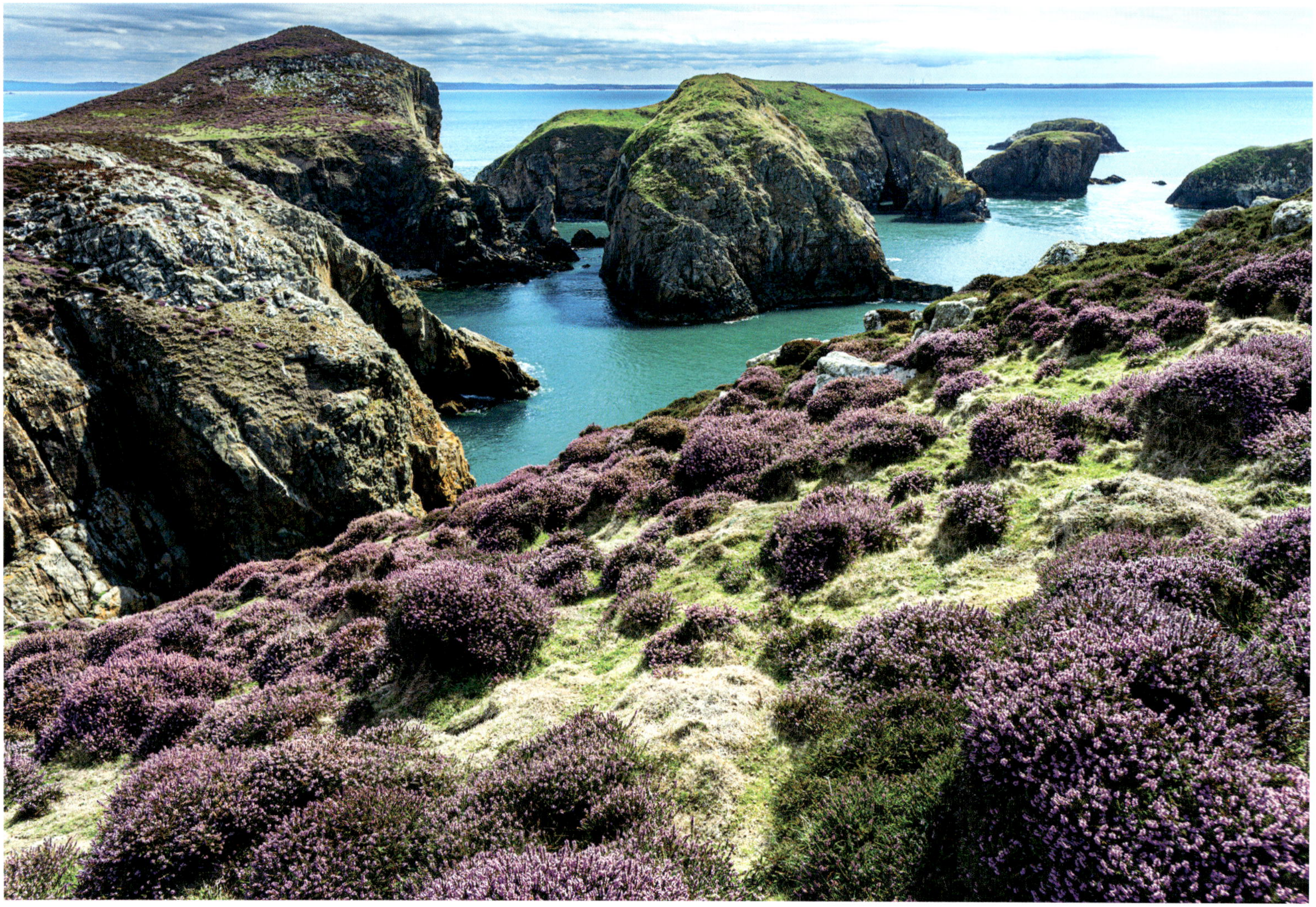

Heather Grug *Calluna vulgaris*

Bell Heather
Grug y Mêl
Erica cinerea

Bell heather tends to flower well before heather, and is perhaps the most outstanding of the heath species, although it is not as frequent as heather and is mainly restricted to drier ground. The Welsh name means 'honey heather', a perfect name for this important nectar source. On warm summer days, the purple heath can smell just like a freshly opened jar of best honey.

Cross-leaved Heath
Grug Croesddail
Erica tetralix

Cross-leaved heath earns its name from the whorls of four slender, grey-green leaves which adorn the length of the stem. In appearance, this is the most delicate of the heaths, with soft, pale pink clusters of bell-shaped flowers at the end of long, waving stems. It thrives in harsh, acidic, wetter areas and bogs. It has been used as a dye in the woollen industry.

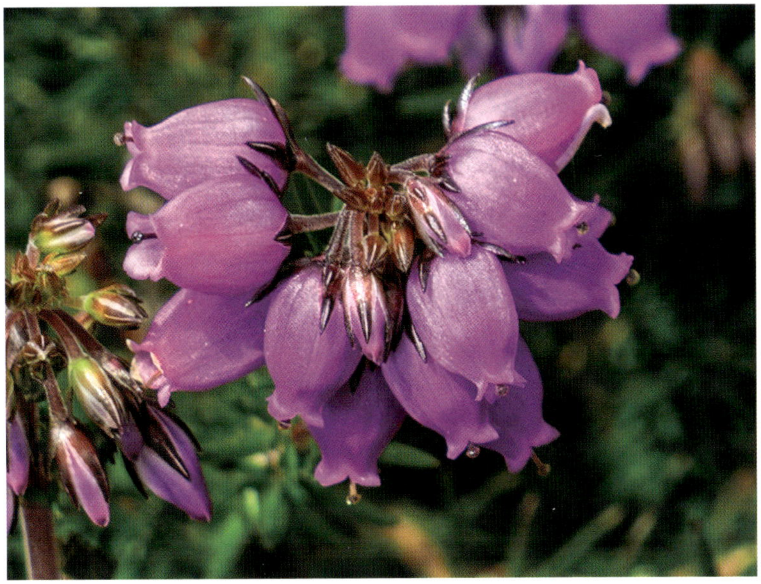

Bell Heather
Grug y Mêl
Erica cinerea

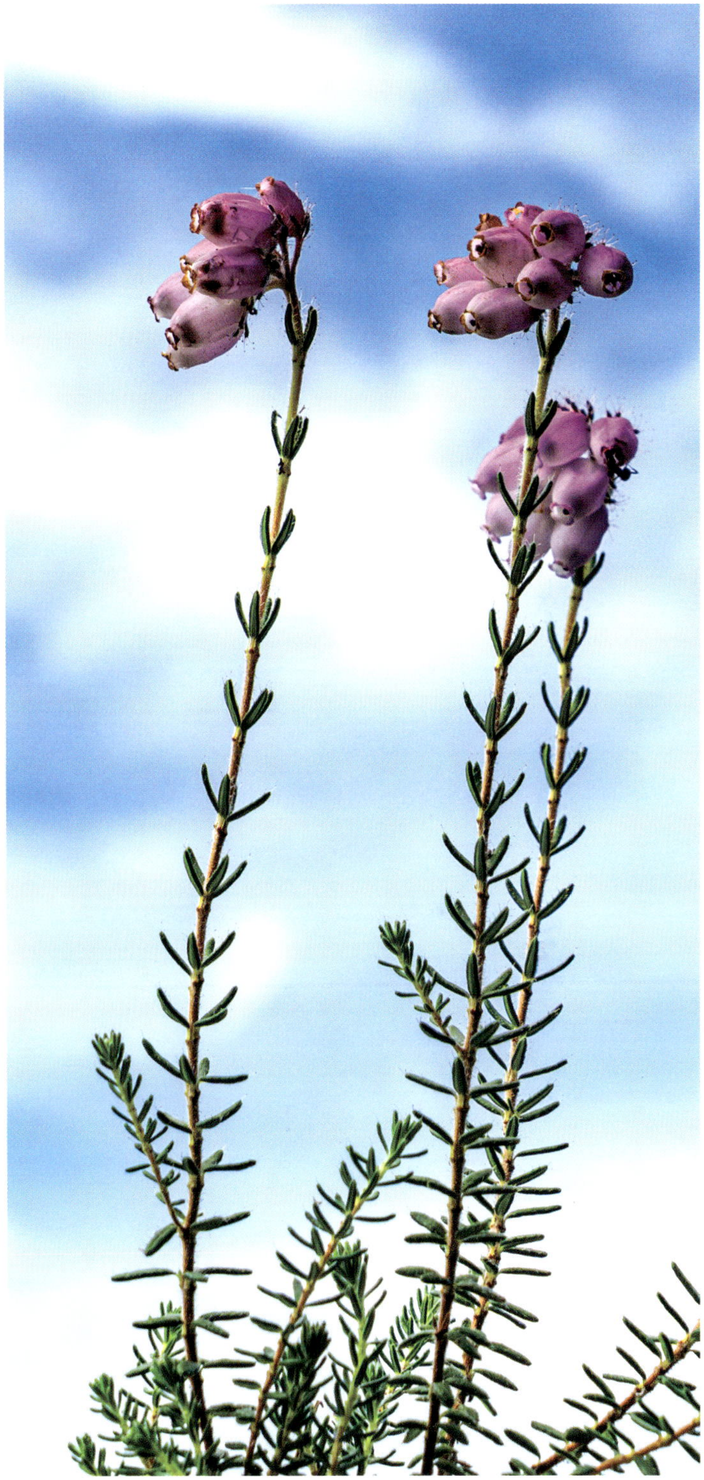

Cross-leaved Heath
Grug Croesddail
Erica tetralix

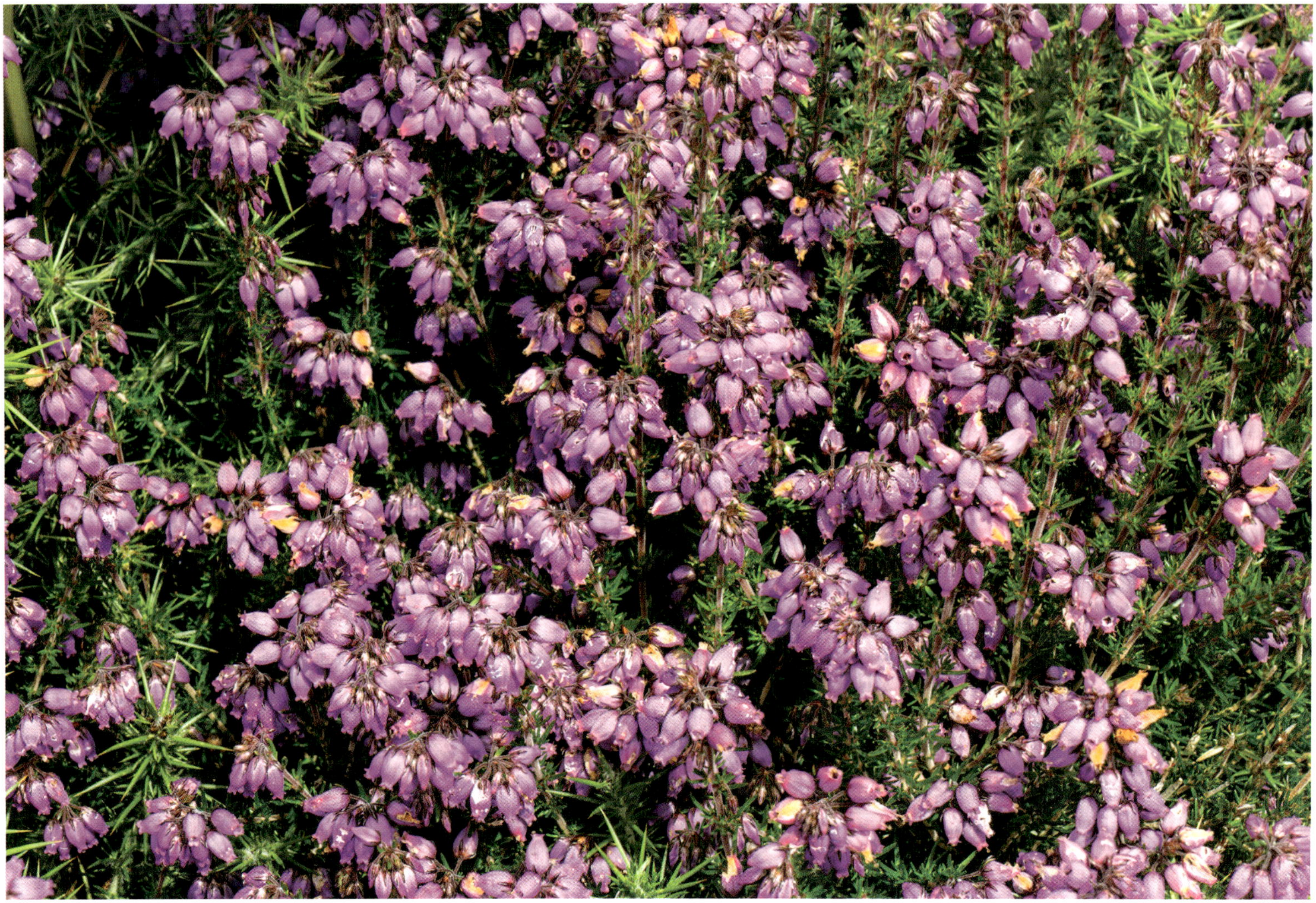

Bell Heather Grug y Mêl *Erica cinerea*

Mynydd Mawr

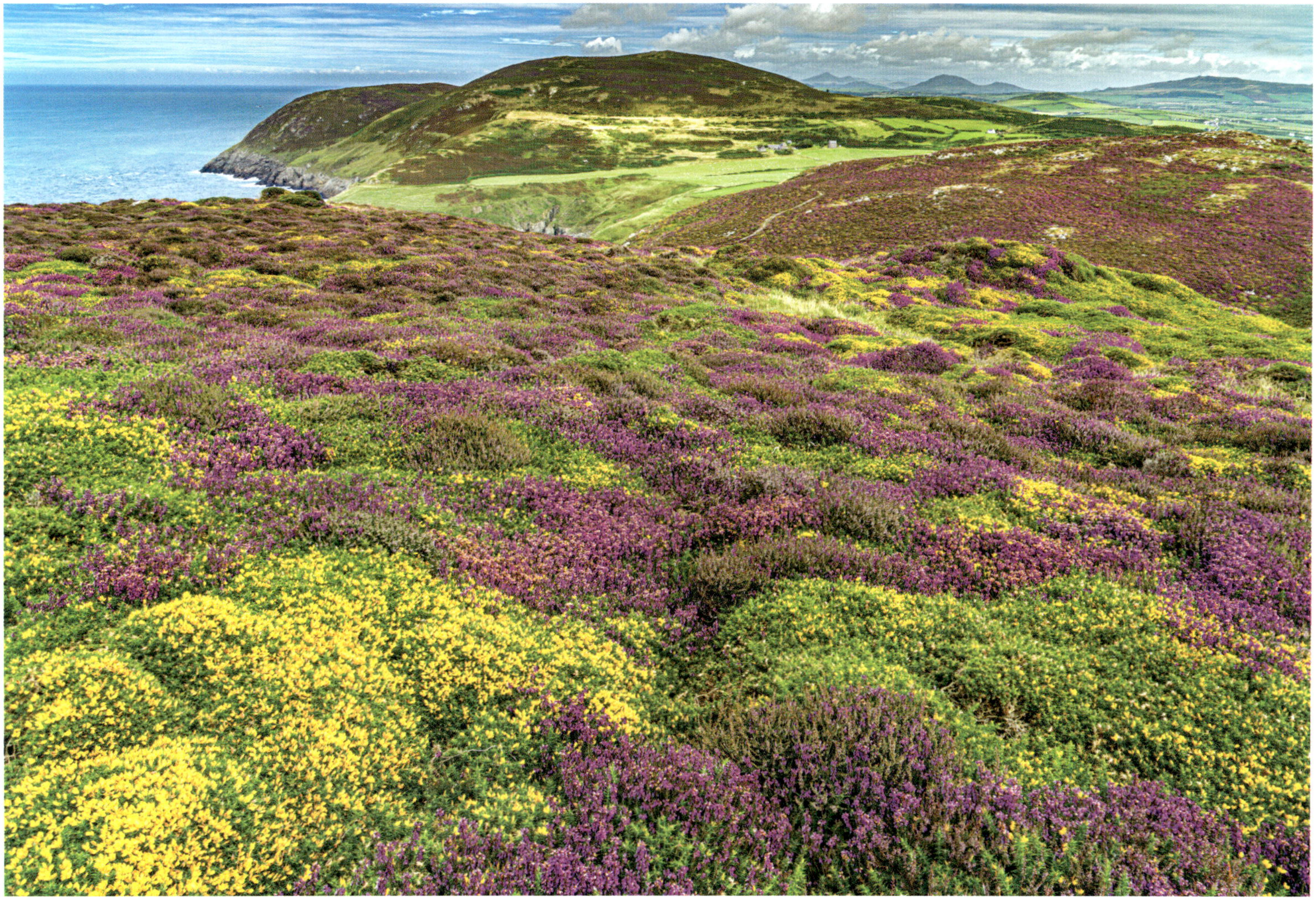

Bell Heather Grug y Mêl *Erica cinerea*

Primrose Family Teulu'r Friallen

Primrose
Briallen
Primula vulgaris

Primroses have a delicate fragrance, which is soft and sweet. Sadly, as we age, our ability to detect the scent fades, until it survives mostly as a memory of springtimes long gone. Perhaps they have such a precious place in childhood recollections because they are one of the first hedgerow flowers to appear at the end of winter (as their name suggests, the first rose of spring), but their gentle beauty alone is more than enough to create long-lasting memories. According to folklore, they are the symbol of youth and (if only I had known!) children who eat them are able to see fairies. In earlier times, both the flowers and leaves were used in salads. It was a popular herbalists' plant, considered a cure for many ailments, and in Wales it was regarded as a treatment for insanity. Primroses occupy a restricted niche on sea cliffs, but you may find them – sometimes in profusion – during March, April and May, on the north-facing or most sheltered steeply sloping, grassy cliff banks. Anne Brontë (1820–49) captures so much of what this flower means to many of us in these lines from the poem 'Memory':

> That I might simply fancy there
> One little flower – a primrose fair,
> Just opening into sight;
> As in the days of infancy,
> An opening primrose seemed to me
> A source of strange delight.

The poem at the bottom of the page is by one of my favourite Welsh poets, Eifion Wyn (1867–1926). I hesitated for some time over including it because it is so sombre, but it is also deeply beautiful. In parts of Wales, Palm Sunday is known as *Sul y Blodau* (Flowering Sunday), traditionally a day when fresh flowers are laid on graves. Eifion Wyn wrote a poem by this name as a tribute to his brother, Goronwy, who died in early childhood. I have included one verse from it below left, with an English translation by J W Wynne-Jones below right.

Cwsg, fy mhlentyn, heb dy fami,
Cwsg yn erw Duw;
Casglu blodau buom iti,
Sul y Blodau yw:
Chwe briallen fach y ddywed
Mai yr haf yw hi,
Cwsg odanynt heb eu gweled
Cwsg, fy rhosyn i.

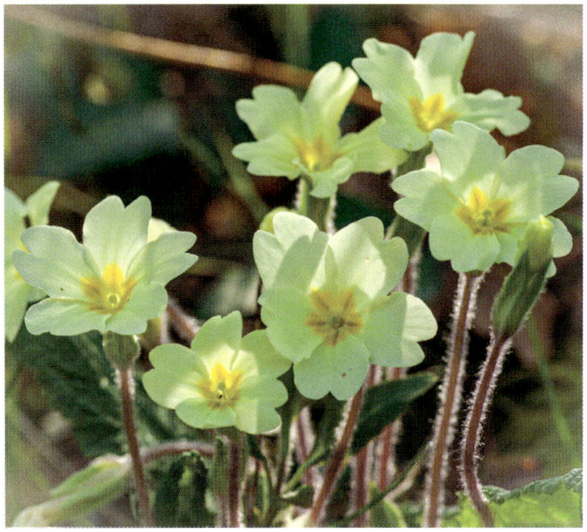

Sleep, my child, without thy mother,
In God's acre rest;
We, this Flower Sunday, gather
Posies for thy breast:
Six small primroses unfolding
Tell of summer mild;
Sleep beneath them, none beholding,
Sleep, my rose, my child.

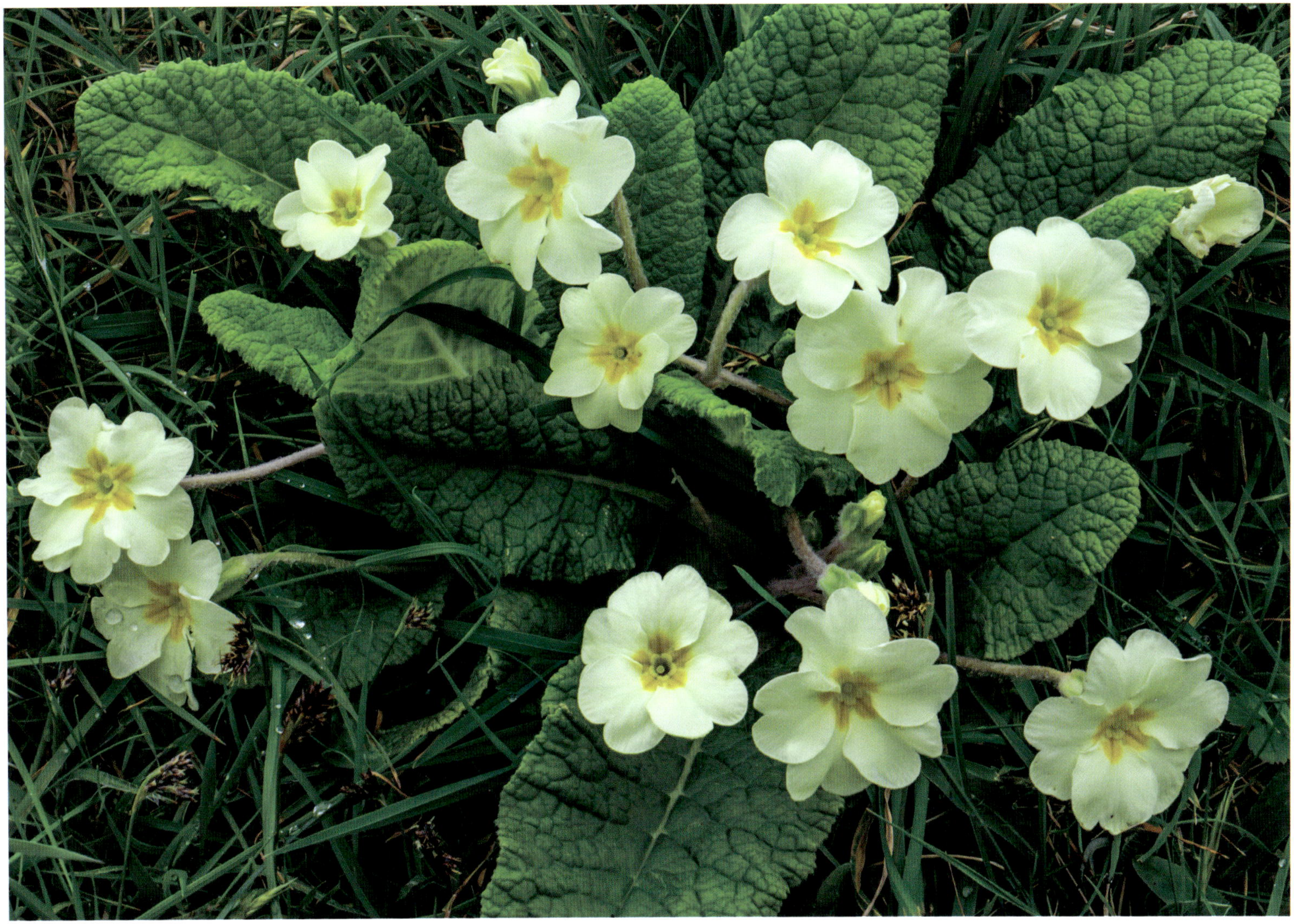

Above and previous page: Primrose Briallen *Primula vulgaris*

Cowslip
Briallen Fair
Primula veris

Cowslip is another familiar member of the primrose family, commonly found on limestone clifftops and mature sand dunes. Their name, derived from 'cowpat', does little justice to this beautiful flower, but it is appropriate for a plant which was once an abundant meadow species. Today, it is most often seen on road verges and, of course, the cliffs of west Wales.

Scarlet Pimpernel
Llysiau'r Cryman
Anagallis arvensis

Scarlet pimpernel is, surprisingly, a member of the primrose family, although it bears little resemblance to its relatives. The name has a familiar ring because of the romantic novel *The Scarlet Pimpernel* by Baroness Orczy, set in the time of the French Revolution. This plant, with its sprawling, orange-red flowers, is known as *llysiau'r cryman* in Welsh. This clumsily translates as 'sickle herb', an excellent name for a typical 'weed' species which will readily take advantage of disturbed ground – possibly ground cleared with a sickle. Scarlet pimpernel favours disturbed and bare areas in sand dunes and on clifftops, which are created by animals grazing, people trampling or natural processes. Pimpernels can look disappointing on dull days, because they only open in sunlight, closing in late afternoon and when skies become overcast.

Bog Pimpernel
Gwlyddyn Mair y Gors
Anagallis tenella

Bog pimpernel is the member of this family least like a primrose in appearance. This is a low, spreading plant of wet places, particularly coastal flushes where water continually percolates through peaty turf. The delicate flowers appear pale pink from a distance, but in close-up the petals are white with dark pink, closely spaced veins. In common with their relatives, the flowers only open in sunlight.

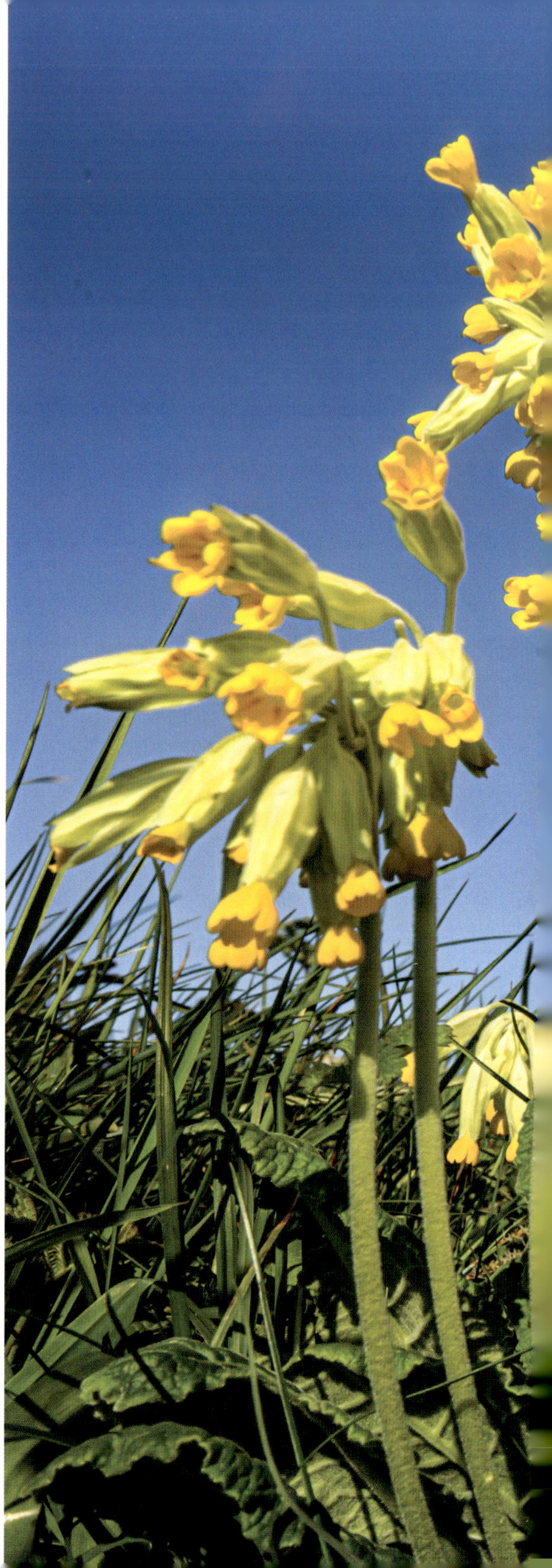

Cowslip
Briallen Fair
Primula veris

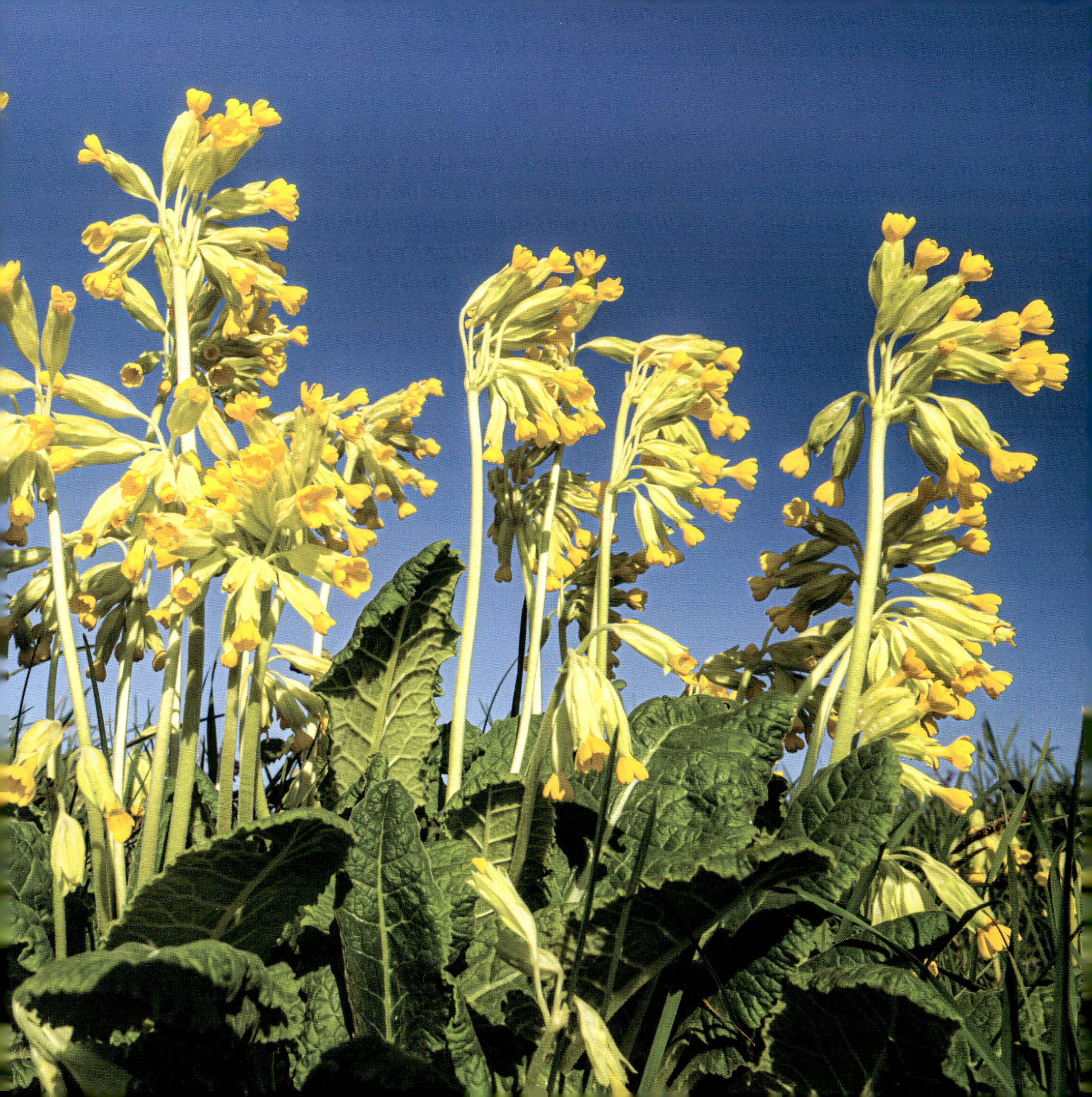

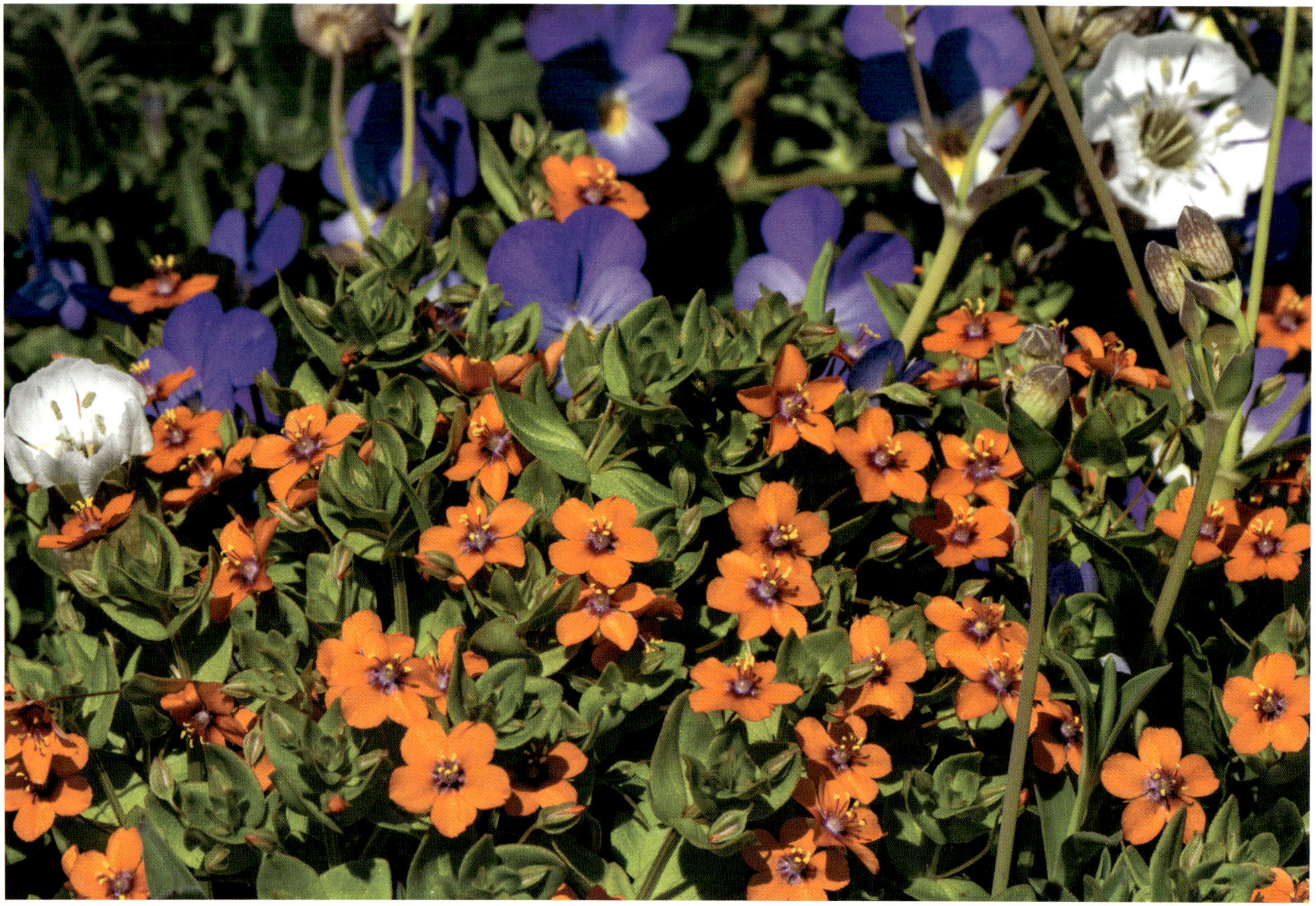

Above: Scarlet Pimpernel Llysiau'r Cryman *Anagallis arvensis*
Next page: Bog Pimpernel Gwlyddyn Mair y Gors *Anagallis tenella*

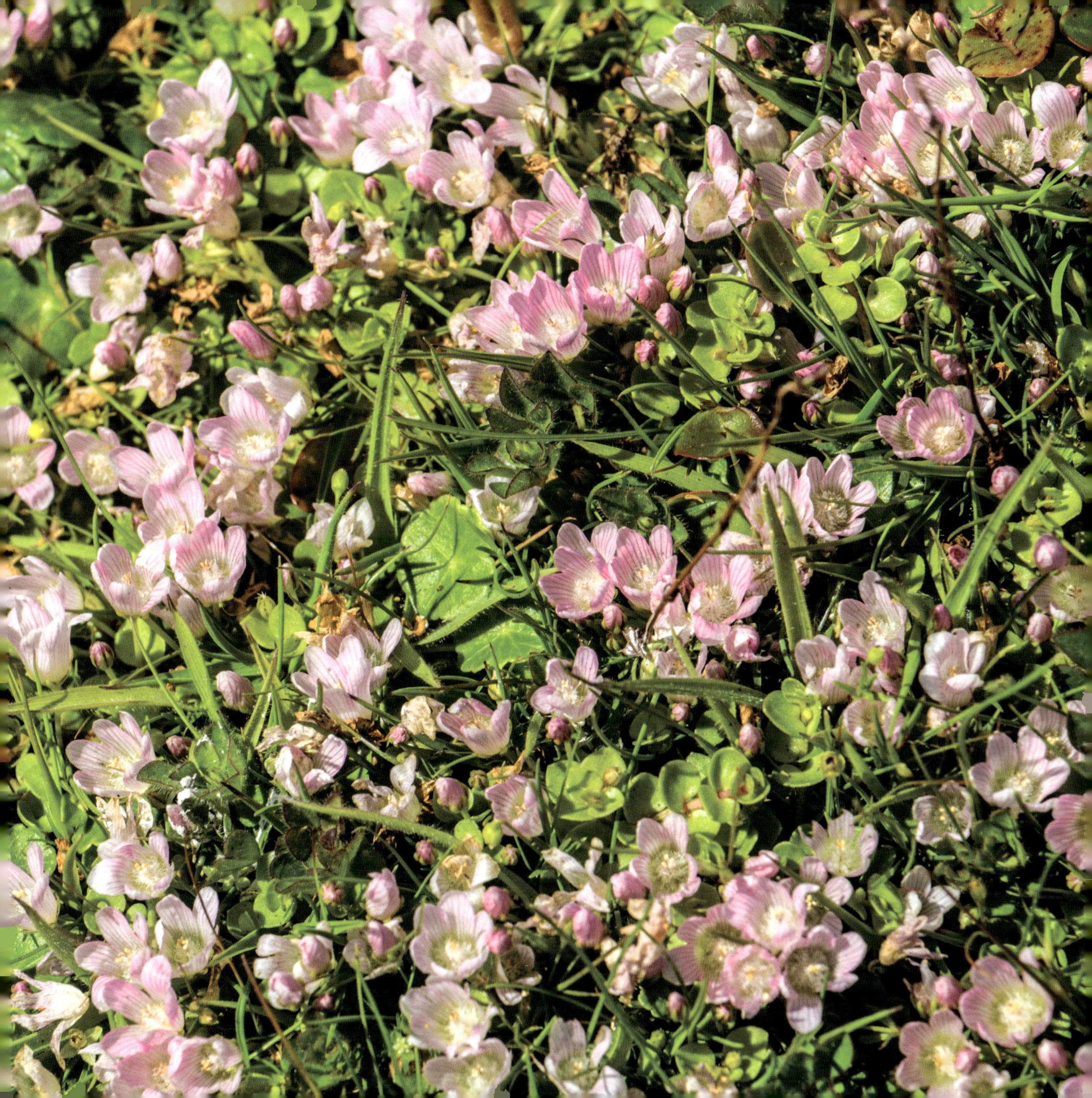

Loosestrife Family Teulu Llysiau'r Milwr

Purple-loosestrife
Llysiau'r Milwr Coch
Lythrum salicaria

Purple-loosestrife stands out among the vivid greens of wet and marshy places with a dappling of brilliant purple or magenta which lasts right through the summer. Usually, solitary plants or small clumps of flowers are scattered through the damp, verdant vegetation, but occasionally they form large, dazzling patches of colour, alive with buzzing insects. It is a persistent and reliable species. Generally, once you have found a patch, you will be able to revisit each year with a high expectation of finding it again. I was enchanted by two vibrant swathes of loosestrife when I first discovered them on Skomer Island back in the 1960s, and they remain special to me, providing continuity as they reappear in the same place year after year. Purple-loosestrife is an extremely popular nectar source for butterflies and other insects, which makes a loosestrife patch on a warm, sunny day a perfect place to sit quietly and watch the shimmer of living things. I took the photograph of the red admiral butterfly on Skomer, in a cluster of loosestrife swarming with bees and other insects, including six different butterfly species. Kenneth Grahame captures the atmosphere wonderfully in just a few words in *The Wind in the Willows*:

> The pageant of the river bank had marched steadily along, unfolding itself in scene-pictures that succeeded each other in stately procession. Purple loosestrife arrived early, shaking luxuriant locks along the edge of the mirror whence its own face laughed back at it. Willow-herb, tender and wistful, like a pink sunset cloud, was not slow to follow.

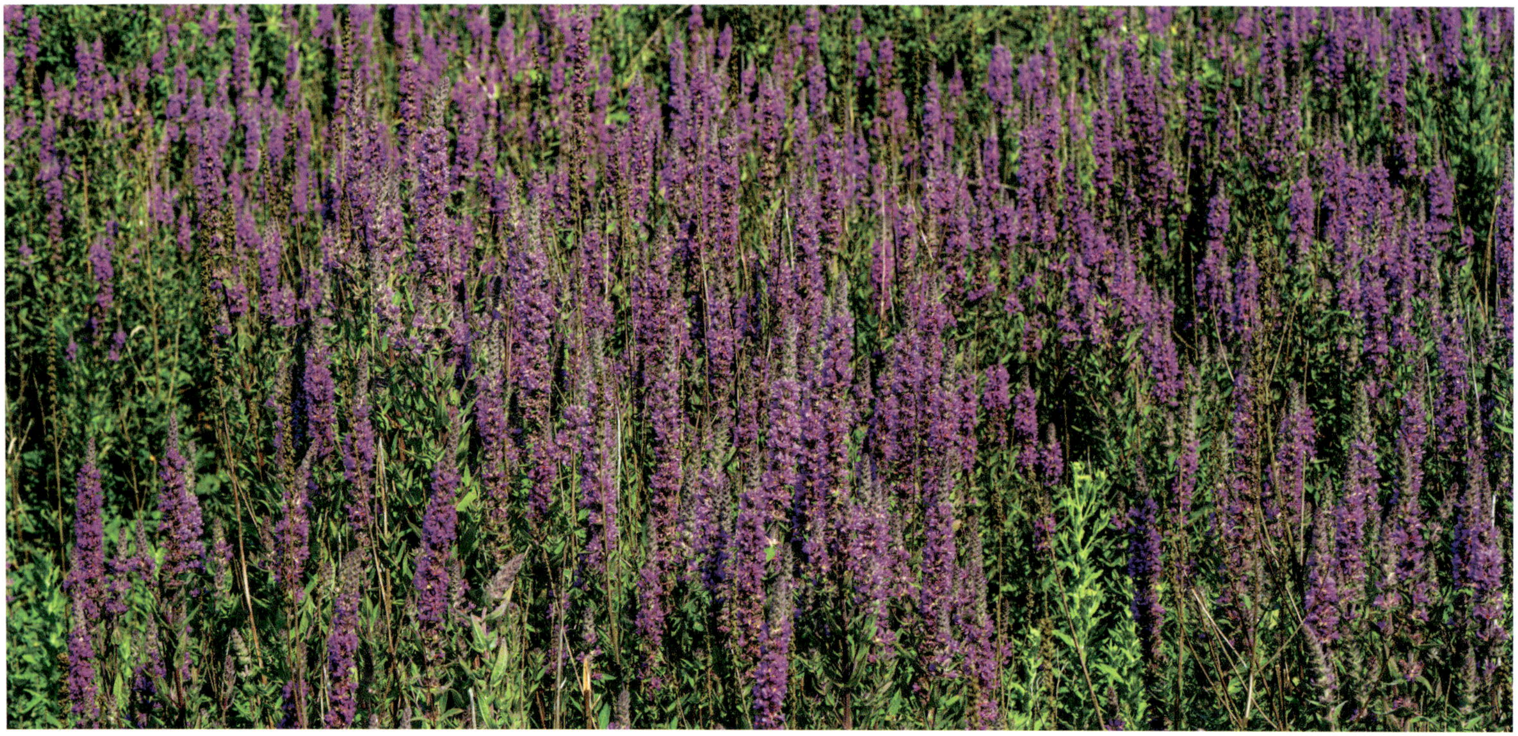

Purple-loosestrife Llysiau'r Milwr Coch *Lythrum salicaria*

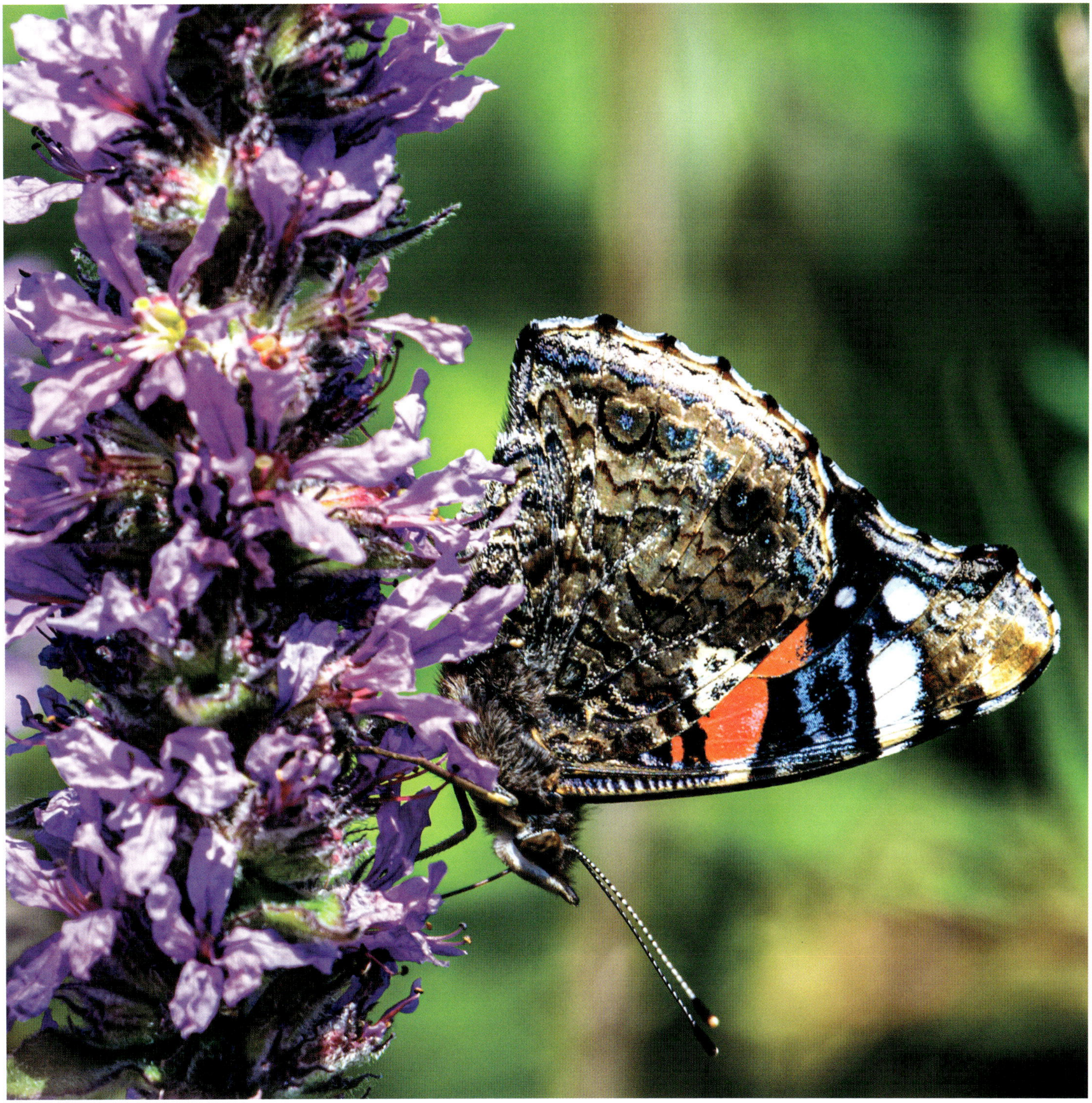

Red Admiral butterfly Mantell Goch *Vanessa atalanta*

Stonecrop Family Teulu'r Friweg

This is a family of hardy, succulent plants, with the characterisically thick, fleshy leaves of many drought-tolerant species. The two stonecrops I have included are different colours, but otherwise have similar tiny flowers, which grow in low mats. The third member of the family, navelwort, is obviously different, with upright flower spikes adorned with whorls of small, bell-shaped flowers.

The family name, stonecrop, is apt, since these are all plants which thrive on rock outcrops, sea cliffs and drystone walls. These tend to be places with little or no soil, which dry out in summer.

Biting Stonecrop
Briweg Boeth
Sedum acre

Biting stonecrop has golden yellow, star-shaped flowers which can grow closely together in low-lying clusters. As its name implies, it has a hot, biting taste and the sap can cause a rash. It was traditionally planted on roofs because it was credited with the magical property of being able to deflect lightning.

English Stonecrop
Briweg y Cerrig
Sedum anglicum

English stonecrop has similar habitat requirements to biting stonecrop. It is widespread and common, probably more so than its golden relative. The sun-loving, star-like flowers are white with a delicate pink tinge.

Navelwort
Deilen Gron
Umbilicus rupestris

Both the English and scientific names of navelwort come from the unusual rounded leaves, which have a navel-like centre. Widespread around the cliffs, these plants favour slightly sheltered places and have a strong affinity for old stone walls with lime mortar. The flower stalks can vary from green to dark red and the flowers shade from pale yellow-green to dark pink. Plants growing in moist, shady places are often completely green, while those growing in sunshine will have altogether redder stalks, leaves and flowers.

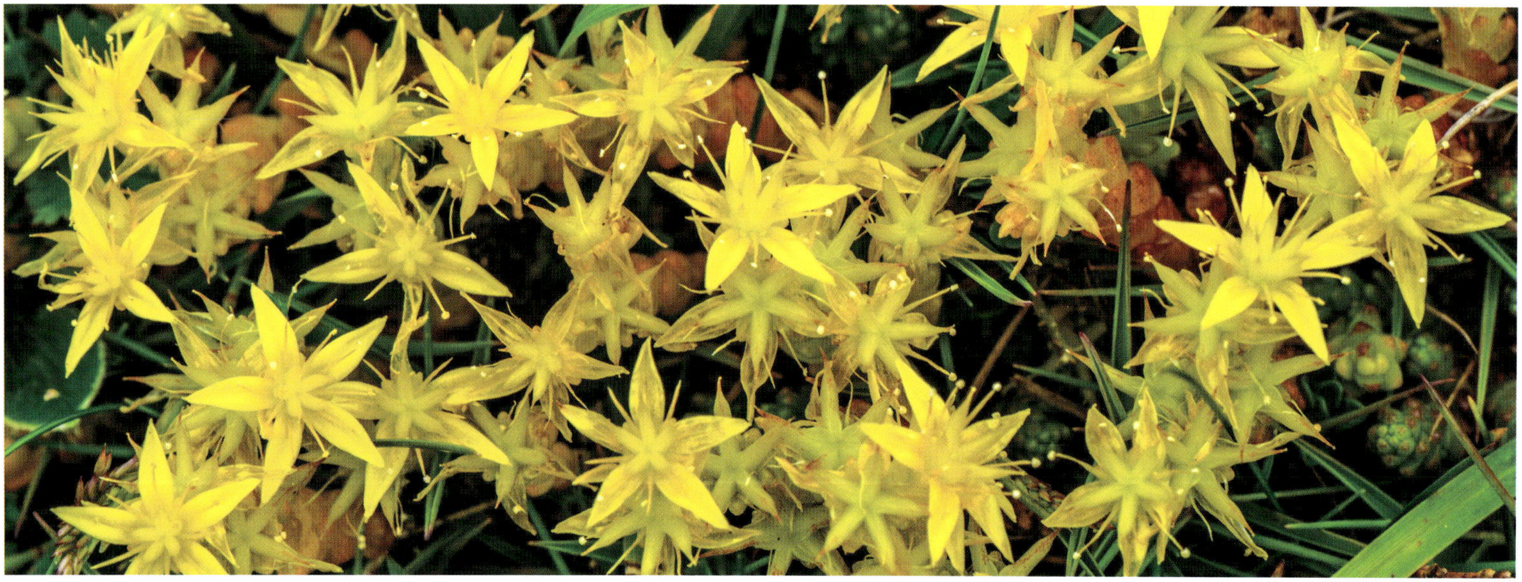

Biting Stonecrop Briweg Boeth *Sedum acre*

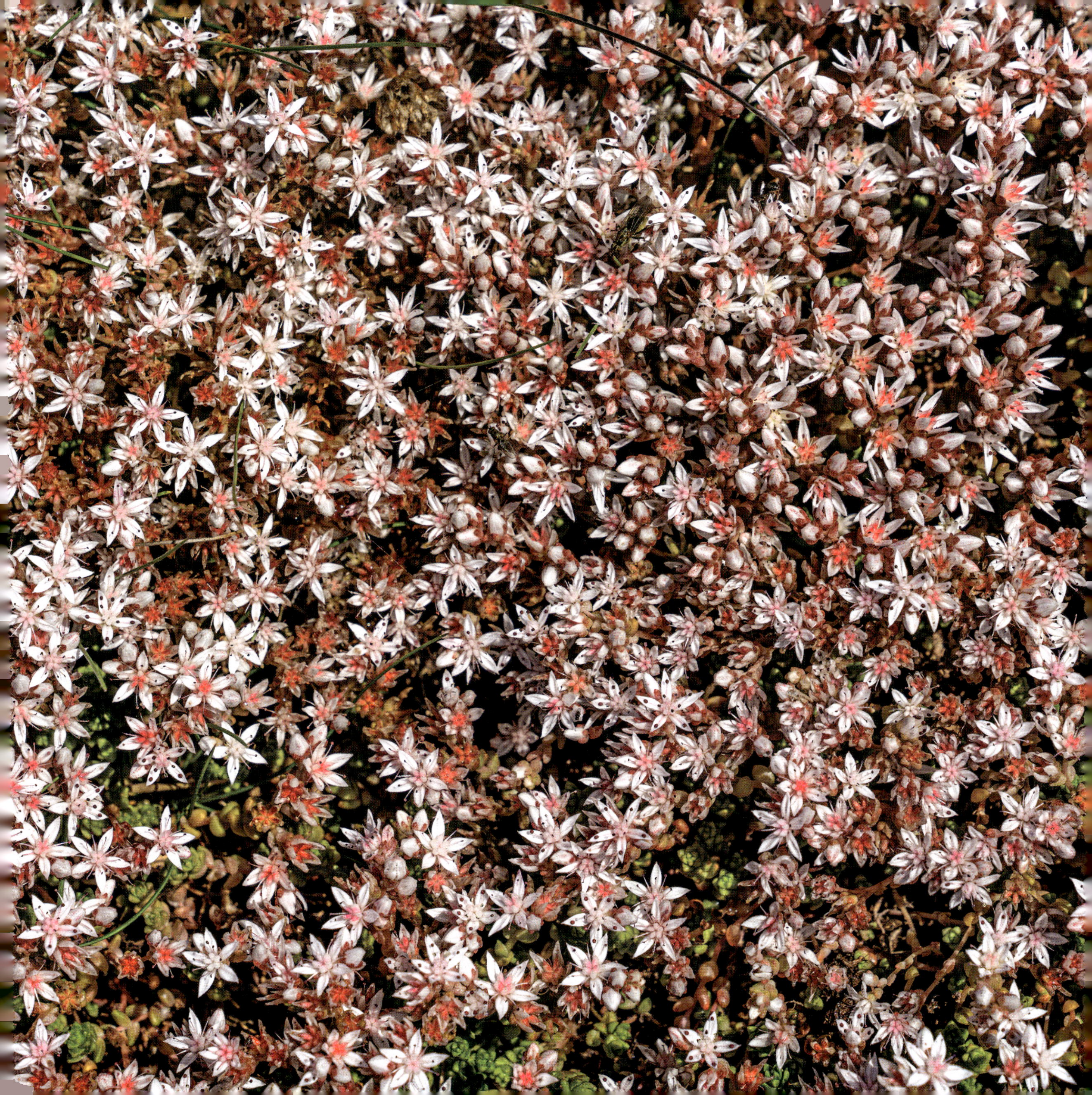

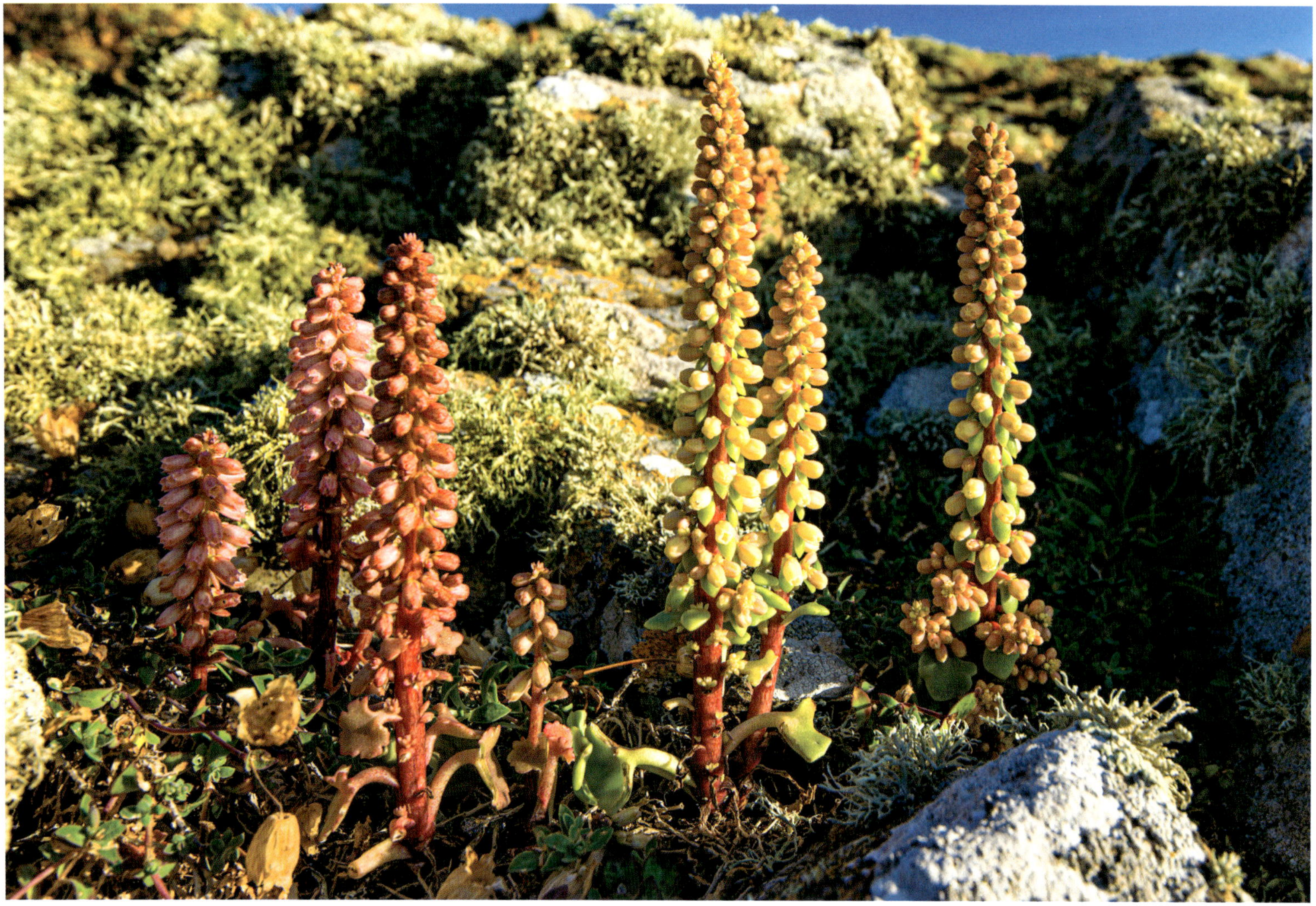

Navelwort Deilen Gron *Umbilicus rupestris*
Previous page: English Stonecrop Briweg y Cerrig *Sedum anglicum*

Rose Family Teulu'r Rhosyn

'We can complain because rose bushes have thorns or rejoice because thorn bushes have roses' is a quote often attributed to Abraham Lincoln, but which in fact seems to come from French writer Alphonse Karr's *A Tour Round My Garden*.

Wild roses have symbolic meanings in many different cultures, including Western, Eastern, Chinese, Japanese and Native American traditions. During the Victorian era in Britain, wild roses achieved high status because in the language of flowers, which became popular at that time, they symbolised love, beauty and elegance. Greek mythology associated the wild rose with Aphrodite, creating a powerful image of the goddess rising from the sea with white foam at her feet, and wherever the foam touched the ground, wild roses sprang into bloom. It is not surprising that, from the earliest times, so many cultures have cherished wild roses. Their subtle, ephemeral beauty is all the more captivating because the delicate blooms have such a short flowering period. After just a few weeks in late spring, their fragile, soft-coloured petals are lost. In contrast, the plants themselves are long-lived. Most years, I make a short pilgrimage to a favourite rose bush, growing at the edge of a field that my uncle once owned. I can still remember my aunt collecting the rose hips to make syrup in the early 1950s. This, however, is nothing compared to the Rose of Hildesheim in Germany. Known as the Thousand-Year Rose, it was planted at least 700 years ago, and is reputed to be the oldest living rose in the world. It is a beautiful wild dog-rose that climbs the outside wall of the cathedral apse.

The wild rose family is large, with many obvious roses, but it also contains numerous species that bear scant resemblance to our image of a typical rose. I have included two clearly recognisable members of the rose family: the burnet rose (because it is a coastal species) and the dog-rose (as they are so common). The third species included in this section is bramble: not a rose, but unmistakably a member of the family. These words of George Meredith (1828–1909), from his poem 'The Wild Rose', set the rose immaculately in one of those soft, warm days we all remember:

> High climbs June's wild rose,
> Her bush all blooms in a swarm;
> And swift from the bud she blows,
> In a day when the wooer is warm;
> Frank to receive and give,
> Her bosom is open to bee and sun:
> Pride she has none,
> Nor shame she knows;
> Happy to live.

Dog-rose
Rhosyn Gwyllt
Rosa canina

Dog-roses always manage to disappoint me. They are gorgeous flowers, but there is never enough time to enjoy them because they have a desperately short flowering season, usually extending to just a few weeks in June. These thorny climbers have clusters of large, sharp, hooked prickles along their stems. They are most often encountered as hedgerow plants, weaving their tangled way through the shrubbery, but they are capable of supporting themselves and standing alone. There are many different species of wild roses, all similar, and all requiring some expertise to identify them. The best approach for most of us is to enjoy the spectacle and not worry too much about identity. We can also look forward to the autumn splendour when the rose bushes are laden with shiny red clusters of hips.

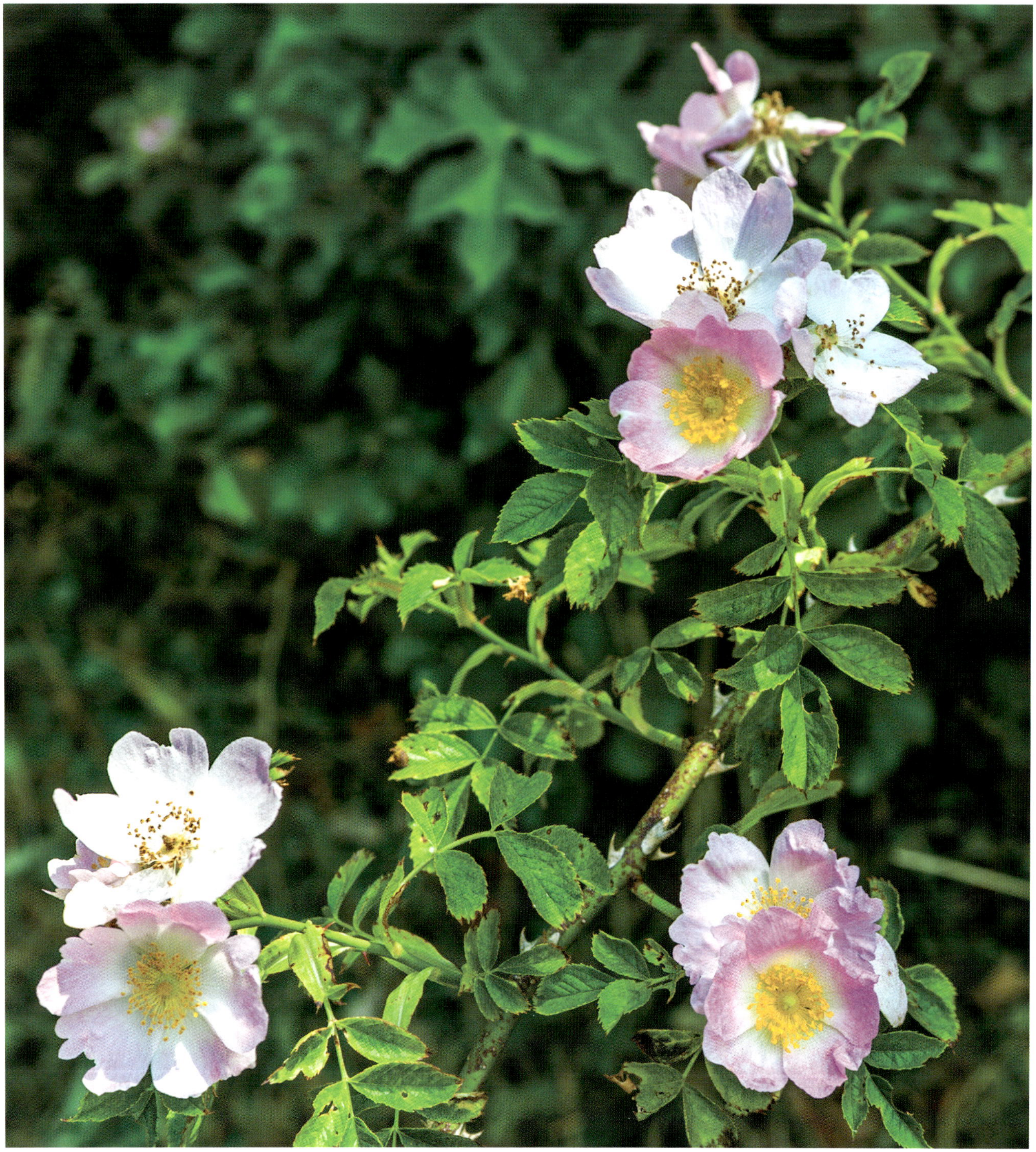

Dog-rose Rhosyn Gwyllt *Rosa canina*

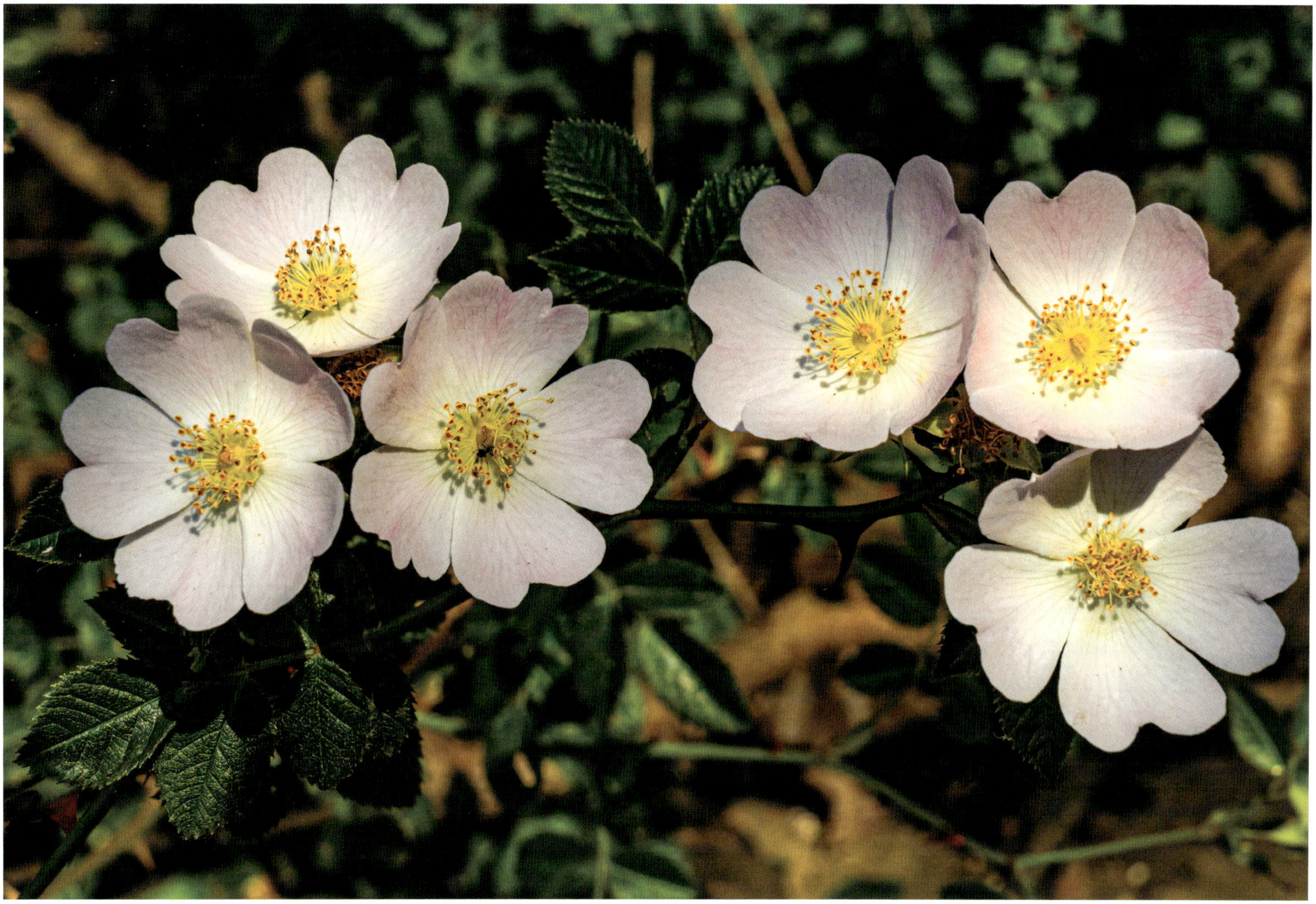

Dog-rose Rhosyn Gwyllt *Rosa canina*

Burnet Rose
Rhosyn Bwrned
Rosa spinosissima

Burnet rose is a coastal species in west Wales, where sand dunes and limestone cliffs are their favoured haunts. This sprawling, low-growing rose has lovely flowers, which are usually white or a subtle creamy colour, and occasionally pink. For me, the greatest find of all is the rare and beautiful variegated variant, with pink-streaked white petals. It would be a mistake to be lulled by such delicate flowers: true to their scientific name, *spinosissima*, the stems are armed with a vicious array of prickles.

The plants can be invasive and locally abundant in the dune grasslands. A good place to see them in a perfect setting is on the sand-covered limestone above Broad Haven, in south Pembrokeshire.

The name burnet, meaning 'dark brown', is derived from the old French, and is a variant of the word 'brunette'. Some authors hold that the burnet rose is so named because, unlike all other wild roses, which have red hips, the burnet rose has dark brown hips, tinged with purple. Another explanation is that the leaves of the burnet rose are similar to salad burnet leaves – another member of the rose family – but I prefer the first version. The burnet rose is also commonly called the Scots rose. It is one of Scotland's most symbolic flowers, second only to the thistle, and has been used as an emblem since the time of Bonnie Prince Charlie (1720–88).

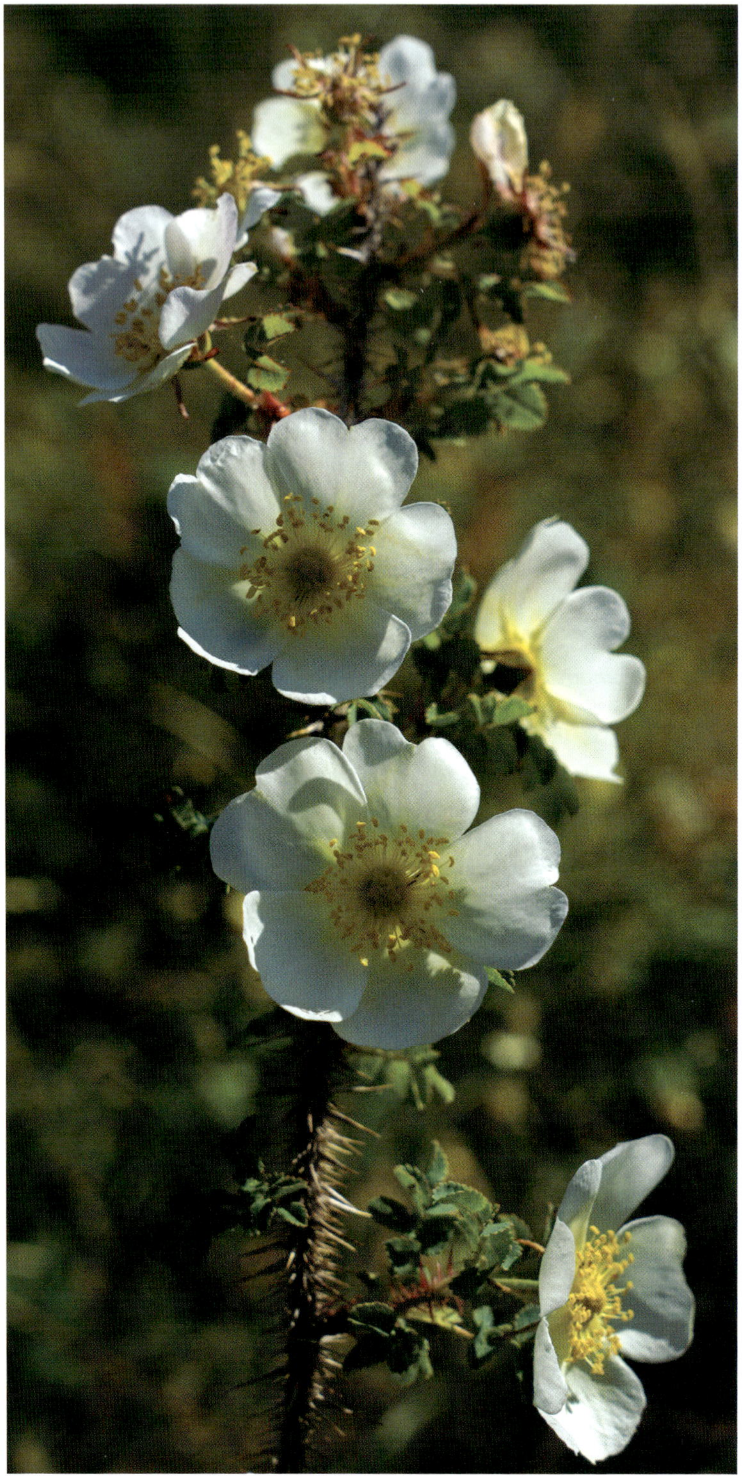

Burnet Rose
Rhosyn Bwrned
Rosa spinosissima

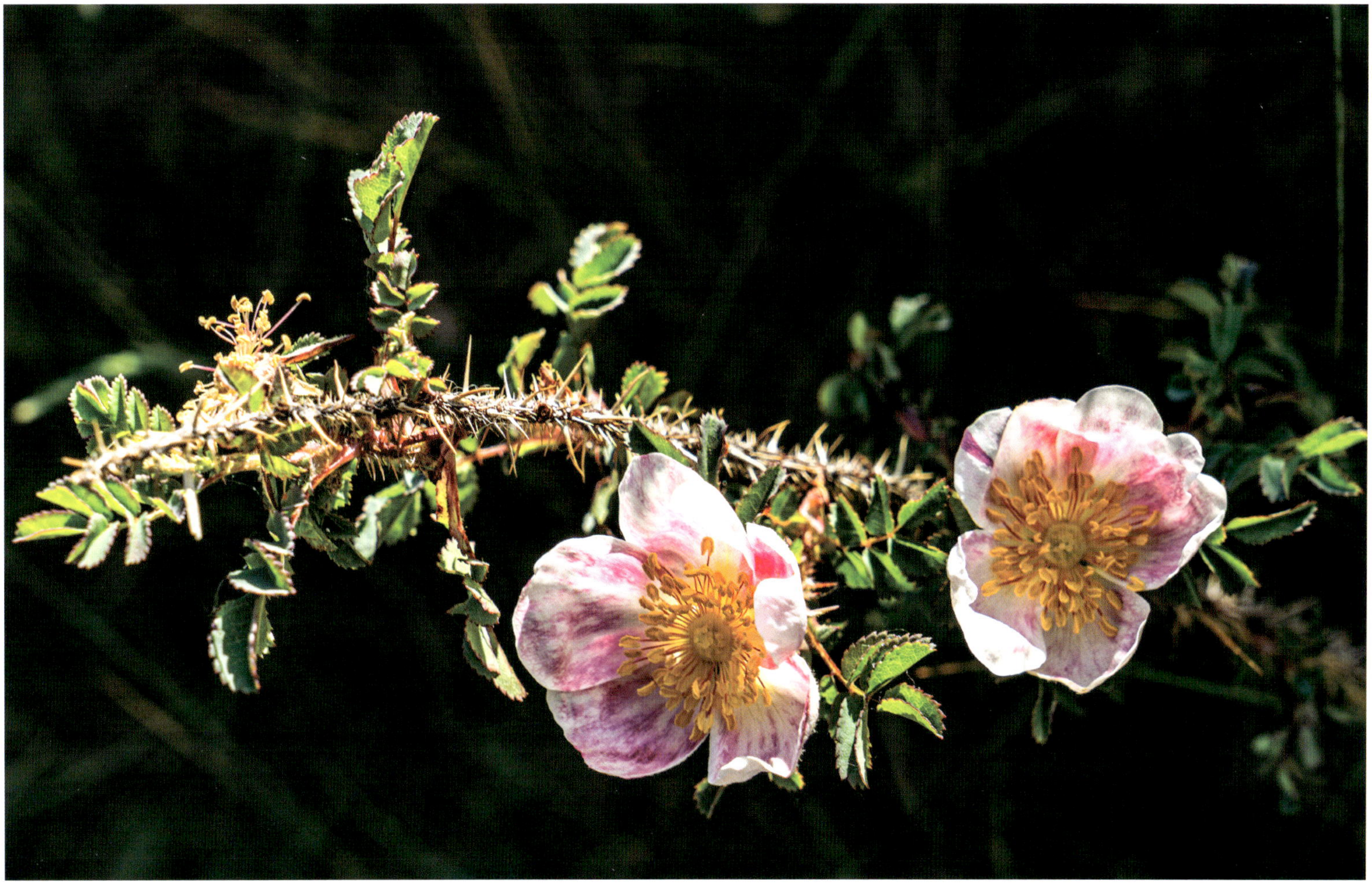

Burnet Rose Rhosyn Bwrned *Rosa spinosissima*

Bramble
Miaren
Rubus fruticosus agg.

Brambles are so common in our countryside that their unassuming, tissue-paper flowers usually go unnoticed, but there is no missing the summer fruit. The inclusion of *agg.* (aggregate) at the end of the scientific name is used to cover a group of similar plants. Brambles are one of our most familiar plants, but they are also one of the most variable. There are over 300 microspecies of bramble in Britain alone, and it requires considerable skill and experience to identify them with any confidence, but this does not distract from our ability to enjoy them. One of my favourite childhood summer activities was blackberry picking, competing with siblings and friends as to who could gather the most, racing from bush to bush and laying claim to the most prolific patches. Then, best of all, teatimes with blackberry tart, crumble, or plain stewed blackberries, and fresh cream from the *crochan* (crock) in the dairy.

Brambles in flower provide an essential nectar source for many different insects, including butterflies. If you want to get close to butterflies, a bramble bush flowering in a sunny location offers great opportunities. I include photographs of four of the more common species of butterfly that make use of brambles as adults.

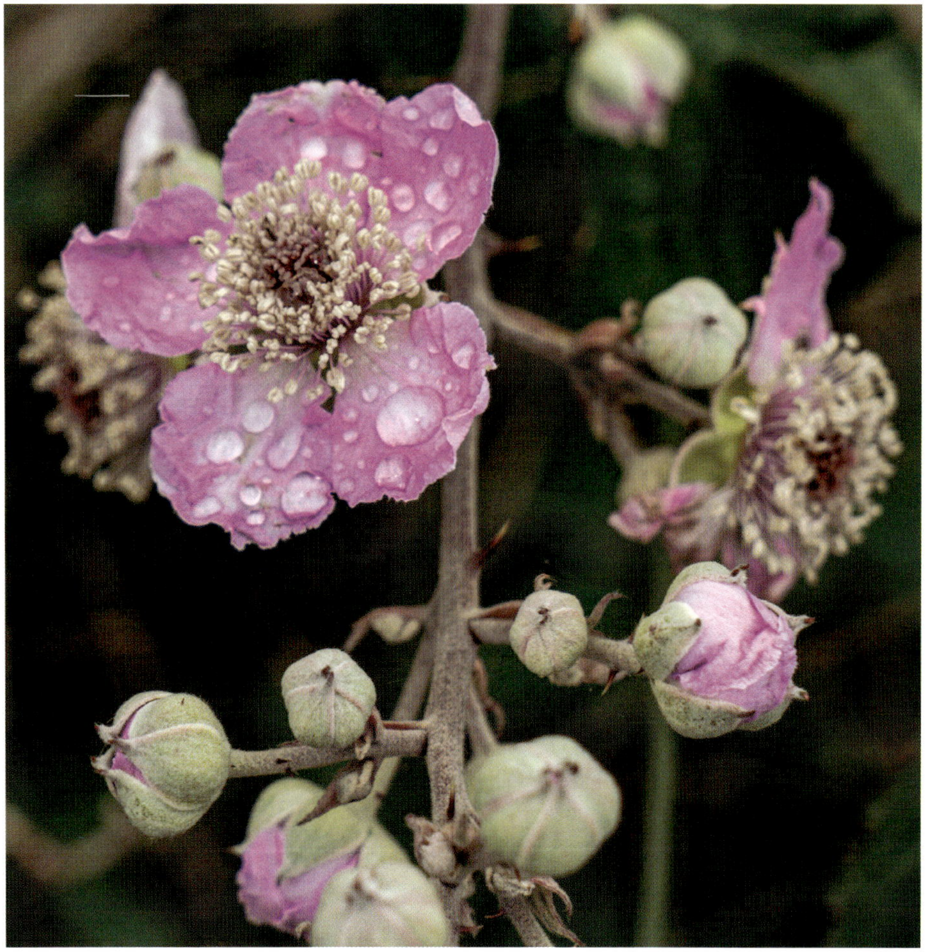

Bramble Miaren *Rubus fruticosus agg.*

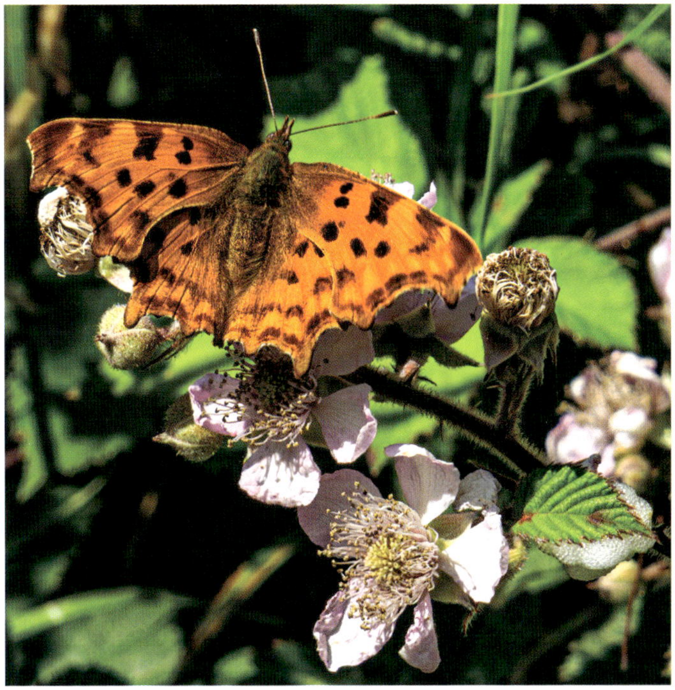

Comma butterfly Mantell Garpiog *Polygonia c-album*

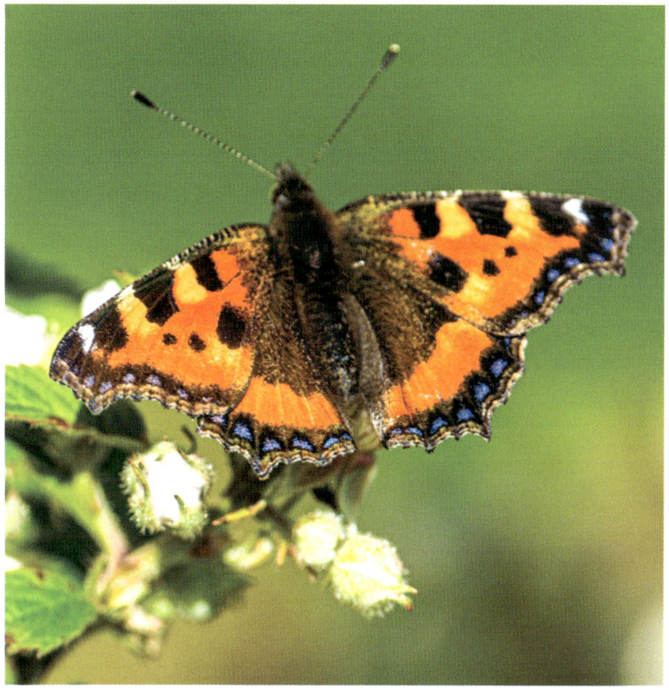

Small Tortoiseshell butterfly Trilliw Bach *Aglais urticae*

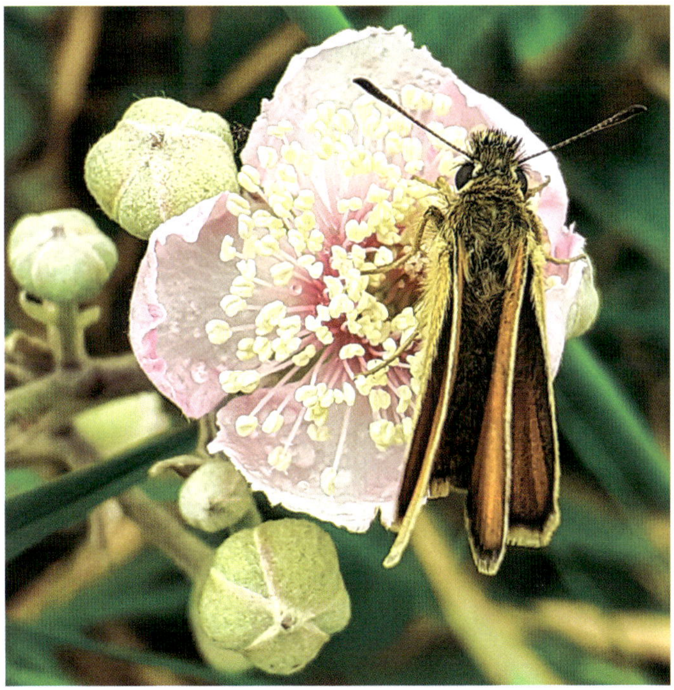

Small Skipper butterfly Gwibiwr Bach *Thymelicus sylvestris*

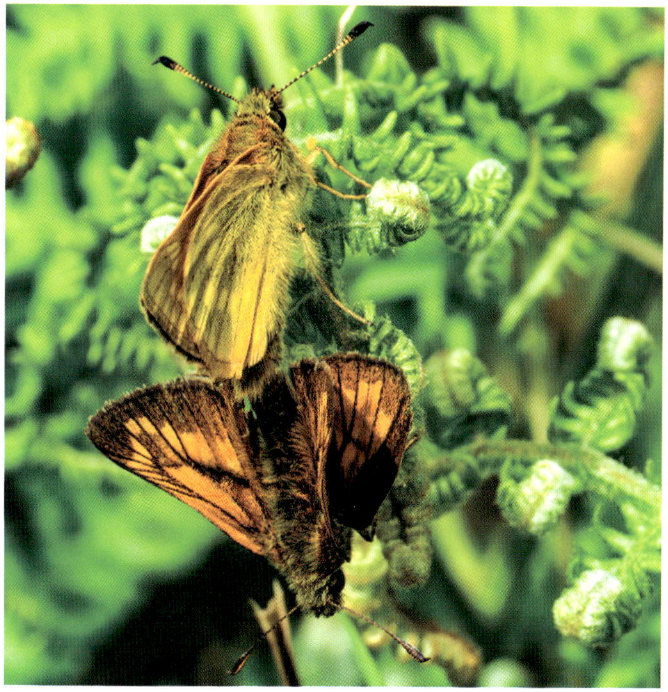

Large Skipper butterfly Gwibiwr Mawr *Ochlodes sylvanus*

Meadowsweet and Cinquefoils Erwain a Phumnalennau

Meadowsweet
Erwain
Filipendula ulmaria

Meadowsweet is a perfect name for this fragrant plant. It is associated with Blodeuwedd, one of the most iconic characters in the Welsh stories of the *Mabinogi*. She is known as the Welsh goddess of spring or flowers, and was created by the legendary wizards Gwydion and Math out of flowers which represented strength, humility and beauty. The following line is taken from the *Mabinogi*:

> *Ac yna y cymerthpwyd blodeu y deri a blodeu y banadyl a blodeu y meillion, ac o'r blodeu hynny y gwnaethpwyd y wreic oreu a'r hardaf a welas dyn eiroed.*
>
> And they took the blossoms of the oak, and the blossoms of the broom, and the blossoms of the meadowsweet, and produced from them a maiden, the fairest and most graceful that man ever saw.

Meadowsweet is a tall, showy plant, which favours damp meadows and similar habitats. The creamy white clusters of flowers are light and elegant, usually standing prominently above the surrounding vegetation. I remember, as a young child, walking along a country lane one late-summer afternoon, with the low sun streaming through the plants and highlighting the glowing, sweet-smelling clouds of petals.

Silverweed
Dail Arian
Potentilla anserina

Silverweed is sometimes called silvery cinquefoil. It gets its name from the silver hairs which cover the fern-like, saw-toothed leaves. In most exposed coastal situations, the plants trail or creep close to the ground, growing in silvery mats, with their solitary lemon-yellow, five-petalled flowers extending above the foliage, but it tends to become more upright when growing in denser vegetation. Silverweed prefers damper places; you will find it on the clifftops and on shingle beaches, often where fresh water percolates through the pebbles, and it will even tolerate occasional inundations of salt water.

In earlier times, it was an important food plant. It is one of the most carbohydrate-rich and palatable of our indigenous plants, and its roots are an excellent source of starch. Accounts of their taste when cooked vary, with some suggesting that they are similar to parsnips and others likening the taste to turnips. Silverweed species were eaten around the world, and there is a fascinating description from North Uist, in the Outer Hebrides, of silverweed cultivation: 'productivity was so great that a man could survive on the roots from a small plot'.

Tormentil
Tresgl y Moch
Potentilla erecta

Tormentil is a common coastal species, found most frequently in places with acid to neutral soils. Unlike most other members of the family, tormentils almost always have four petals instead of the usual five. The yellow flowers often grow in dense clusters on low-lying clumps. In taller vegetation, they can grow much more upright and less crowded.

I am always surprised to learn how many of our common and, today, overlooked wild plants had a significant place in early medicine, folklore, food and trade, and tormentil is yet another example. The roots of tormentil were valued as a source of red dye, called tormentil red, which was used in the tanning trade to colour leather and was also used to make red ink.

The scientific name, *potentilla*, comes from the Latin for 'powerful', while tormentil comes from the Latin for 'colic'. Apparently, the roots, when boiled in milk, were used to cure diarrhoea.

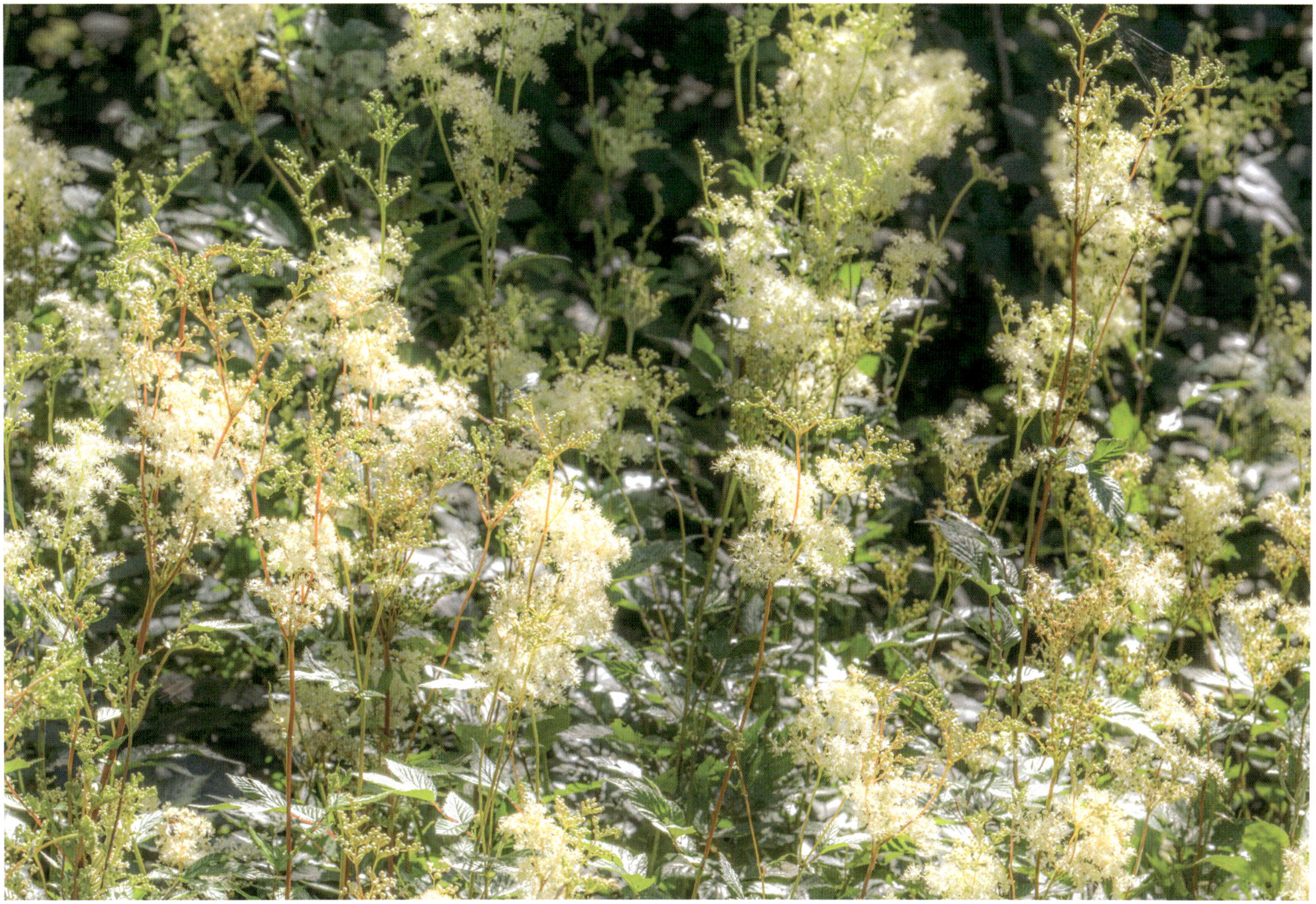

Meadowsweet Erwain *Filipendula ulmaria*

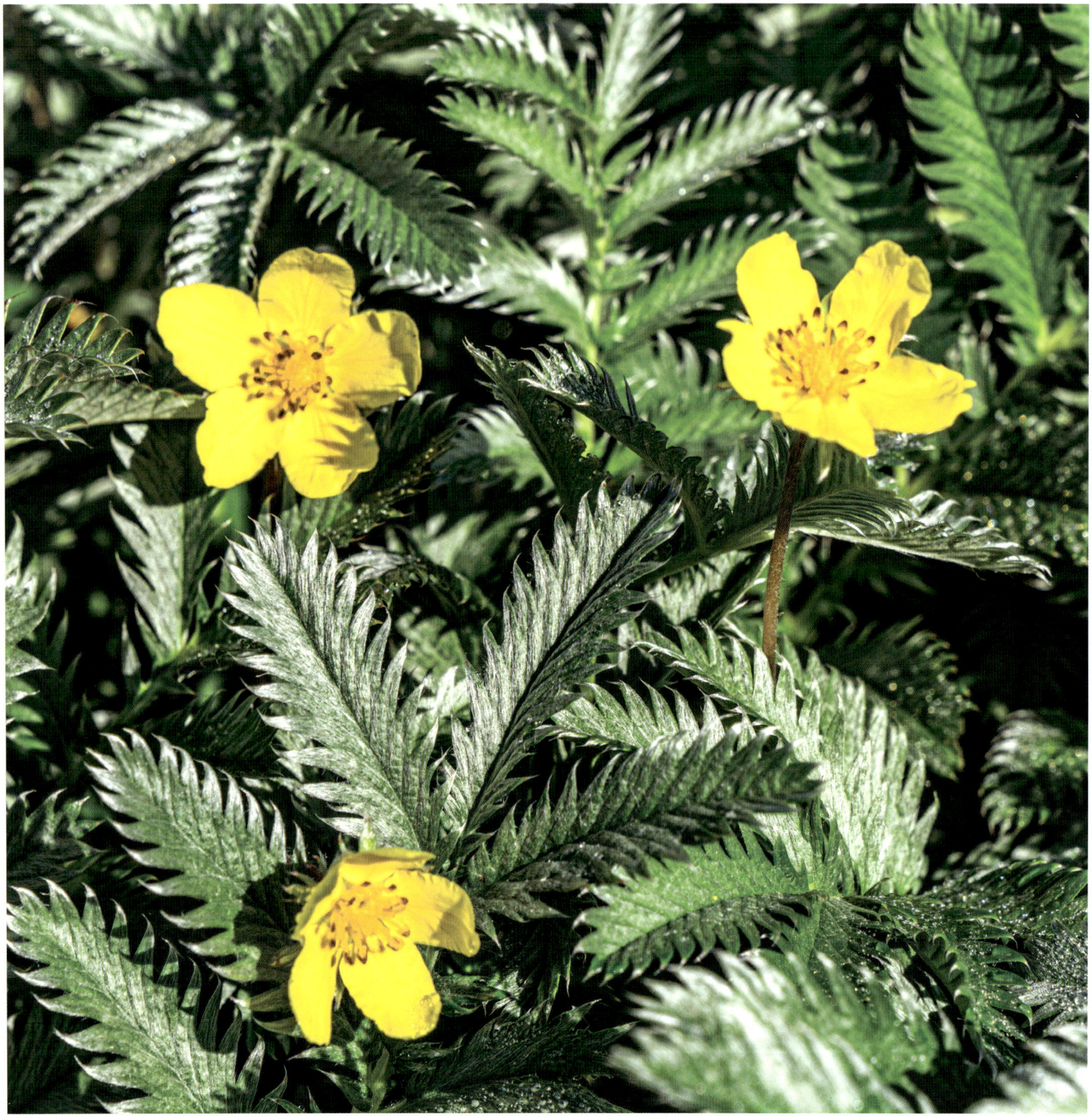

Above: Silverweed Dail Arian *Potentilla anserina*
Next page: Tormentil Tresgl y Moch *Potentilla erecta*

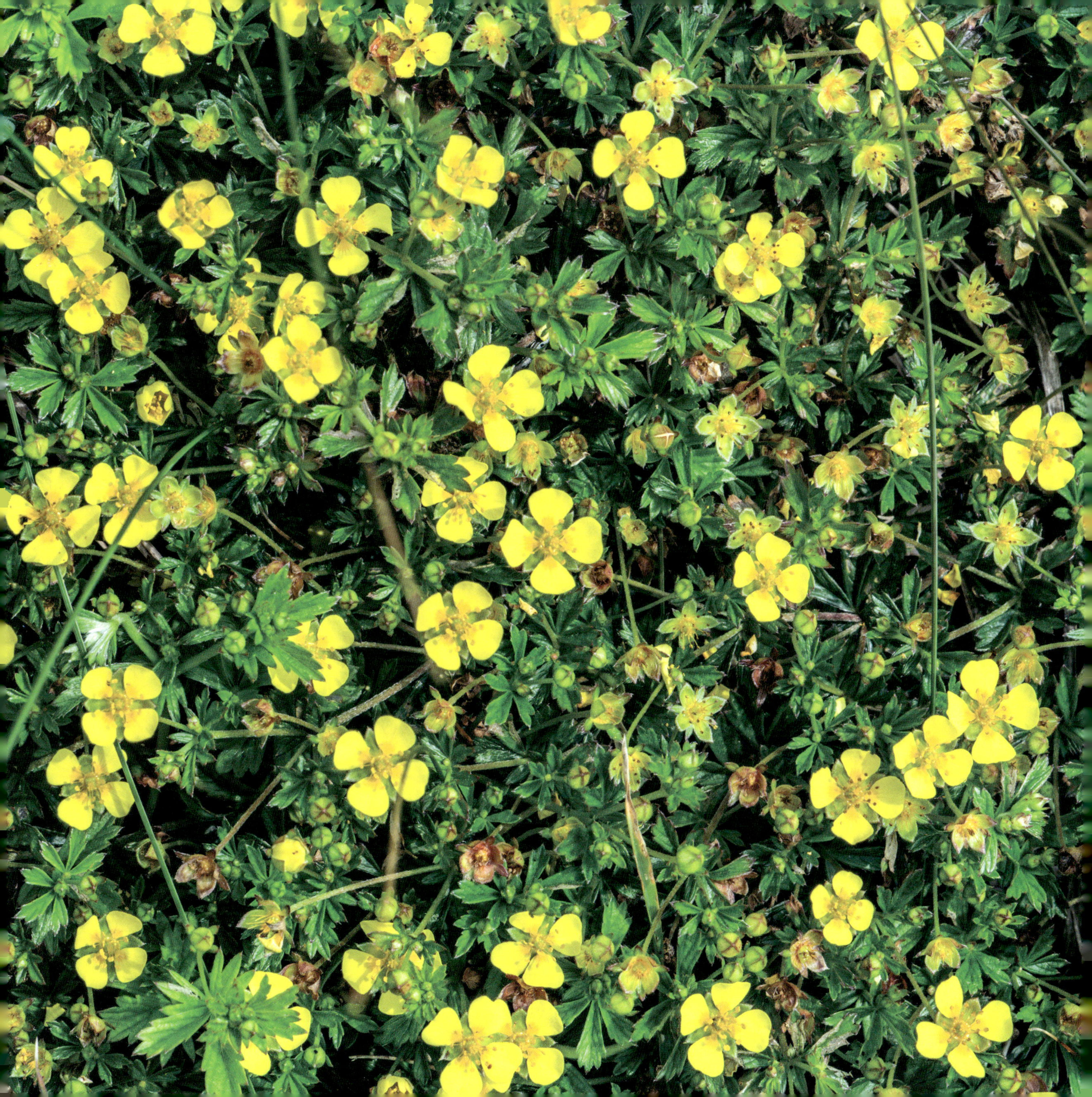

Creeping Cinquefoil
Pumnalen Ymlusgol
Potentilla reptans

Creeping cinquefoil has a name derived from the Vulgar Latin *cinque*, meaning 'five', with *foil* meaning 'leaf'. The creeping plant usually has five toothed leaflets, hence the name – but, just to confuse, sometimes there are more. The flowers, often described as being similar to buttercups, have five yellow petals. This is not an uncommon species, and may often be found along the edges of coastal footpaths. Unfortunately, identification can sometimes be a challenge, because they hybridise with tormentil, the previous flower in this section. The cinquefoils are bigger than tormentil, with distinctly larger flowers and leaves, but the frequent hybrids are confusing. They can look like large-flowered tormentil or small-flowered cinquefoil.

In the Middle Ages and later, supernatural magical properties were attributed to cinquefoils. Plants were hung over doorways to repel witches, with the added benefit that it was said to bring luck and prosperity. This species was occasionally carved in relief in Christian churches, with Gothic arches also frequently shaped to resemble these five-petalled flowers.

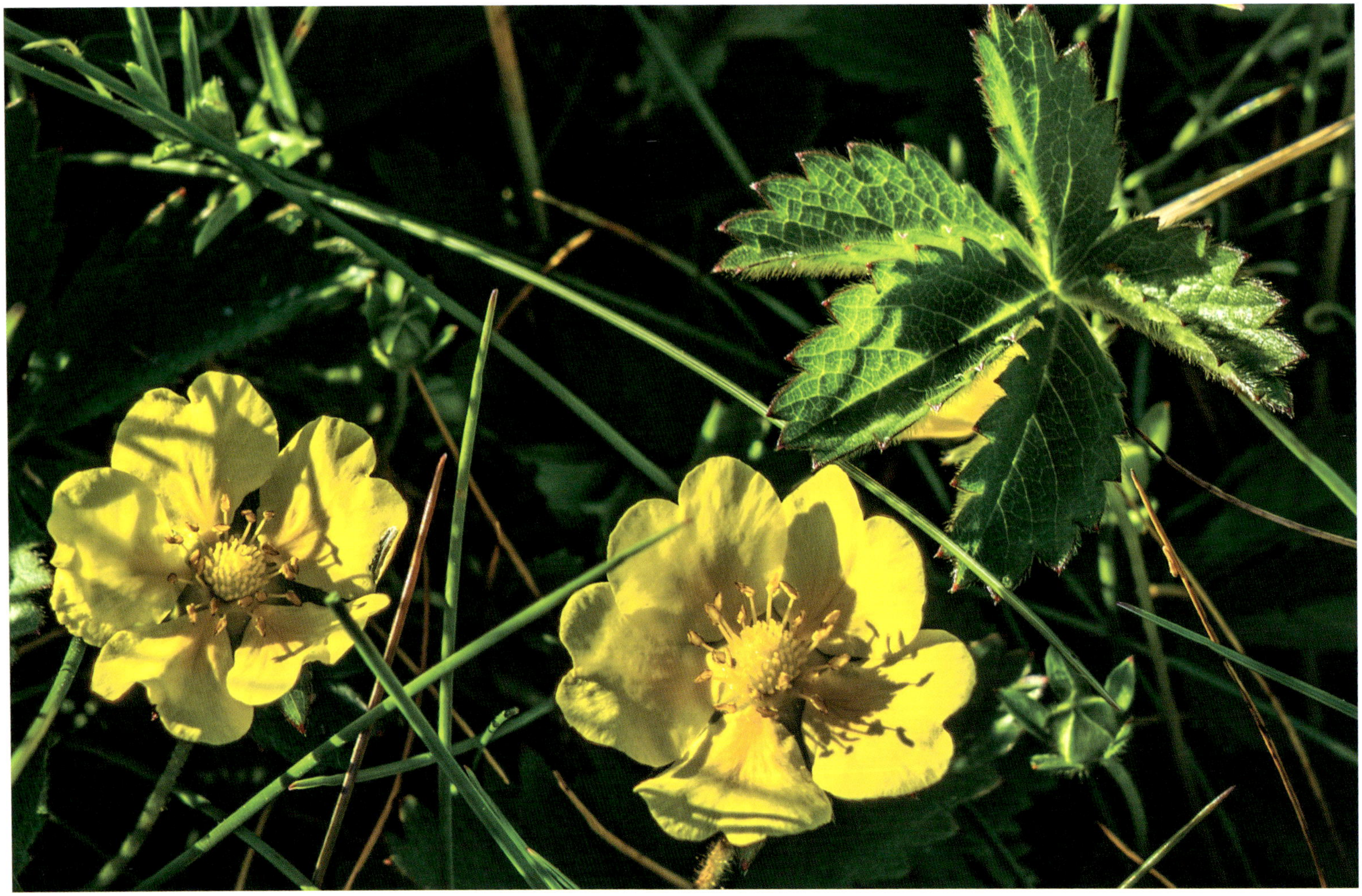

Creeping Cinquefoil Pumnalen Ymlusgol *Potentilla reptans*

Hawthorn and Blackthorn Draenen Wen a Draenen Ddu

These two common and widespread thorny species are found in many habitats, including the coast. Of the two, blackthorn is the most tolerant of coastal exposure and can colonise the most extreme cliff edges. Both these species can be problematic: in the absence of traditional grazing they can become dominant, out-competing the less robust coastal species. They are, however, valuable habitat for invertebrates and also provide both shelter and nest sites for birds.

Hawthorn
Draenen Wen
Crataegus monogyna

Hawthorn is commonly called the may tree in most of Britain, though we used to call it the mayflower in west Wales, with both names clearly a reflection of its flowering season. Sadly, climate change brings flowering forward, and, in time, the name may become less relevant. The blooming of the may tree is undoubtedly a highlight of any spring, as there is little to compete with the dazzlingly exuberant clusters of flowers. The petals are white, most with a tinge of pink, and their odour is strong and distinctive. I have heard them described as foul-smelling, but I like the scent, probably because it is so evocative of sunny days in May.

Hawthorn is a desirable and common hedgerow species, and is frequently cultivated as such. I always think of it as having two clear seasons: may trees in glorious springtime bloom and, equally special, laden with red berries (or, to be accurate, haws) in autumn. Years ago, cold winters could almost be guaranteed to bring avian refugees from Scandinavia: great flocks of redwings and fieldfares would descend on the bushes, quickly stripping the nourishing fruit.

Although the wide medicinal use of hawthorn was first recorded by Dioscorides in the first century AD, its apparently successful use in treating heart disease in the late nineteenth century created great interest, and it is still used today as a herbal supplement for heart health.

Blackthorn
Draenen Ddu
Prunus spinosa

Blackthorn had a deliberately cultivated fearsome reputation. When I was a child, my aunts – who had been born long before the advent of antibiotics – took every opportunity to tell cautionary tales about neighbours who had been pricked by a blackthorn and quickly died of blood poisoning. I remember the old roadmen with a *cryman* (sickle) and the thickest of pig-leather hedging mittens, so that they could safely handle the thorns.

Blackthorn has a remarkable ability to establish itself in some of the most hostile, exposed coastal environments. It is likely that an occasional seed, dispersed by a feeding bird, will survive if it germinates in a crevice or small, sheltered hollow, sometimes behind a rock. Once successfully established, blackthorn can spread rapidly, sending up suckers from the roots, and in a short time it can form an impenetrable thicket. The side facing into the prevailing wind will be vigorously pruned, but each sucker that survives provides shelter for those behind it: windward growth is prevented or restricted, but the leeward side may advance inland.

Hawthorn grows in slightly more sheltered areas, away from salt-washed cliff edges. Look out for blasted shrubs of both blackthorn and hawthorn, bending away from the prevailing wind. The wonderful, sculpted forms – nature's topiary – are a typical feature of the hedgerows and exposed headlands along the coasts.

I always associate the fruit of the blackthorn with sloe gin, perhaps because an elderly family friend was famed for the quality of his annual production. I once helped gather the purplish, white-bloomed fruit, which looked deceptively delicious. I can clearly remember him sitting at his kitchen table, laboriously pricking each sloe with a needle – although, sadly, I was too young to be given a taste of the end product. In today's recipes, the sloes are frozen to help release the juice.

Little Haven

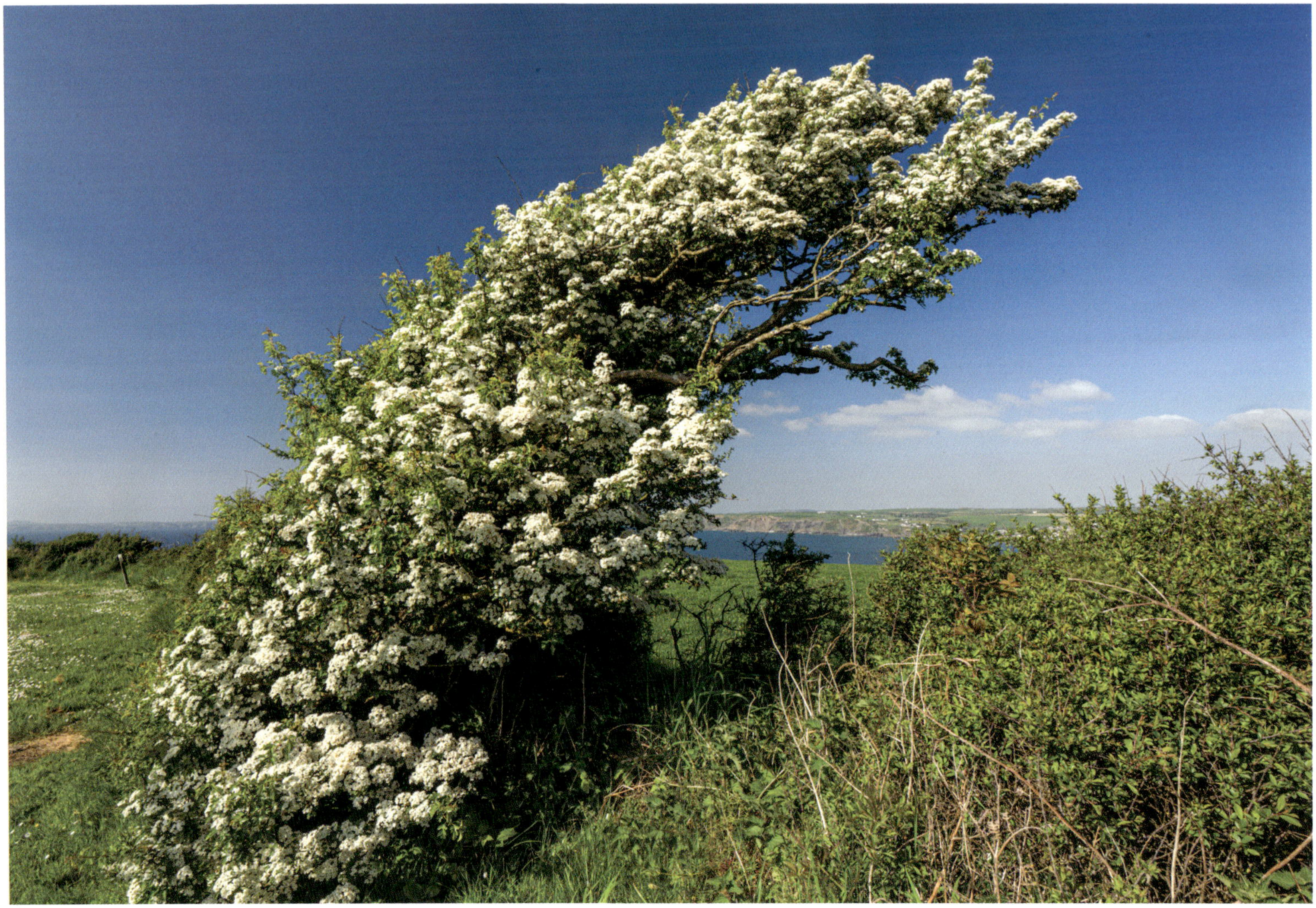

Hawthorn Draenen Wen *Crataegus monogyna*

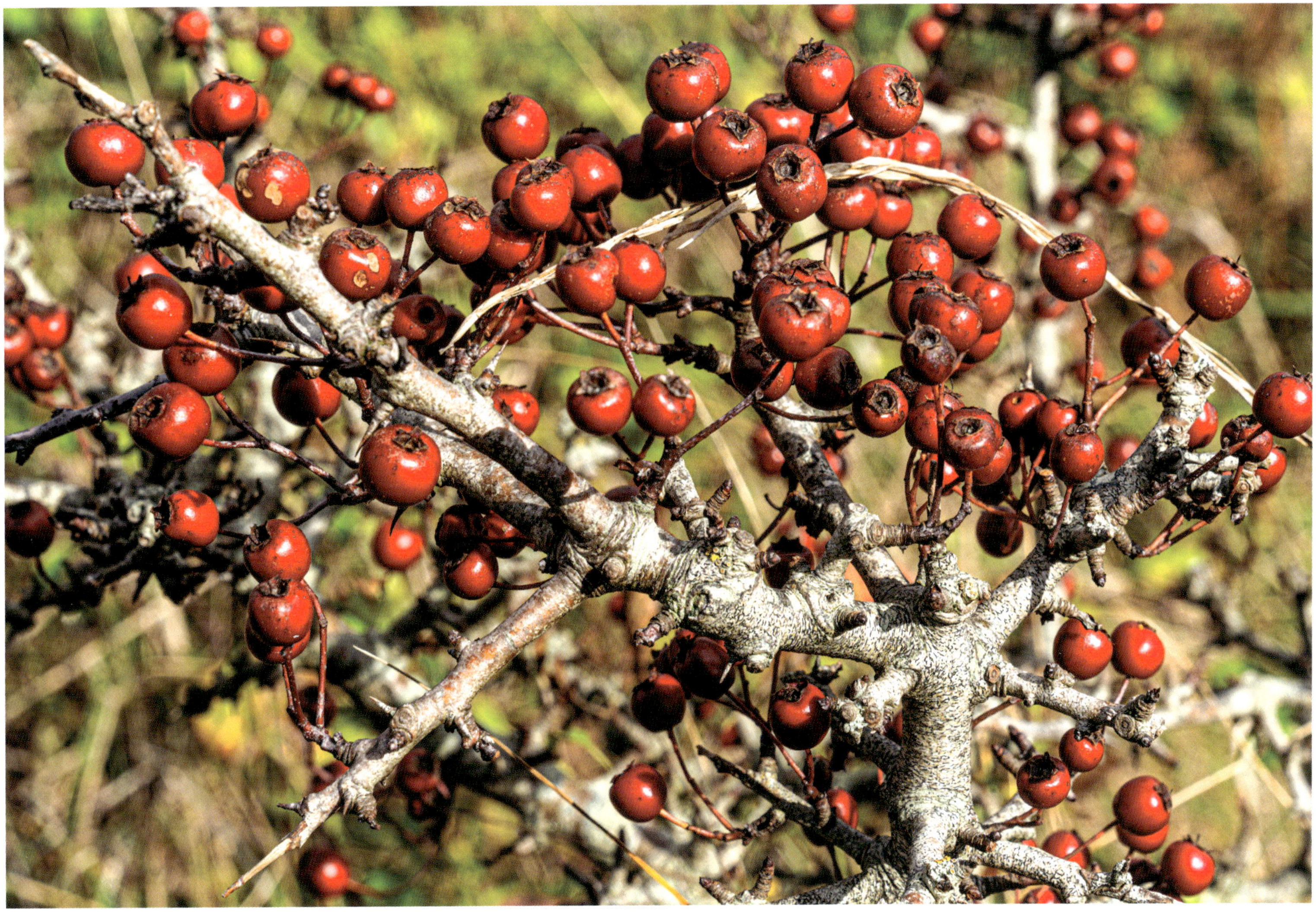

Hawthorn Draenen Wen *Crataegus monogyna*

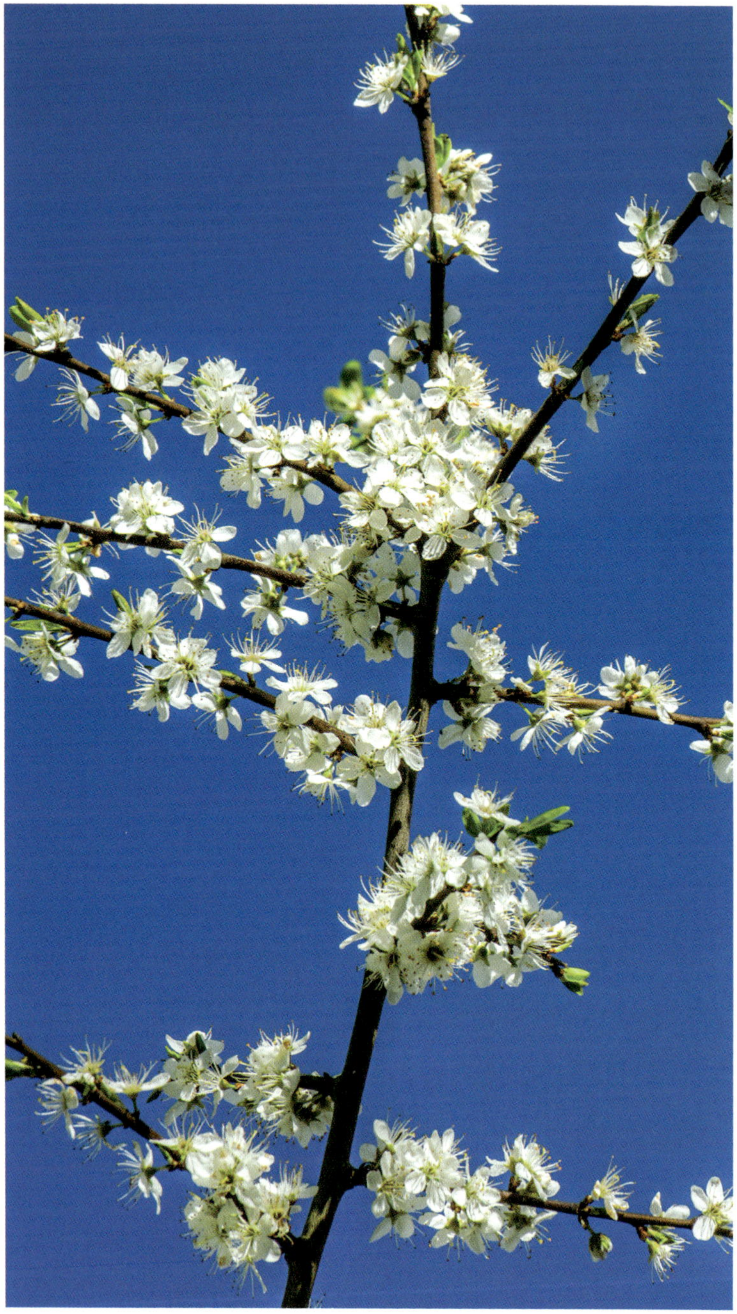

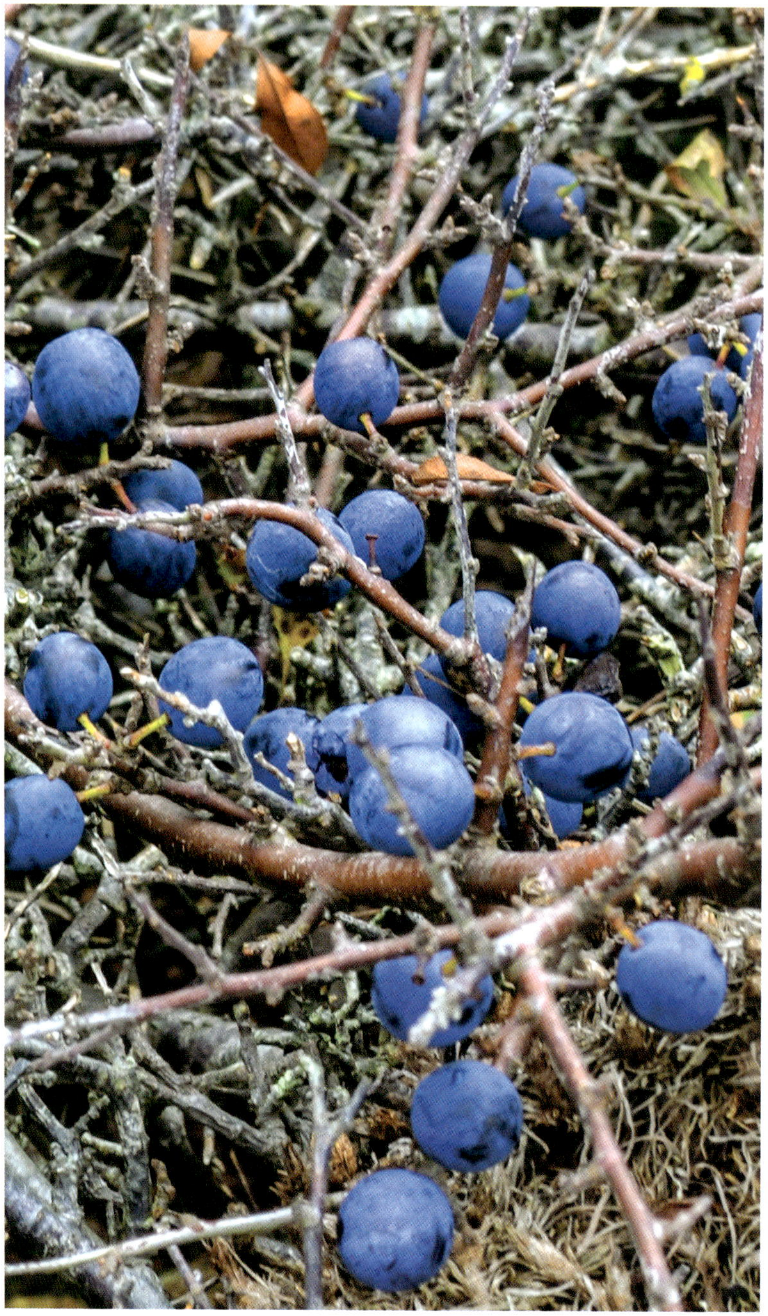

Blackthorn Draenen Ddu *Prunus spinosa*

Pea Family Teulu'r Bysen

I think that it is worth occasionally reminding ourselves of how important plants are to human existence and wellbeing. The *Fabaceae*, commonly known as the legume or pea family, is a spectacular example of a large and agriculturally important family which provides human food, animal fodder and green manure. The complete list of species is enormous, and includes countless varieties of beans, peas, soybeans, chickpeas, lentils, peanuts, alfalfa, clover, and even the highly prized tropical rosewoods. Global food security is recognised as one of the biggest challenges facing humankind, and legume crops could play a critical role in securing our future. We all know that legumes are an essential source of high-quality food, but less well known is the fact that they release five to seven times less greenhouse gas than most other crops. They also fix nitrogen in the soil, which has been recognised by farmers for a long time, and in earlier crop-rotation systems, various legumes were grown as a key constituent of the cycle. Members of the pea family are reasonably easy to identify because they all have similarly shaped flowers. These are bilaterally symmetrical, which means that they have two matching halves, rather like a butterfly, and they even have a pair of wings. This contrasts with flowers like daisies, which are radially symmetrical (with similar parts regularly arranged around a central axis).

Kidney Vetch
Plucen Felen
Anthyllis vulneraria

Kidney vetch is frequent all around the coast, although possibly a little more common on the limestone calcareous soils. The low-lying foliage is topped with clusters of yellow, 'woolly' flowers. It is a spreading, or colonising, species, and one of the first to cover bare ground. A field near Martin's Haven, on the Marloes Peninsula, was ploughed a few years ago and left bare. Kidney vetch was among the first species to appear, and after a few years it dominated great sections of the field with an astonishing display of soft yellow cushions. The photograph is of a typical vetch rosette growing in clifftop grassland opposite Ramsey Island.

Common Bird's-foot-trefoil
Pysen y Ceirw
Lotus corniculatus

Bird's-foot-trefoil has small flowers, egg-yolk-yellow or orange in colour, and is common in all kinds of coastal and grassy places. The flowers may look a little like fairy slippers, but it is the seed pods which provide their name, because they really do have the appearance of birds' feet. This is a good nectar plant, tempting many different butterflies, so I have included a photograph of a rare silver-studded blue, taken on the cliffs above Bullslaughter Bay. Similarly, I could not resist adding a photograph of a six-spot burnet moth resting on this, its larval food plant. Although these moths are common around the coast, I think they are one of the most elegant day-flying moths seen in Wales.

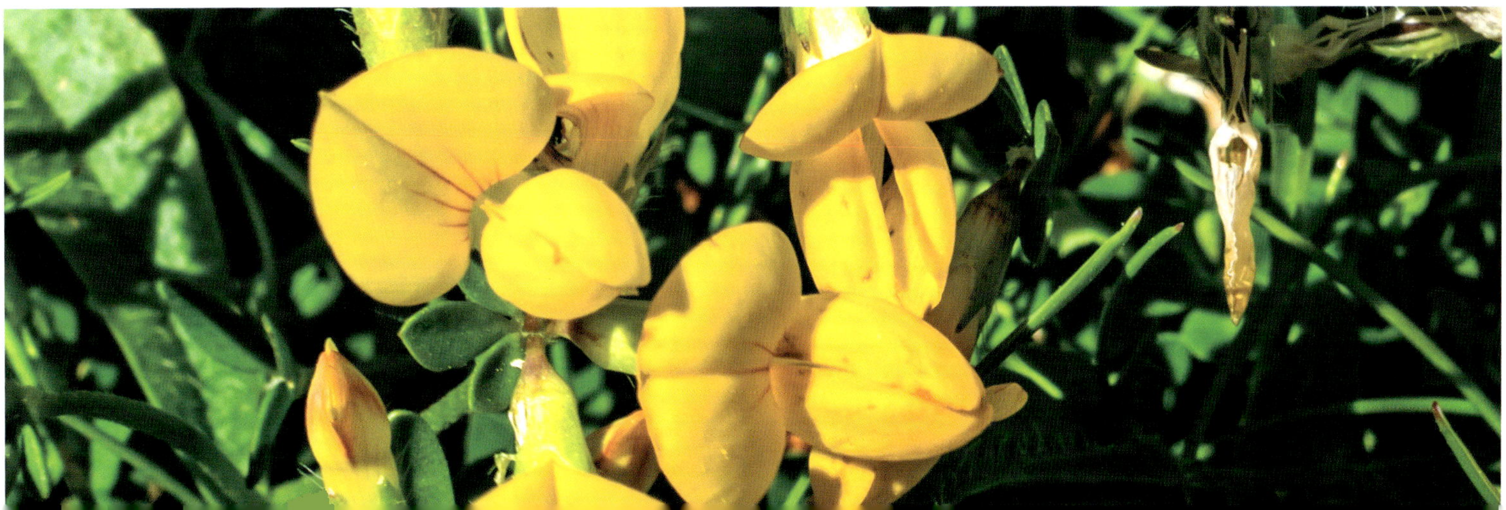

St Justinian and Ynys Dewi (Ramsey Island)

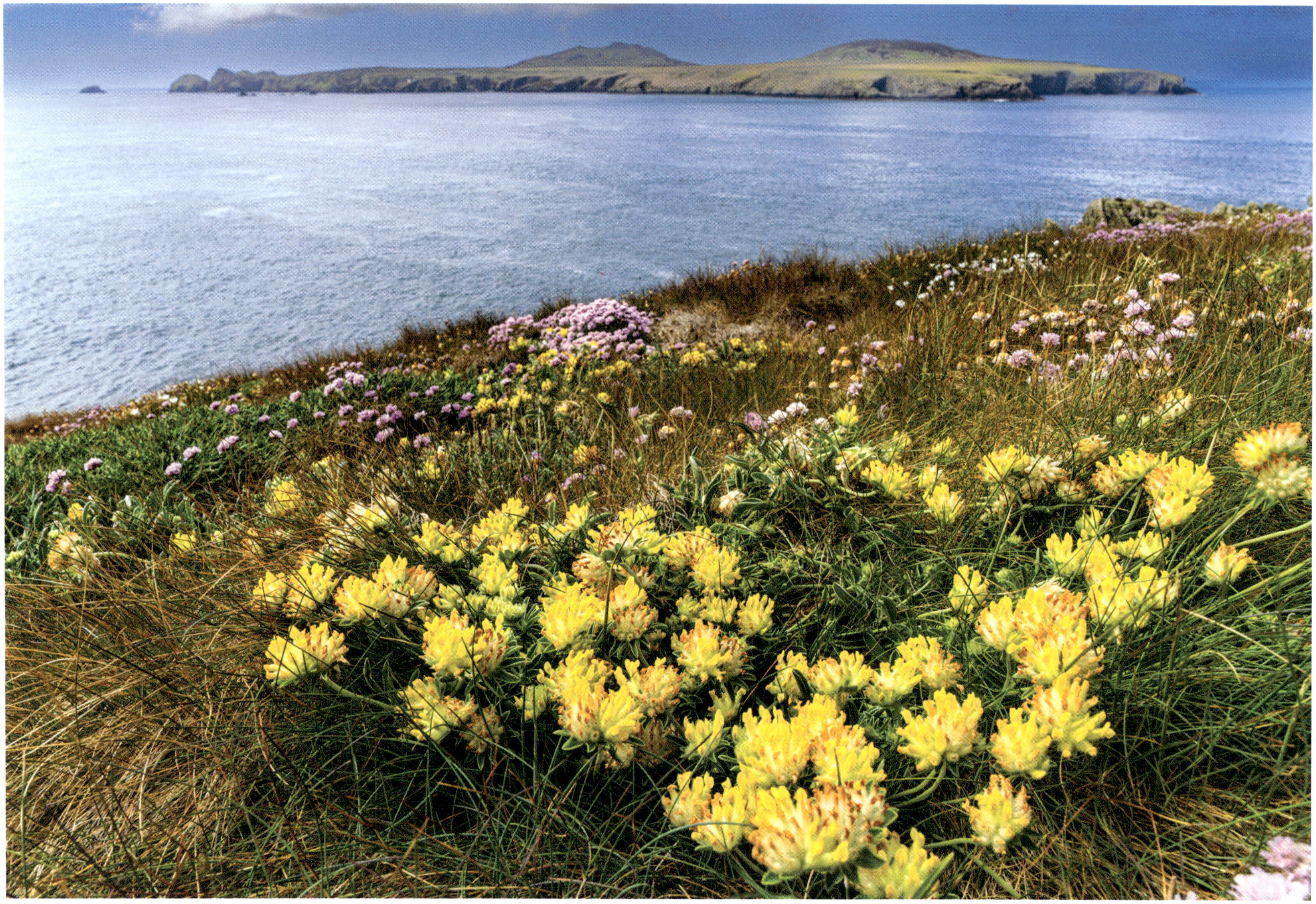

Kidney Vetch Plucen Felen *Anthyllis vulneraria*

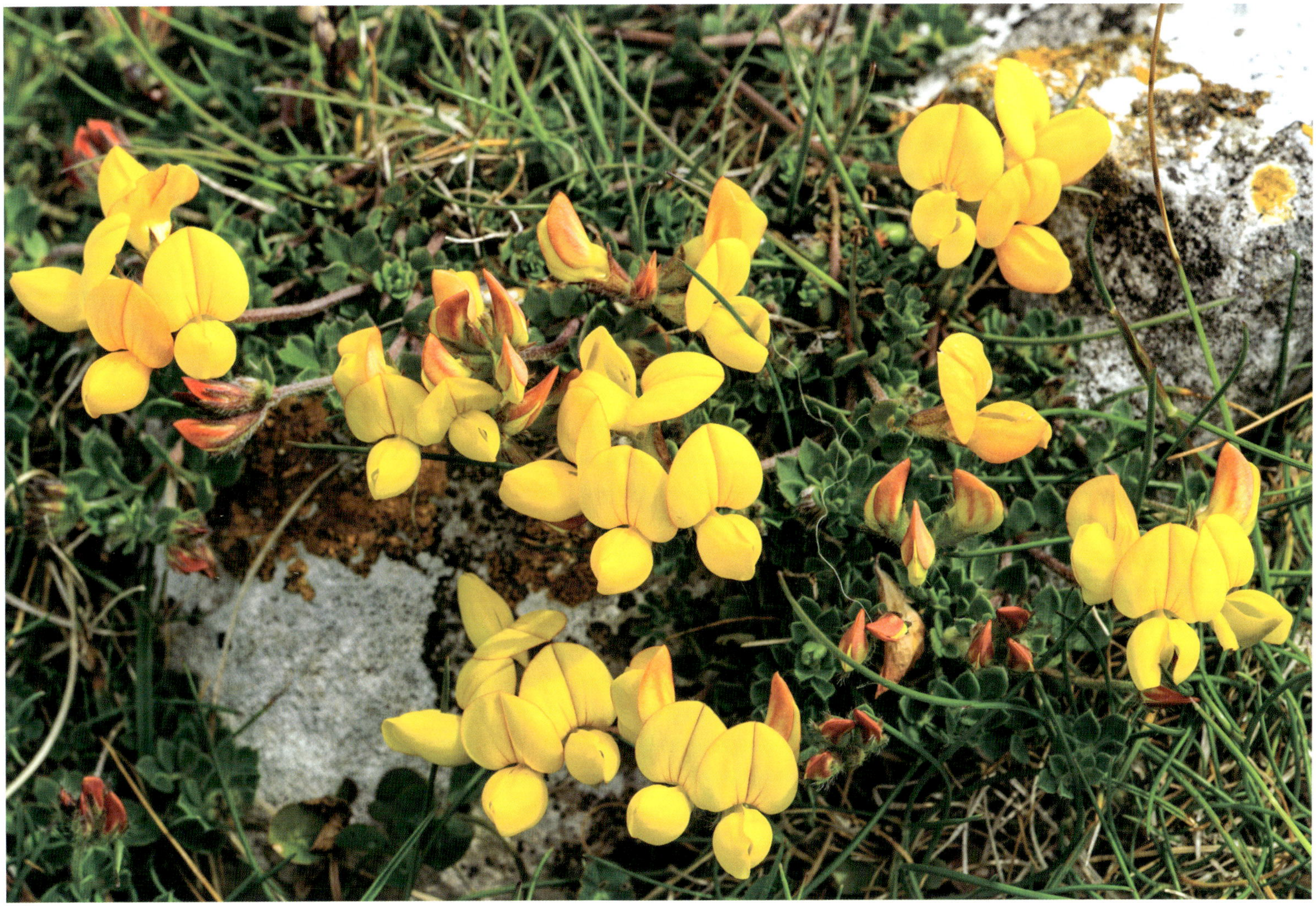

Common Bird's-foot-trefoil Pysen y Ceirw *Lotus corniculatus*

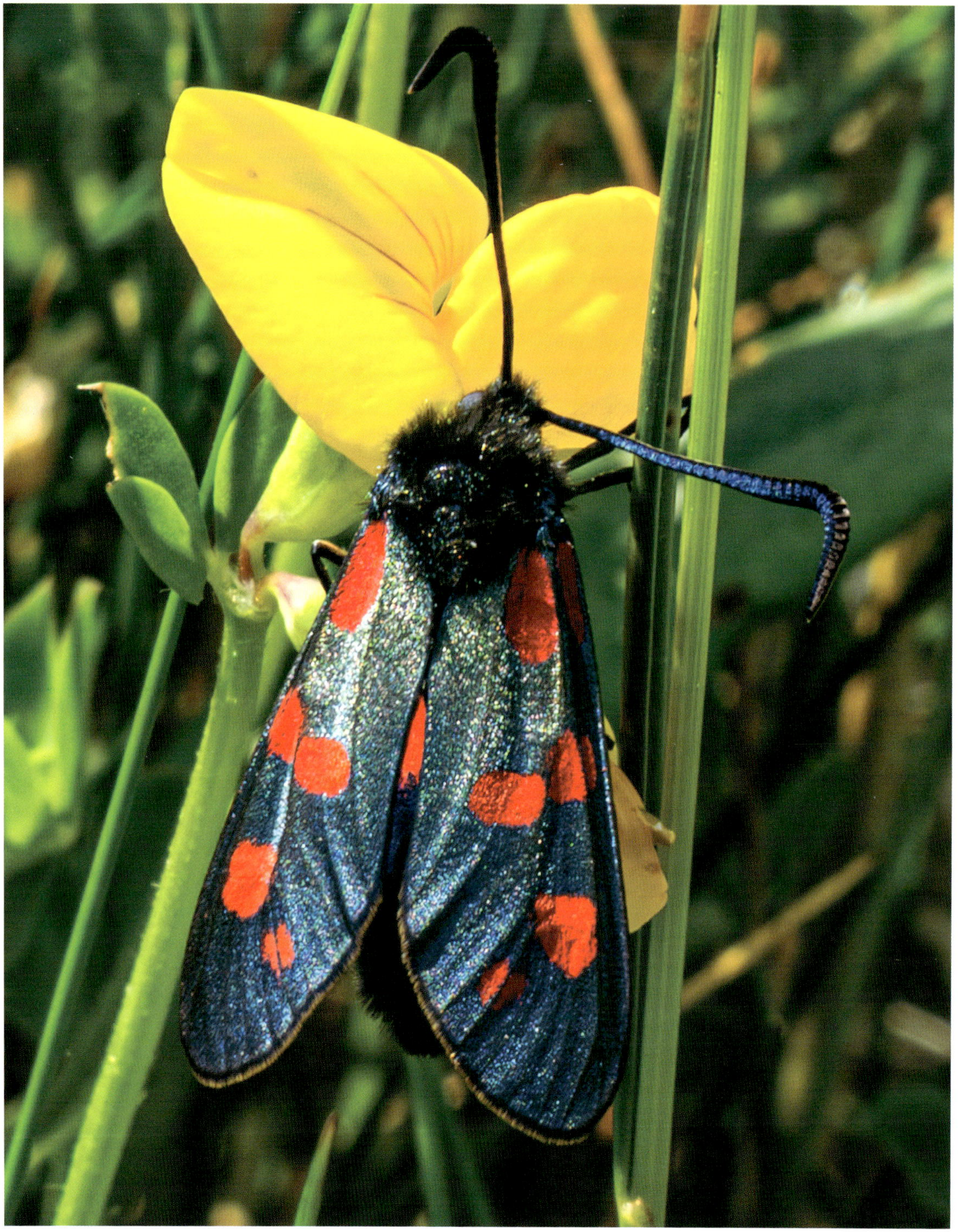

Six-spot Burnet moth Bwrned Chwe Smotyn *Zygaena filipendulae*

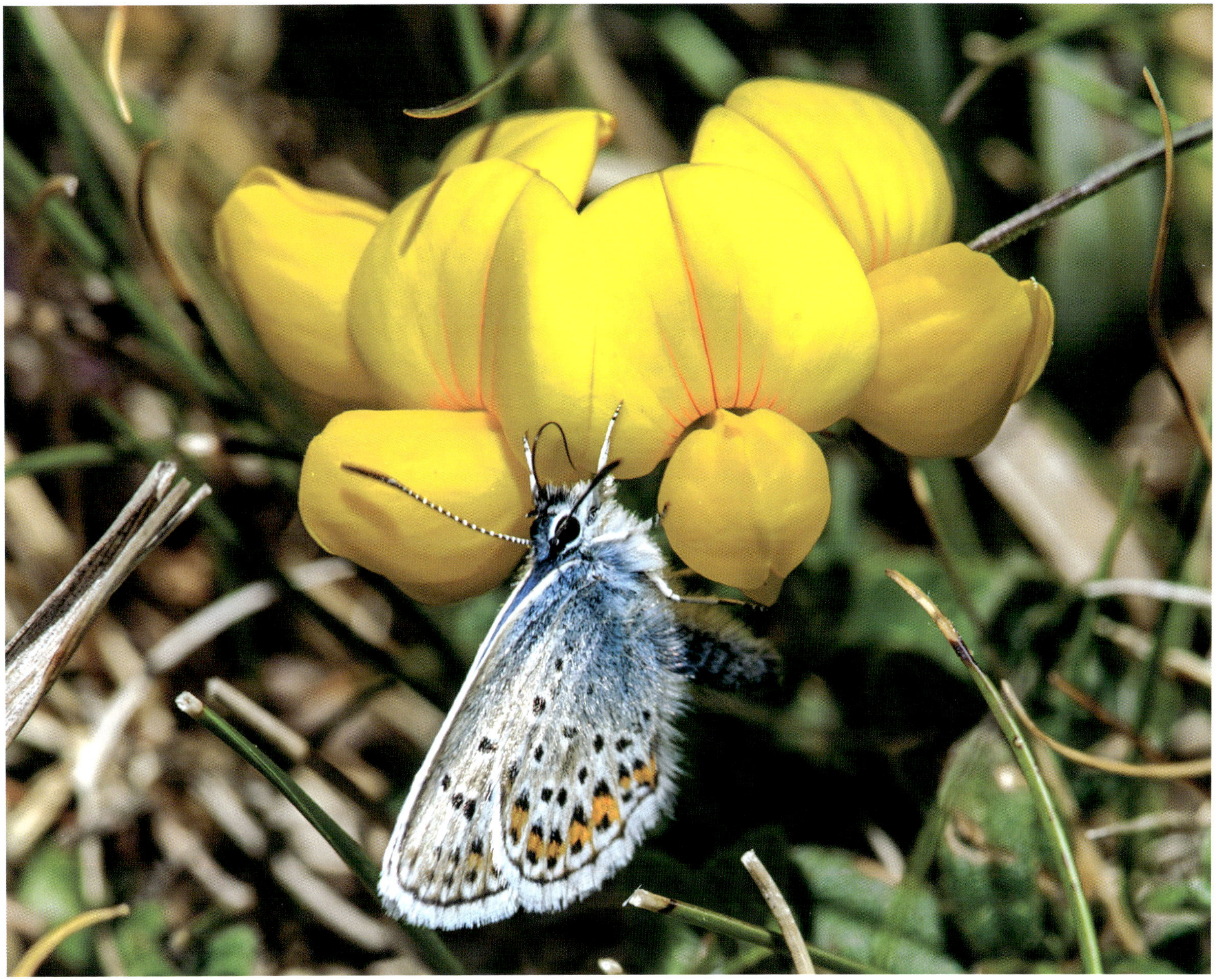

Silver-studded Blue butterfly Glesyn Serennog *Plebejus argus*

Clovers Meillion

When St Patrick returned to Ireland to convert the Irish to Christianity, he found it difficult to explain the concept of the Holy Trinity and so he used a three-leaf clover – three leaves in one leaf – to represent it. Clovers are also, unsurprisingly, called trefoils (meaning 'three-leaved'). They were, and remain, a hugely significant agricultural plant, providing tasty and highly nutritious animal fodder. They also fix nitrogen in the soil and grow vigorously, despite repeated harvesting or heavy grazing. I have included the two most familiar species and one which is a favourite of mine.

Red Clover
Meillionen Goch
Trifolium pratense

Red clover is a common plant of grassy areas. It has typical trefoil leaves, each with a V-shaped white mark. The round pink flower-heads are an excellent source of nectar.

White Clover
Meillionen Wen
Trifolium repens

White clover has off-white, often pink-washed, flowers. It has the highest digestibility of any grassland species and is greatly valued by stock farmers. However, it is not always welcome, particularly in precious relict, species-rich meadows and pastures, where it is an indicator that fertilisers have been used. As clover increases in the sward, the diversity of colourful wildflowers decreases.

Hare's-foot Clover
Meillionen Gedenog
Trifolium arvense

Hare's-foot is my favourite clover. Although it is not common around the coast, it will occasionally appear in profusion. The soft, downy hairs covering the pale pink flowers create the impression of an animal's foot, giving rise to its name.

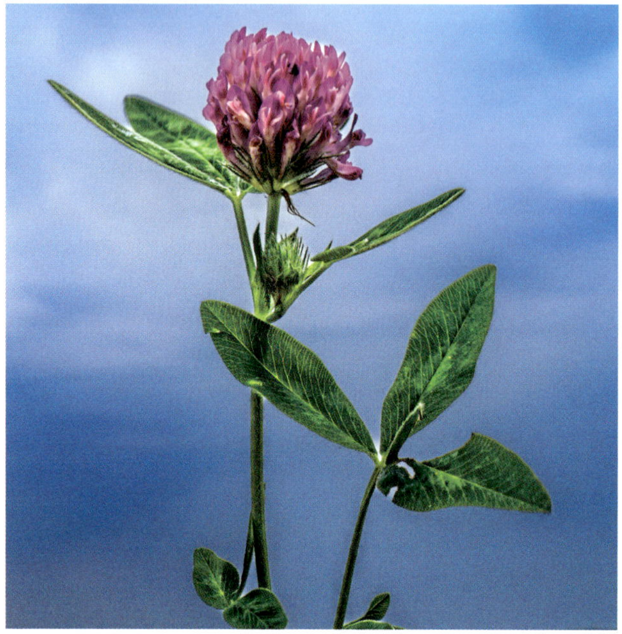

Red Clover Meillionen Goch *Trifolium pratense*

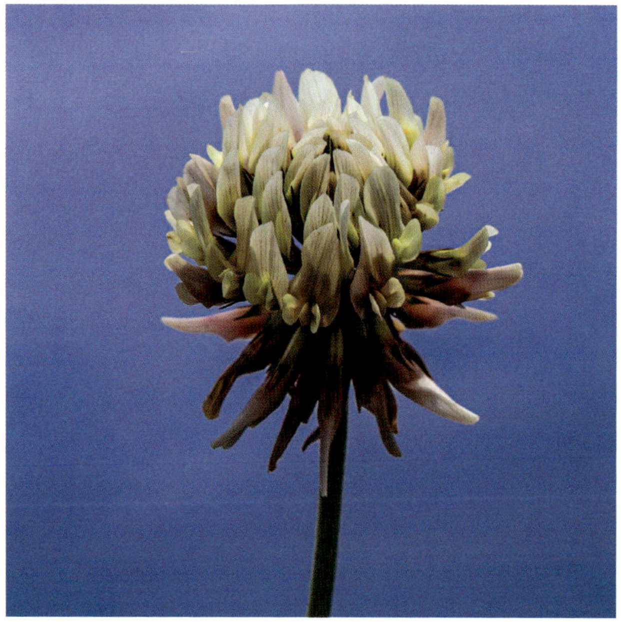

White Clover Meillionen Wen *Trifolium repens*

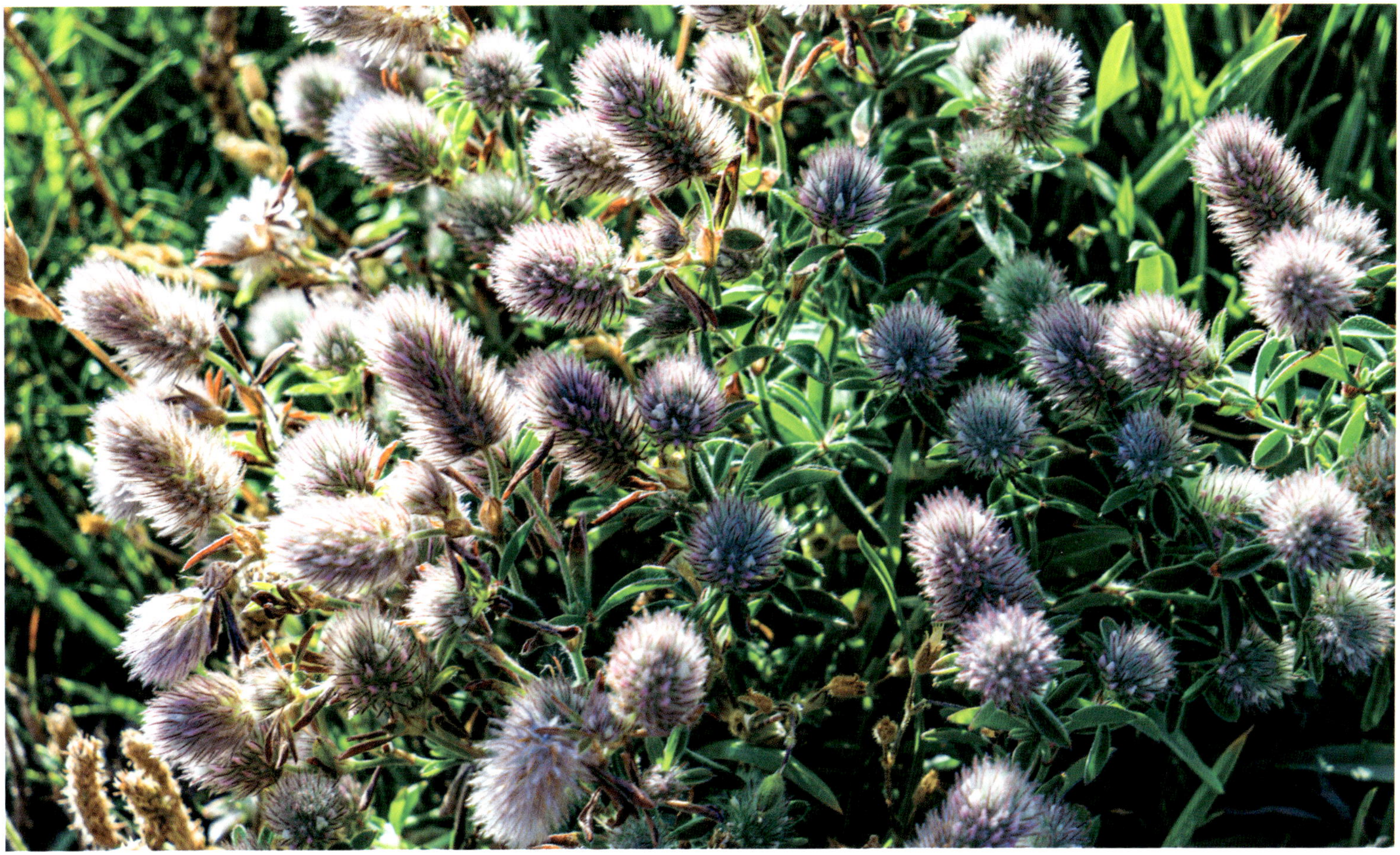

Hare's-foot Clover Meillionen Gedenog *Trifolium arvense*

Restharrow Tagaradr

Common Restharrow
Tagaradr
Ononis repens

Restharrow is a low-growing species found frequently around the coast, especially on sand dunes. The pink and white flowers are unmistakably pea-like. It was widely unpopular with farmers, being regarded as a problematic arable weed. There are two different stories of how it got its name, both fascinating, and a reminder of our pastoral heritage. Some people suggest that when restharrow was a common agricultural weed, it could grow so densely, and had such tough roots, that it could tangle the tines of a harrow and prevent the horse from making any progress. A horse-drawn harrow was a little like a plough but, in place of the single cutting blade, it had rows of curved tines, which broke up the soil following the plough.

The second story of the name's origin comes from the practice of crop rotation. Before the advent of artificial fertiliser, farmers relied on crop rotation to fertilise and condition the soil. There were many versions of the rotation system, but it might typically be a year of oats, then grass and clover, followed by wheat and finally a fallow year. In earlier times, the ground was left uncultivated during the fallow year and a host of 'weed' species, including restharrow, would provide green fertiliser. The appearance of restharrow showed that farmers had rested their harrows for a year. I have no idea which is the better story, but I would like to think that there is some truth in both of them.

As a further blow to its reputation, an alternative Welsh name is *cas gan arddwr*, which roughly translates as 'hated by gardeners'.

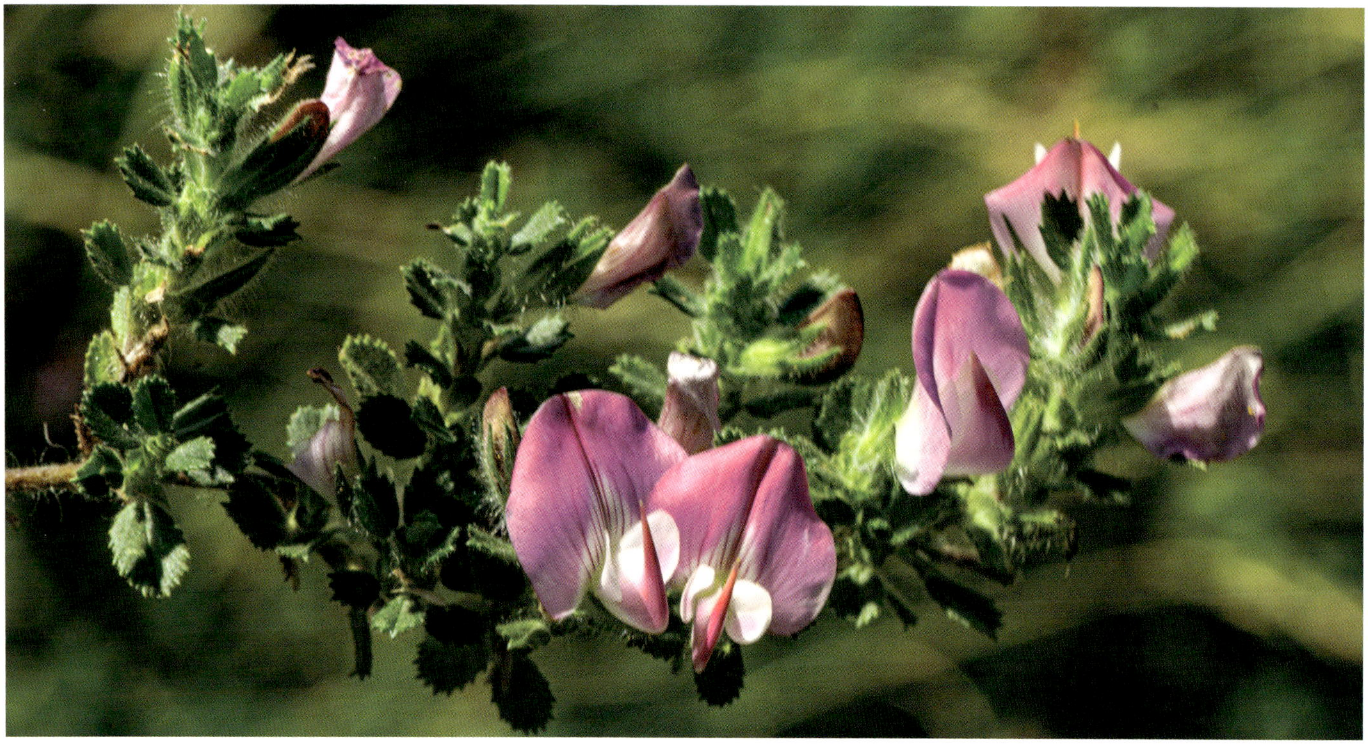

Common Restharrow Tagaradr *Ononis repens*

Greenweed and Gorse Corfanhadlen ac Eithinen

The final three in my list of legumes are all similar, with pea-like flowers in various shades of yellow. These are not strictly coastal species, but they all thrive in the extreme coastal conditions and are some of the most abundant members of coastal scrub and heath communities.

Hairy Greenweed
Corfanhadlen Flewog
Genista pilosa

Hairy greenweed is the rarest and most delicate member of this group. It is low-lying, occasionally forming spectacular yellow mats. The leaves are small, green and very hairy. The hairs, which help the plant to conserve moisture, give it a silvery appearance, and an alternative name is silkleaf broom. The first picture shows it growing in profusion on the mainland cliffs opposite Ynys Dewi (Ramsey), and the photograph including flowering hawthorn was taken at the same location.

Gorse
Eithinen Ffrengig
Ulex europaeus

Gorse is a native British species, despite its scientific name, *europaeus*, and its Welsh name translating as 'French gorse'. And yet it is often treated as an undesirable, invasive visitor – perhaps occasionally with good reason, because it does dominate the west Wales coast in places. It is, however, a beautiful and important habitat, ideally suited to many butterflies and other invertebrates. Birds also abound among gorse scrub, which is particularly attractive to warblers. You might even be lucky enough to spot a colourful Dartford warbler, and you would be unlucky not to see stonechats. I am sure that if yellowhammers ever make a comeback, this is where we will find them. Gorse was originally grown as a fodder crop, and you come across the place name Felin Eithin in Wales, being the Welsh for 'furze (or gorse) mill'. Gorse was rolled and crushed between spiked rollers and used as green winter fodder, an important food for the ewes lambing in spring.

Western Gorse
Eithinen Fan
Ulex gallii

Western gorse is a diminutive gorse, native, as its name implies, to the wild Atlantic coasts of Britain. Apart from the size difference, the two gorse species can be easily distinguished because they have different flowering periods. Common gorse is an early spring-flowering species, while western gorse blooms in late summer. Its flowering season coincides spectacularly with that of the purple bell heather. Together they dominate the most colourful of all the western coastal heath plant communities. It is worth a special August pilgrimage to enjoy the vibrant yellow-purple spectacle of two stunning complementary colours.

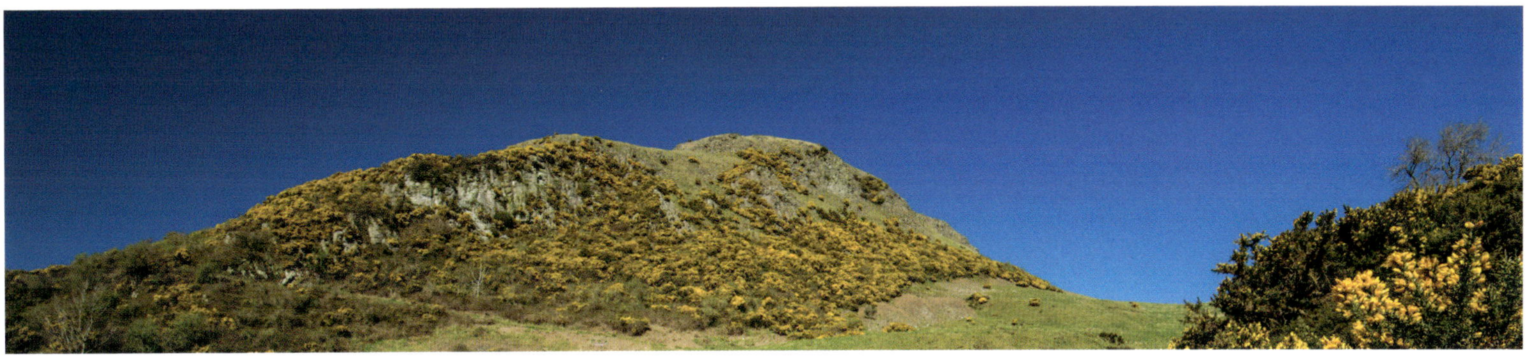

Penrhyn St Ioan (Point St John)

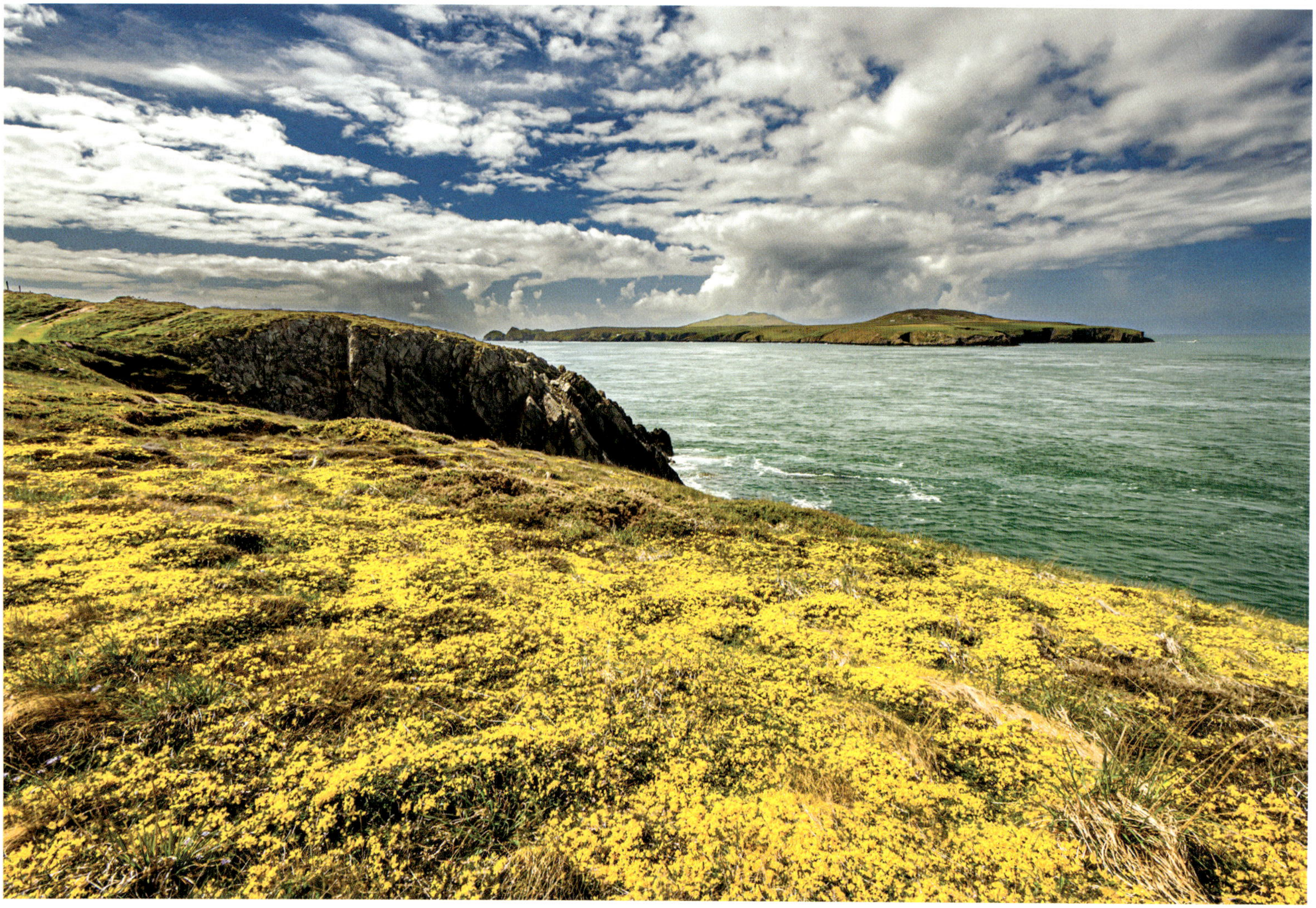

Above: Hairy Greenweed Corfanhadlen Flewog *Genista pilosa*

Next page: Hairy Greenweed Corfanhadlen Flewog *Genista pilosa* *and* Hawthorn Draenen Wen *Crataegus monogyna*

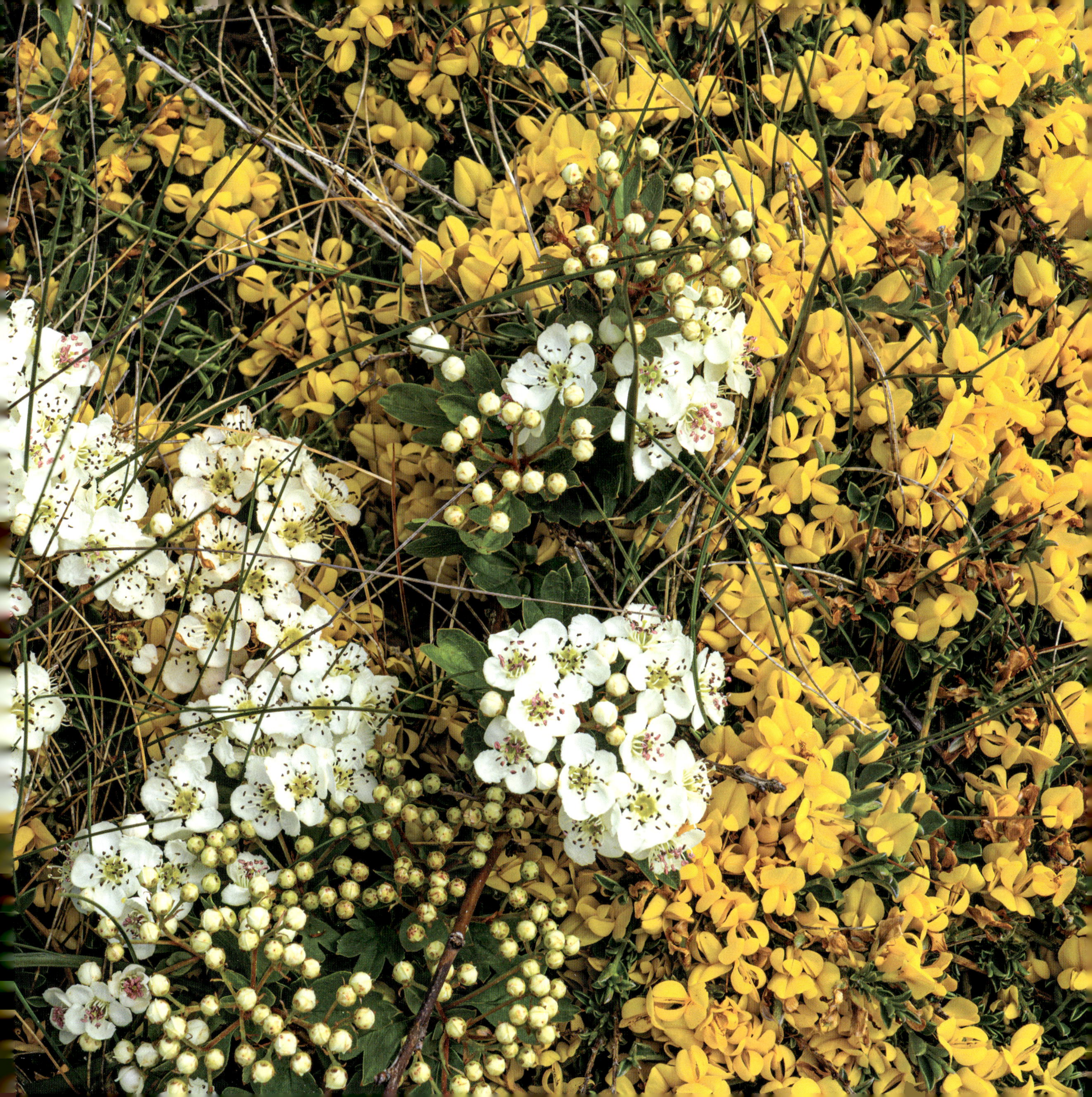

Barafundle

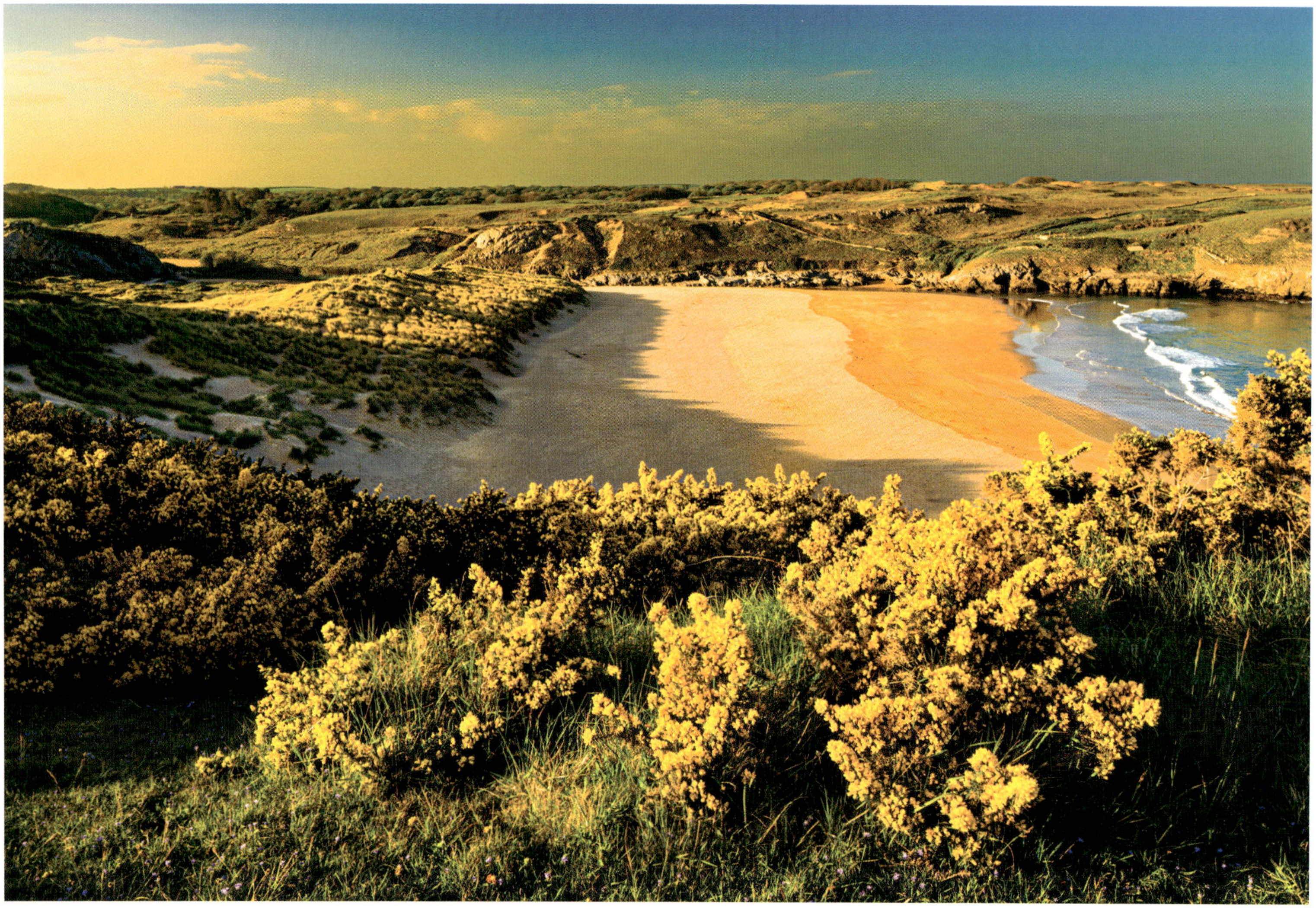

Gorse Eithinen Ffrengig *Ulex europaeus*

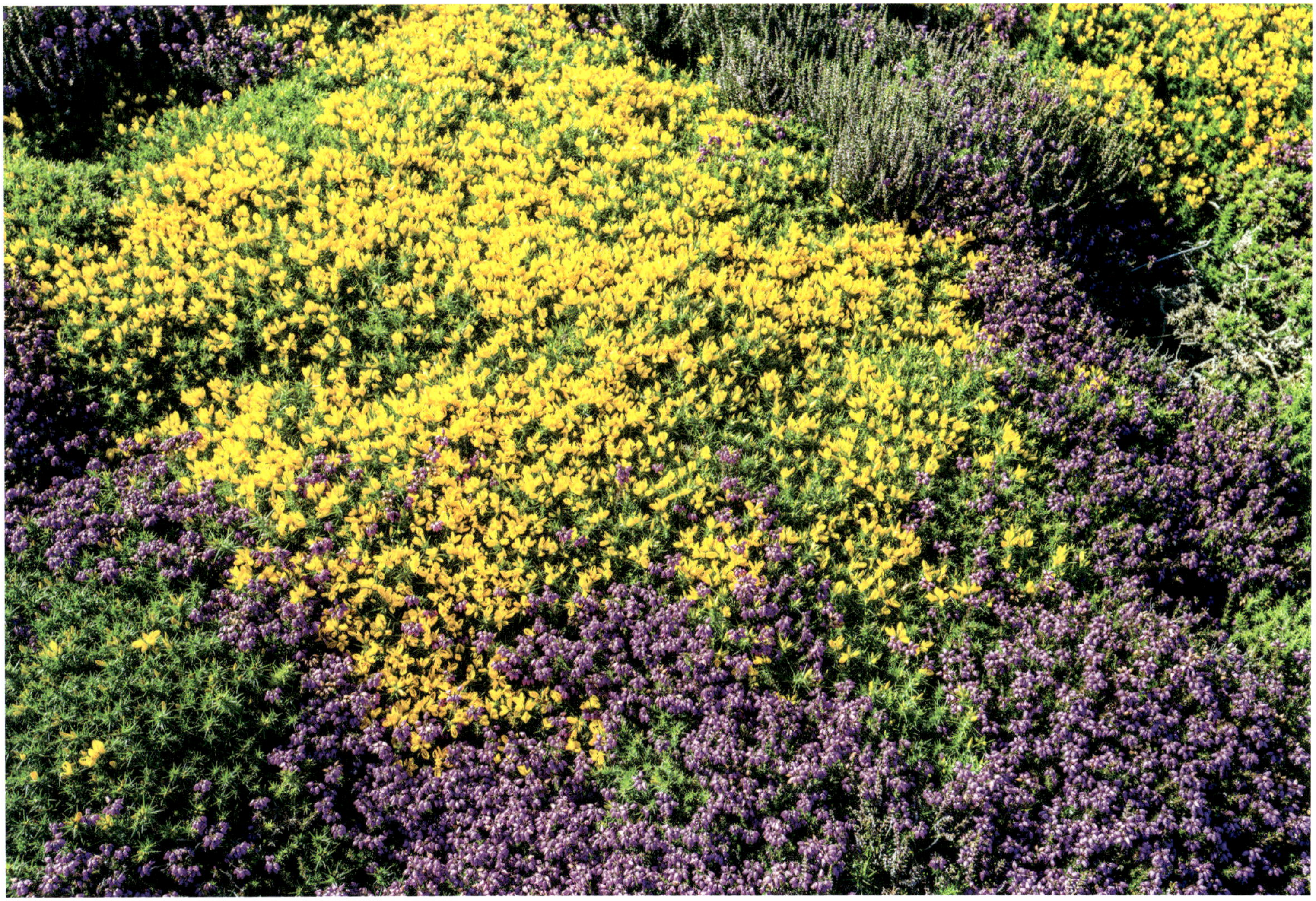

Western Gorse Eithinen Fan *Ulex gallii*

Willowherb Family Teulu'r Helyglys

Rosebay Willowherb
Helyglys Hardd
Chamaenerion angustifolium

Rosebay willowherb is a tall, elegant pink flower, which usually grows in dense, spreading stands. The name 'rosebay' is from the superficial resemblance of the flowers to pink wild roses and the flawed suggestion that the leaves are similar to bay. The name first appears in Gerard's *Herball* in 1597, so this is a long-standing misnomer. Regardless of name, these are lovely flowers.

Rosebay willowherb can appear almost anywhere around the coast, but has a preference for disturbed mature sand dunes. It is known as fireweed in North America, where it colonises bare ground following forest fires. In parts of Britain it is known as bombweed, because of its rapid appearance on bomb sites during the Blitz of World War II. The blueish-pink flowers bloom progressively from bottom to top, producing a gently tapering cone. The blooms are followed by slender, upright seed capsules, which peel open to reveal tiny seeds, all equipped with a white 'silken' parachute. An individual plant can produce as many as 80,000 wind-dispersed seeds, and this is the secret of their ability to rapidly colonise bare ground. Apparently, the heat from fires can help the seeds to germinate. Although it is a common species today, in the 1800s it was considered rare. Its rapid expansion is attributed to the development of Britain's railway system and the associated soil disturbance, with some botanists citing the arrival of the North American form as being an important factor. Once seedlings have become established, the plants can quickly reproduce vegetatively by sending out spreading rhizomes. In some situations, this ability to aggressively colonise and dominate can be threatening to other species.

Rosebay willowherb is valued for its medicinal properties, including anti-inflammatory and analgesic effects. It is good for headaches and muscle pain, and can also be used to treat infected wounds, coughs, bronchitis, stomach disorders and asthma.

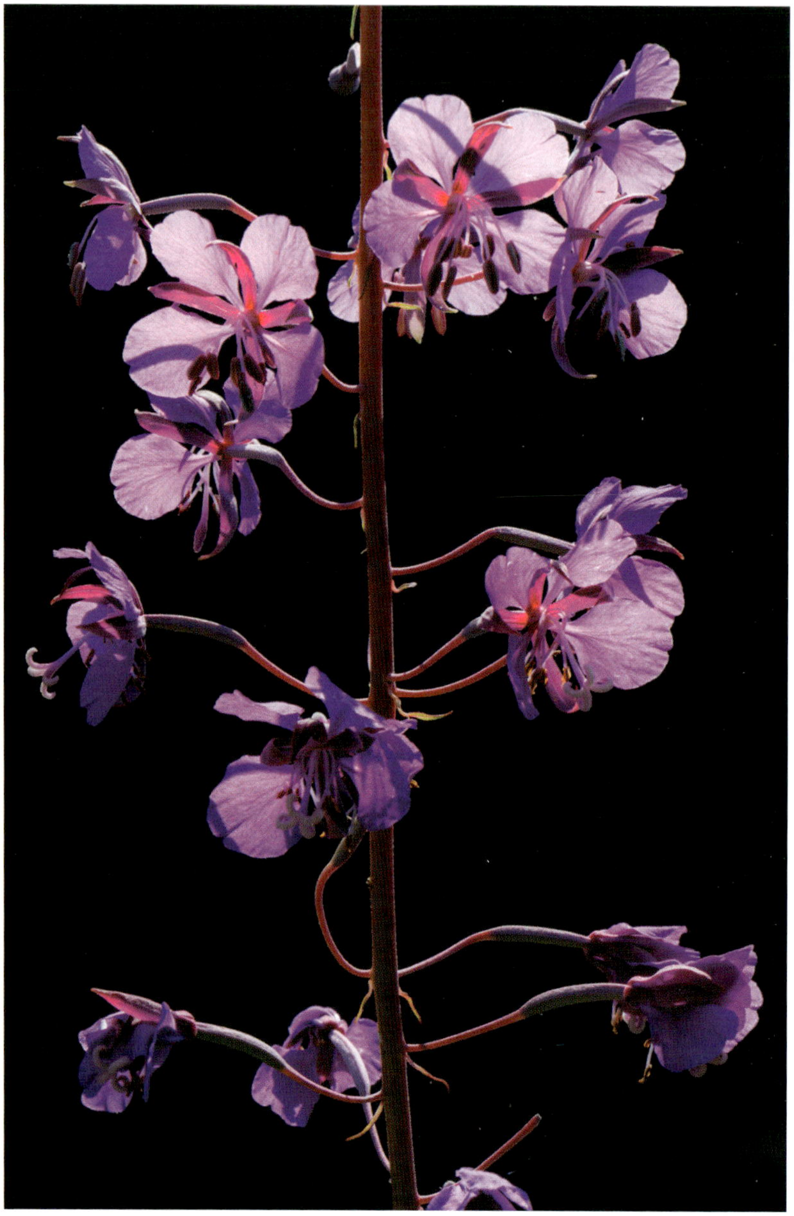

Rosebay Willowherb
Helyglys Hardd
Chamaenerion angustifolium

Spurge Family Teulu'r Llaethlys

Spurges, or euphorbias, are a large and diverse family, distinguished by a poisonous white, viscous sap. Since it can cause skin irritation, stomach upsets and even blindness, the sap is best avoided, though in some parts of the world, toxic sap from members of this family was traditionally used to make poisoned arrows. The English name, spurge, derives from the Middle English *espurge*, meaning to purge, because the sap was used as a purgative. The flowers are green and have no sepals or petals, or indeed much that resembles a typical flower. There are many different euphorbias, from tiny annuals to 30-metre-high trees. The most familiar members of the family are the popular Christmas poinsettias.

I have included two members of the family, both of which are found mainly, although not exclusively, on sand dunes. These are good examples of the typical specialised plants with adaptations that allow them to conserve water and survive hot dry summers in the arid mobile sandy areas at the seaward edge of the dunes. Both species are also able to tolerate the salt sea spray on their leaves and can even thrive in salty soils.

Portland Spurge
Llaethlys Portland
Euphorbia portlandica

Portland spurge is the more delicate of the two spurges that frequent our coasts. They appear as whorls of fleshy, blue-green leaves around a red stem. Despite the lack of typical blooms, the array of small greenish-yellow bracts (modified leaves inside which the flower grows) makes an appealing and interesting addition to the vegetation.

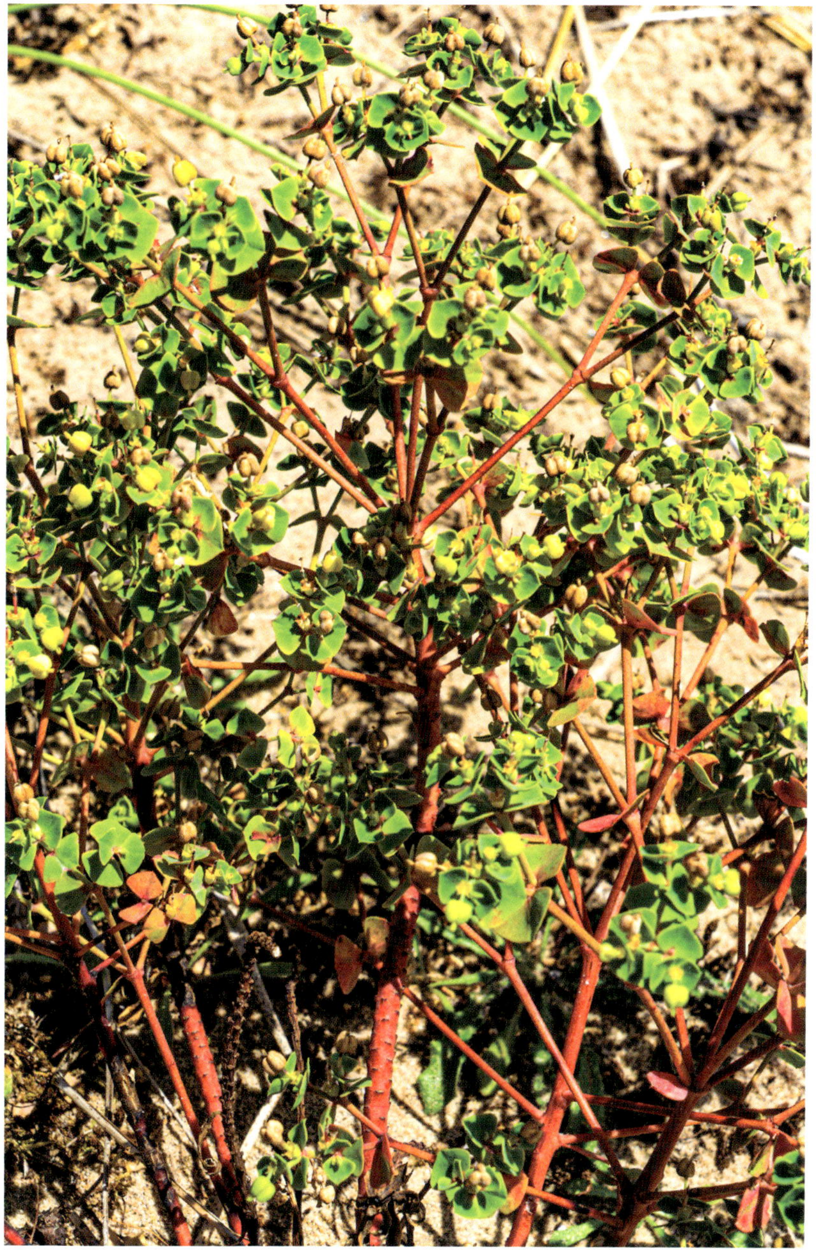

Portland Spurge
Llaethlys Portland
Euphorbia portlandica

Sea Spurge
Llaethlys y Môr
Euphorbia paralias

Sea spurge is larger and more robust than Portland spurge. It is fleshier and greener, with less red on the stems. The upright stems, with crowded whorls of slender, stalkless leaves, are topped with cup-shaped bracts. These are eventually replaced by dark, wrinkly fruit capsules, each containing three seeds, which burst open when mature, expelling the seeds several metres from the parent. The seeds are buoyant and durable, capable of surviving long-distance dispersal in the sea currents. This is a robust and resilient species, which comes equipped with a highly effective seed-dispersal mechanism. In Australia, it is an extremely successful invasive naturalised species, seriously threatening coastal areas.

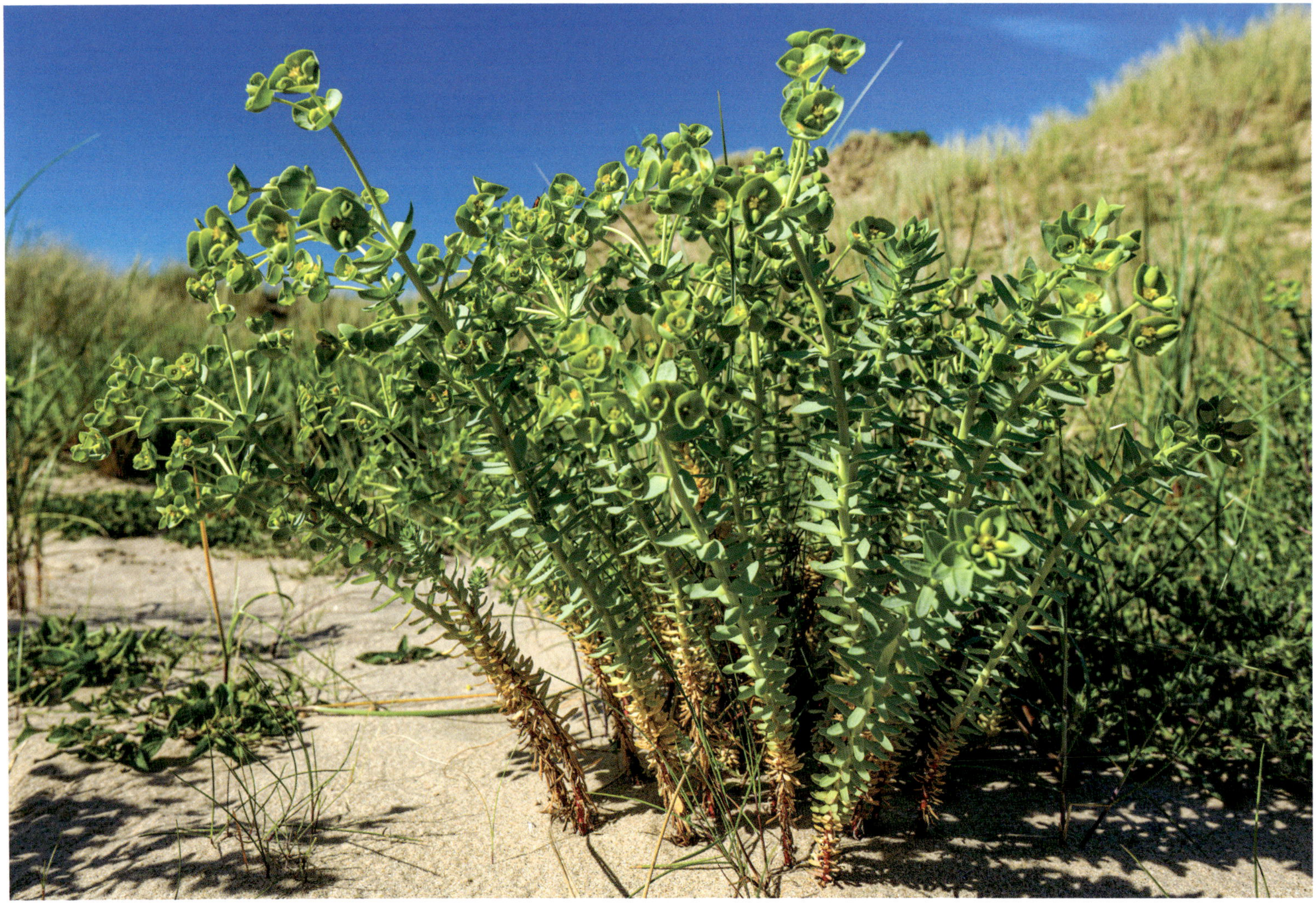

Sea Spurge Llaethlys y Môr *Euphorbia paralias*

Carrot Family Teulu'r Foronen

This family contains many large species, with flowers that may not be considered conventionally pretty and could never be described as colourful, being mostly white or greenish off-white. They often seem to be the unnoticed background in a landscape, but in some settings they come into their own, providing the pale froth that highlights the flower arrangement. Springtime hedge-banks in west Wales, with tall, overhanging swathes of cow parsley and hogweed, are perfect examples. The flower heads, called umbels, give this family its scientific name, *umbelliferae*. Umbels are umbrella-shaped inflorescences, with clusters of small, often delicate, flowers, borne on a number of short stalks radiating from the top of the main stalk. It is not surprising that both terms are derived from the Latin word *umbella*, meaning parasol. Some members of the carrot family are edible, while others are poisonous (a few extremely so). Although appreciation of smell is subjective, some have a strong and pungent aroma which could be considered unpleasant. Sadly, members of the carrot family are often regarded as invasive, undesirable pests by gardeners and farmers.

St Ann's Head

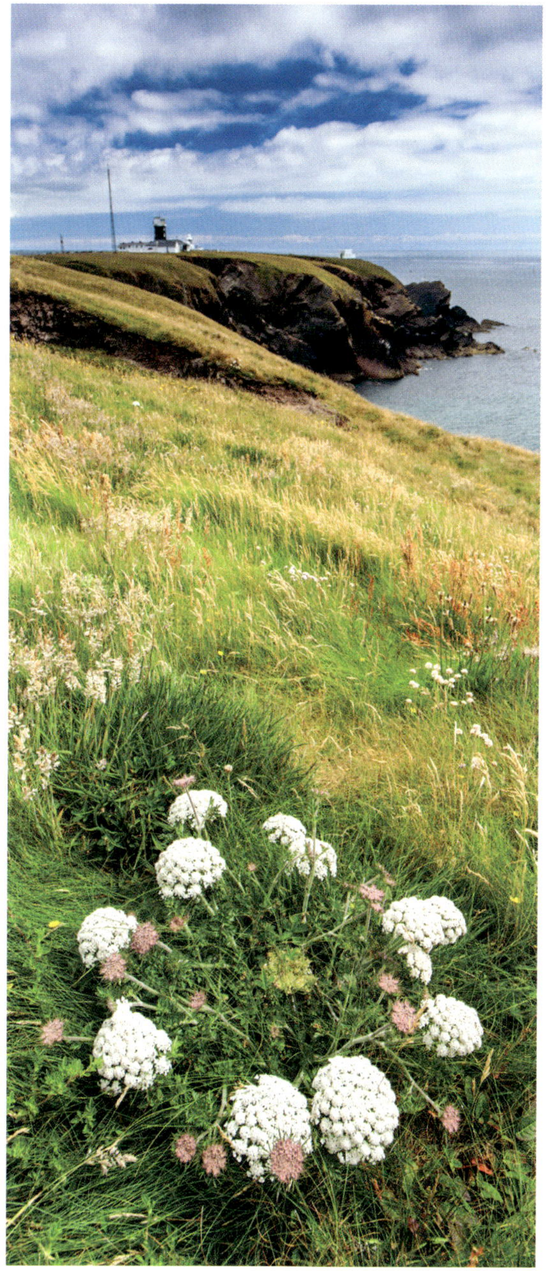

Sea Carrot
Moronen Arfor
Daucus carota ssp. gummifer

Hogweed
Efwr
Heracleum sphondylium

Hogweed is an abundant plant of hedgerows, roadsides, waste ground and rough pasture, which can rapidly colonise cleared land. I always think of it as the heavyweight of the family: a powerful and sturdy plant with thick-ribbed and hairy (or bristly), hollow stems. The pinnate leaves, which are also hairy, are divided into 3–5 lobes. White or pinkish flowers are displayed in the large umbels typical of this family. The flowers are followed by brown, untidy-looking masses of flattened, winged seeds. This is an edible species and all parts can be eaten: the stem chopped in salad and the leaves used as a seasoning, while the seeds can be used in cakes, shortbread, chutneys and curries. The photograph is of a display of hogweed completely dominating a coastal field which was ploughed and then, for some reason, left uncultivated for a few years.

Sea Carrot
Moronen Arfor
Daucus carota ssp. gummifer

Sea carrot might not look like a cultivated carrot, but it certainly smells like carrots. This is a relatively rare coastal subspecies of the much more widespread wild carrot. The sea carrot does not grow as tall as many members of the family, and when growing along the exposed coasts, it will usually spread out low and

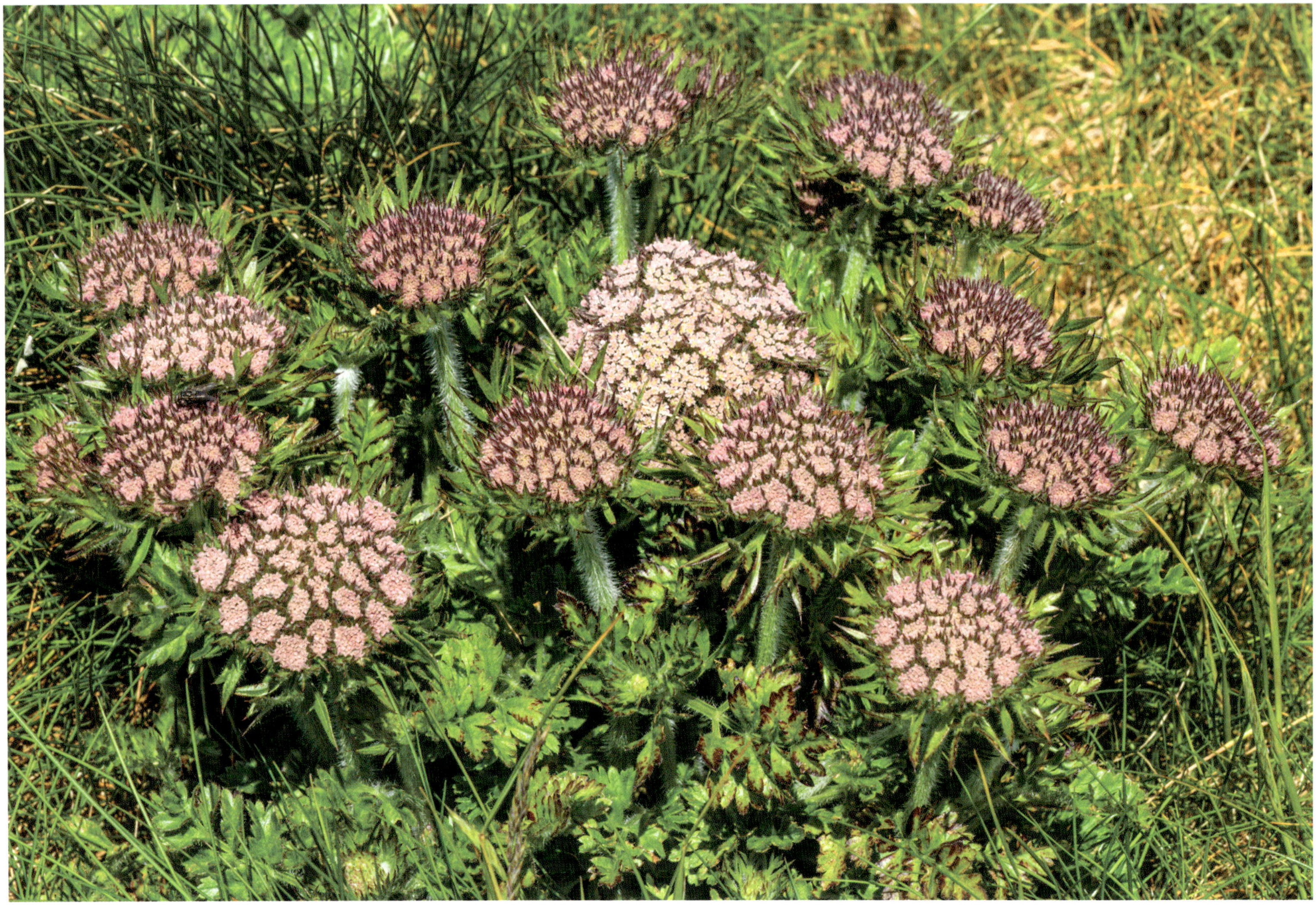

Sea Carrot Moronen Arfor *Daucus carota ssp. gummifer*

close to the ground. The flowers, borne on strong, hairy stems, are pale pink before they are fully open, maturing to white, domed umbels. The flower ripens into a wonderful seed head which, at first glance, looks like a mass of intertwined, leggy insects, or perhaps a bird's nest, which gives the plant the common names of bird's nest and bee's nest. The long, feathery leaves are vaguely reminiscent of a cultivated carrot, and possibly responsible for giving the species yet another name, Queen Anne's lace. It is described as delicious and nutritious, and is used in a variety of both sweet and savoury dishes. The first photograph of a sea carrot was taken looking towards St Ann's Head, at the entrance to Milford Haven.

Wild Angelica
Llysiau'r Angel
Angelica sylvestris

Wild angelica is a beautiful and elegant member of the carrot family. It is tall, erect and robust, bearing large, domed umbels, which can be white or a subtle shade of lilac. Angelica is famed for its incense-like fragrance. Even the roots are scented, and they are an important ingredient used in making perfumes. Reputed to possess angelic attributes, its medicinal properties were revealed to a monk by Archangel Michael during the plague. The second part of its scientific name, *sylvestris*, is usually given to woodland plants. Angelica is, in fact, a species of damp places, including coastlands, meadows, ditches, riverbanks and wet woodlands. The wild species is closely related to the domesticated angelica: both are edible and can be used to produce candied angelica. The photographs were taken above Bull Hole, on the north coast of Skomer Island. This has long been my favourite location for spectacular, and occasionally colourful, angelicas.

Hemlock Water-dropwort
Cegiden y Dŵr
Oenanthe crocata

Hemlock water-dropwort is a poisonous plant, deadly to humans and animals, and considered to be the most toxic plant growing in Britain. It shares the name dead man's fingers with a number of different species. It is named after the cluster of finger-like white roots, which look and smell like parsnips but are the most toxic part of the plant. The roots are occasionally washed out of the soil during flooding and end up along the seashore. Hemlock water-dropwort contains a powerful neurotoxin called oenanthotoxin, which triggers unpleasant symptoms, including uncontrolled muscle spasms and convulsions, sometimes followed by sudden death. There have not been many reported cases of poisoning in humans in the UK over the last century or so, but most involved children and 70% were fatal. This is a species that must be avoided and never handled, as the toxin is able to enter the body through the skin. It is reasonably common around the coast and always restricted to damp places, particularly the edges of flushes and streams exiting along the cliffs. This tall and robust species is very obvious, with thick, hollow, branched stems and large pinnate leaves, bearing 3- or 4-lobed, or toothed, leaflets. The flowers are large domed umbels, typical of this family.

Alexanders
Dulys
Smyrnium olusatrum

Alexanders is one of the earliest coastal plants to bloom. Often, in springtime, the lanes and footpaths closest to the coast are transformed into lush green avenues of alexanders. The tall, hollow stems, with dark green foliage, can grow over a metre high, topped with contrasting, pale green umbels. Alexanders have a strong, sweet, spicy smell, attracting clouds of pollinating insects. Many authors claim that the seeds smell of myrrh, and I wish I was familiar enough with that scent to confirm the claim. The association with myrrh, however, has an excellent pedigree: it dates to the first century AD in Ancient Rome, when the naturalist Pliny called alexanders *smyrnium*, because of the myrrh-like smell.

Alexanders are a Mediterranean species, apparently introduced to Britain by the Romans as a food plant. The stem, leaves and flowers are all edible and have a taste similar to celery. The distinctive black seeds were added to food for extra flavour. An earlier English name was parsley of Alexandria.

Bull Hole, Skomer

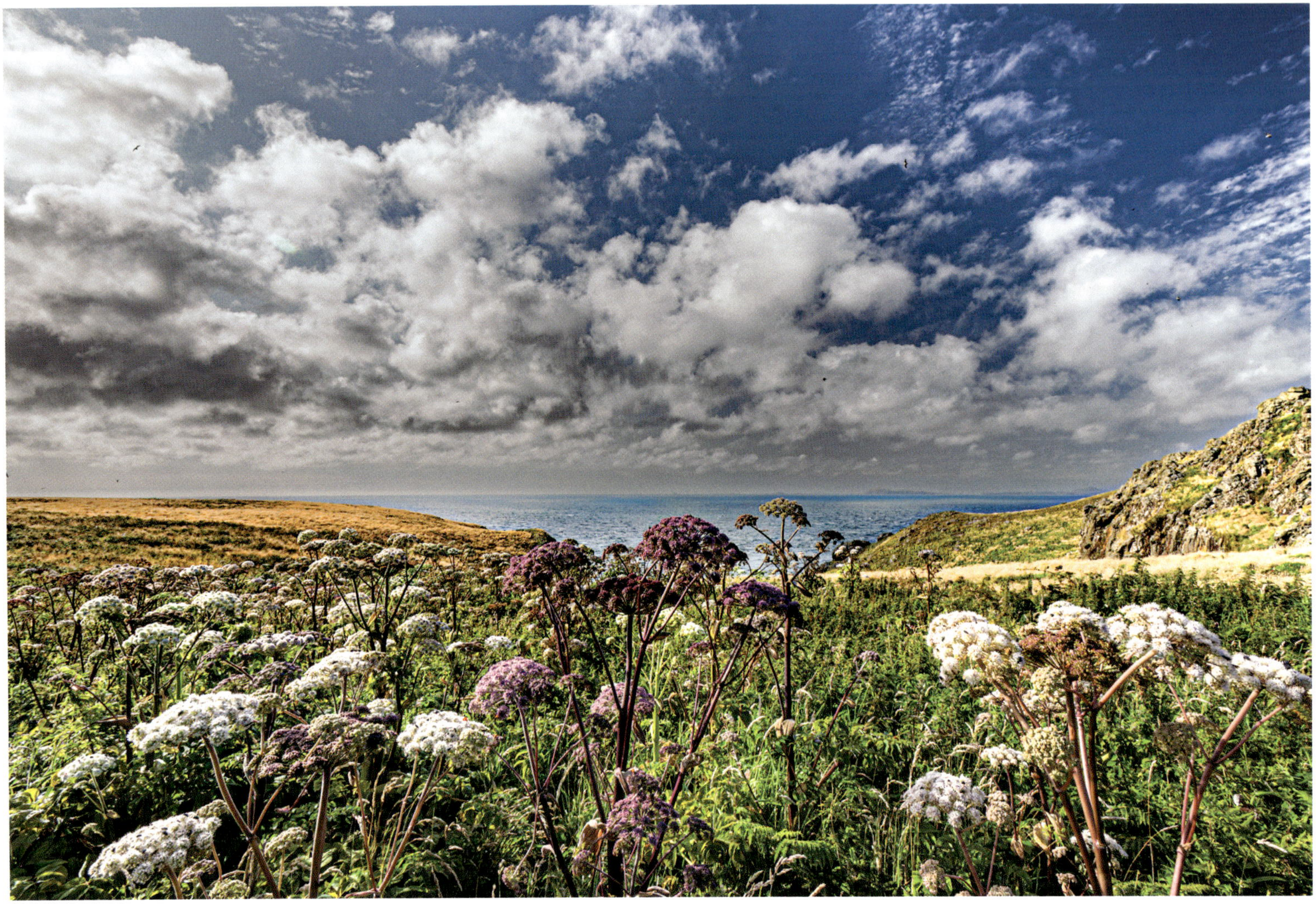

Wild Angelica Llysiau'r Angel *Angelica sylvestris*

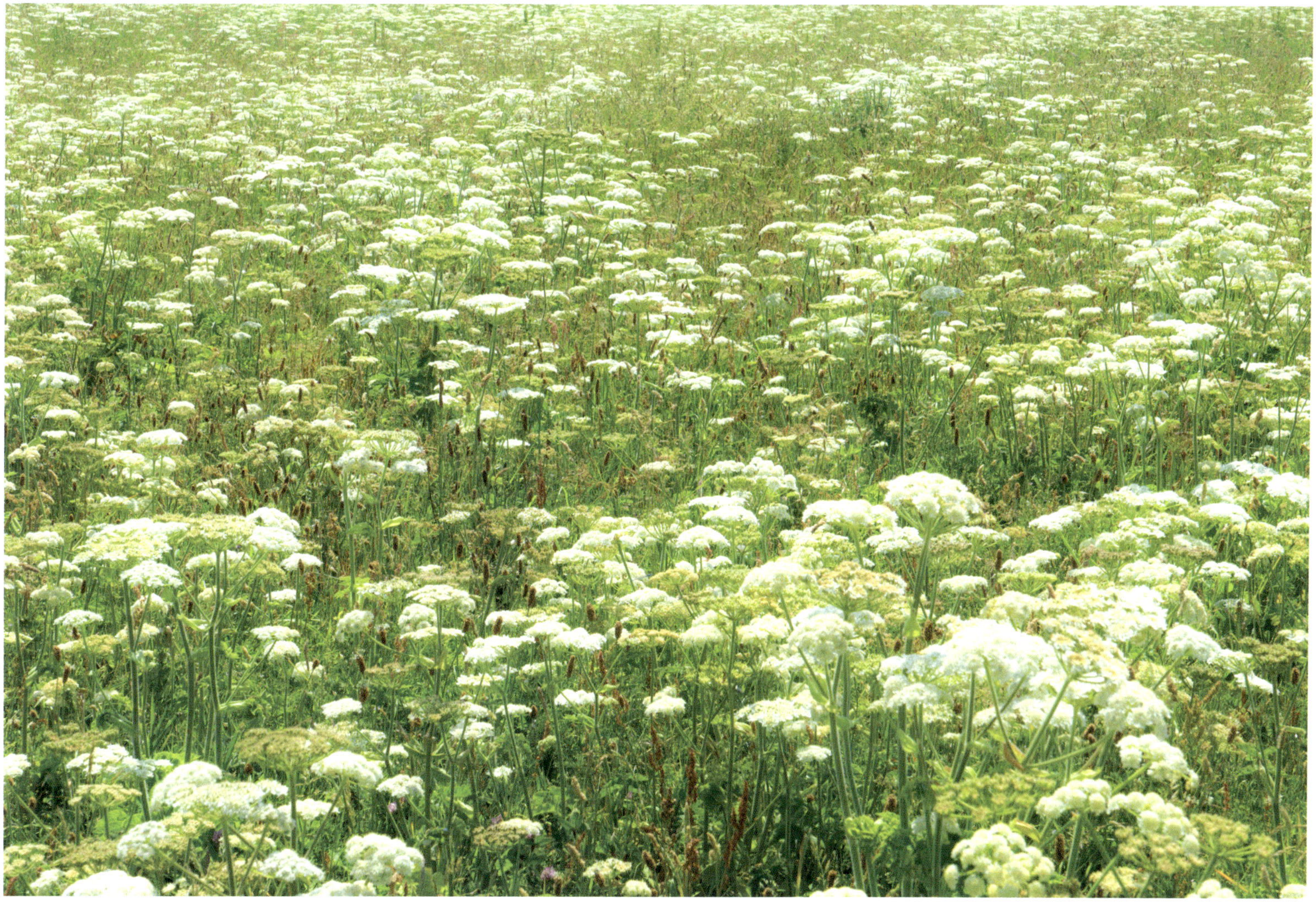

Hogweed Efwr *Heracleum sphondylium*

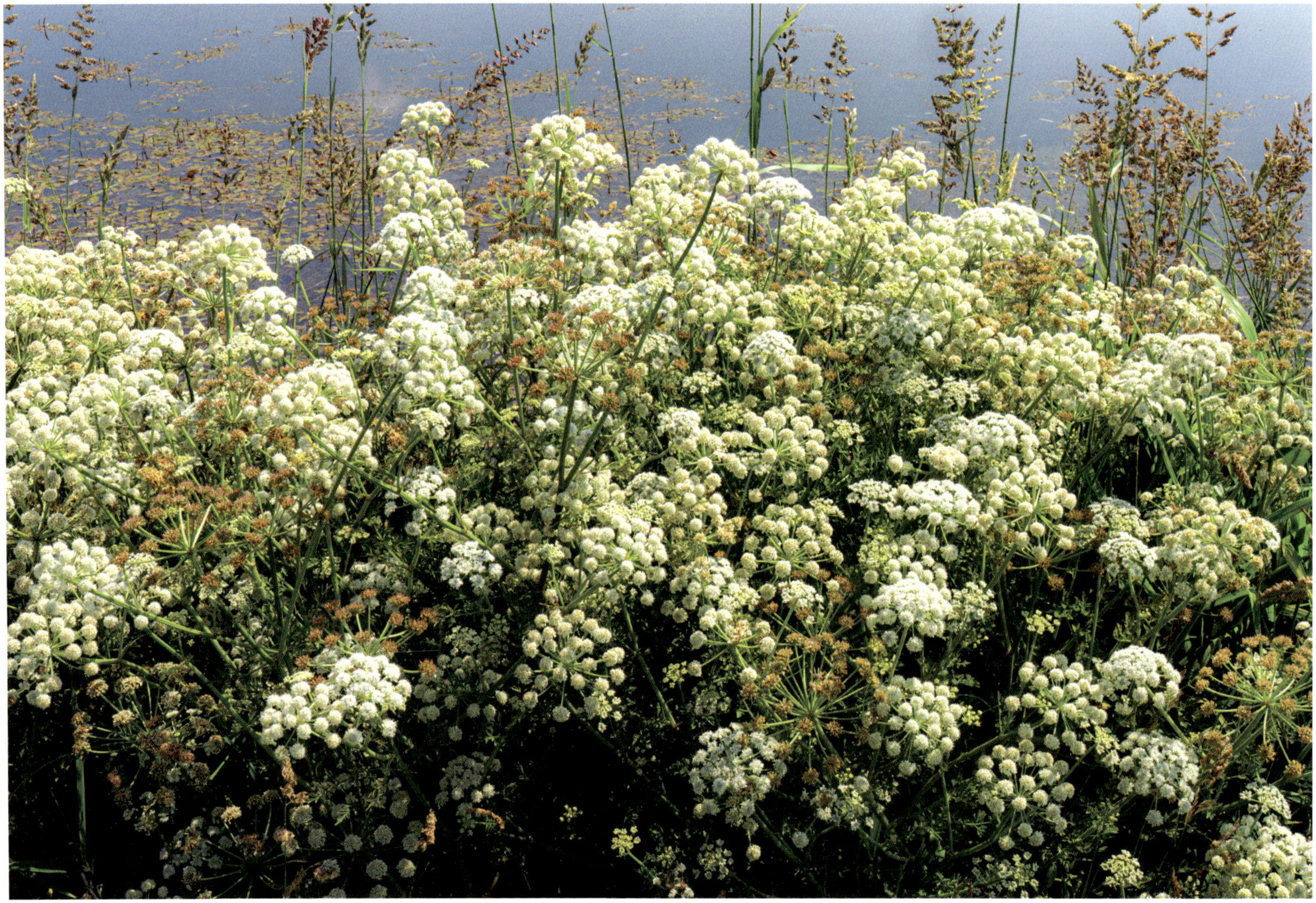

Hemlock Water-dropwort Cegiden y Dŵr *Oenanthe crocata*

Porthmawr

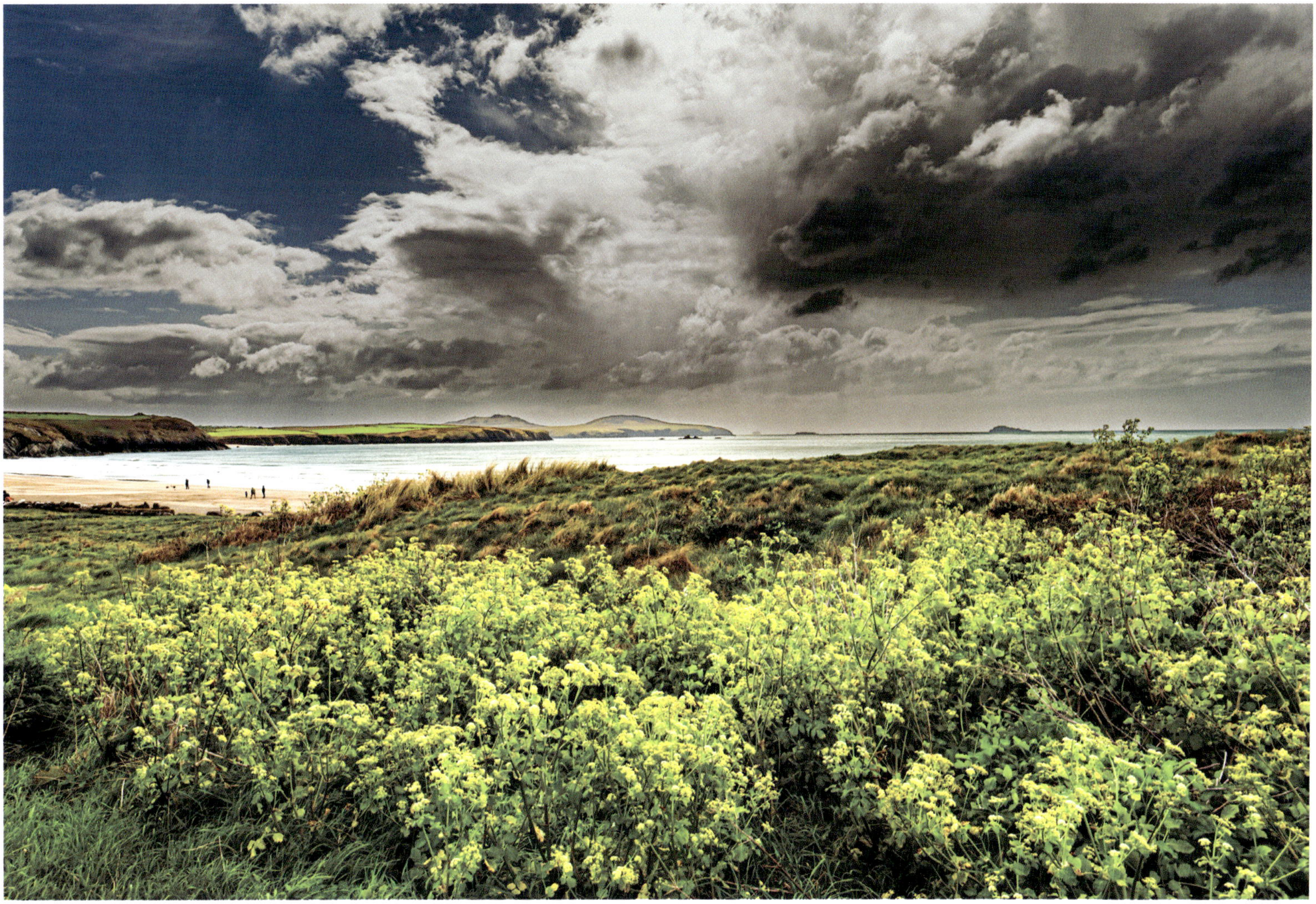

Alexanders Dulys *Smyrnium olusatrum*

Sea-holly and Rock Samphire Celynnen y Môr a Chorn Carw'r Môr

These are two atypical members of the carrot family. It is hard to find any obvious family traits in sea-holly, while rock samphire bears perhaps just a passing resemblance to its relatives.

Sea-holly
Celynnen y Môr
Eryngium maritimum

Sea-holly is a magnificent plant, with electric-blue stems and flowers, and glaucous-green leaves patterned with a tracery of the same brilliant blue. The shape of the plant, with its many-branched stems and whorls of thick, spiny leaves, is equally eye-catching. This is a plant of the sunny open dunes, a pioneer species with adaptations for surviving drought, including deep taproots for water storage and leaves with a waxy cuticle which helps to conserve water. In Elizabethan times, the roots were candied to make a confection which was claimed to be an aphrodisiac. This is another species mentioned by Shakespeare, conjured up by Falstaff in *The Merry Wives of Windsor*:

> My doe with the black scut!
> Let the sky rain potatoes,
> Let it thunder to the tune of 'Greensleeves',
> Hail kissing-comfits, and snow eryngoes;
> Let there come a tempest of provocation,
> I will shelter me here.

Rock Samphire
Corn Carw'r Môr
Crithmum maritimum

Rock samphire is also a species which thrives in harsh conditions, and, as its name implies, is often found on the rocky cliffs. Bushy cushions of succulent, elongated grey-tinged leaves cling to the tiniest crevices on the cliff faces. The yellow-green flowers grow in small umbels. This is a highly prized edible plant, but I am not entirely fond of its faintly petrol-like taste, which comes from pinene, a component of turpentine. By coincidence, the second of this unusual pair of plants is also mentioned by Shakespeare, this time in the words of Edgar in *King Lear*:

> …Here's the place. Stand still. How fearful
> And dizzy 'tis to cast one's eyes so low!
> The crows and choughs that wing the midway air
> Show scarce so gross as beetles. Halfway down
> Hangs one that gathers samphire – dreadful trade;
> Methinks he seems no bigger than his head.
> The fishermen that walk upon the beach
> Appear like mice…

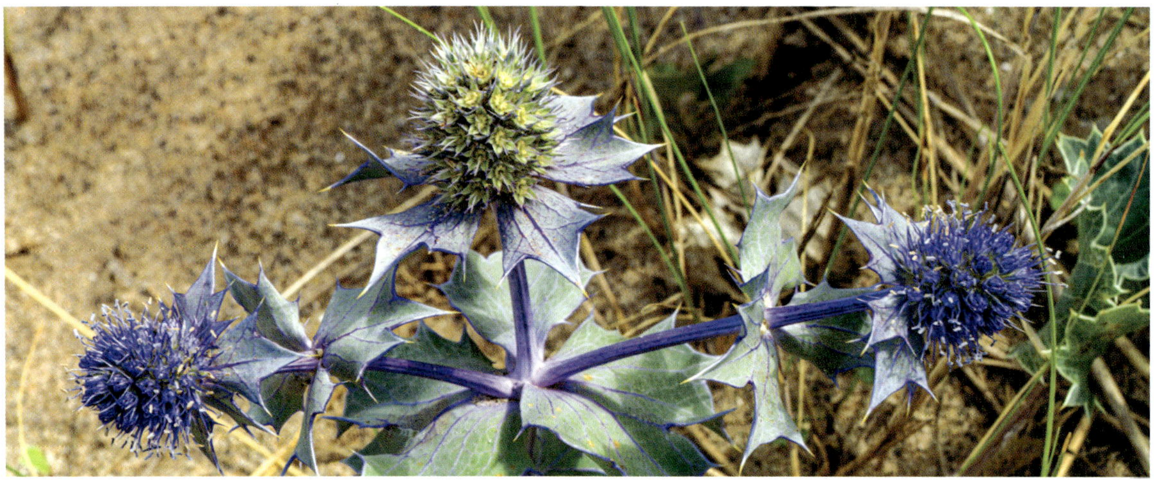

This and next page:
Sea-holly
Celynnen y Môr
Fryngium maritimum

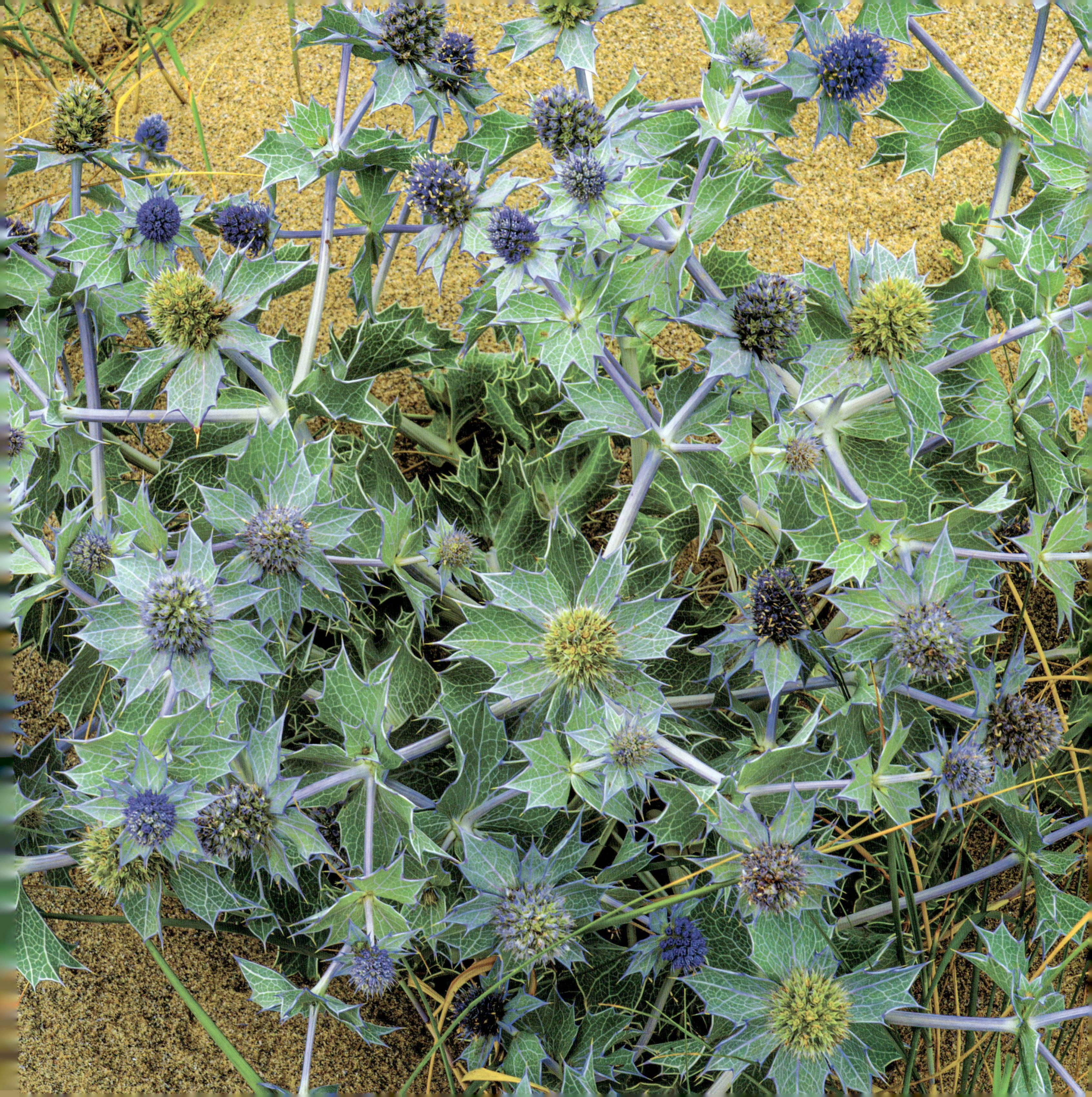

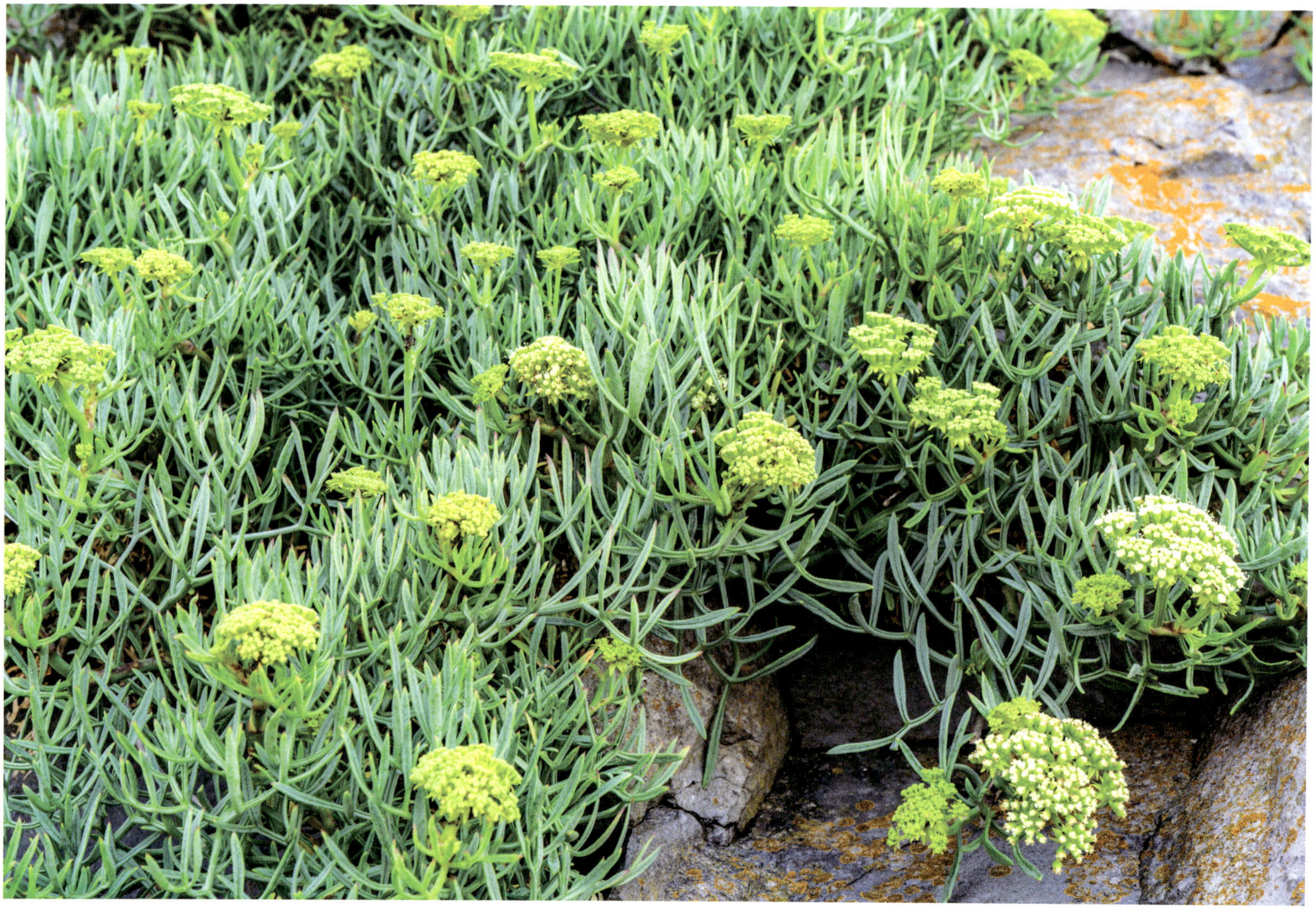

Rock Samphire Corn Carw'r Môr *Crithmum maritimum*

Gentian Family Teulu'r Crwynllys

I have included three members of the gentian family. The name 'centaury' comes from Greek mythology. Chiron was a centaur, son of Titan god Cronos, and was famed for his healing skills and use of medicinal herbs. Irish Christians regarded centaury as a 'blessed herb', and brought it into their houses for good luck between the Annunciation (25 March) and the Assumption of the Blessed Virgin Mary (15 August).

Common Centaury
Y Ganrhi Goch
Centaurium erythraea

Common centaury is a low-growing species found on sand dunes, coastal heaths and dry grasslands. It has small, five-petalled pink flowers in clusters at the top of the stems. The fleshy dark-green, lance-shaped leaves grow in an alternate pattern around the stem. Common centaury has a long history as a traditional medicine used to aid digestion and stimulate appetite. One of the best places to find common centaury is the sandy, limestone clifftops above Broad Haven beach, in South Pembrokeshire.

Slender Centaury
Y Ganrhi Goch Fain
Centaurium tenuiflorum

Slender centaury is, as the name suggests, more slender and upright than common centaury, although it is very similar. There is little in folklore or literature relating to this plant, suggesting that, in earlier times, people did not differentiate between the species, which happens quite commonly.

Yellow-wort
Y Ganrhi Felen
Blackstonia perfoliata

Yellow-wort is a plant of limestone grassland and sand dunes. It has cup-shaped yellow flowers, which appear in clusters, atop almost impossibly slender upright stems. Pairs of pointed blue-green leaves grow at intervals along the stem. The pairs are fused together around the stem, giving the appearance of a single leaf.

This is another flower easily found on the limestone grassland above Broad Haven.

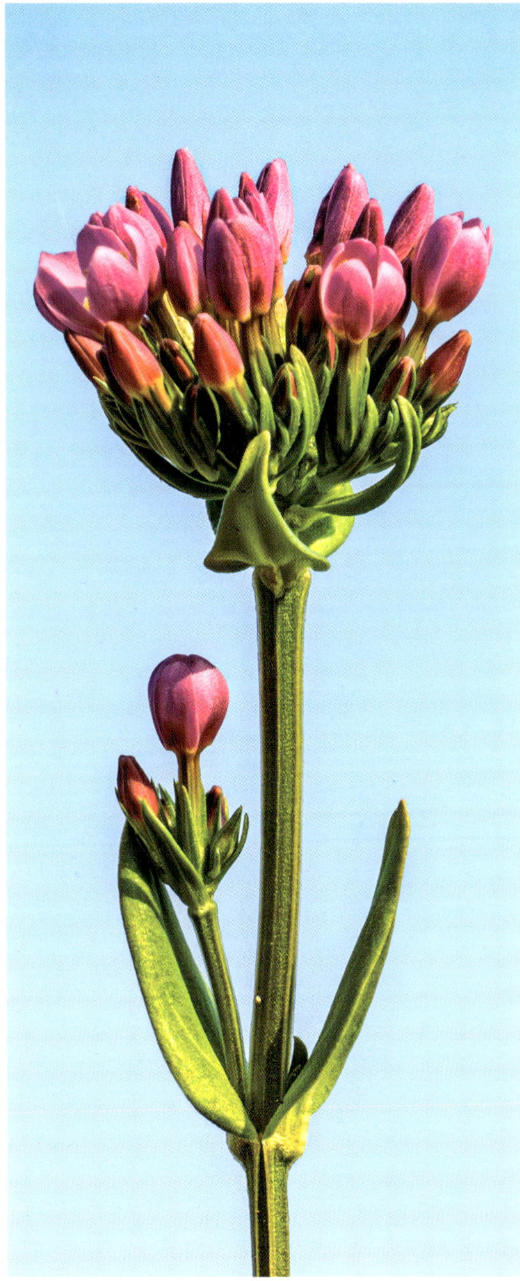

Common Centaury
Y Ganrhi Goch
Centaurium erythraea

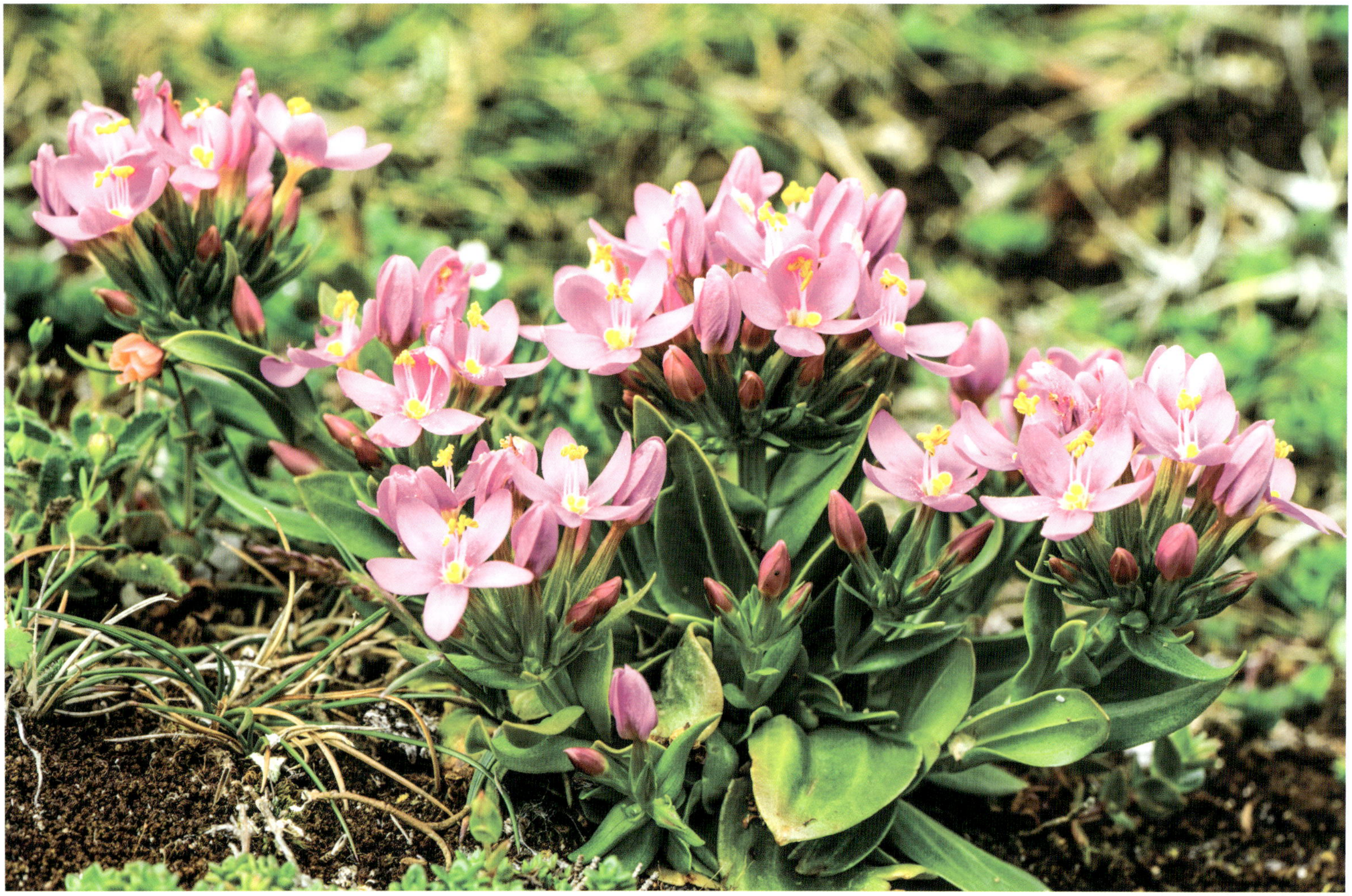

Common Centaury Y Ganrhi Goch *Centaurium erythraea*

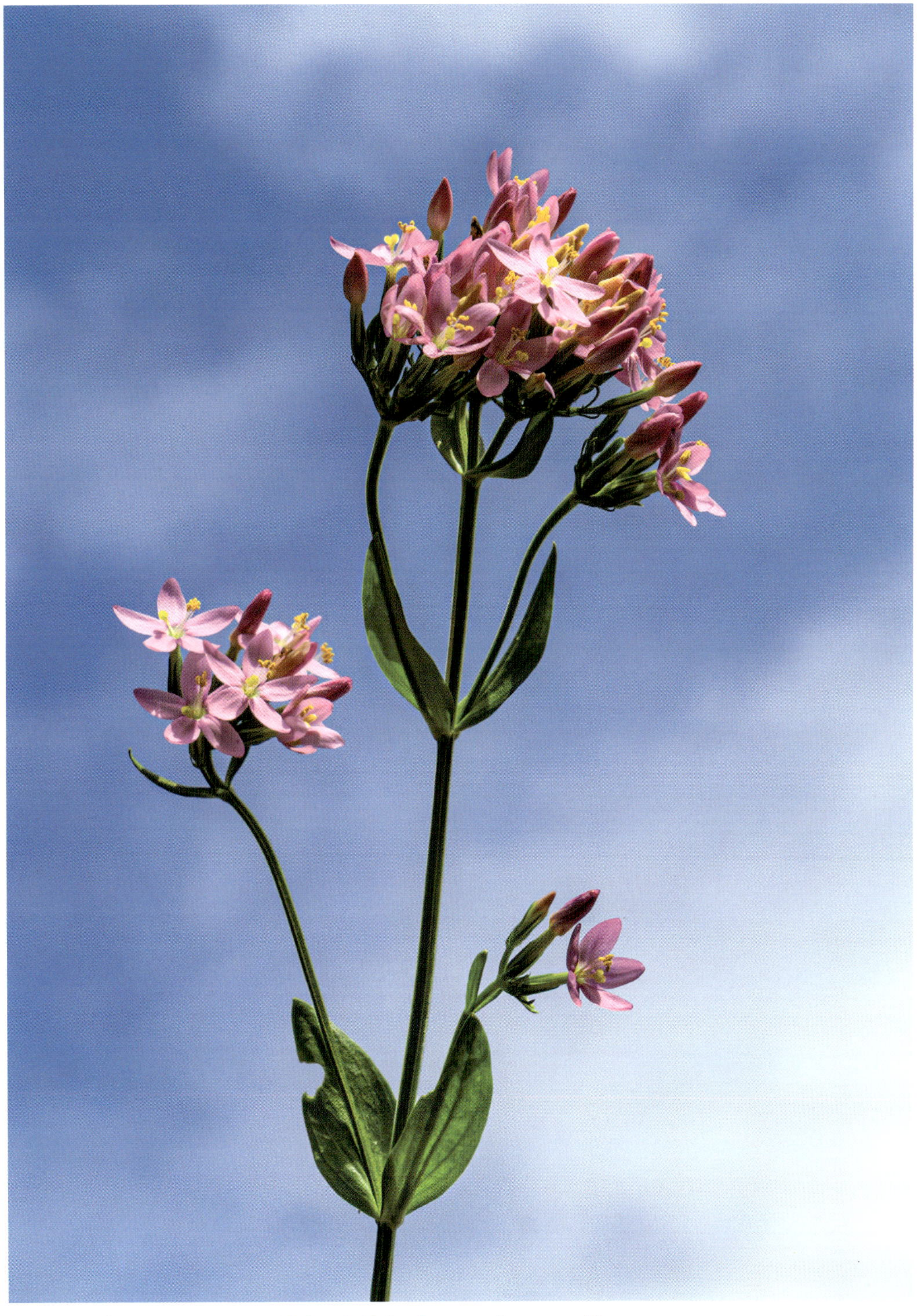

Slender Centaury Y Ganrhi Goch Fain *Centaurium tenuiflorum*

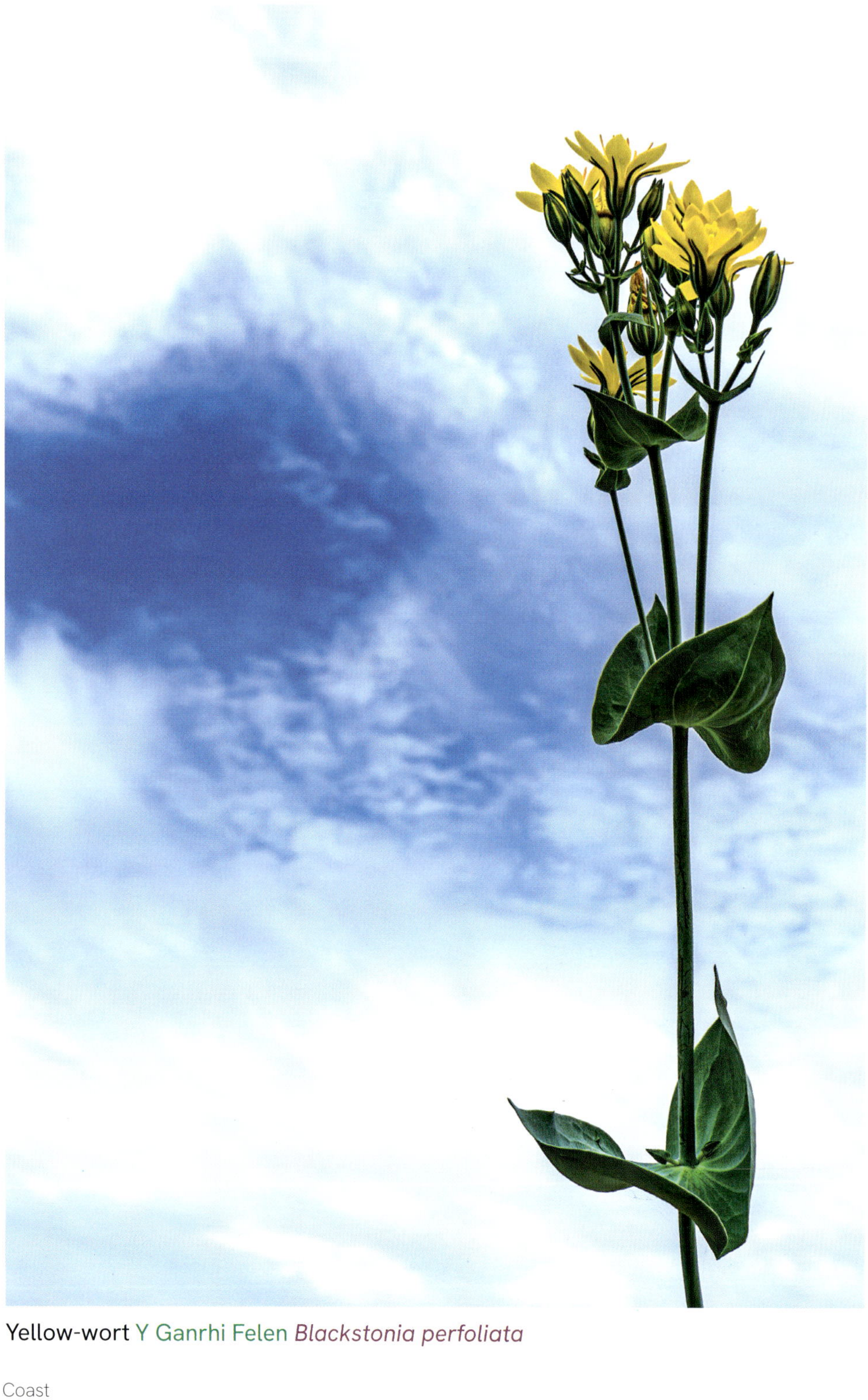

Yellow-wort Y Ganrhi Felen *Blackstonia perfoliata*

Nightshade Family Teulu'r Codwarth

Bittersweet
Elinog
Solanum dulcamara

Bittersweet is a vine that scrambles through other plants and is supported by them. The small flowers grow loosely in clusters, with five purple petals which curve backwards and surround protruding deep-yellow stamens. The flowers are quickly followed by shiny green berries, which turn red. Flowers and fruit are often seen together on a plant. The flowers look like tomato or potato flowers and the fruit is like a tiny tomato. Unsurprisingly, bittersweet, potatoes and tomatoes are all members of the same family. The berries are poisonous, but they are important in the diet of many species of songbirds, which are immune to the poison. Poisoning cases in humans are rare, apparently because the berries are intensely bitter, but the aftertaste is described as sweet, hence the name bittersweet. Regarded in earlier times as a symbol of fidelity, it was used in Christian bridal wreaths during the Middle Ages.

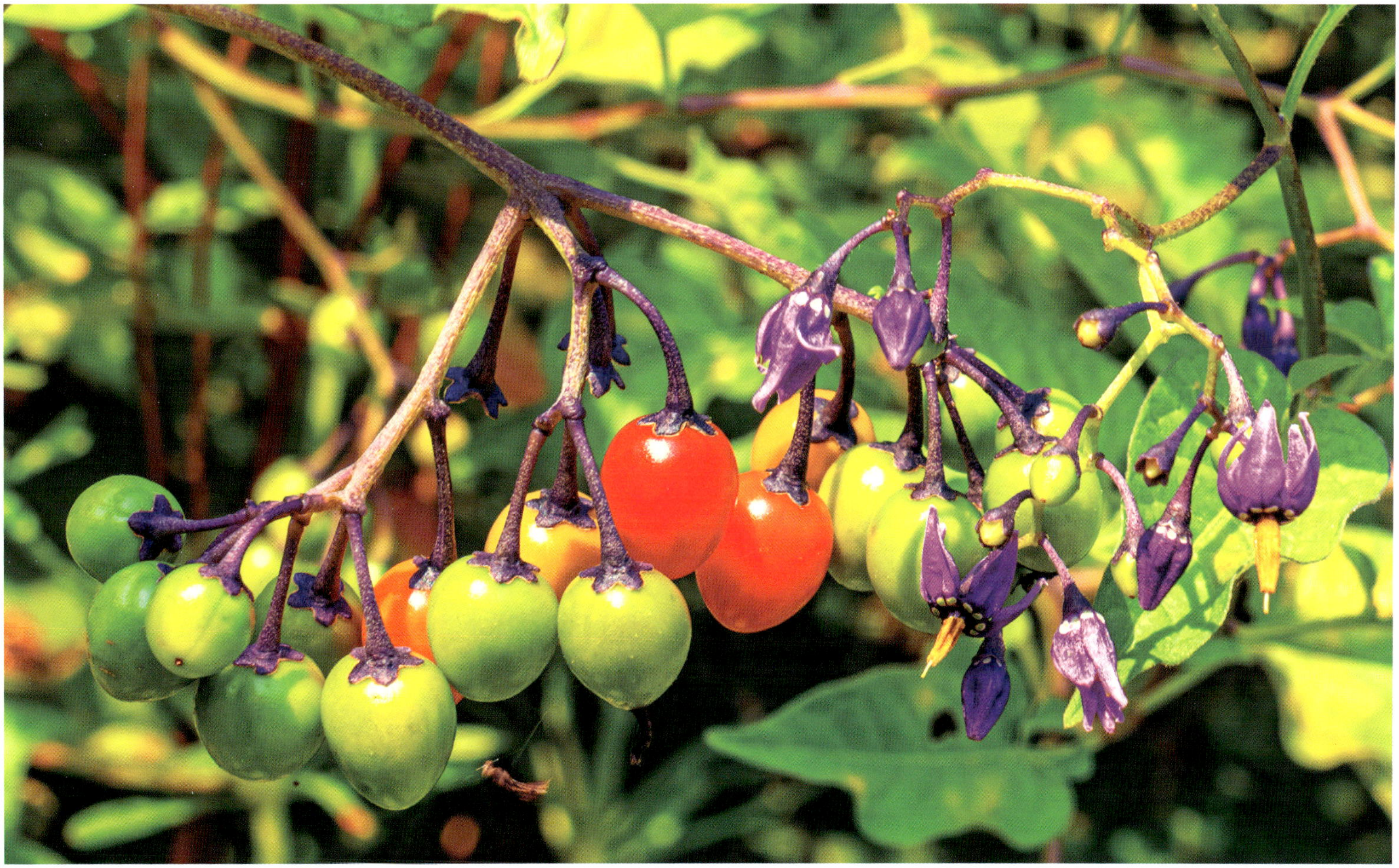

Bittersweet Elinog *Solanum dulcamara*

Bindweed Family Teulu'r Taglys

Sometimes called morning glories, this is a large family of mainly vines. The stems are usually winding, which is how they earned the name convolvulus, from the Latin *convolvere*, 'to coil or interweave'.

Field Bindweed
Cwlwm y Cythraul
Convolvulus arvensis

Field bindweed creeps through coarse grasses and other vegetation, usually at ground level. The arrowhead-shaped grey-green leaves grow in spirals along the stem. The delicate trumpet-shaped flowers can be pink, white or pink and white striped. Sadly, it is often regarded as an aggressive garden weed. The Welsh name, *cwlwm y cythraul*, translates as 'devil's knots', probably for good reason. It is, nevertheless, a beautiful flower, which is widespread around the coast, and can also be found along the verges of country roads.

Sea Bindweed
Taglys Arfor
Calystegia soldanella

Sea bindweed is also known as shore convolvulus and beach morning glory. It is similar to field bindweed but has larger flowers, usually pink or violet, with five white radial stripes. This is primarily a sand dune or shingle species, capable of growing just above the strandline, where they are occasionally sea washed. The leaves are dark green, shiny, fleshy and kidney-shaped; quite different to the arrowhead leaves of field bindweed.

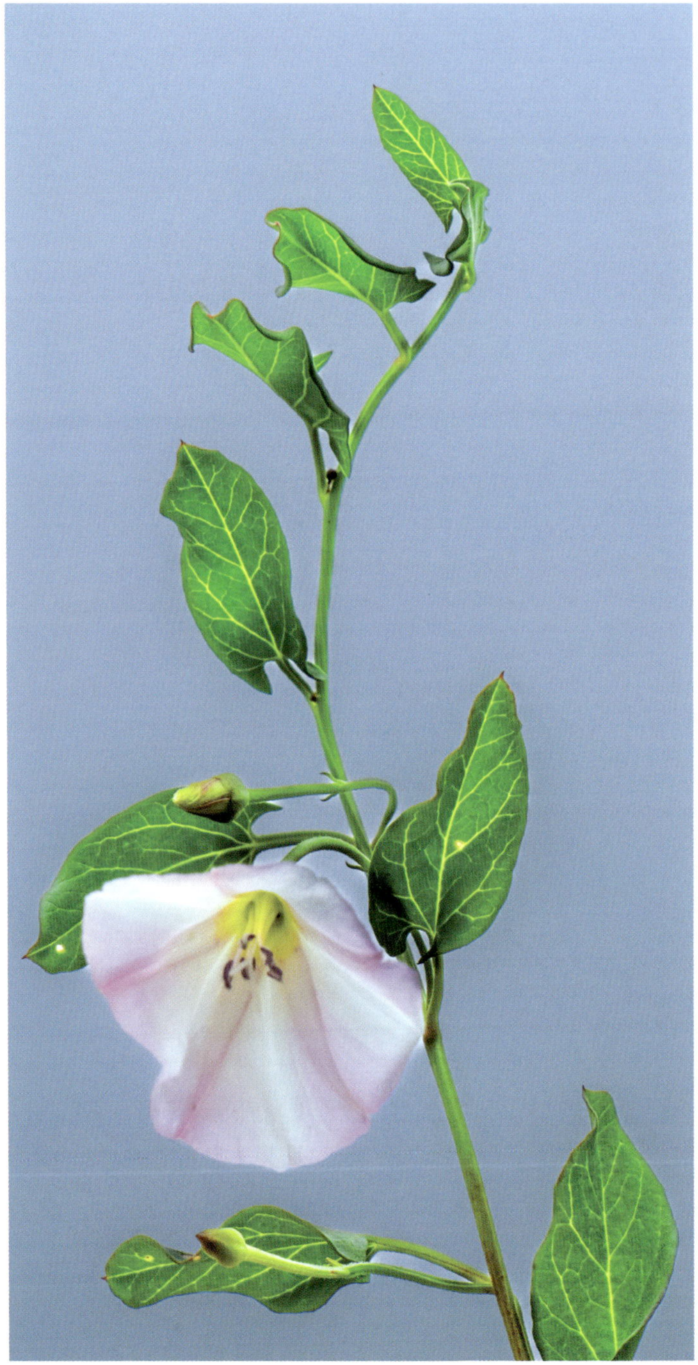

Field Bindweed
Cwlwm y Cythraul
Convolvulus arvensis

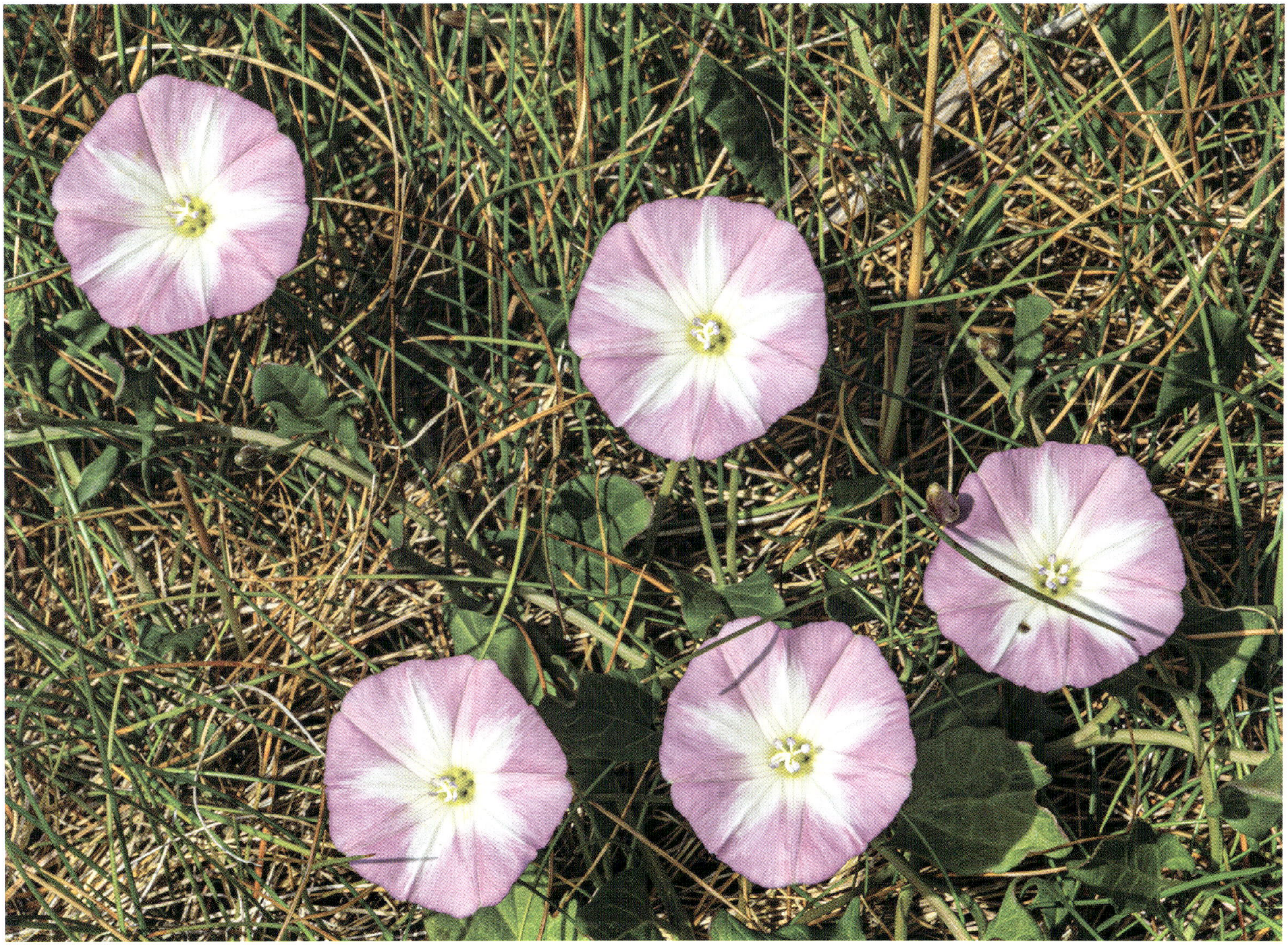

Field Bindweed Cwlwm y Cythraul *Convolvulus arvensis*

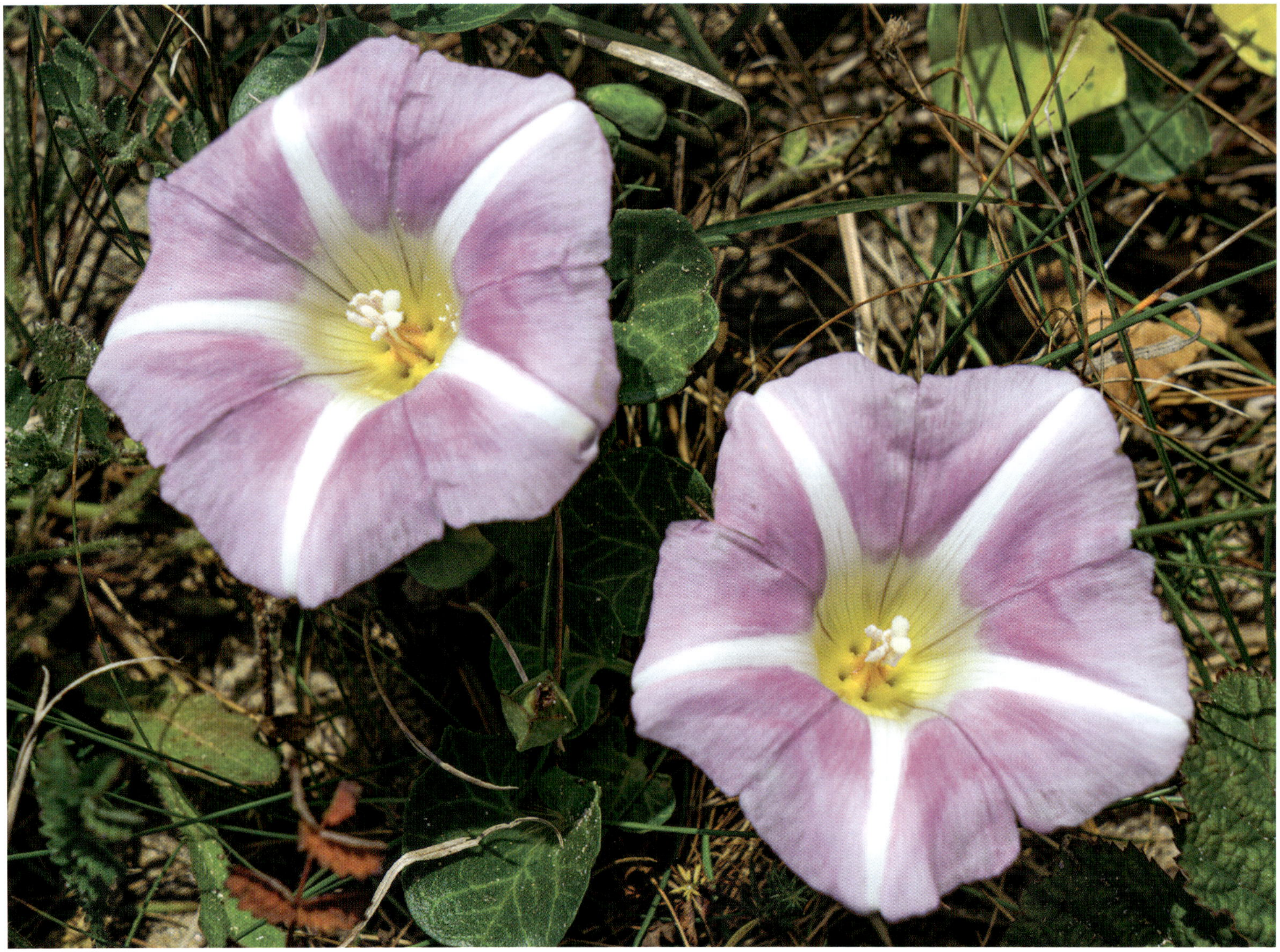

Sea Bindweed Taglys Arfor *Calystegia soldanella*

Borage Family Teulu Tafod yr Ych

I have included two very different members of this family. Both are interesting, but in different ways.

Viper's-bugloss
Gwiberlys
Echium vulgare

Viper's-bugloss is a long-standing favourite of mine. The tall flower spikes emerge pink, turning brilliant blue as they mature. The stamens remain red, contrasting vividly with the intense blue. The flowers always seem to be teeming with insects, including bees and butterflies. The best places to find them are on the thin, drought-prone soils along the edges of limestone cliffs. The common name is from the spotted stem, which some claim looks like a viper. Bugloss is derived from the Greek, meaning 'ox tongue', because the rough leaves are tongue-shaped. The Welsh name, *gwiberlys*, is from *gwiber*, meaning viper, and *llys*, which means 'plant' or 'herb'.

Hound's-tongue
Tafod y Bytheiad
Cynoglossum officinale

Hound's-tongue is considered by some to be a noxious weed – mainly in North America, where it was accidentally introduced and soon became a seriously invasive species. I first learned to identify hound's-tongue by smell. It has a slightly unpleasant mouse-pee odour, and a popular alternative name is rats and mice. The name hound's-tongue comes from the leaves, which are long and tongue-shaped, covered in soft white hairs and with a strong central vein. The flowers are small and discreet, ranging in colour from dull red to burgundy, with both colours sometimes appearing in the same cluster. They develop into seeds which have a hard, shiny husk, covered in sharp barbs. The barbs will cling tenaciously to grazing animals and wildlife, which then disperse the seeds. Look for hound's-tongue in sand dunes and on limestone cliffs, but don't be tempted to touch the plants, all parts of which are toxic and can cause contact dermatitis. However, it is not all bad news, since bumblebees love it. It also had various medicinal uses: in Culpeper's day the root was used for coughs, colds, difficulty breathing and piles, and the leaves as a cure for dysentery and to ease the pain of a burn.

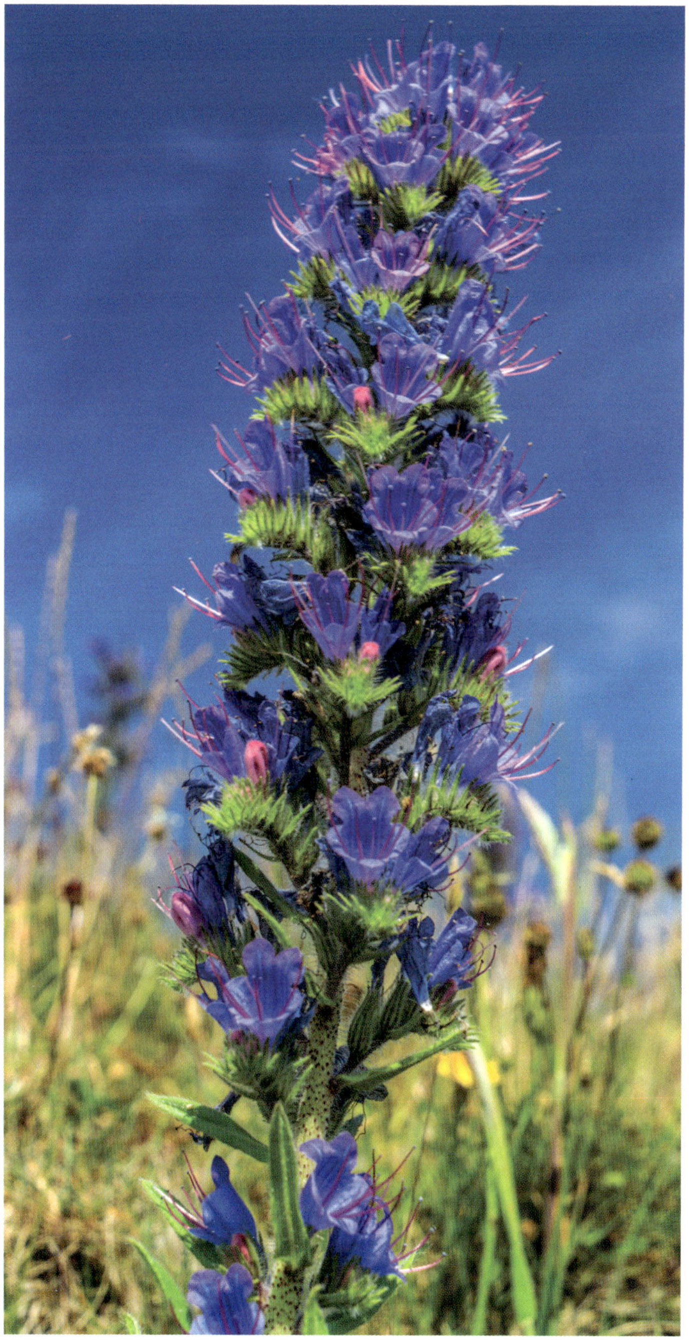

Viper's-bugloss Gwiberlys *Echium vulgare*

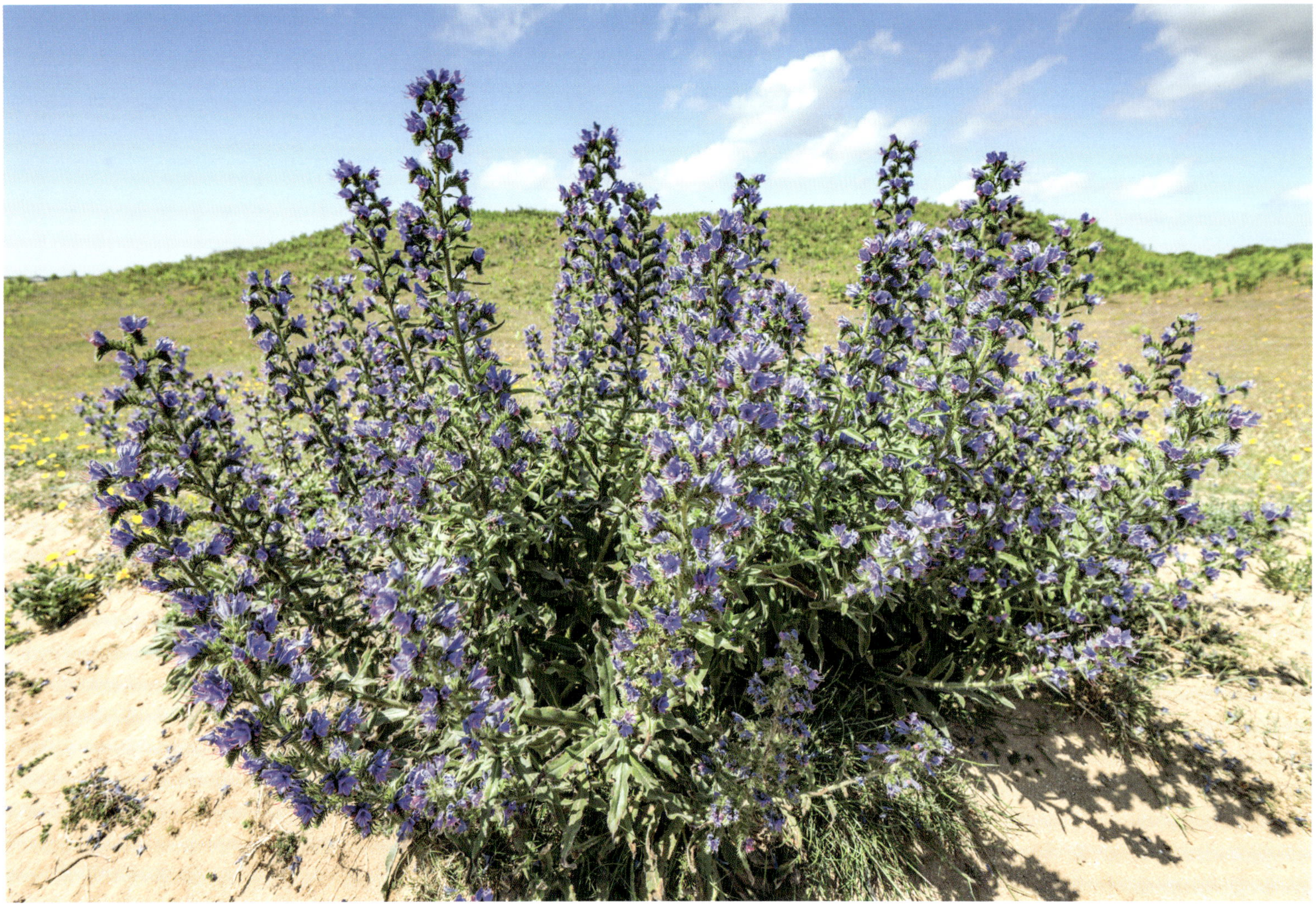

Viper's-bugloss Gwiberlys *Echium vulgare*

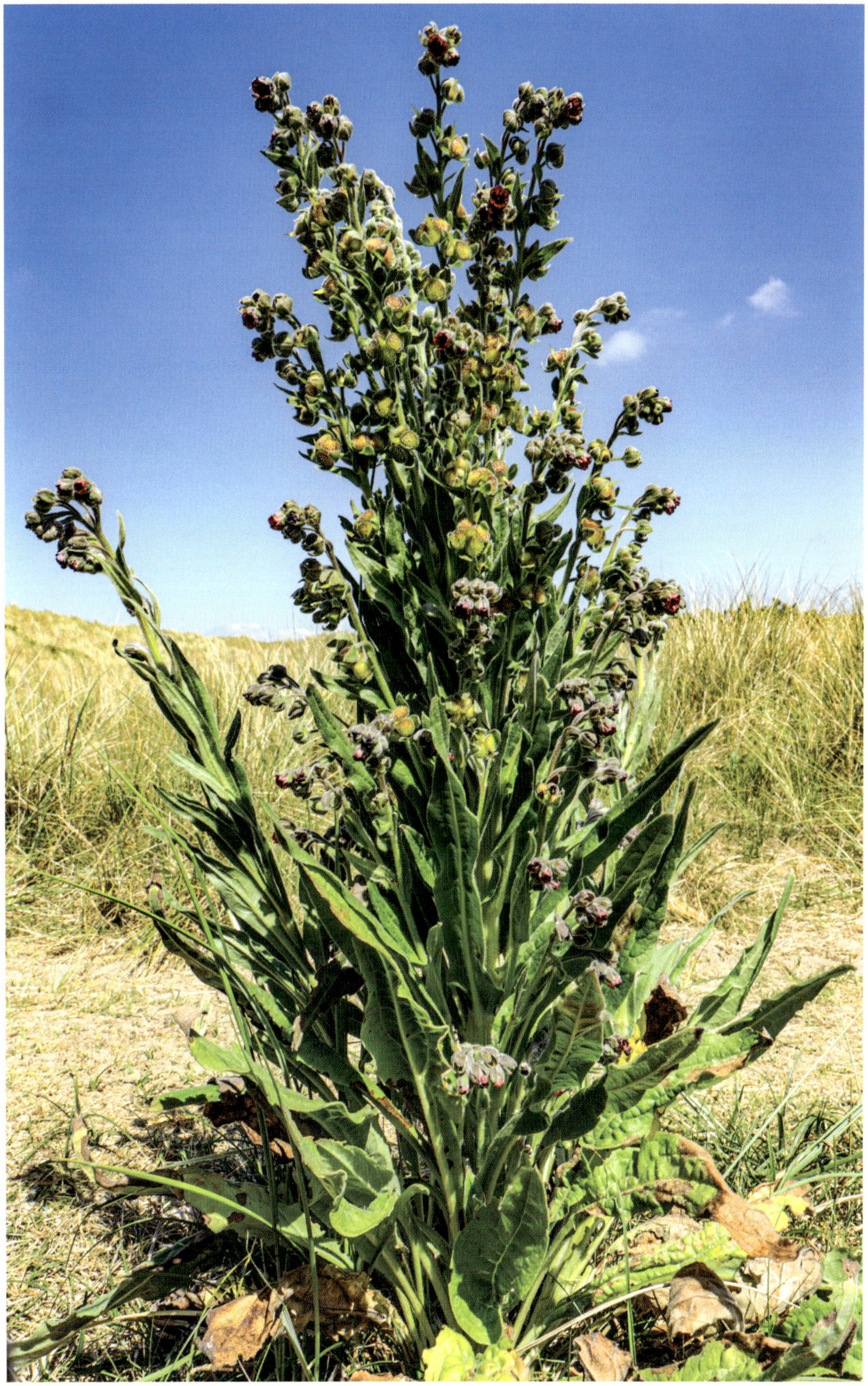

Hound's-tongue
Tafod y Bytheiad
Cynoglossum officinale

Dead-nettle Family Teulu'r Farddanhadlen

This is a family of not particularly flamboyant species. They tend to be hairy or downy, are often aromatic, and they all have square stems. It is a relatively common family that frequents most coastal habitats. I have chosen to include a selection of typical species, and most will be recognisable as common culinary herbs.

Betony
Cribau San Ffraid
Stachys officinalis

Betony has pretty purple to red flowers, which stand proud on erect, square stems, with toothed foliage that is dark green and wrinkled. It will grow in grasslands, rough ground and hedgerows. Betony has a significant place in history, folklore and traditional medicine. It was mentioned by Gaius Plinius Secundus (AD 23/24–AD 79), commonly known as Pliny the Elder. He wrote in his Natural History that betony was, 'a plant more highly esteemed than any other'. He also claimed that betony would protect a house from harm. A fourth-century herbal listed almost 50 uses for the species. Culpeper, who called it woody betony, provided an enormous list of ailments which it could cure, including epidemical diseases, indigestion, belching, palsy, gout, worms, agues of all kinds, obstructions of the liver and spleen, pains in the back, toothache, bruises and wounds. Betony really was regarded as an almost universal cure-all. A Welsh connection is that it was prescribed by the famous twelfth-century Physicians of Myddfai (*Meddygon Myddfai*), who believed that it could control dreams, and recommended that its juice should be drunk before sleep. They also used betony to treat colic, eye troubles and deafness. The Welsh name, *Cribau San Ffraid*, is intriguing: it translates as 'St Bride's combs'. St Bride apparently came to Wales from Ireland

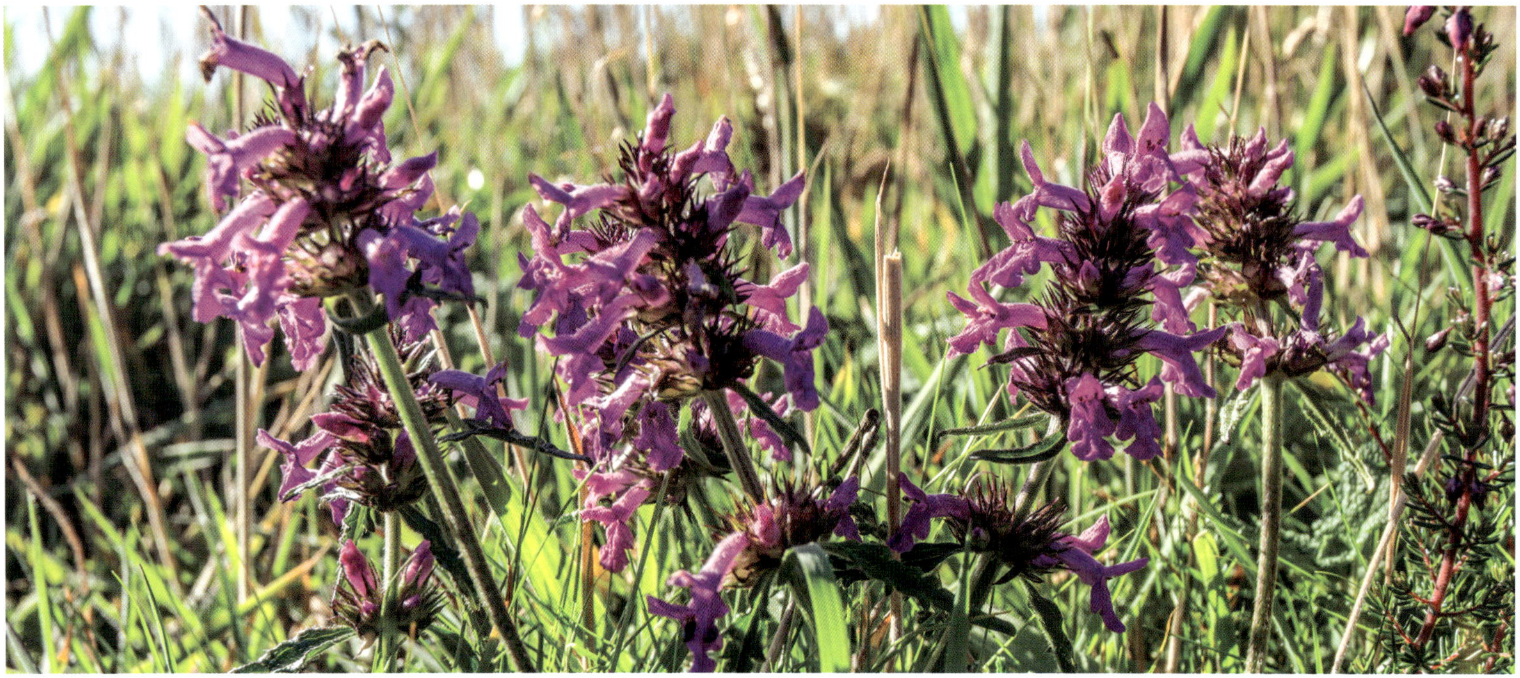

Betony Cribau San Ffraid *Stachys officinalis*

floating on a piece of turf, and landed in the Pembrokeshire bay which today bears her name.

Wild Thyme
Teim Gwyllt
Thymus polytrichus

Wild thyme has such a delightful fragrance that I can never resist getting close enough to enjoy the full sensory experience. It flowers from June to September, forming mats of deep purplish pink in the close-grazed coastal pastures, on lime-mortar walls and on the rocky cliffs. For some reason, it also favours the dry soil on anthills.

It is a close relative of a Mediterranean species which is widely used to flavour food. Thyme (though not this species) was used by the Egyptians for embalming, while the Ancient Greeks used it as incense, and in the Middle Ages it was placed under pillows to ward off nightmares. Wild thyme is still used for seasoning barbecues, fish and meat dishes, and as edible ornamentation in salads. Thyme is an excellent source of nectar, attracting more than its share of pollinators. I have included a photograph of the brilliant metallic-green rose chafer, and another of a painted lady butterfly, feeding on thyme.

This is another quote from Shakespeare's *A Midsummer Night's Dream*. In the prelude to the scene where Oberon decides to play a trick on Titania, he describes her location to Puck:

> I know a bank where the wild thyme blows,
> Where oxlips and the nodding violet grows,
> Quite over-canopied with luscious woodbine,
> With sweet musk-roses, and with eglantine:
> There sleeps Titania sometime of the night.

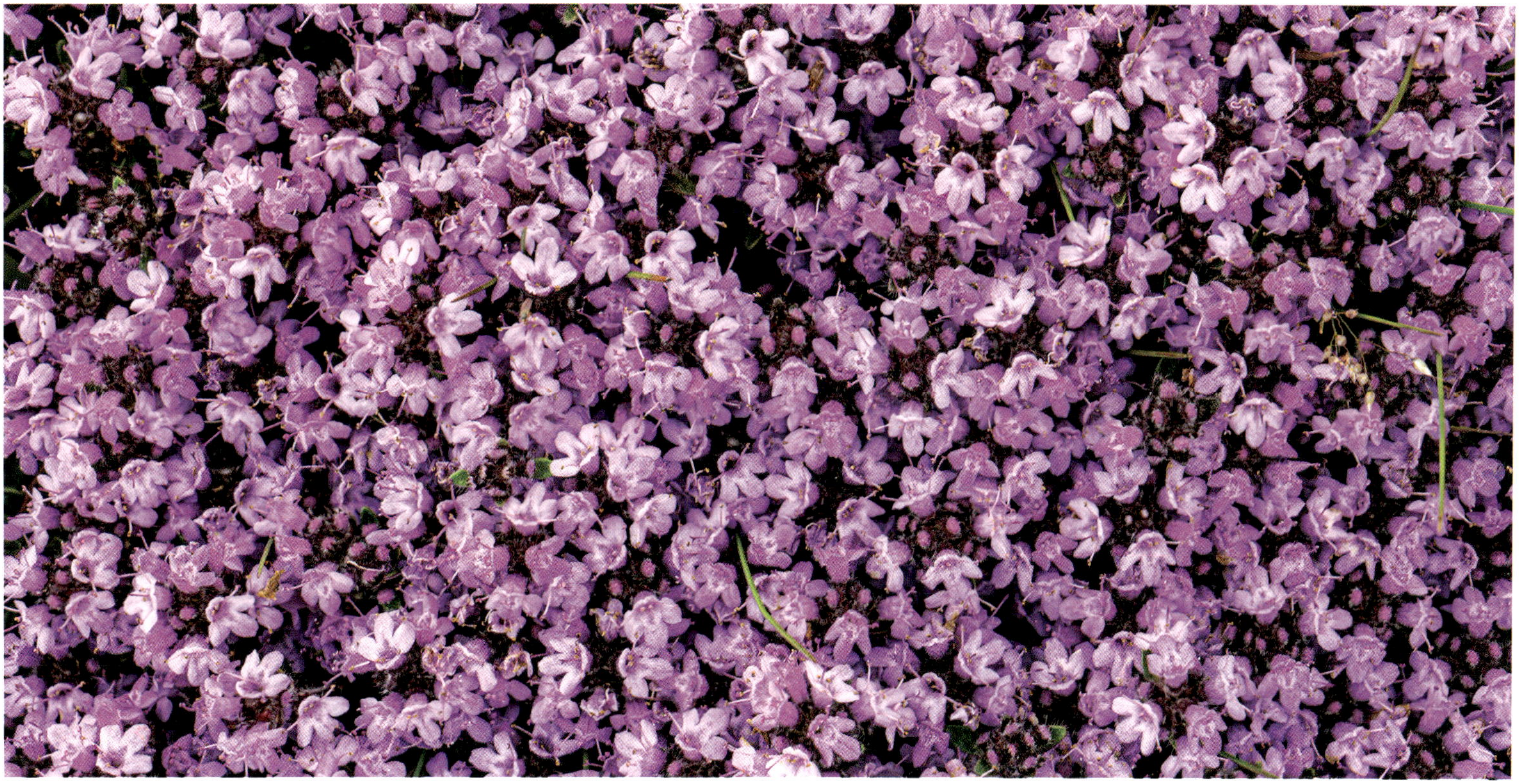

Wild Thyme Teim Gwyllt *Thymus polytrichus*

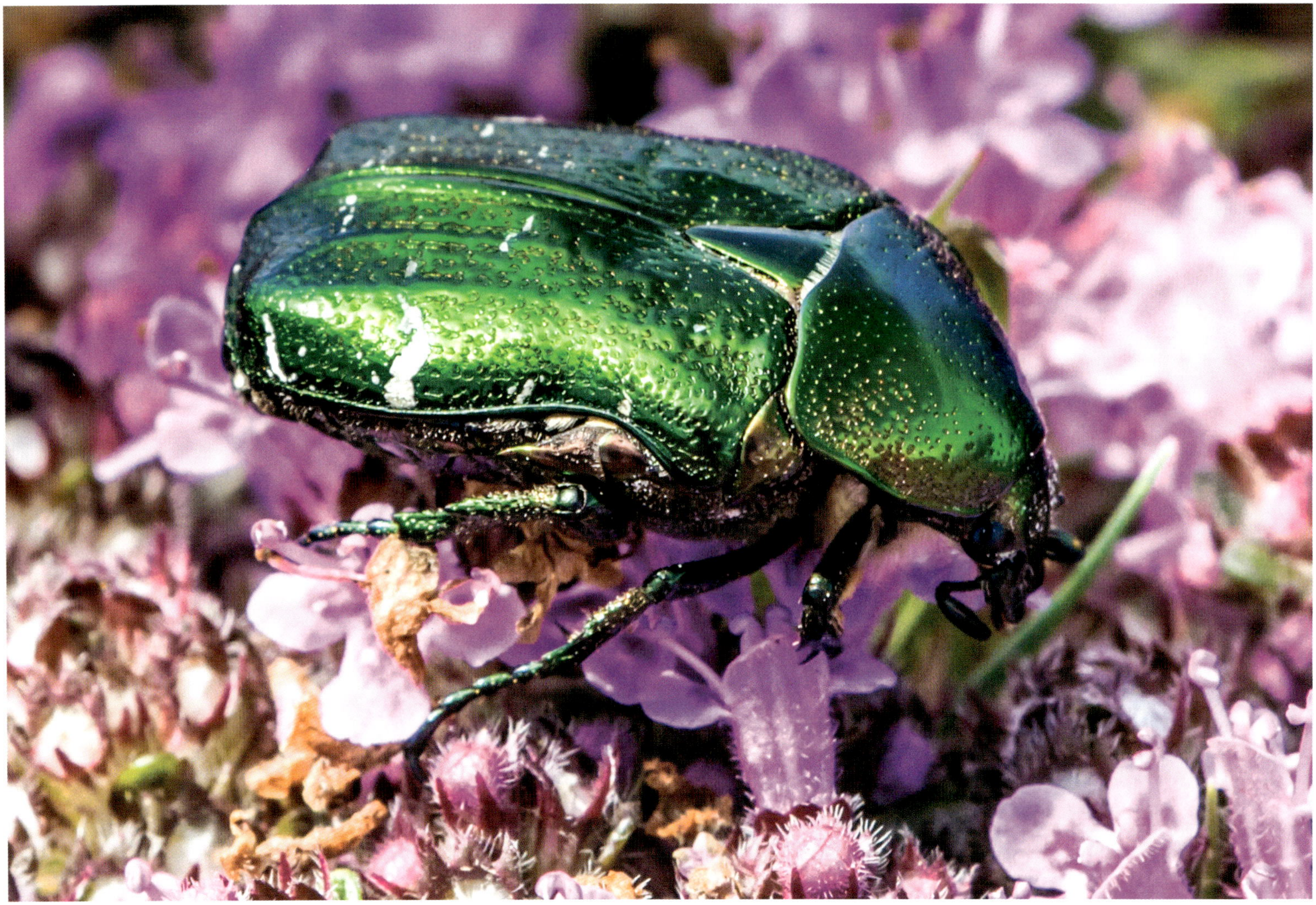

Rose Chafer beetle Chwilen y Rhosod *Cetonia aurata*

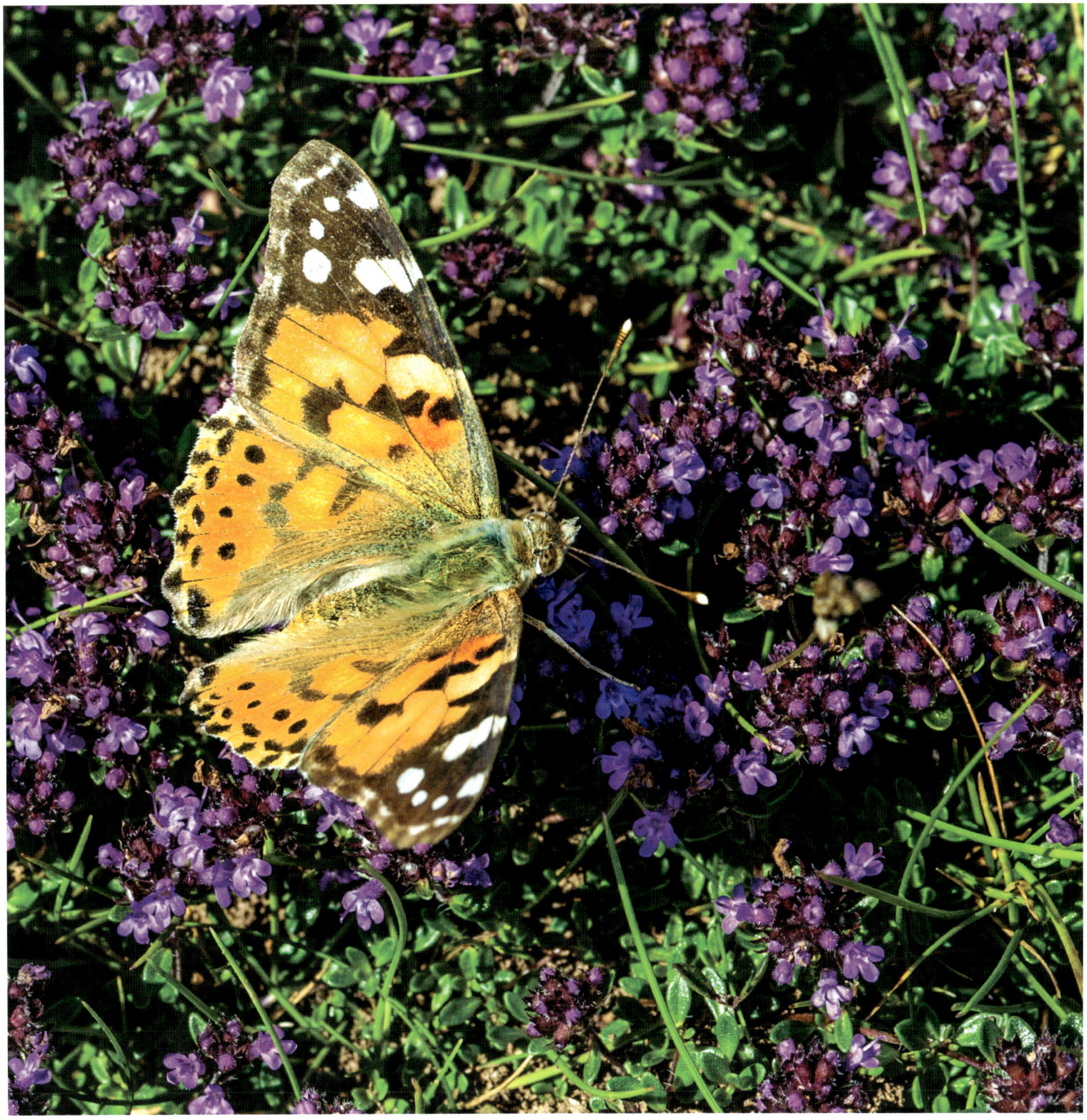

Painted Lady butterfly Mantell Dramor *Vanessa cardui*

Marjoram
Penrhudd
Origanum vulgare

Marjoram is a popular aromatic culinary herb. Look for it on limestone, where it will flower later in the summer, between July and September. It can grow quite tall, and has red stems with oval pointed leaves arranged in pairs along them. The soft clusters of tiny, tufted flowers are delicate pink, with an aromatic fragrance. Marjoram oil can be distilled from the flowers.

Wood Sage
Chwerwlys yr Eithin
Teucrium scorodonia

Wood sage is not an edible herb, having little scent and an unpleasant flavour. As its name implies, it is usually regarded as a woodland – or, more accurately, woodland edge – species, but it is also a widespread and common coastal plant. The islands of Skomer and Skokholm have large populations of rabbits, which manage to eat almost everything they consider edible. This reduces competition and allows the unpalatable plants, including wood sage, to thrive and become extremely prolific. It is easily identified by its close similarity in appearance to the familiar culinary herb.

Selfheal
Y Feddyges Las
Prunella vulgaris

Selfheal is another common and widespread species. The flowers, which are usually purple but occasionally white, appear as a spike at the end of a vertical stem, and it is sometimes suggested that the individual flower looks like a mouth. I couldn't resist including this flower, because the close-up photograph is one that I love. Whenever I look closely at selfheal, there are wicked little faces staring back at me, which I can never now unsee. Traditionally, this was an important medicinal herb, so much so that it was cultivated for that purpose. In the sixteenth century, the herbalist John Gerard claimed that there was no better herb for wounds than selfheal. It is used today as an infusion to relieve bites and scratches. The Welsh name, *y feddyges las*, translates as 'the blue (or verdant) doctor'. Surprisingly for a medicinal herb, it is also a good addition to salads and similar dishes.

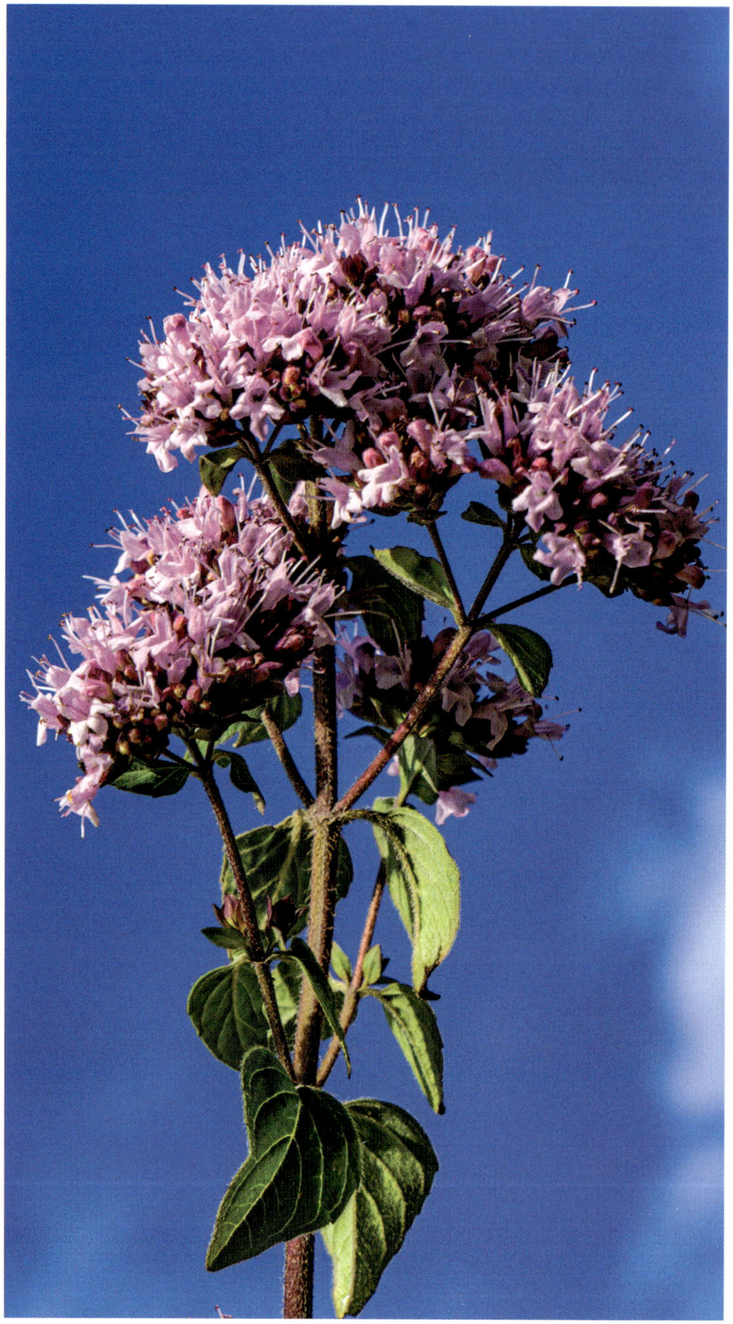

Marjoram Penrhudd *Origanum vulgare*

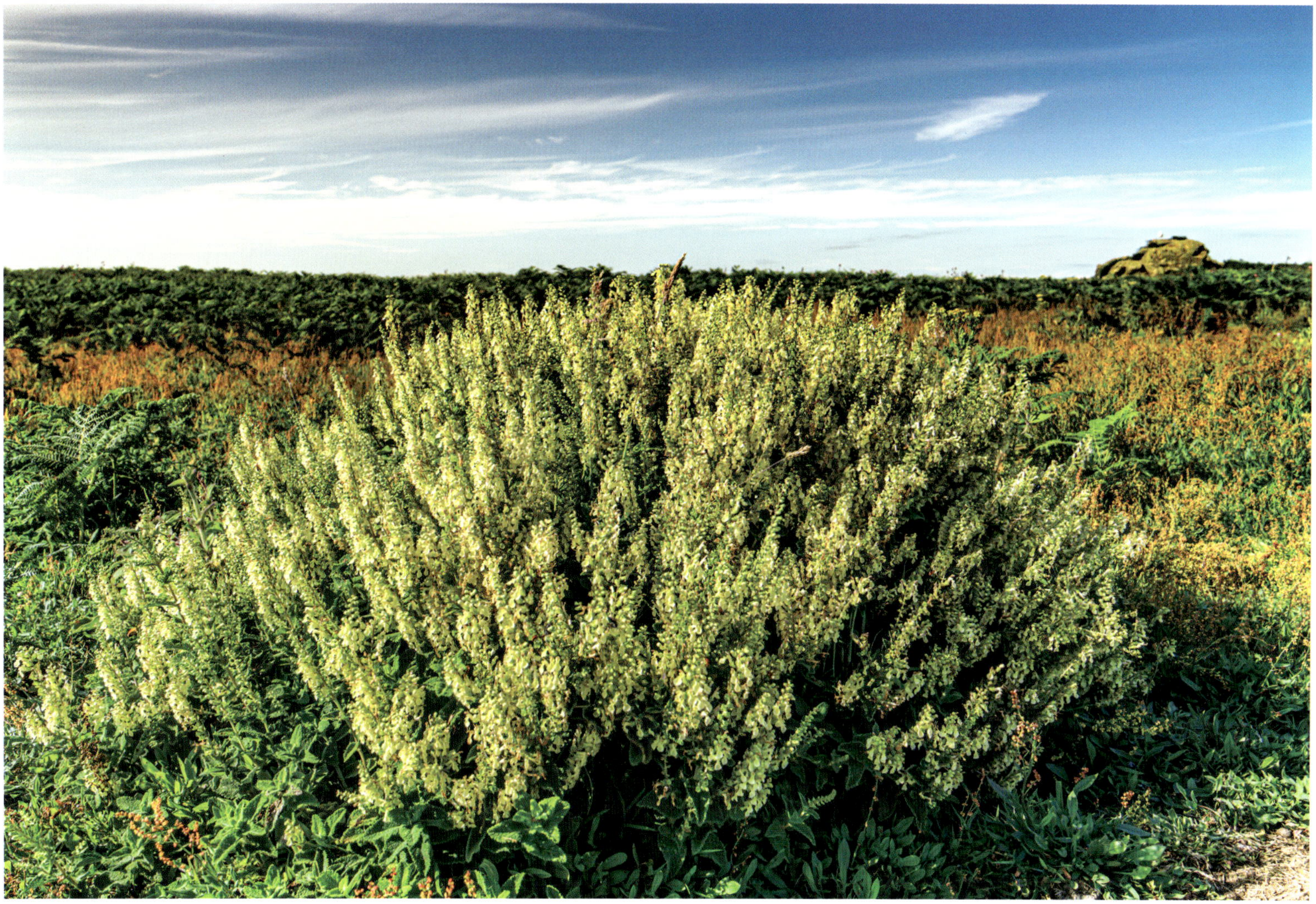

Wood Sage Chwerwlys yr Eithin *Teucrium scorodonia*

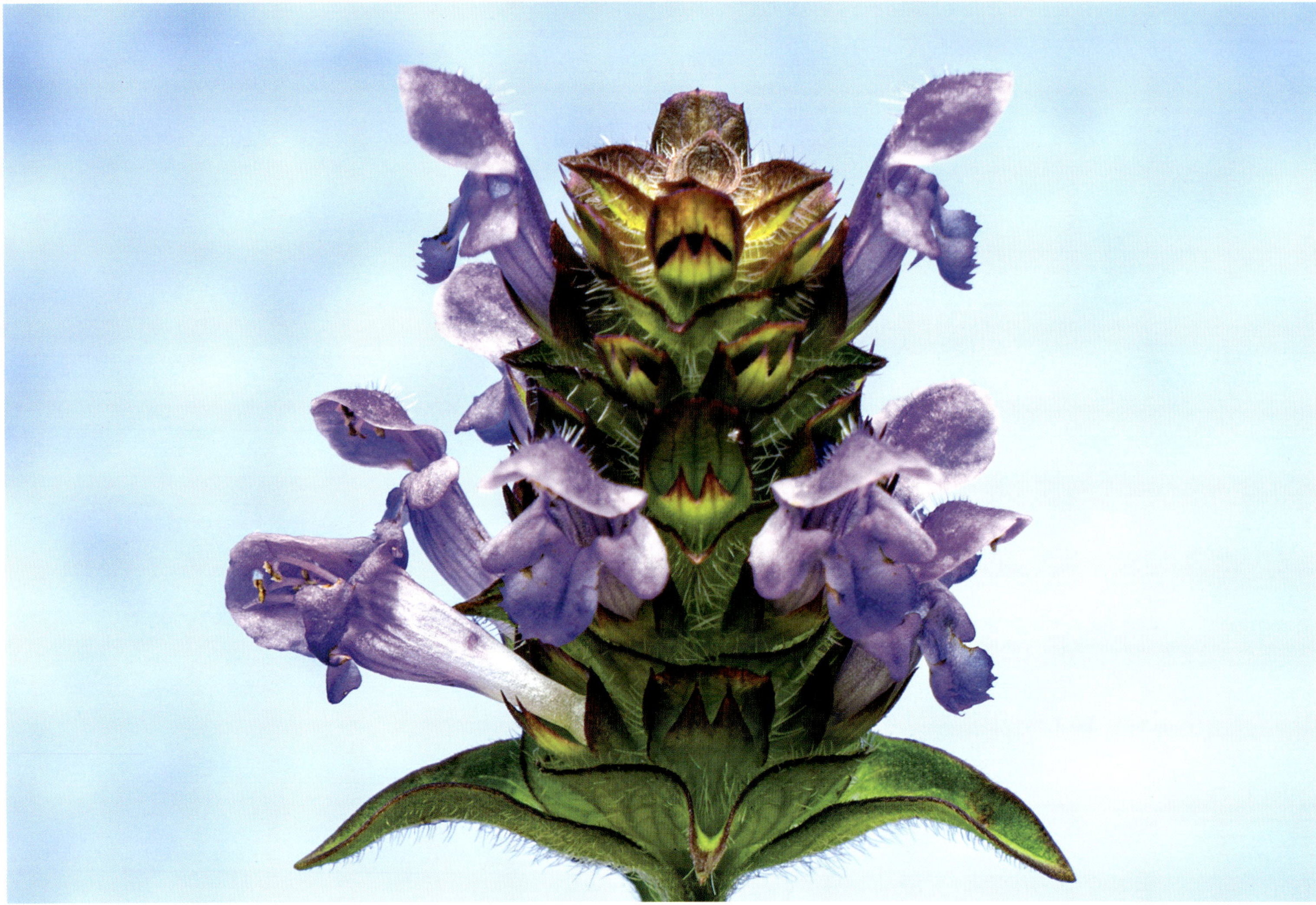

Selfheal Y Feddyges Las *Prunella vulgaris*

Figwort Family Teulu Bysedd y Cŵn

The figwort family contains a diverse variety of plants which, on first acquaintance, bear little resemblance to one another. I have included four common, but very different, members of the family.

Foxglove
Bysedd y Cŵn
Digitalis purpurea

Foxglove is among the most beautiful of all wildflowers. Their tall, elegant pinkish-purple flower spikes are unmistakeable. They seem to be able to grow almost anywhere, especially when the soil has recently been disturbed. You will find them in woodland, scrub, heath, wasteland, road verges and in abundance on the coast. They are, however, ephemeral, and, although they can rapidly colonise and dominate newly disturbed areas, they are usually out-competed in the longer term. During their first year after germinating, the plant produces a small non-flowering basal rosette, and it is not until the second year that the flower spikes appear. It is almost worth experiencing drought years or even occasional fires for the profusion of foxgloves that often follows. My photograph of foxgloves was taken on a section of coast where the heath had been reduced to bare ground by fire two years previously.

Foxglove contains a chemical called digitalis, the word coming from the scientific name and meaning 'finger-like' – a reference to the tubular flowers. Digitalis has been used since the time of Ancient Rome as a herbal remedy, and was brought into proper medicinal use for dropsy and epilepsy in the eighteenth century by William Withering.

There is speculation that toxicity from digitalis, possibly used to treat his epilepsy, might have influenced the intense yellows used in van Gogh's later works. Certainly, his only surviving portrait of his doctor depicts him with a sprig of foxglove. Digitalis, or digoxin, is still used to treat various heart conditions.

There are many explanations for the origin of the name foxglove. The most frequent is that foxes wear the flowers on their paws to go silently when hunting. Another, more interesting, account is that the original name was folk's gloves, with 'folk' referring to fairies. There are many Welsh names, the most common being *bysedd y cŵn*, or 'dogs' fingers'. A less familiar name, which is similar in origin to the English folk's gloves, is *menig ellyllon*, which translates as 'elves' gloves'. The *ellyllon* are pigmy elves, who haunt the groves and valleys, and are similar to, but not the same as, English elves.

Common Toadflax
Llin y Llyffant
Linaria vulgaris

Common toadflax has easily identifiable yellow and orange flowers with long, tapering spurs, which are crowded together on tall spikes. If you look closely at the individual flowers, you will see that they are like miniature snapdragons, the popular garden plant which is also a member of the figwort family. Toadflax is widespread around the coast, but you are most likely to see it growing on roadside verges and in hedgerows. The plants attract a variety of pollinators, but only the stronger insects are able to prise open the flower lip to reach the nectar.

Germander Speedwell
Llygad Doli
Veronica chamaedrys

Germander speedwell, the boldest and brightest of the speedwells, is the traditional good luck charm for travellers. Speedwell is derived from 'speed you on your way'. Germander is probably a corruption of its scientific name, *chamaedrys*, which has an Ancient Greek origin, meaning 'on the ground'. True to its name, germander speedwell is a ground-hugging wildflower, adorned with clusters of small shining, sky-blue flowers. It is a common species, found in a wide variety of habitats, including grasslands, hedge-banks and the edges of woodland.

The Welsh name, *llygad doli*, or 'doll's eye', is wonderfully descriptive, and one of my favourites, probably because I learned it during primary school nature walks.

Next page: Foxglove Bysedd y Cŵn *Digitalis purpurea*

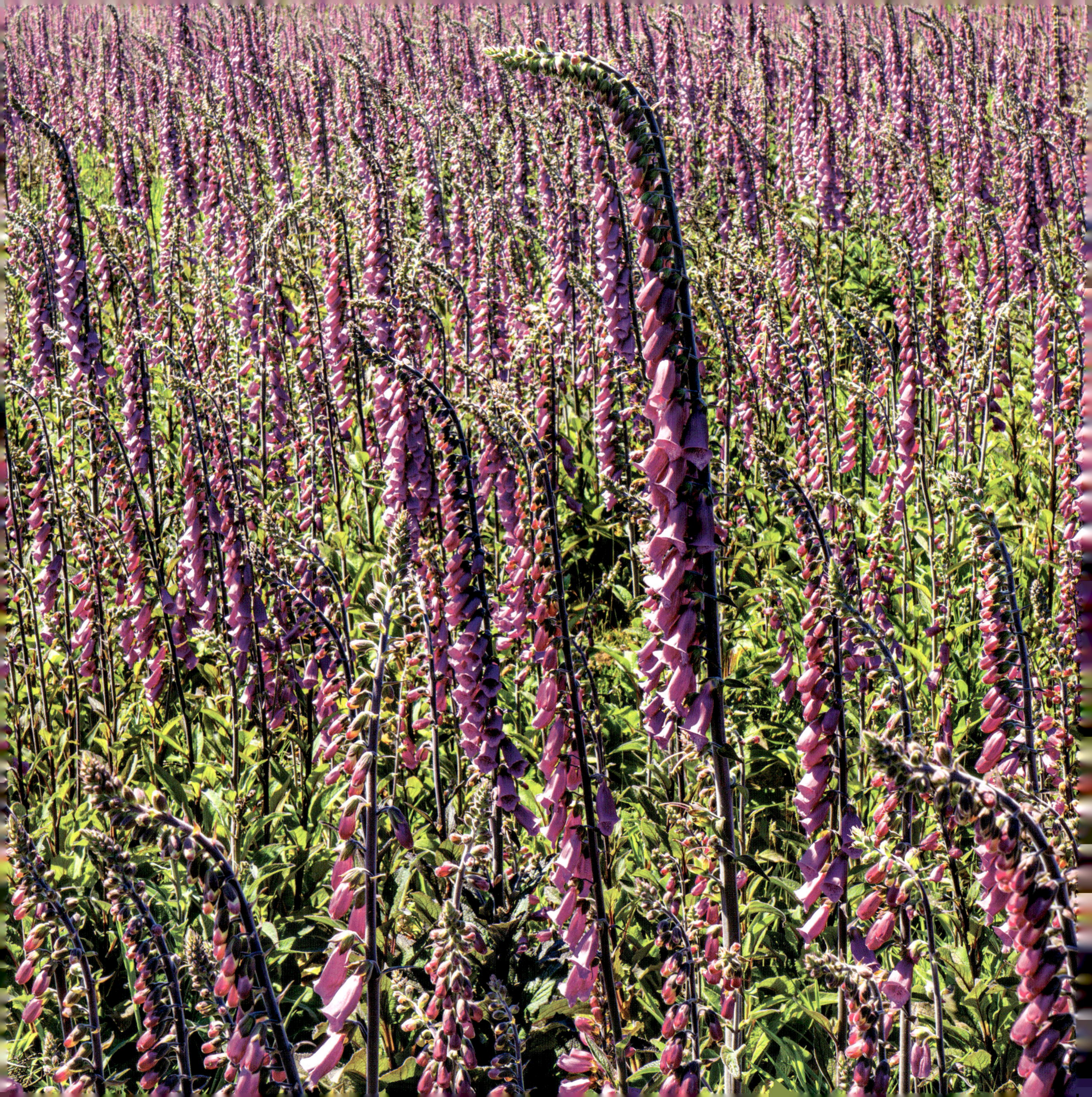

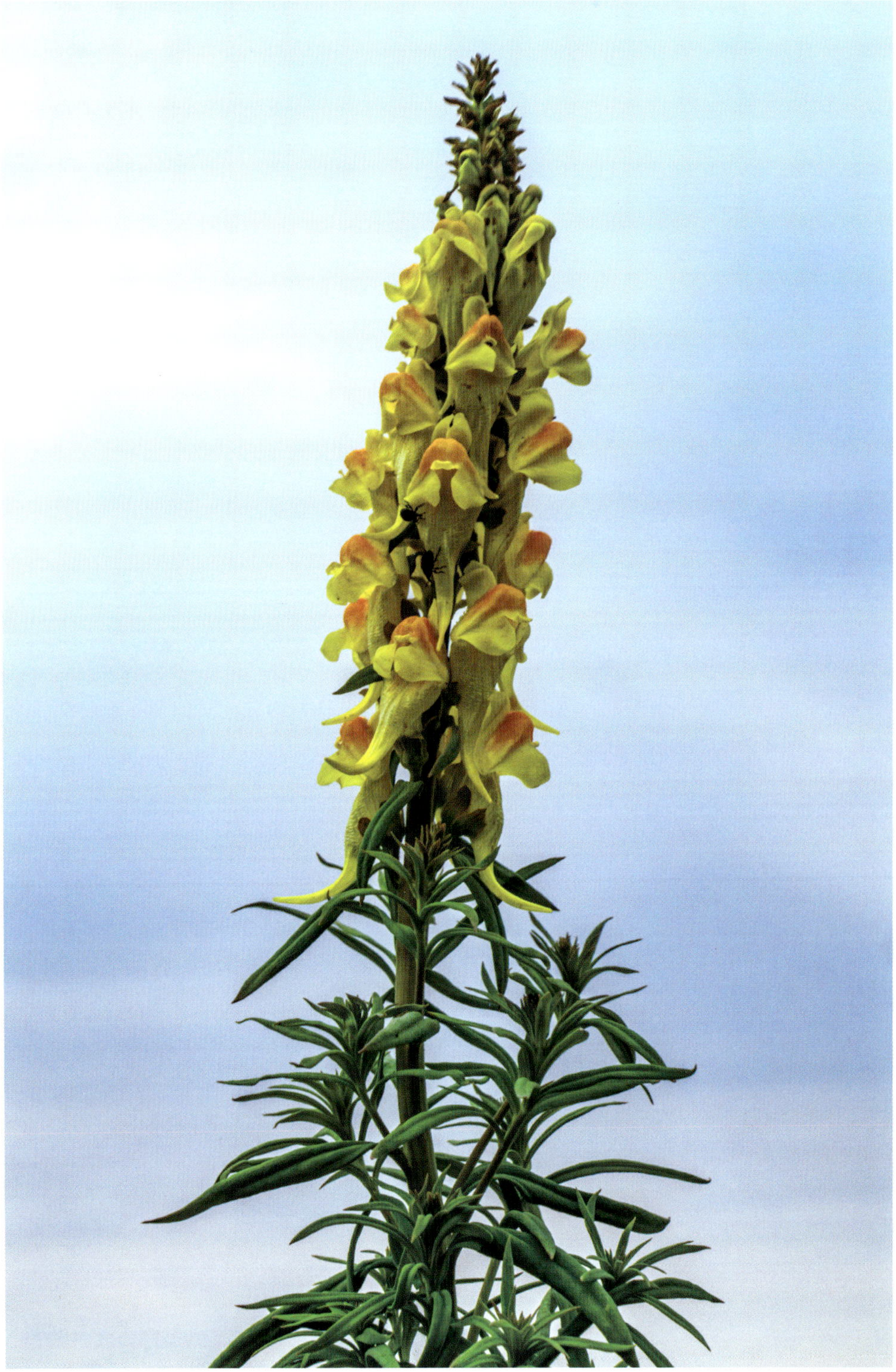

Common Toadflax
Llin y Llyffant
Linaria vulgaris

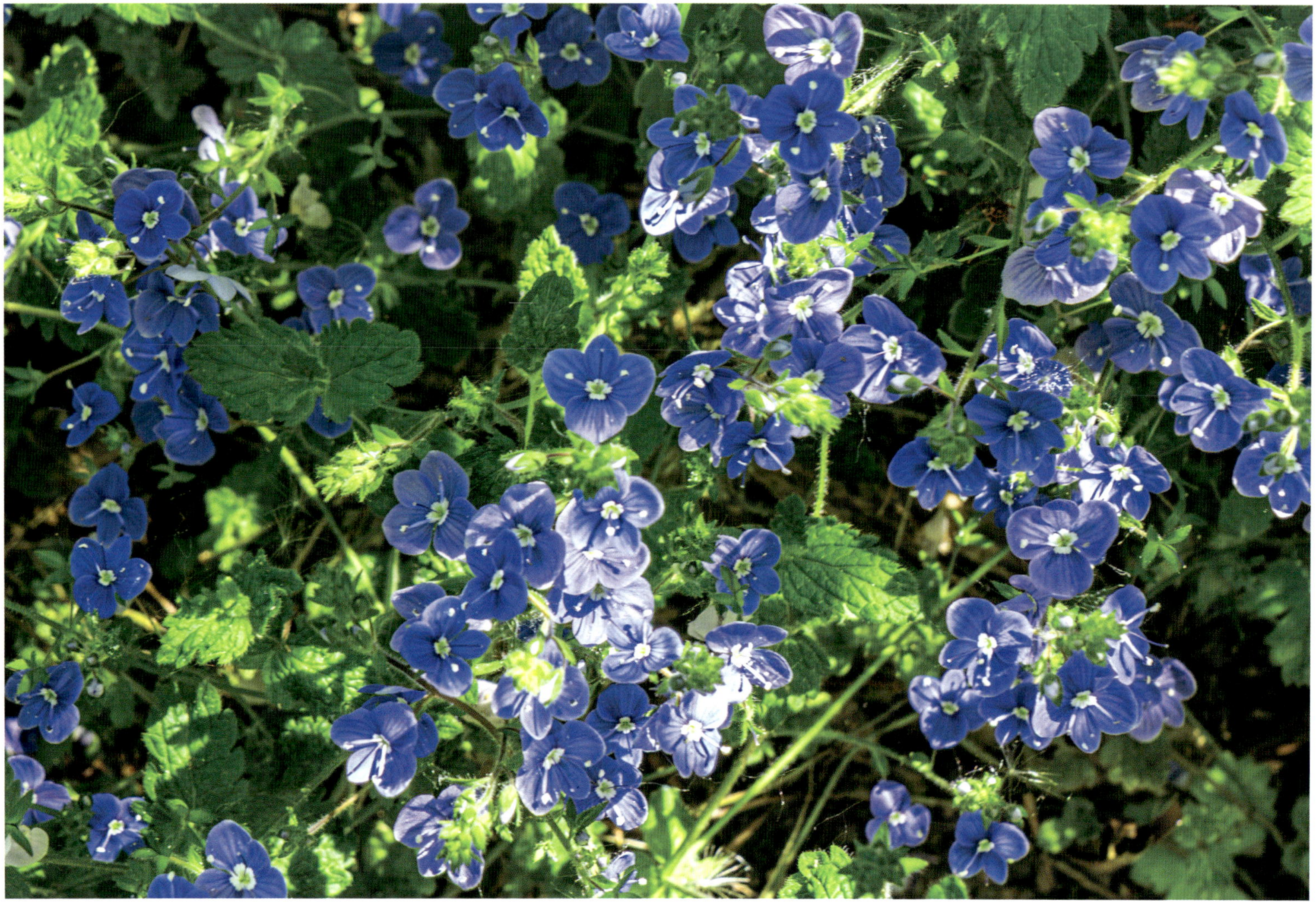

Germander Speedwell Llygad Doli *Veronica chamaedrys*

Yellow-rattle
Cribell Felen
Rhinanthus minor

Yellow rattle is a special plant which can play an exceptionally important role in grassland management. It has pale yellow tube-like, hooded flowers. The sessile leaves, growing directly from an upright stem, are slender, serrated and spear-like. Once the flowers have been pollinated, the calyxes turn brown and, as they ripen, fill with tiny black seeds, which rattle loudly when disturbed. This characteristic sound is the obvious reason for their common name. Yellow rattle is a hemiparasitic plant which targets grasses, reducing their vigour and ability to compete with other delicate meadow flowers. Farmers despair of this species, recognising it as an indicator of poor agricultural grassland, but it is now also valued as an essential aid in re-establishing flower-rich meadows, and is often described as the meadow maker.

The photograph on the next page of a glorious sward dominated by sorrel and yellow rattle, was taken at Stackpole Head, in south Pembrokeshire. In the early 1950s, as part of the drive for national self-sufficiency and the need to grow as much food as possible, the entire headland was ploughed and cultivated. The post-war legacy was a highly improved, species-poor grassland, dominated by white clover and rye grass, but, despite this, there was sufficient residual wildlife value for the area to be declared a National Nature Reserve. Many years ago, the then reserve warden, Bob Haycock, an outstanding conservationist and naturalist, decided to try introducing yellow rattle. He gathered seeds from a nearby source and simply spread them at Stackpole Head. The response was spectacular, and I think that my photograph says everything about the successful outcome.

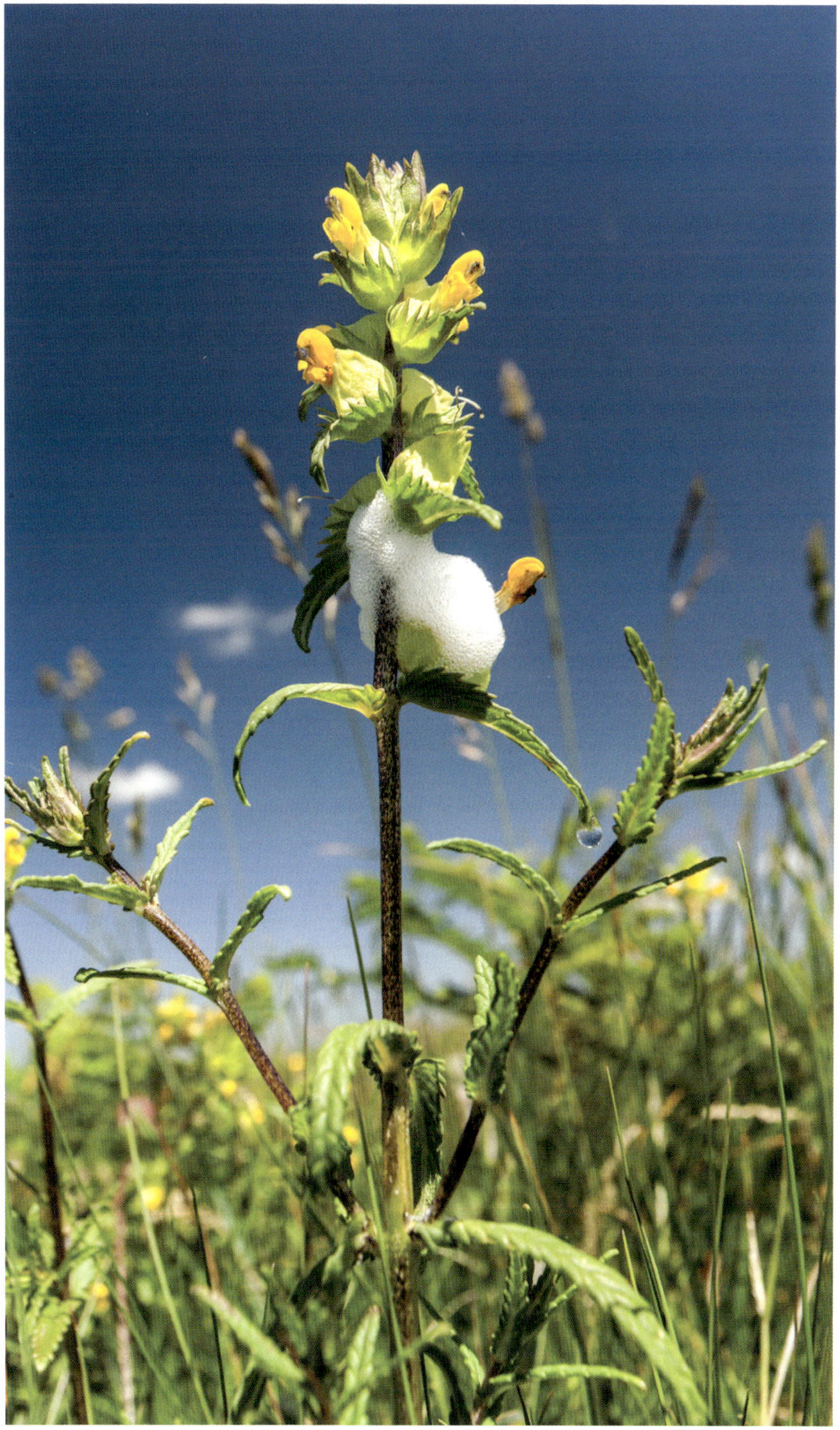

Yellow-rattle Cribell Felen *Rhinanthus minor*

Stackpole Head

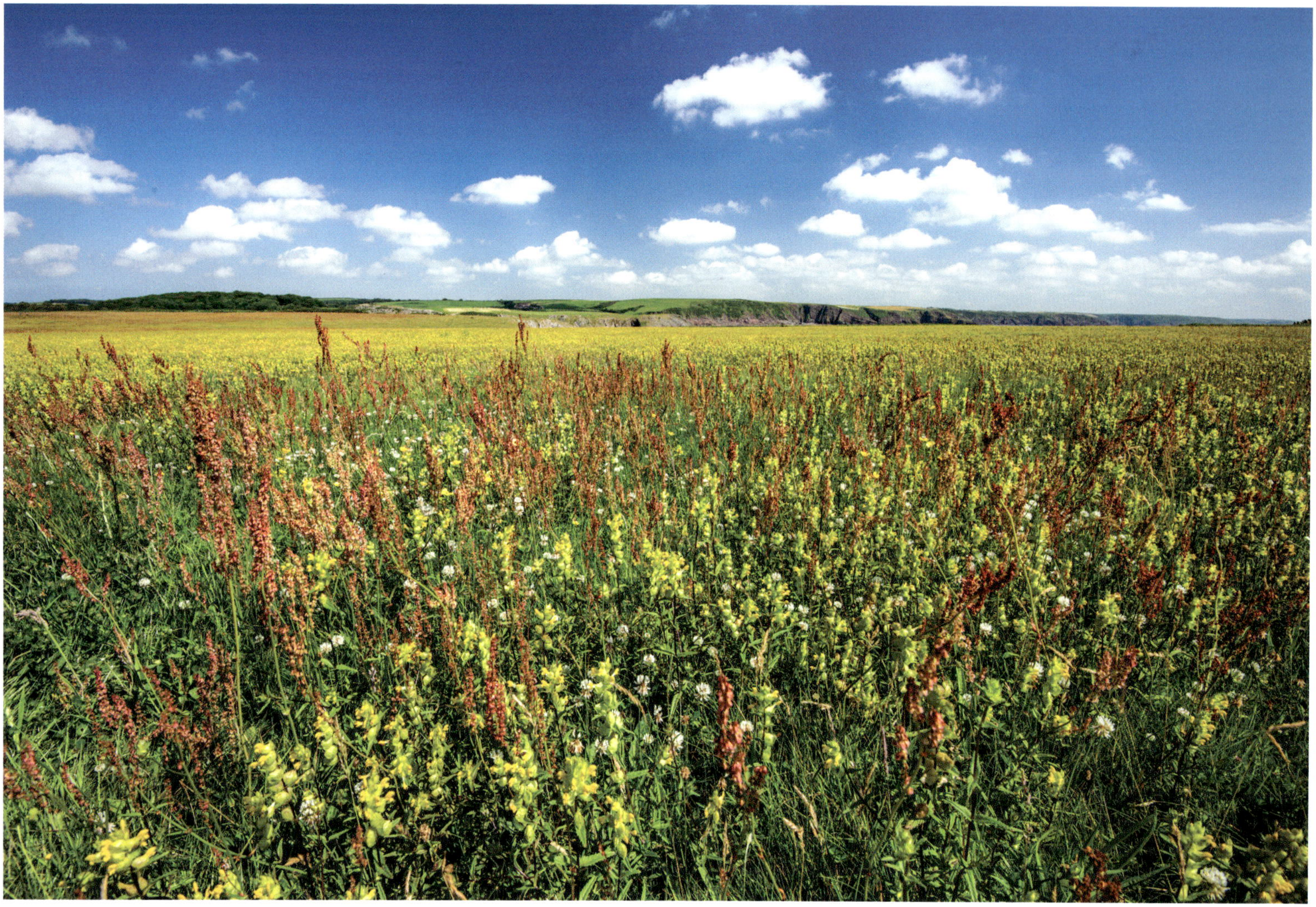

Yellow-rattle Cribell Felen *Rhinanthus minor*

Broomrape Family Teulu'r Gorfanhadlen

Eyebrights
Effros
Euphrasia

Eyebrights were formerly regarded as members of the figwort family but more recently have been moved to the broomrape family. Eyebrights are low-growing species found in grasslands, heaths and on clifftops. There are around 20 species and 60 hybrids, all of which are similar, making them difficult to identify. Eyebrights are hemiparasitic: plants which obtain water and mineral nutrients from their host species, but are also able to photosynthesise and produce their own food. The roots of eyebrights attach themselves to those of nearby grasses and other plants. The name eyebright comes from its traditional use as a treatment for eye infections. The scientific name, *euphrasia*, is linked to one of the three Greek *Charites* or Graces, Euphrosyne, who was also the goddess of mirth, merriment and joy. According to legend, linnets used eyebright to clear the sight of their young and passed this knowledge on to humankind.

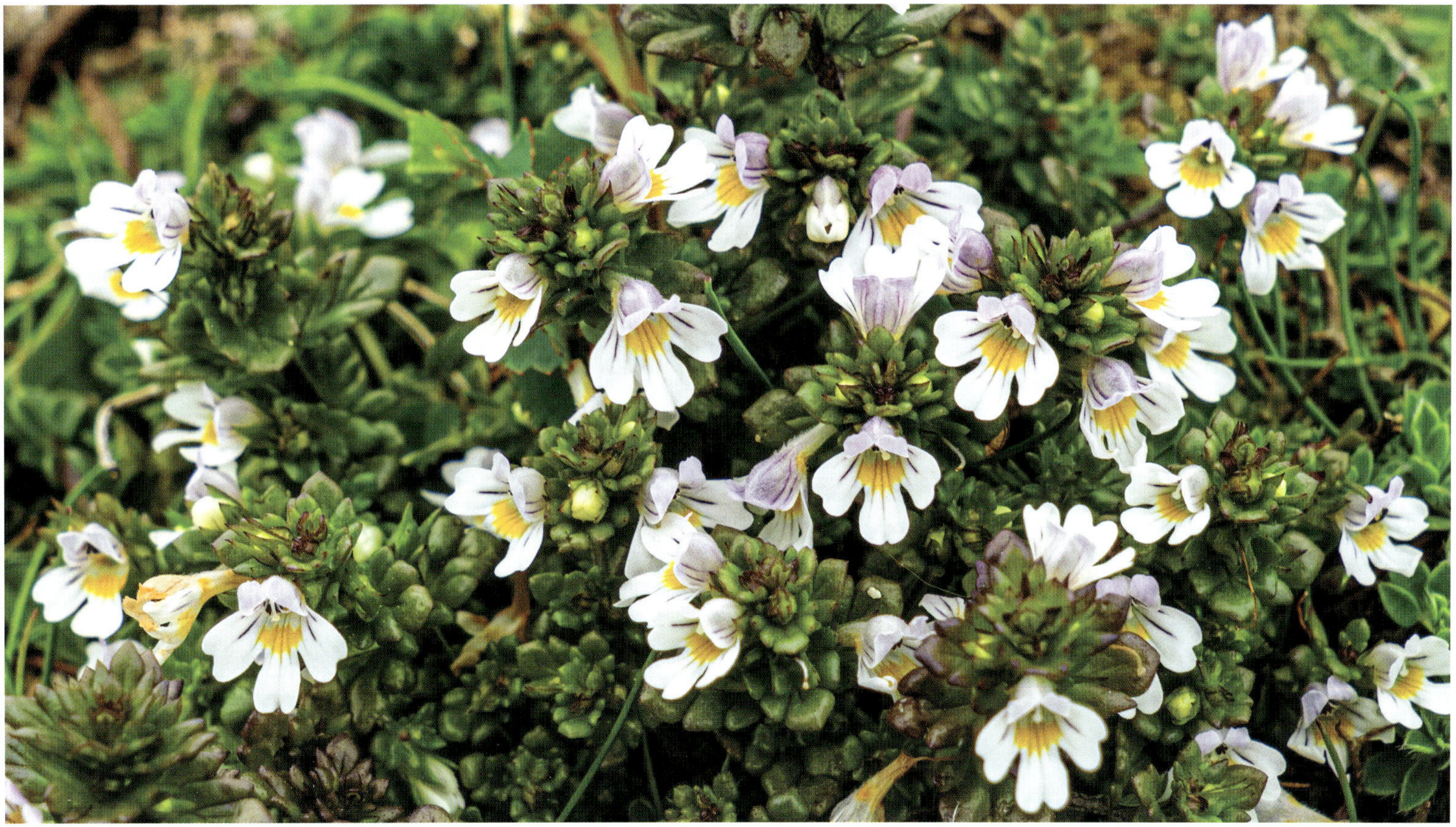

Eyebrights Effros *Euphrasia*

Plantain Family Teulu'r Llyriad

This is a family of plants that is so unobtrusive that they can often be completely overlooked. Two members of the family, sea plantain and buck's-horn plantain, can be regarded as mainly coastal species, while ribwort plantain is more widely distributed inland, away from the coast.

Sea Plantain
Llyriad Arfor
Plantago maritima

Sea plantain is most obvious growing on hedge-banks along the coastal footpath. It thrives in the most exposed sections, where most other plants succumb to the regular drenching with sea spray. Sea plantain is capable of enduring twice-daily immersion in the tide of a salt marsh. The cylindrical flower spikes, on wiry stems, are similar to the flowers of all the other plantains. The leaves are long and very narrow, giving it a grass-like appearance when not in flower.

Buck's-horn Plantain
Llyriad Corn Carw
Plantago coronopus

Buck's-horn plantain has a rosette of leaves with antler-shaped, forked ends, very different to the slender, grassy leaves of sea plantain. Buck's-horn is common and widespread along the Welsh cliffs, and can be found everywhere from the rich limestone cliffs to the most acid of coastal soils. One of the biggest issues to confound any budding botanist is the extreme variation found within a species, and buck's-horn plantain is a notorious example of this, being exceptionally variable in form. At one extreme, it grows as tiny, recumbent florets, usually found along the drier, grazed and trampled edges of the coastal path. These contrast spectacularly with the succulent giants, found mainly on the guano-enriched cliffs of Skomer and Skokholm islands. When they first discovered these giants, earlier botanists believed that they must be a new species, but they are now recognised as ecotypes which display adaptations to their particularly nutrient-rich environment.

Ribwort Plantain
Llyriad yr Ais
Plantago lanceolata

Ribwort plantain is, for me, full of childhood memories. As children, we would weaponise it by taking a firm grip of the stem, curling part of it into a loop below the flower head, and then using it to flick the flower as hard as possible at our friends. More usefully, it provides a window into the history of land use, since the presence of ribwort pollen in a peat sample is regarded as an indicator of past agricultural disturbance. Today, it is most often found growing on the better soils in grassy places, and it has some tolerance of sea spray. Ribwort has a long history of exploitation as a food plant: the leaves can be eaten when young, and it is often used to make tea or as a herbal remedy. It is an excellent first aid treatment for insect bites, and apparently more effective than the popular dock leaf.

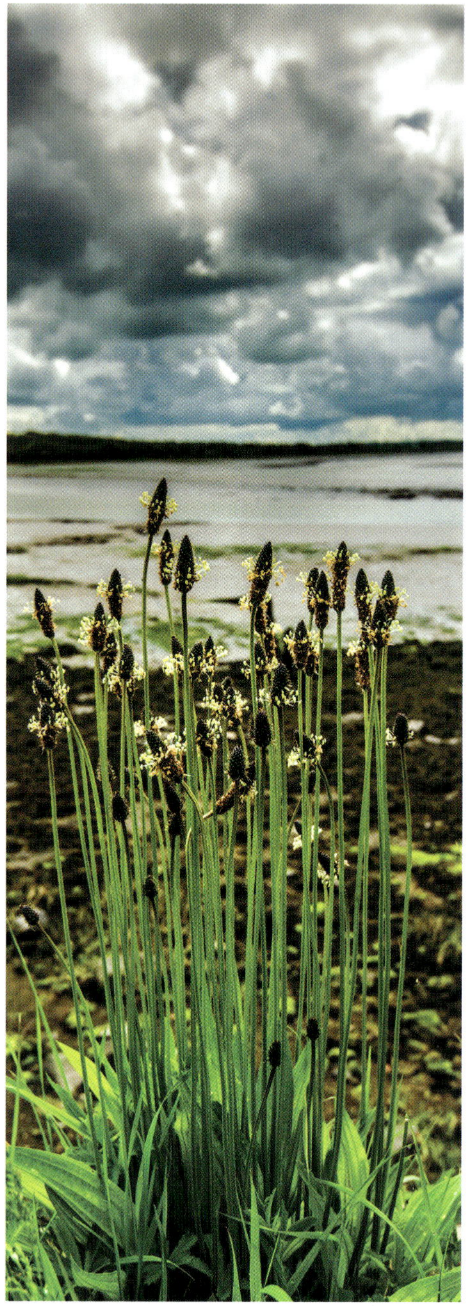

Ribwort Plantain
Llyriad yr Ais
Plantago lanceolata

St Brides, with Stack Rocks in the background

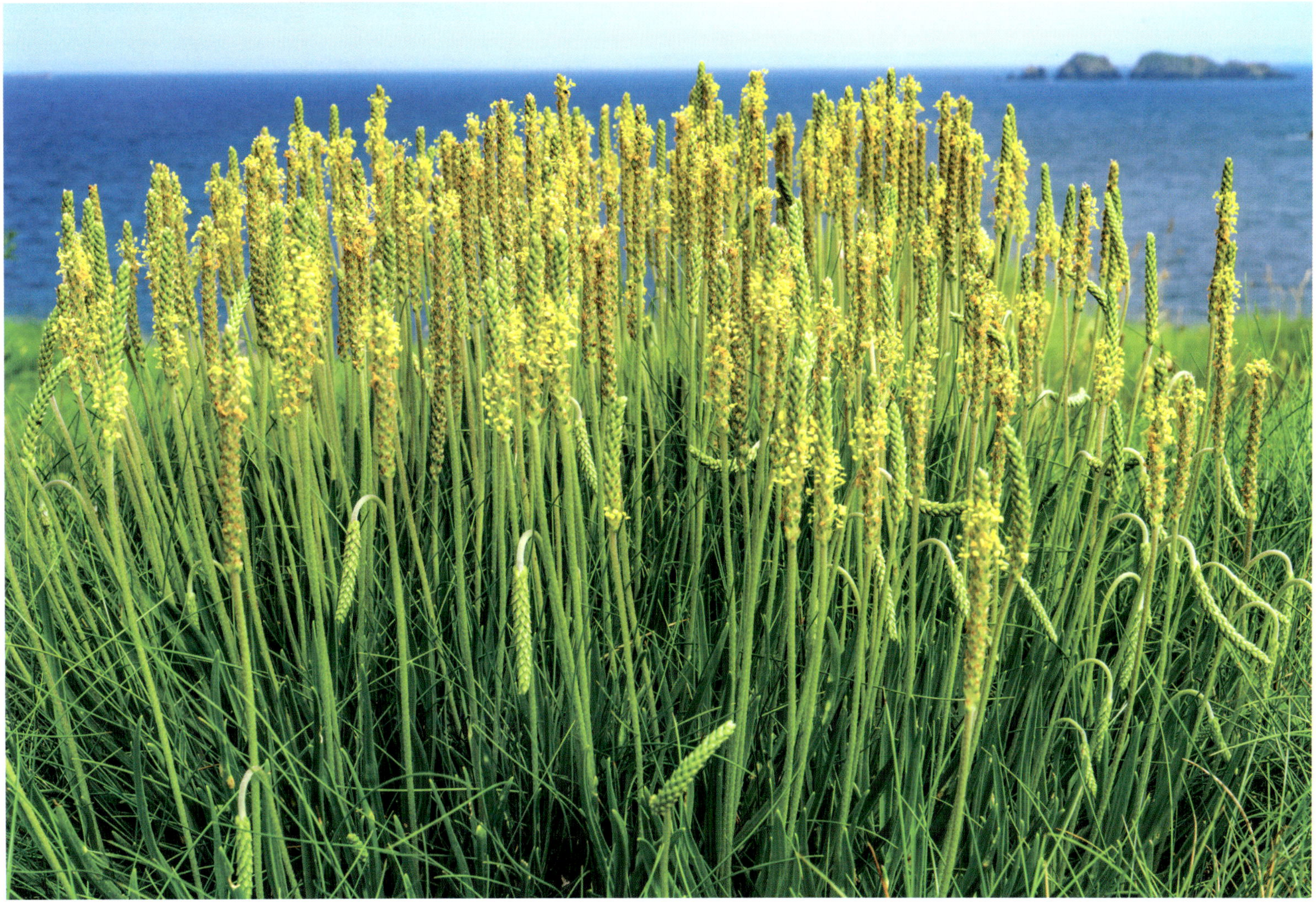

Sea Plantain Llyriad Arfor *Plantago maritima*

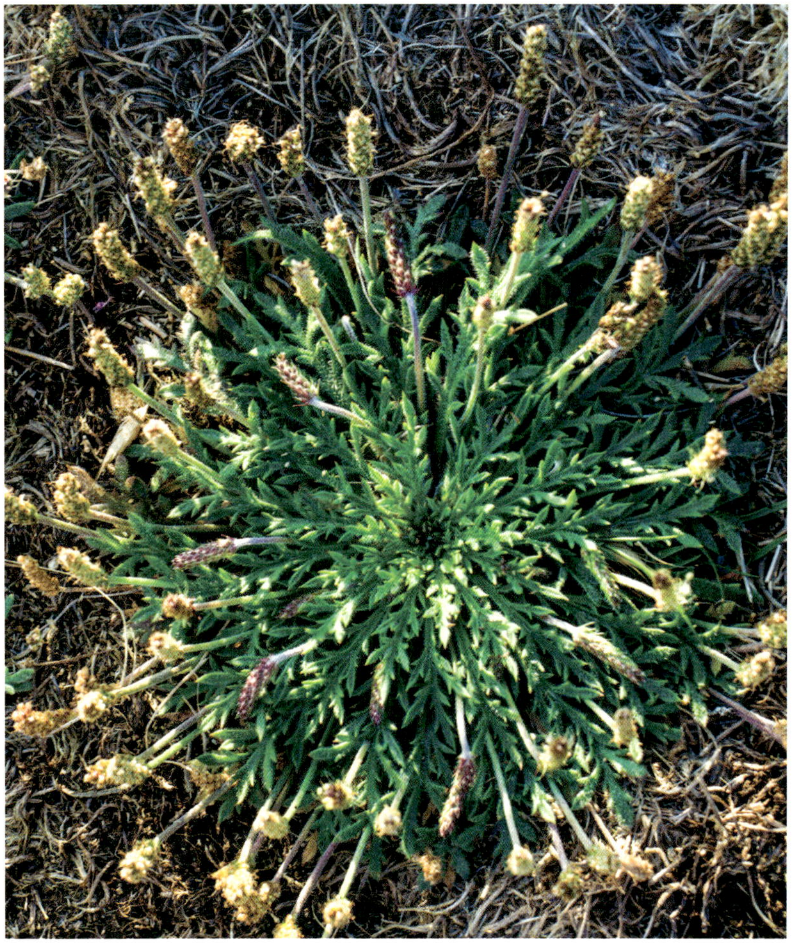

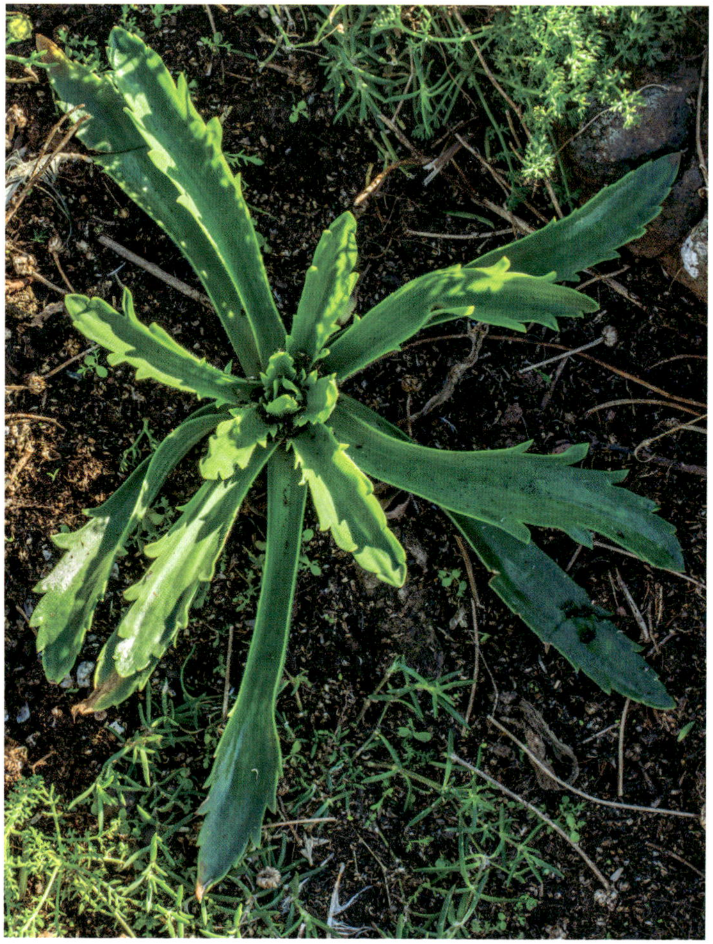

Buck's-horn Plantain Llyriad Corn Carw *Plantago coronopus*

Bellflower Family Teulu'r Clychlys

Sheep's-bit
Clefryn
Jasione montana

Sheep's-bit is a member of a diverse family of plants named after their most recognisable feature, the bell-shaped flowers. The family member that I have included is an exception to the rule, since the flowers are not easily recognised as being bell-shaped. They are a fluffy, domed cluster of up to 200 tiny, brilliant blue tube-like flowers. These eye-catching plants favour the more acid, thin, dry soils, and are often found in the stony hedge-banks alongside the coast footpath. They are often called sheep's-bit scabious because the flowers are similar to plants of the scabious genus, which are members of the honeysuckle family.

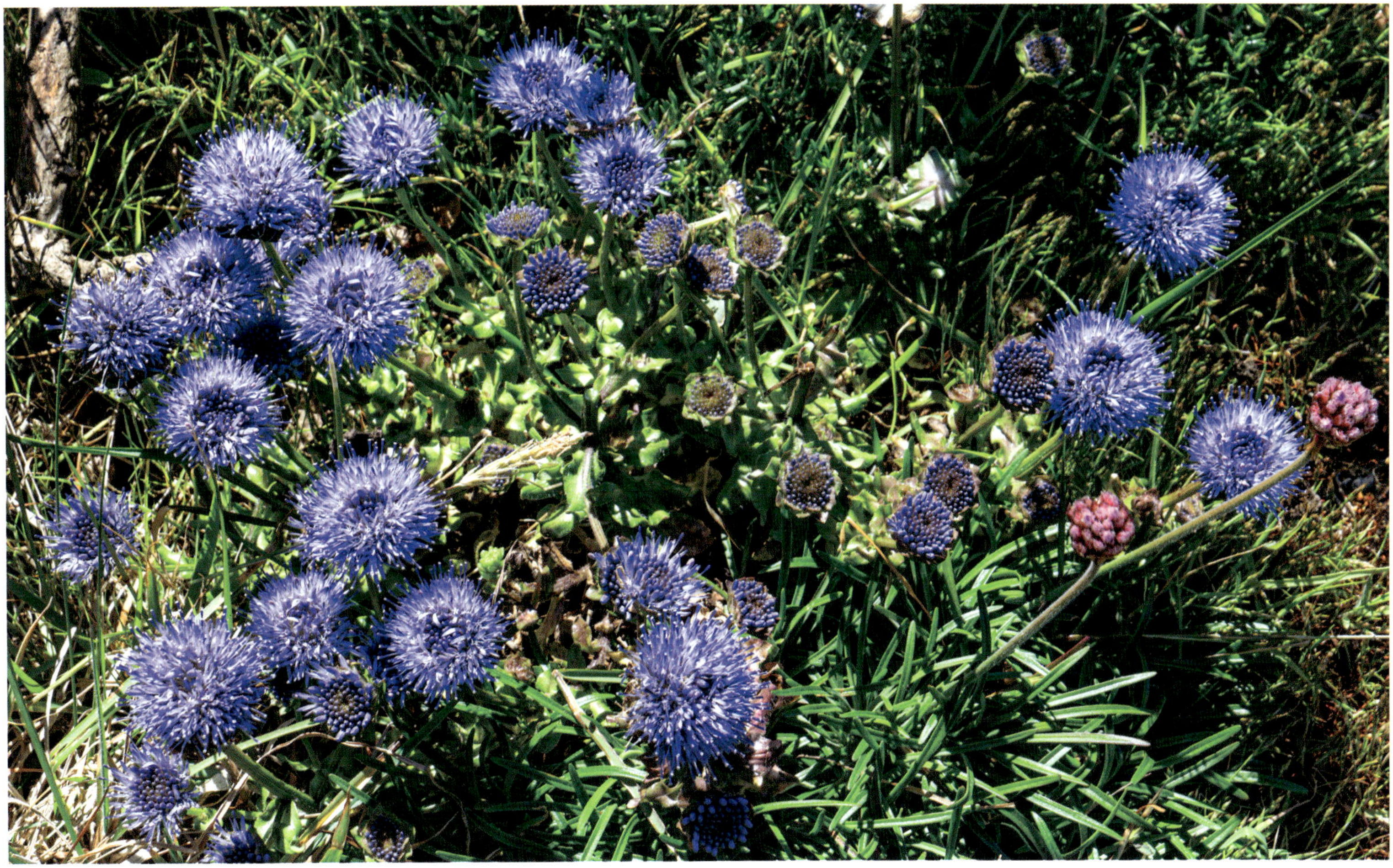

Sheep's-bit Clefryn *Jasione montana*

Bedstraw Family Teulu'r Friwydden

This is a family of slender, sprawling herbs, which spread over the ground and other vegetation. The most familiar species is cleavers, with its dense, smothering network of 'sticky' stems and insidious little spherical fruits all covered in tiny hooks, which cling to animals and to our clothing.

Heath Bedstraw
Briwydden Wen
Galium saxatile

Heath bedstraw produces a mat of tiny white flowers. The leaves, which are stalkless, oval and pointed, grow in whorls around a sprawling square stem.

The plant has a long history of use as a traditional medicine, being used to treat skin ailments, digestive and menstrual problems. In Wales, it was mixed with butter to make an ointment used to soothe shingles.

Lady's Bedstraw
Briwydden Felen
Galium verum

Lady's bedstraw is sometimes called yellow bedstraw or bed flower. It produces a froth of golden-yellow, honey-scented flowers, which were once used to stuff mattresses. Apparently, when dry, they smell like hay, hence the name 'bedstraw'. The addition of 'lady' to the name is possibly because the mattresses were used for women in childbirth. Perhaps a further indication of their usefulness is that the scent was said to repel fleas.

Another name for lady's bedstraw, rennet weed, comes from the fact that it contains an enzyme that curdles milk and can be used as an alternative to rennet in cheese-making. Look for lady's bedstraw in coastal grassland, heaths and sand dunes from June to September. I took the photograph on the limestone cliffs near St Govan's Head. The sweet-smelling mix of bedstraw and thyme often covers anthills around the cliff edge.

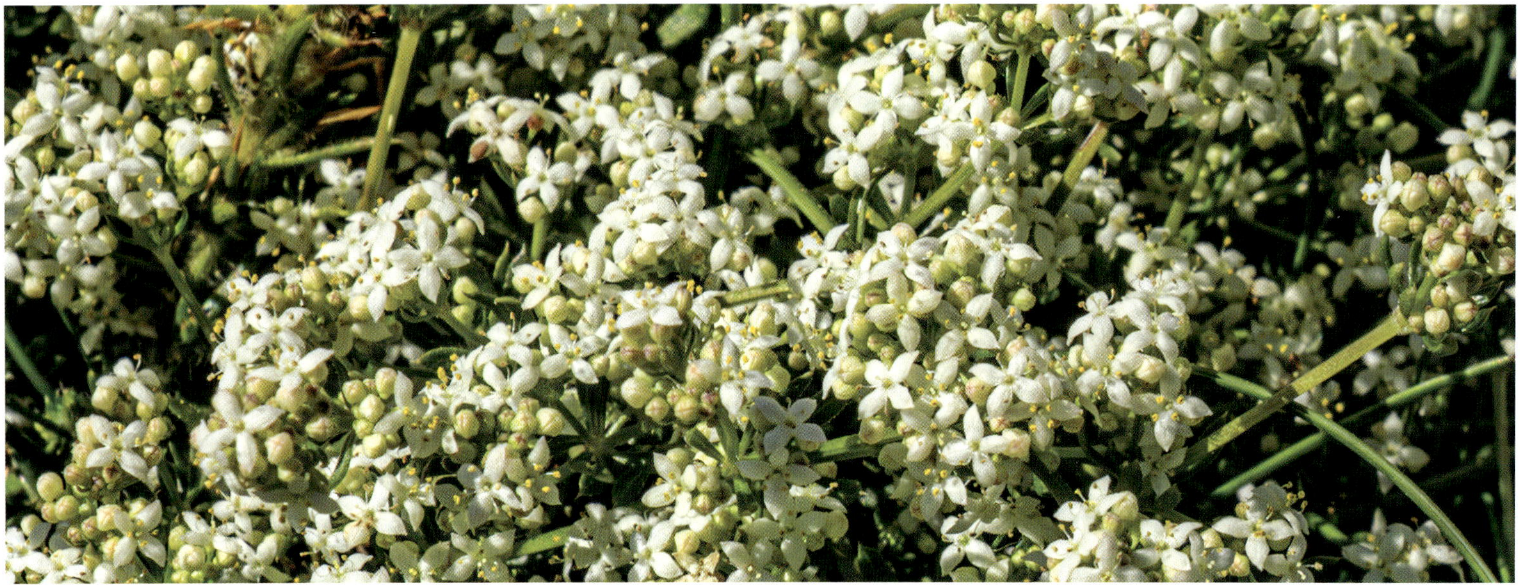

Heath Bedstraw Briwydden Wen *Galium saxatile*

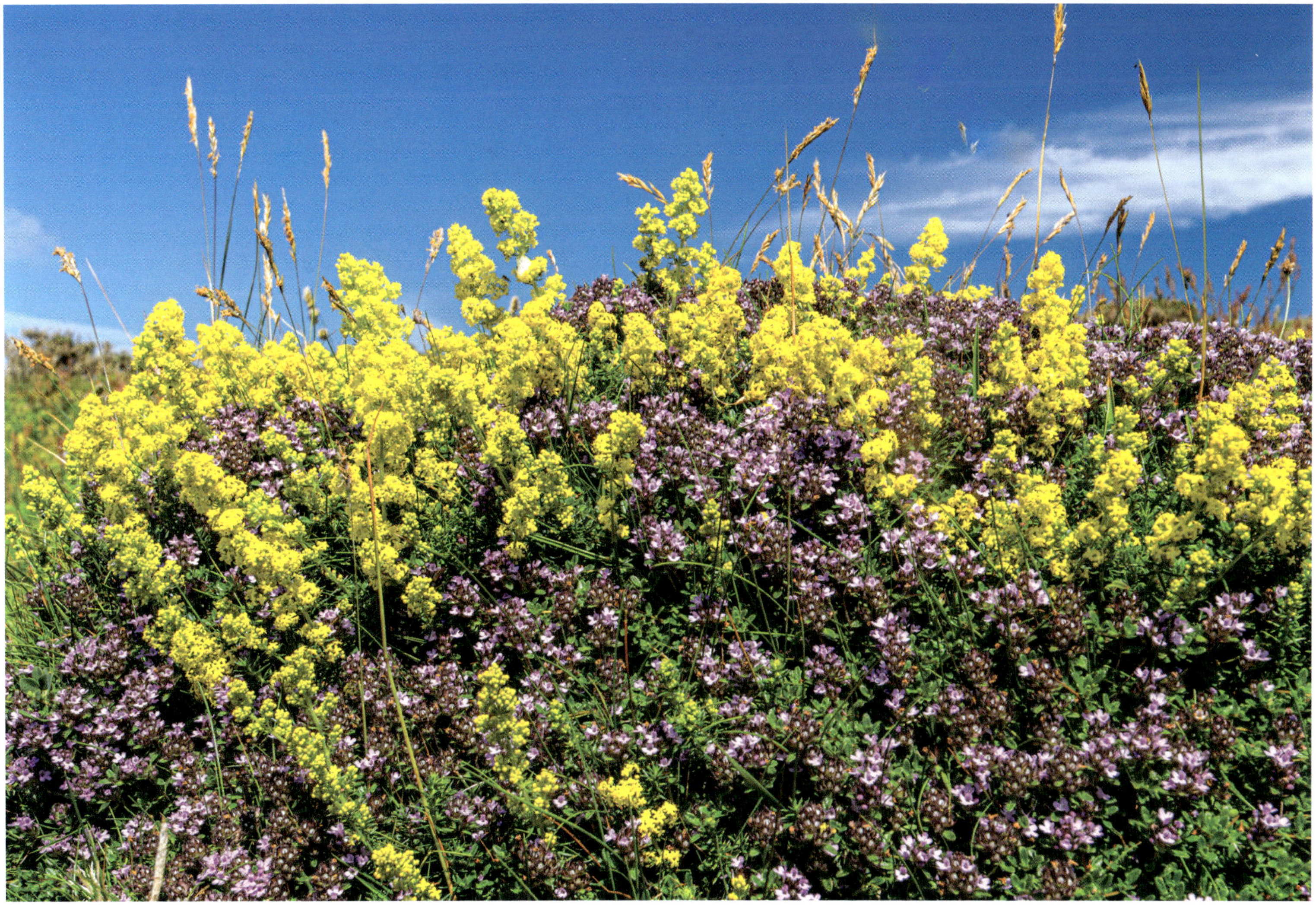

Lady's Bedstraw Briwydden Felen *Galium verum*

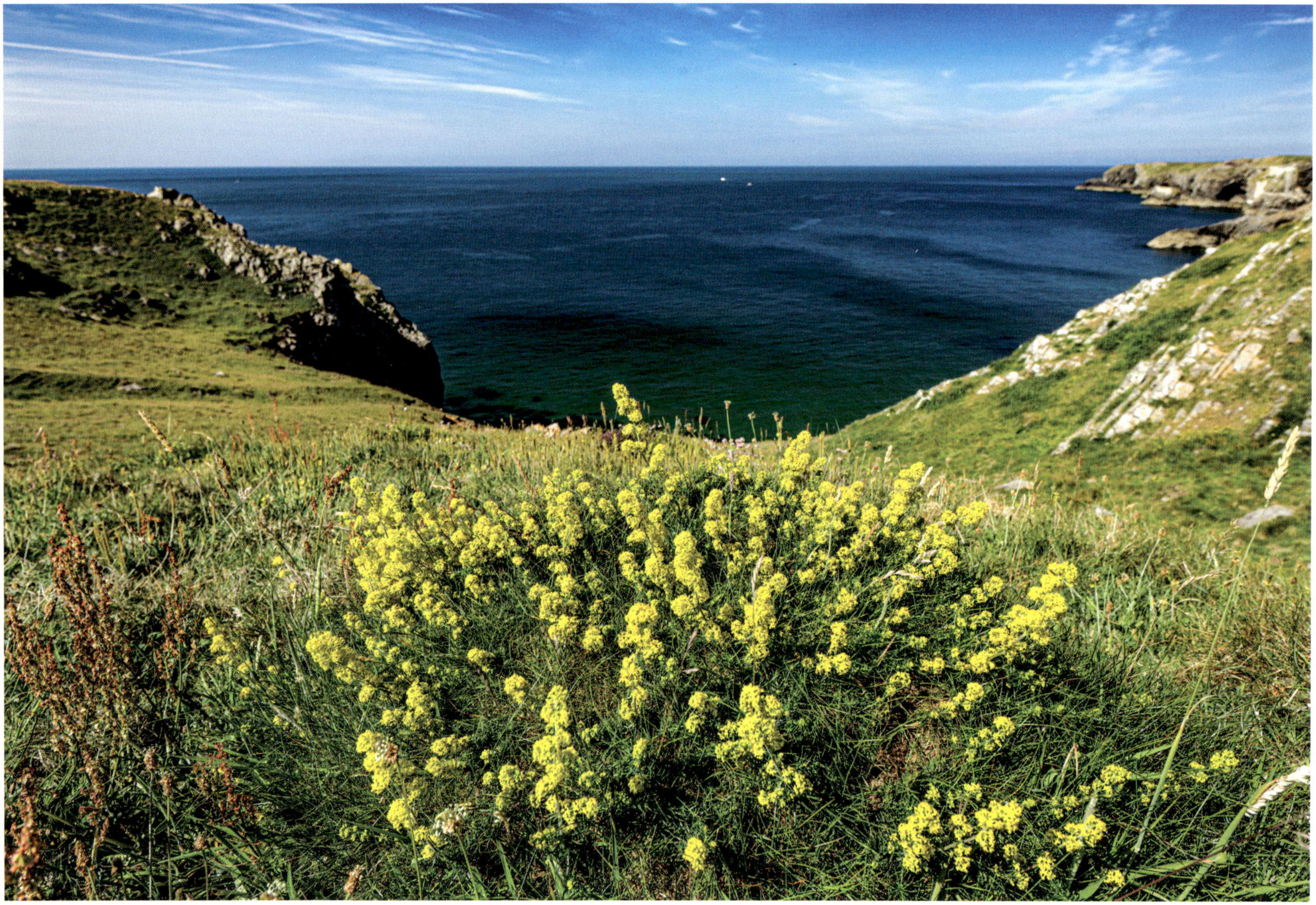

Lady's Bedstraw Briwydden Felen *Galium verum*

Honeysuckle Family Teulu'r Gwyddfid

Honeysuckle
Gwyddfid
Lonicera periclymenum

Honeysuckle is a climbing plant that we would usually expect to see in woodlands and hedgerows, but it is also found in coastal heaths, scrub and, occasionally, growing on rocky cliff faces. The sweet and heady fragrance is strongest at dusk. Just as the sun is setting, wafts of perfume drift through the evening air, announcing the flowers even before they come into view. Whorls of trumpet-like pale yellow or cream flowers, with a hint of pink and red, cluster at the ends of the winding stems. In autumn, the flowers are followed by masses of poisonous red berries.

Honeysuckle always winds clockwise around other plants. Walking stick makers place a high value on the stems of hazel or other shrubs that have been twisted into unique shapes by the entwining honeysuckle, which sculpts the sticks as they grow. People once grew honeysuckle around the entrances to their homes in the belief that it would bring good luck and repel evil spirits. The flowers, seeds and leaves are used in medicines for the treatment of a wide range of ailments, including digestive disorders, dysentery, colds, influenza, pneumonia, diabetes and many more. The photograph of honeysuckle growing on a rocky outcrop was taken on Carn Llidi, St Davids, looking south-west towards Ramsey Island.

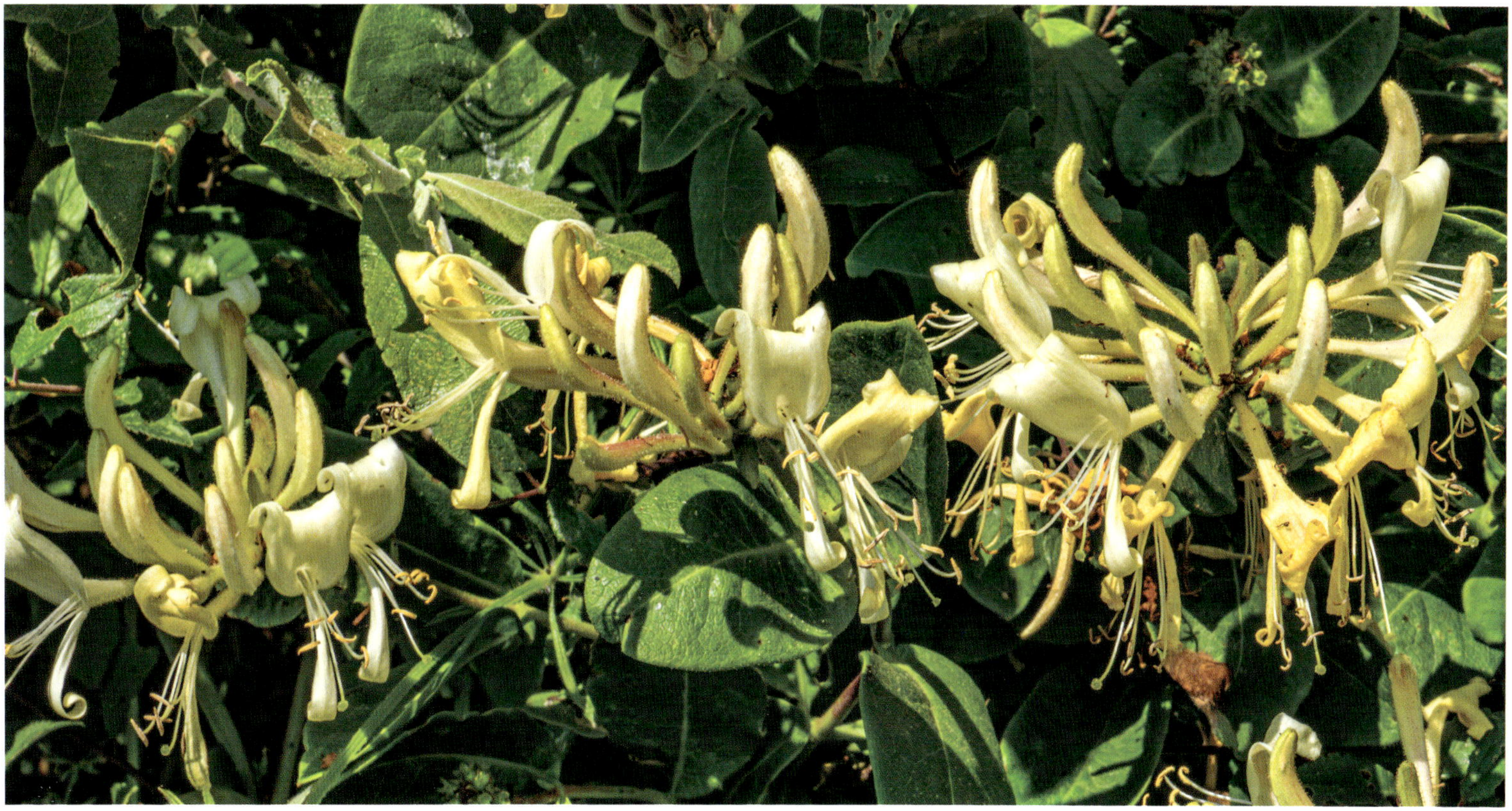

Honeysuckle Gwyddfid *Lonicera periclymenum*

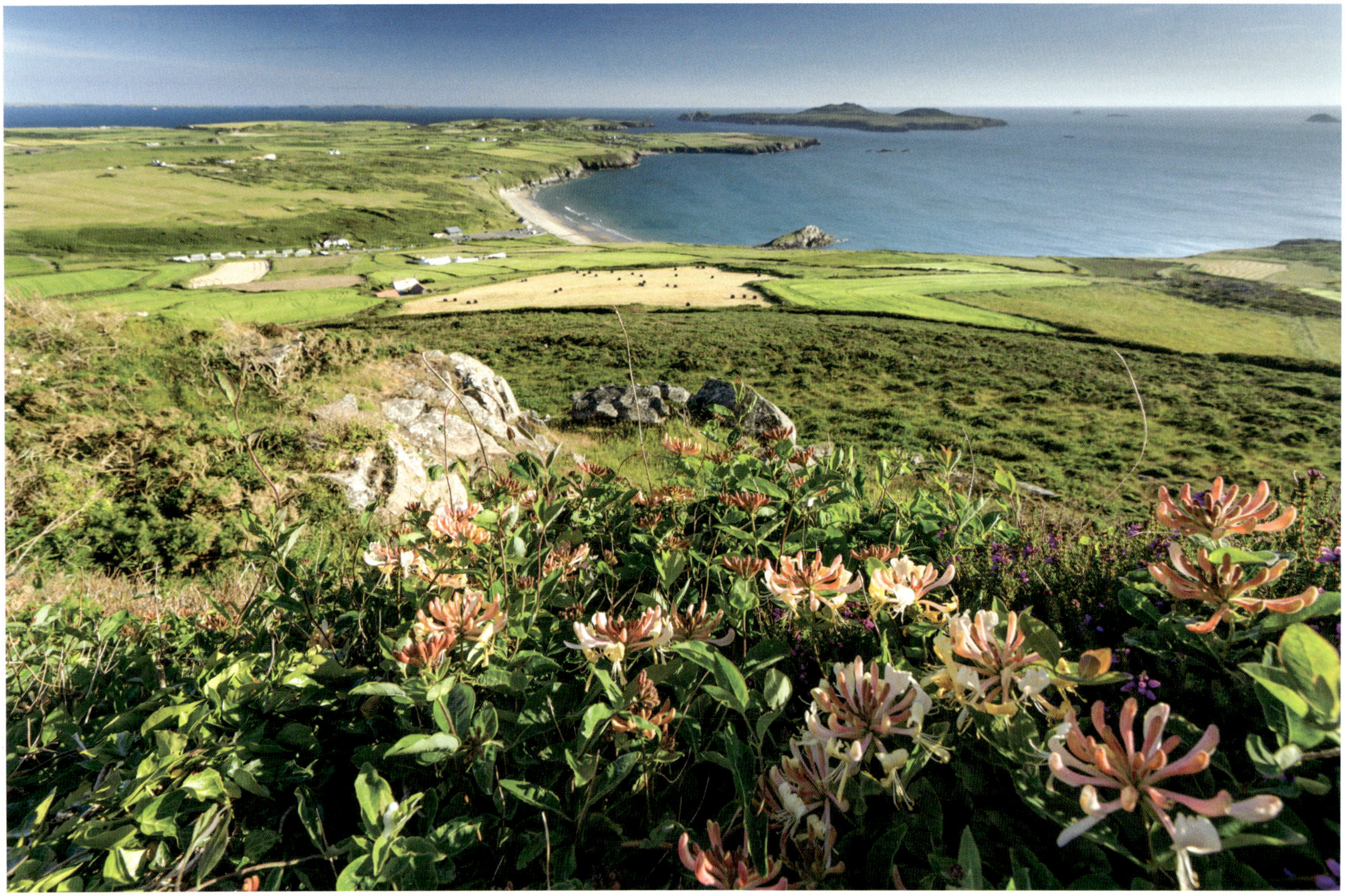

Honeysuckle Gwyddfid *Lonicera periclymenum*

Teasel Family Teulu'r Cribau'r Pannwr

Teasel
Cribau'r Pannwr
Dipsacus fullonum

Teasel is another of those plants that I learned to treasure as a boy. It was not common where I grew up and so the occasional discovery was very special. The stories associated with plants made them easier for me to remember and always heightened my interest in them. I loved to hear my Uncle Jeff, a farmer, describing how teasels were once important in the woollen industry. The seed heads, with their strong curved or hooked spines, were bound together and used to comb the surface of damp woollen cloth, making it soft and fluffy. The teasels used in cloth-making were, in fact, a cultivar with stronger hooks than the wild teasel.

This is a species best known for its magnificent seed heads, sitting on top of many-branched robust, thorny stems, which can be taller than most people. The flower-heads deserve close inspection, because they are surprisingly beautiful. The mass of delicate violet flowers begins opening in a strip around the middle of the oval flower-head, progressively blooming upwards and downwards, creating distinct bands of colour. When in flower, teasels are popular with bees and other pollinators, while, later in the year, they provide a good source of winter food for goldfinches and other seed-eating birds.

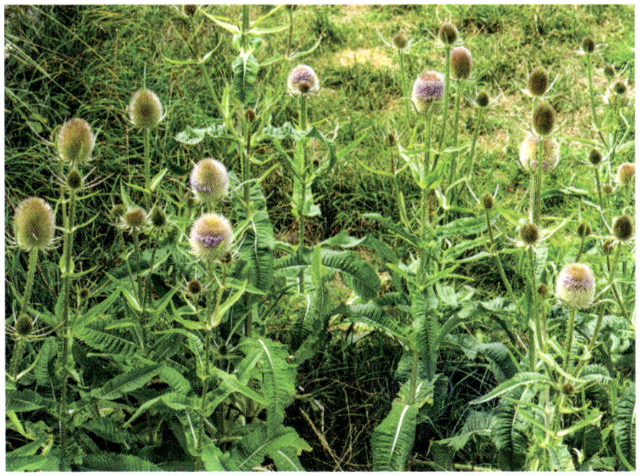

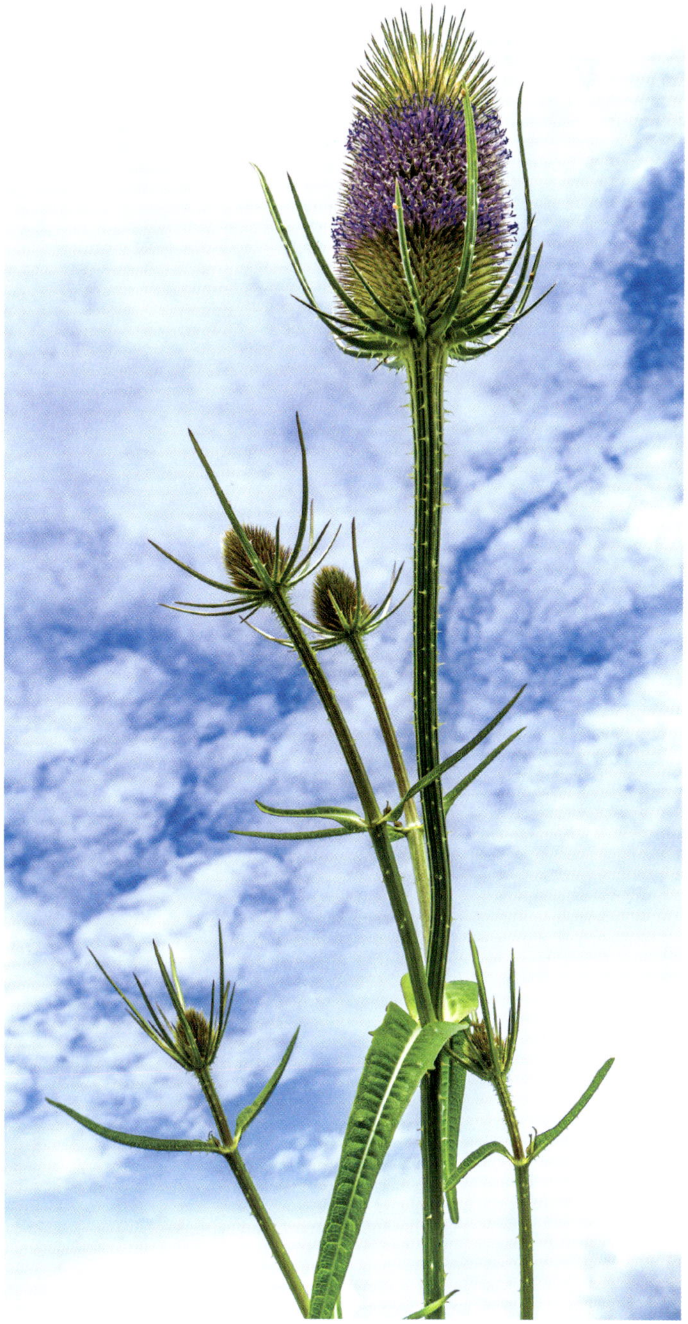

Left and right:
Teasel
Cribau'r Pannwr
Dipsacus fullonum

Daisy Family Teulu Llygad y Dydd

Daisies provide the quintessential image of a flower. Any child asked to draw a flower will almost always produce something which is daisy-like: a central disc surrounded by radiating petals. The daisy is in fact a composite, with each 'petal' being an individual flower. The name daisy comes from the Old English, *dægeseage*, which means day's eye, a fitting name for a flower which only opens during the daytime (or, more accurately, in sunshine). Daisies can be a symbol of innocence, purity and new beginnings. They are the largest family of flowering plants in the UK, a family which includes plants with typical daisy-like flowers, yellow ragworts, knapweeds, thistles, dandelions and a host of dandelion-like flowers, and, finally, sow thistles. I have had to choose a small but, I hope, representative selection of the species most likely to be seen around the coast.

Daisy
Llygad y Dydd
Bellis perennis

Daisies need no description, since they are such familiar flowers, and one of the first that we can name as children. I am sure I am not alone in having a wonderful memory of sitting with friends on a sunny, grassy bank making daisy chains, which would then become the most ephemeral of necklaces or bracelets, fading long before the day was over. The photograph shows a daisy-covered footpath, subtly edged with yellow buttercups, so perfect that it could almost have come from a fairy tale, but which, rather more prosaically, gives a lovely visual demonstration of how daisies can tolerate both compaction and trampling. The soil on the footpath has been compacted and the vegetation trampled, giving daisies a significant advantage in the centre of the path, allowing them to out-compete the buttercups. These daisy paths are most obvious when the grassland is closely grazed by sheep, and the best that I have seen are at Stackpole Head, in south Pembrokeshire. As with the English, the Welsh name, *llygad y dydd*, translates as 'eye of the day'.

Sea Mayweed
Amranwen Arfor
Tripleurospermum maritimum

Sea mayweed is a typical daisy, with a yellow centre and white outer petals. It has bright green, slightly succulent, finely divided, feathery leaves, which help the plants to survive in an extreme marine environment. In the older herbals, it is usually confused with chamomile, and in fact, when crushed, it does smell faintly of chamomile. Today, mayweed is used in the skincare industry. Apparently it is good for a balanced complexion (whatever that means!).

The photograph of sea mayweed was taken late on a summer evening, with the last rays of sunlight streaming through the mass of flowers. On Skomer, these flowers make a luminous backdrop for the puffins gathered around the cliff edges.

Yarrow
Milddail
Achillea millefolium

Yarrow is one of the toughest of plants, flowering from June right through to the end of November. It has flat-topped clusters of white to pinkish flowers and dark green feathery leaves. The plants are aromatic: some say reminiscent of pine needles, while others claim chrysanthemums, with a few saying that it smells like cabbage. The most useful description I came across, which may help to unravel the confusion, was that 'the aroma can vary depending on growing conditions'.

The scientific name, *achillea*, is derived from the Greek warrior, Achilles, who carried it to treat battle wounds. *Millefolium* is from the feather-like, divided leaves. The common name, yarrow, comes from the Greek word *hiera*, meaning 'holy herb', while other common names include nosebleed plant and woundwort. Yarrow leaves are, in fact, used to stop nosebleeds, by staunching the flow of blood, numbing the pain and acting as an antiseptic.

Stackpole Head

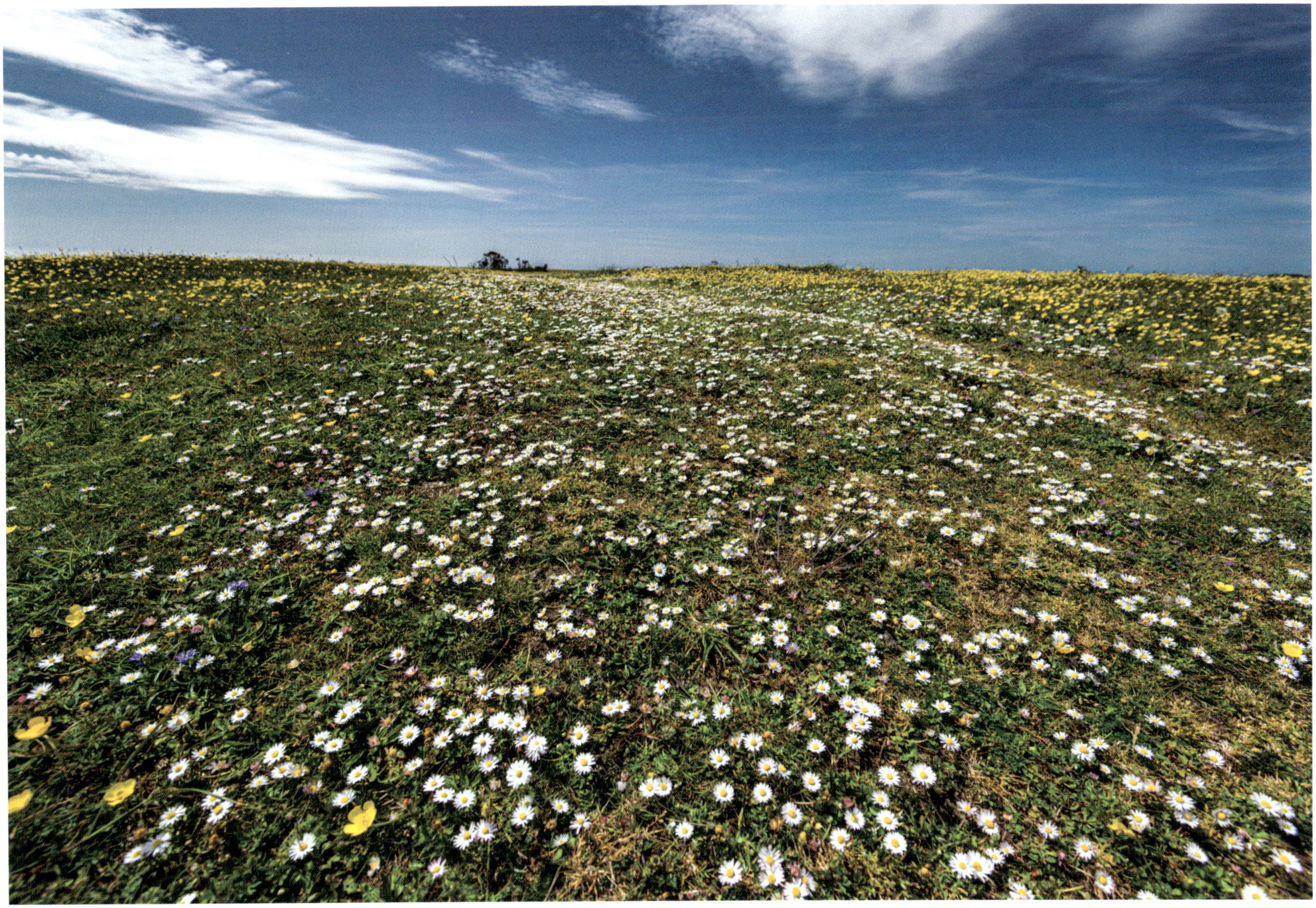

Daisy Llygad y Dydd *Bellis perennis*

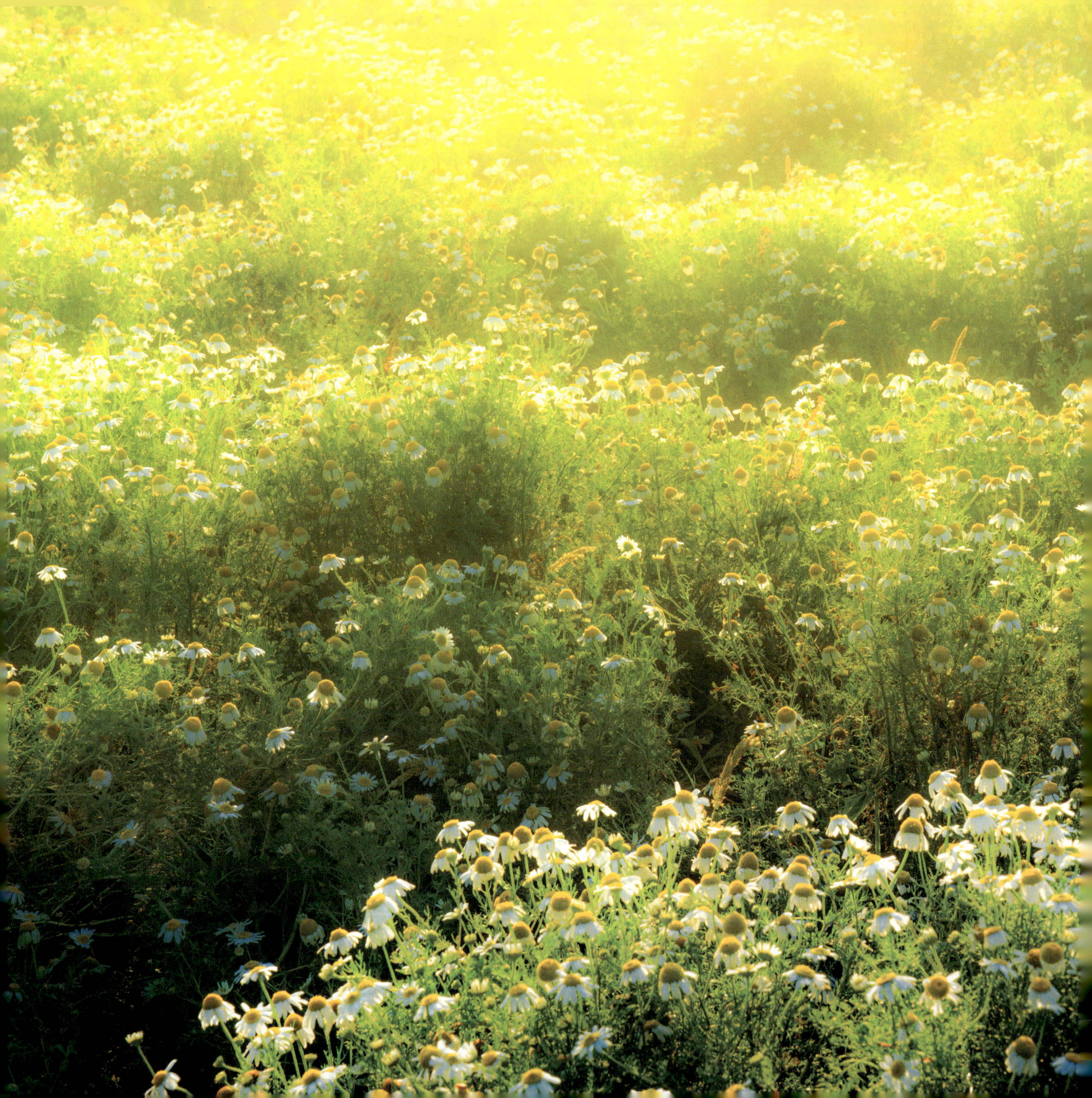

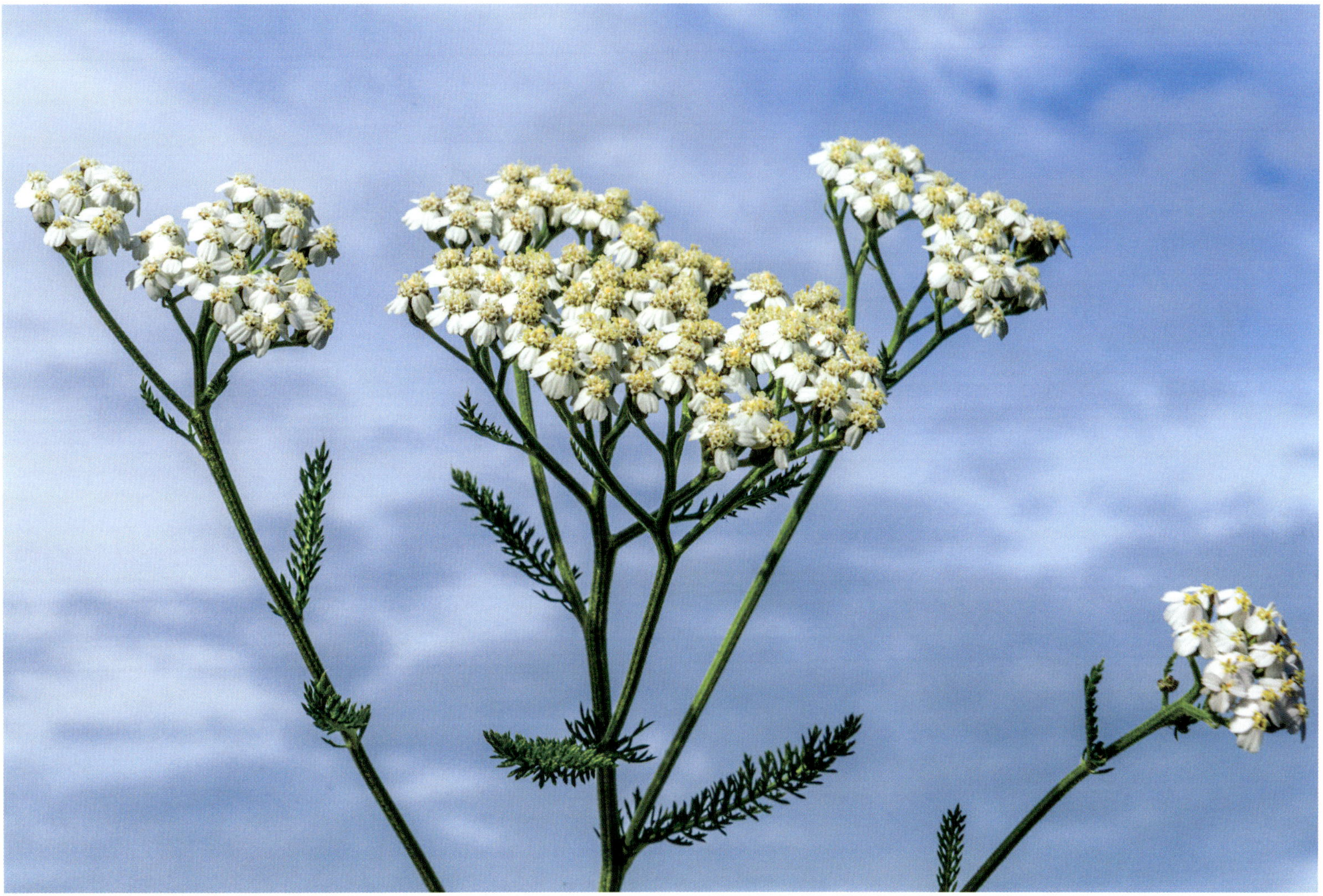

Above: Yarrow Milddail *Achillea millefolium*
Previous page: Sea Mayweed *Amranwen Arfor Tripleurospermum maritimum*

Oxeye Daisy
Llygad-Llo Mawr
Leucanthemum vulgare

Oxeye daisies are stunning, cheerful flowers, often growing in vast swathes along roadsides, and are easy to identify. They are a common species, but one that you are perhaps more likely encounter on your way to the coast than when you arrive. Growing up in south Wales, I was more familiar with the name dog daisy. Botanists sometimes use the word 'dog' to denote something that is considered second best, and I could never imagine how such an ostentatiously beautiful flower could have earned that name. Traditionally, the flower used in the petal-pulling game 'he loves me, he loves me not' was an oxeye daisy.

St Justinian

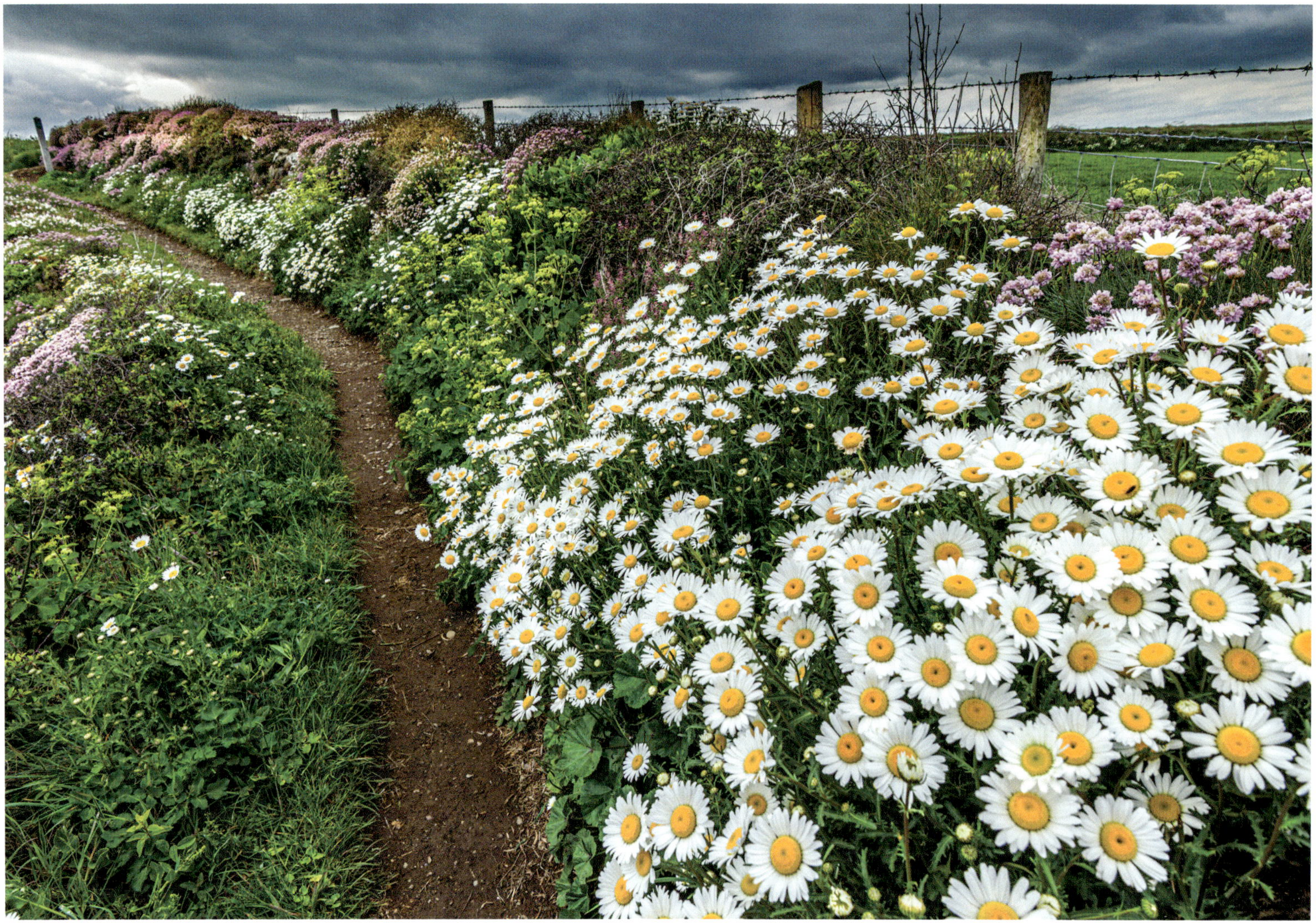

Oxeye Daisy Llygad-Llo Mawr *Leucanthemum vulgare*

Ragwort, Golden Samphire and Goldenrod
Llysiau'r Gingroen, Cedowydd Suddlon ac Eurwialen

Common Ragwort
Llysiau'r Gingroen
Senecio jacobaea

Common ragwort is a controversial species. It is subject to legislation in Wales, requiring widespread control. It is a vigorously invasive species, which can germinate wherever the soil surface is exposed. After a dry year, a few ragwort plants may emerge. The following year, dense areas of plants at the rosette stage can appear, but a year later the area could be covered with swathes of tall golden flowers. Usually, cinnabar moths appear in small numbers at this point. These are day-flying moths with unmistakable red, or cinnabar, spots and stripes on their black forewings, and equally bright red hind wings edged in dusty black. As the ragwort comes into flower for the second or third years, there is frequently a cinnabar population explosion, and the ragwort is rapidly stripped bare by hordes of black and yellow hooped caterpillars. Ragwort, despite its bad name, is an excellent pollinator, drawing in bees and butterflies.

Golden Samphire
Cedowydd Suddlon
Inula crithmoides

Golden Samphire is a plant that I always associate with the exposed rocky sea cliffs, but it also grows in salt marshes. It has yellow flowers and linear, fleshy and succulent leaves. It nearly always grows in the same places as rock samphire, and, as with rock samphire, the leaves are edible. Perhaps this is why it shares its second name with a completely unrelated species. The name samphire is a corruption of the French *Saint Pierre*, the patron saint of fishermen.

Goldenrod
Eurwialen
Solidago virgaurea

Goldenrod is not a spectacular plant, and is mostly found in small, untidy clusters. It can become invasive and rapidly colonises disturbed ground. In common with so many of our coastal species, it was introduced to North America, where it is now regarded as a problem invasive species. Goldenrod is not generally a problem in Britain, but there is an interesting issue on Skokholm Island where, since the 1960s, goldenrod has spread rapidly, engulfing a sizeable area of vegetation. Unfortunately, it is beginning to invade the otherwise pristine sea-cliff plant communities. Though once highly prized for treating wounds, it fell from favour in the seventeenth century.

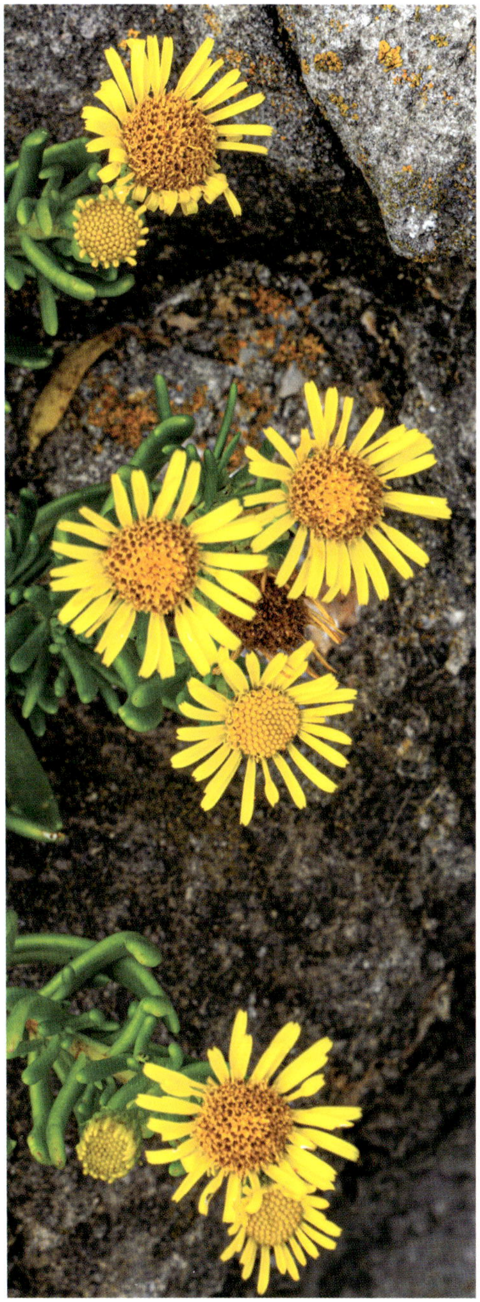

Golden Samphire
Cedowydd Suddlon
Inula crithmoides

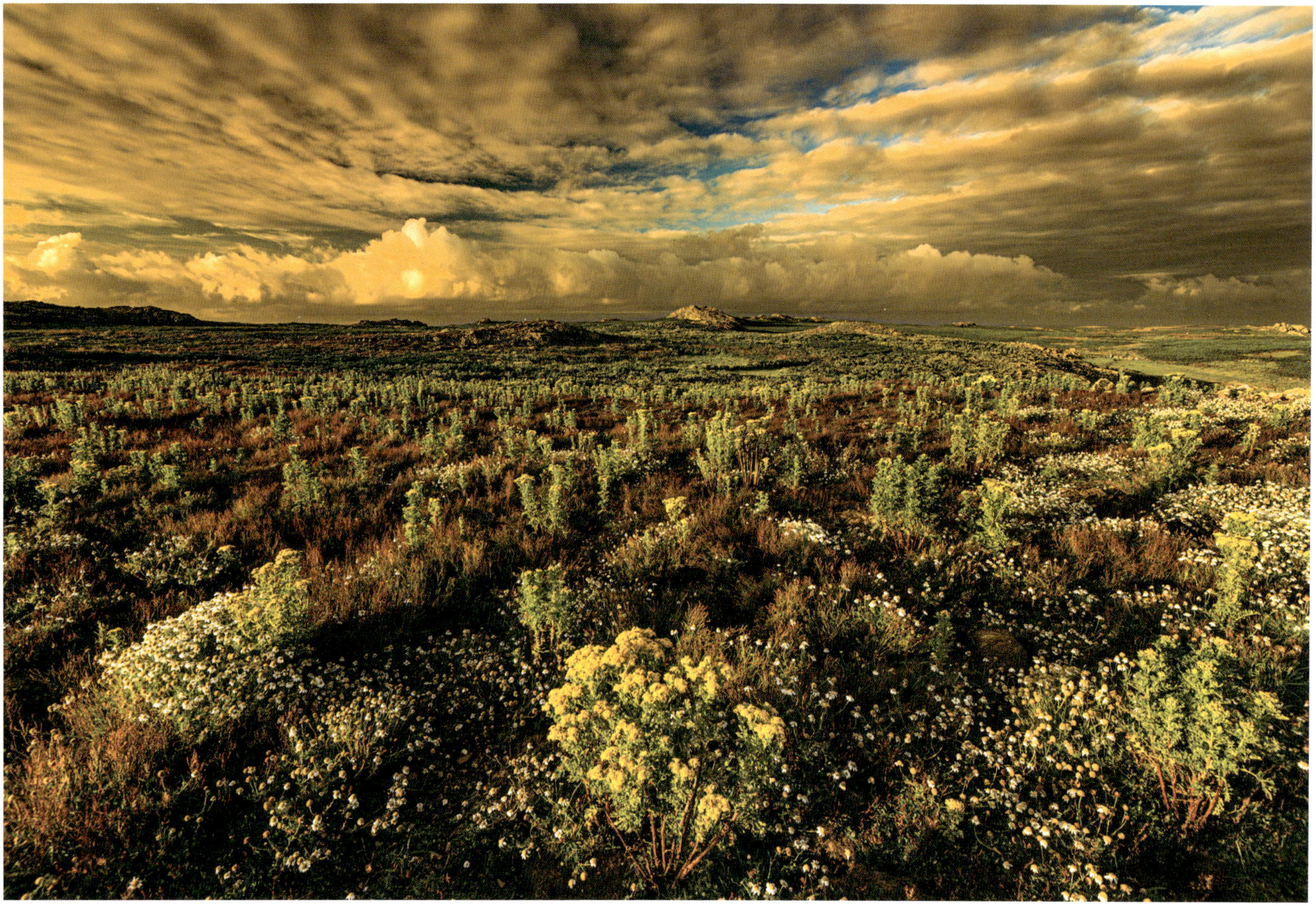

Common Ragwort Llysiau'r Gingroen *Senecio jacobaea*

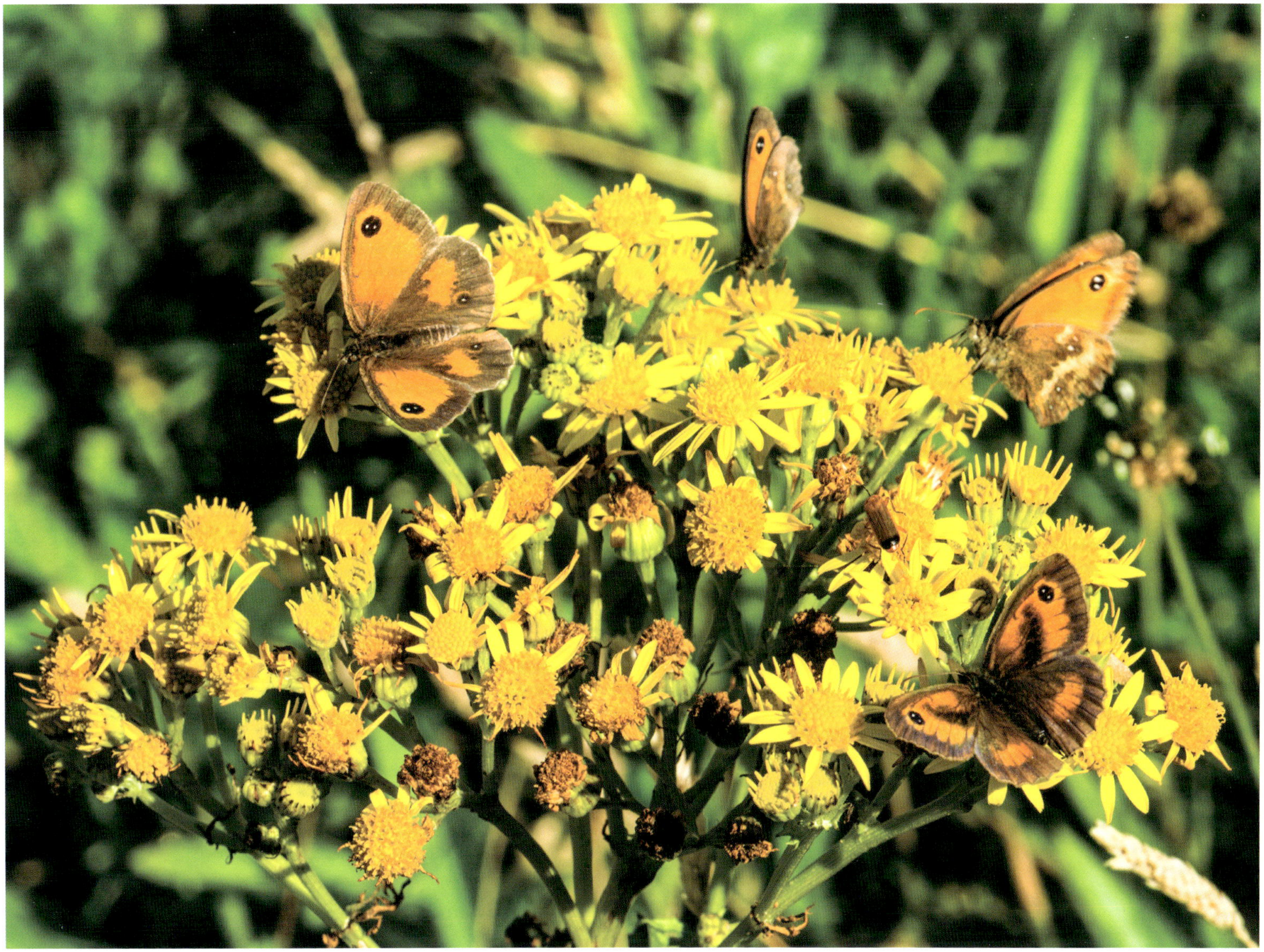

Gatekeeper butterfly Gweirlöyn y Perthi *Pyronia Tithonus*

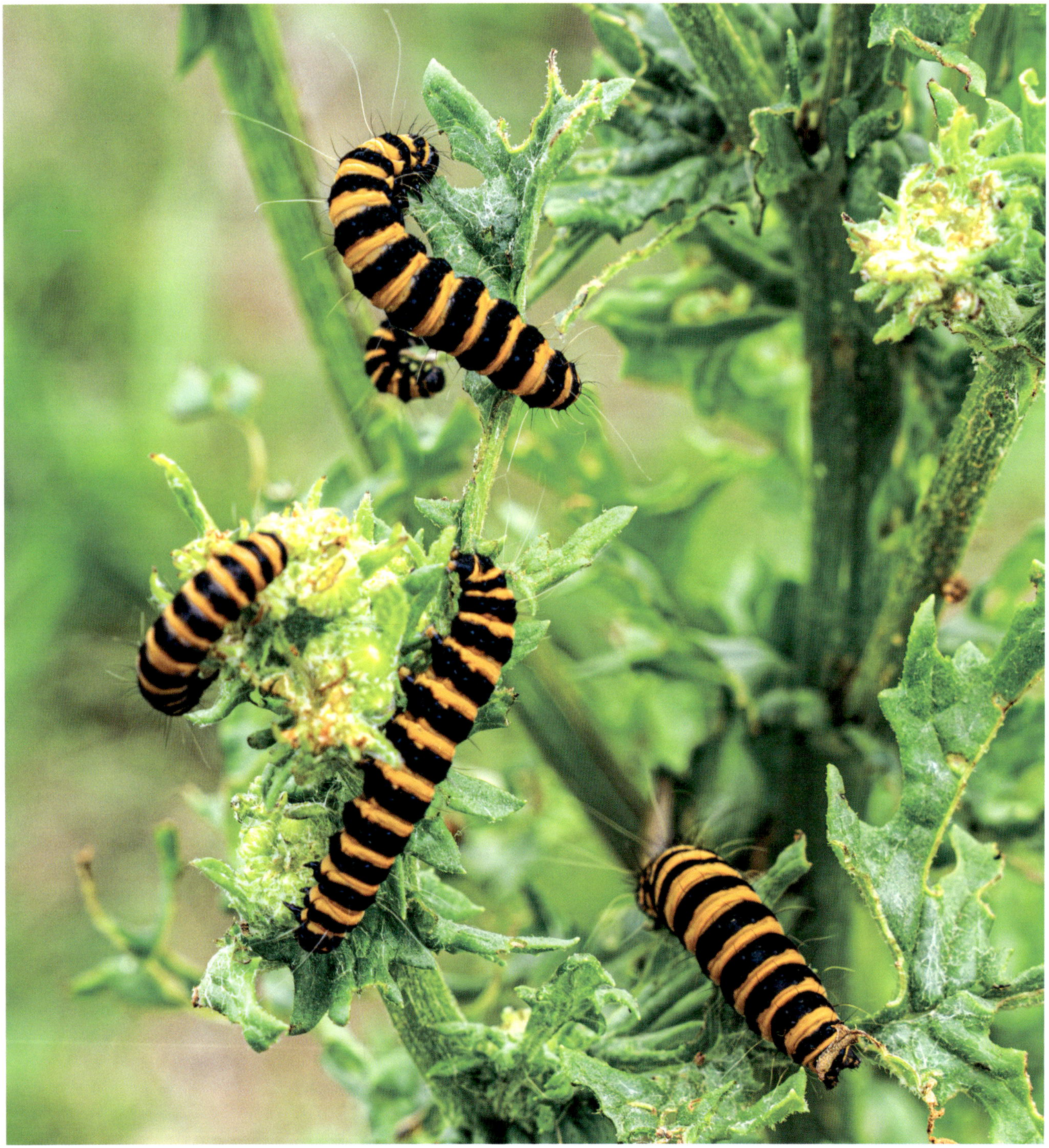

Cinnabar moth caterpillar lindysen Teigr y Benfelen *larva Tyria jacobaeae*

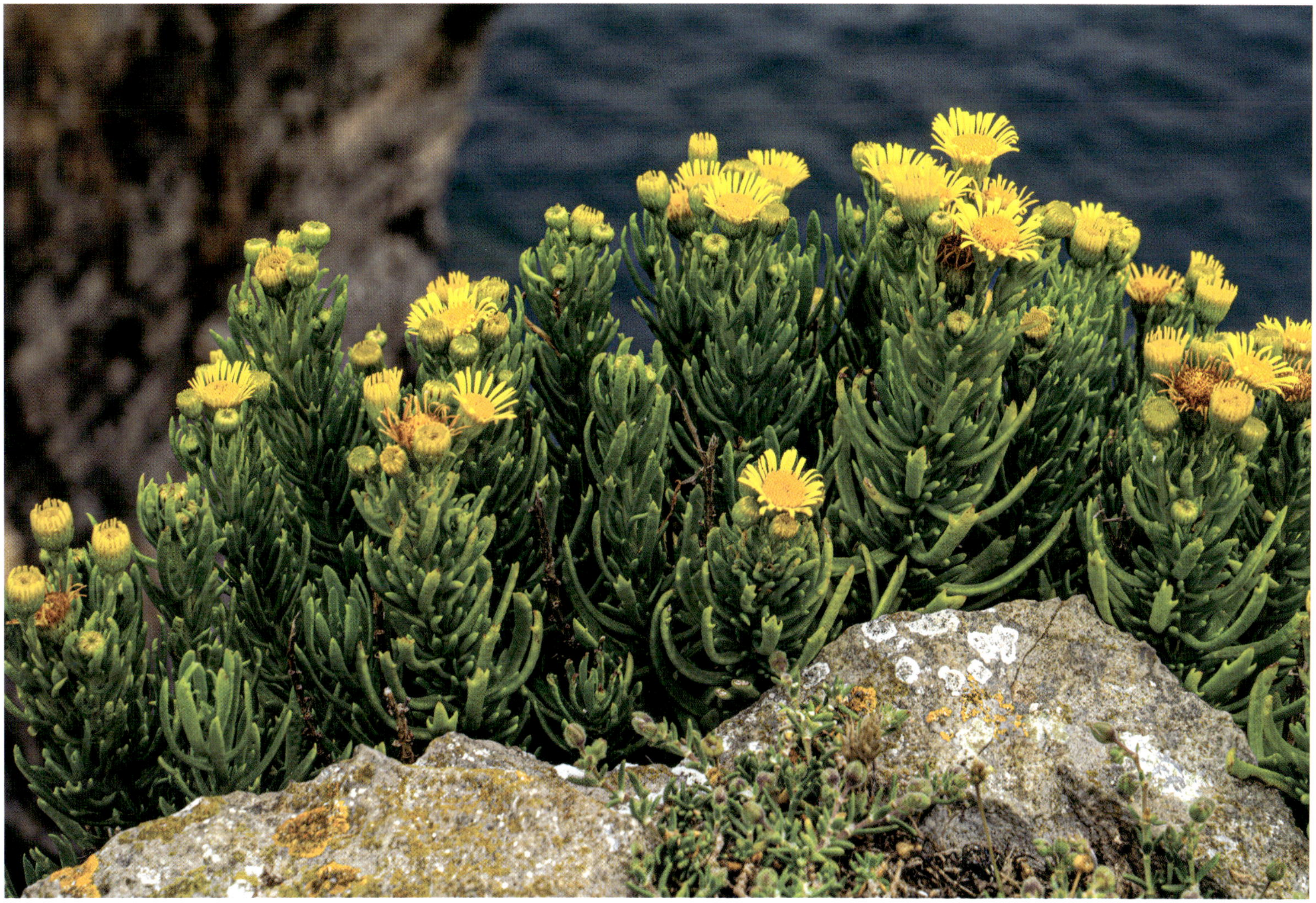

Golden Samphire Cedowydd Suddlon *Inula crithmoides*

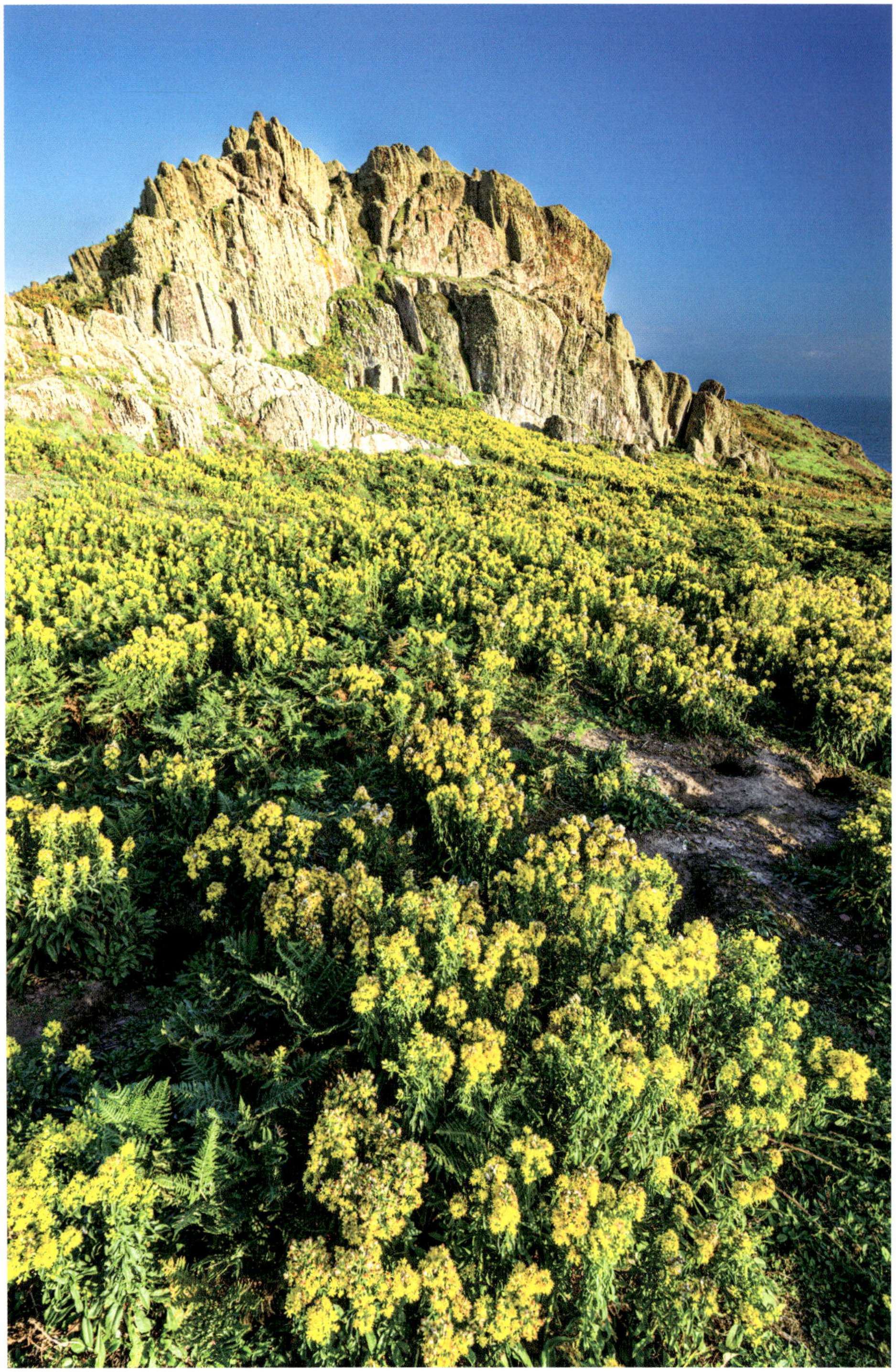

Goldenrod
Eurwialen
Solidago virgaurea

Carline Thistle Ysgallen Siarl

Carline Thistle
Ysgallen Siarl
Carlina vulgaris

Carline thistles are not actually thistles. They are named after Charlemagne, King of the Franks from 768 to 814. When searching for a cure for the plague, an angel told him to shoot an arrow into the sky and the plant that it landed on would provide a cure. The Welsh name *Siarl* means Charles.

This is a species of sunny, dry places, including limestone cliffs and shell-rich sand dunes. It is a strikingly attractive, if not conventionally beautiful, plant. Apart from the period before flowering, it has the appearance of a dried-out daisy or thistle. The composite flower heads are, in fact, a collection of tiny brown flowers, surrounded by a spiky fringe of golden-yellow bracts, or leaf-like structures. The dried flower heads, with silver bracts and yellow centres, persist right through the winter and can often be seen among the new spring thistles.

It has a long history of use in folk medicine, being valued for its anti-inflammatory and pain-relieving properties. It is also a popular plant in mythology. In one tale it was said to have grown from the tears of a fairy, mourning the death of her lover, and in another it is claimed to be the food of unicorns. It was also used to ward off evil spirits. Today it is increasingly declining, so if you do have the good fortune to find one, please take a moment to appreciate this rare, slightly self-effacing but undeniably delightful plant.

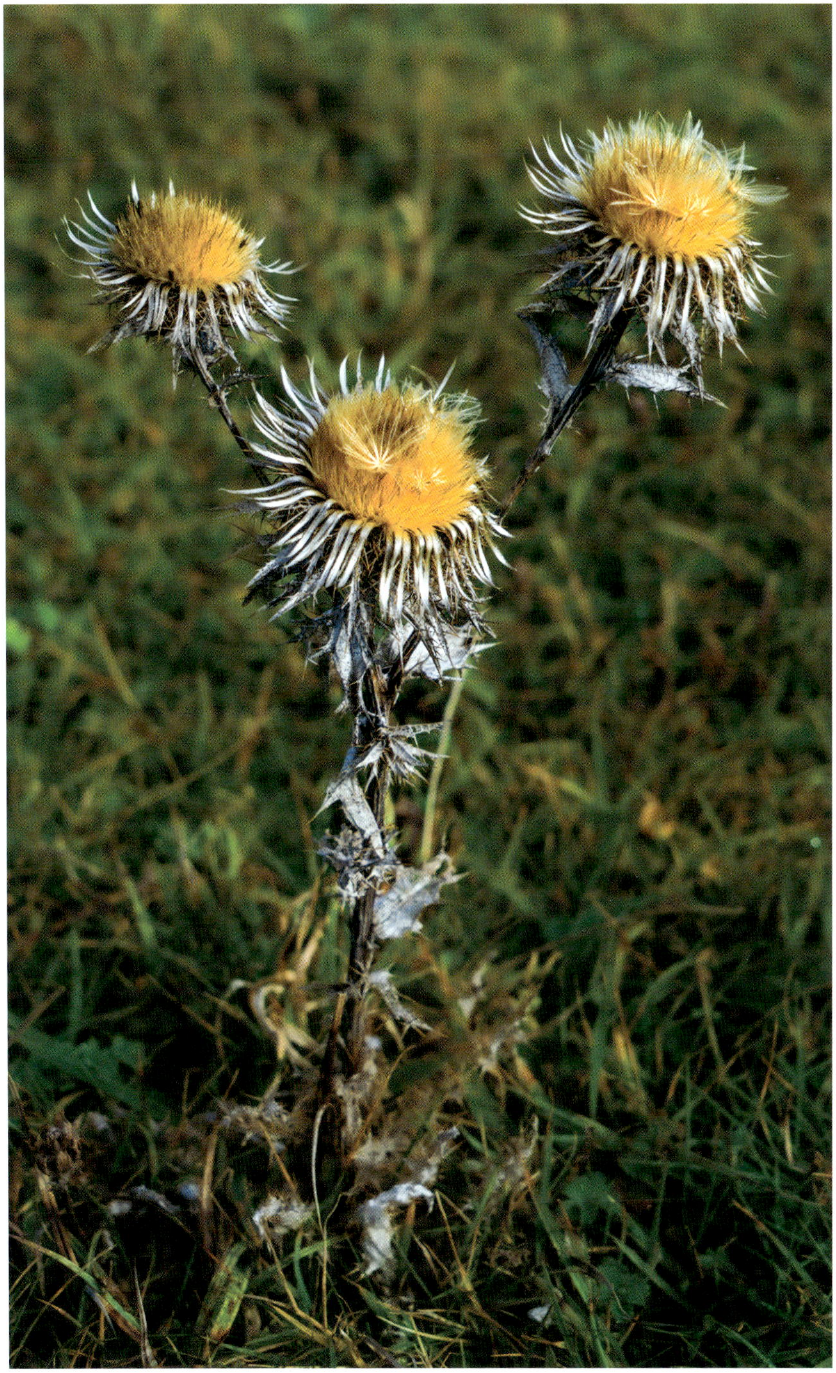

Carline Thistle
Ysgallen Siarl
Carlina vulgaris
in winter (right), and in summer (next page)

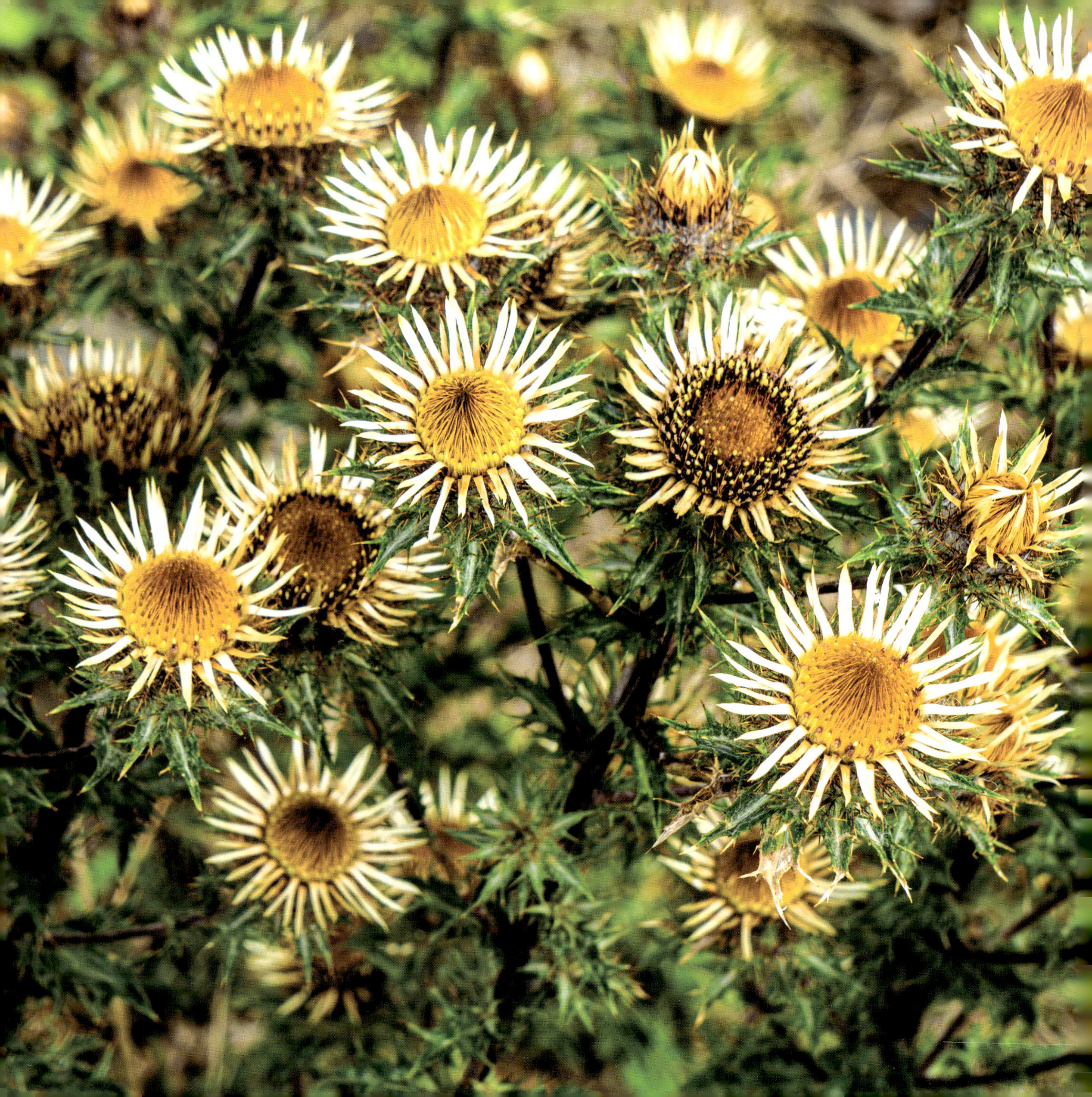

Knapweeds Y Bengaled

Common Knapweed
Y Bengaled
Centaurea nigra

Knapweed is another plant I have loved for most of my life. My Uncle Jeff was a hill farmer and, even as late as the 1960s, he used horses for much of the work on the farm. His hay crop was invariably taken in late July, giving the wildflowers ample opportunity to produce seeds. Above all, I remember a profusion of knapweed in the meadows – the plant that my uncle spoke of in Welsh as *pengaled* (hard head). This was a place so full of life: the sward was alive, jumping with grasshoppers; insects, including butterflies and bees, clouded the air; frogs and small mammals were constantly darting out of the path of the slow, horse-drawn mower; swallows and martins wheeled around us, dipping low to catch the disturbed insects. It is such an idyllic scene that it now seems hard to imagine that the countryside could have been like this as recently as my own lifetime.

This sturdy, thistle-like purple flower, which has always made me think of an old-fashioned shaving brush, can be found in almost any kind of grassland and, of course, on grassy roadside verges. Knapweed attracts many species of butterflies and other pollinators, and has been an important medicinal herb, used to treat bronchitis, coughs, sore throats and gum disease. The genus name, *centaurea*, comes from the centaur Chiron, who used the flowers as a poultice for an infected wound.

This anonymous poem highlights the belief among some that knapweed could tell a maiden's future:

> A maiden plucks a flower,
> Tucks it inside her blouse for an hour.
> With hopeful heart and eyes that gleam,
> She waits to see if love's sweet dream will stream.
>
> The unexpanded florets, tight and shy,
> Hold secrets of fate, as time ticks by.
> When the plant is removed, petals unfurl,
> A silent promise whispers: "Soon, your love will swirl."

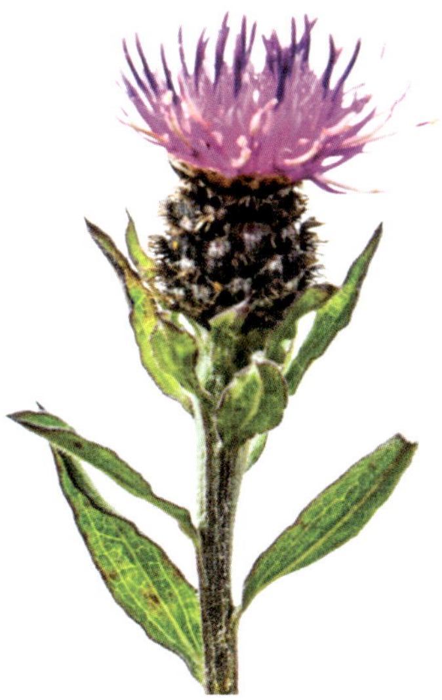

Above and next page: Common Knapweed Y Bengaled *Centaurea nigra*

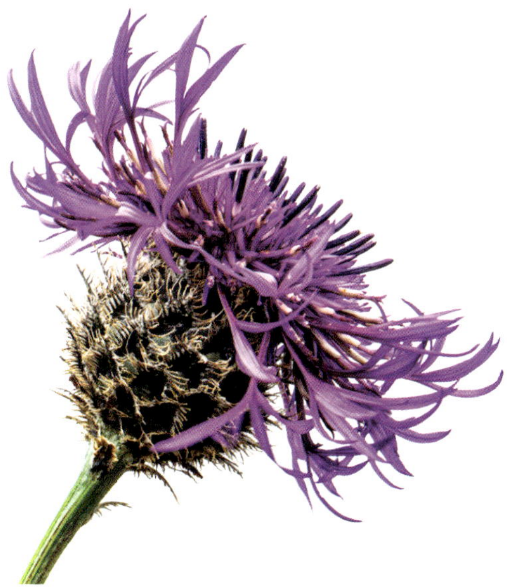

Greater Knapweed Y Bengaled Fawr *Centaurea scabiosa*

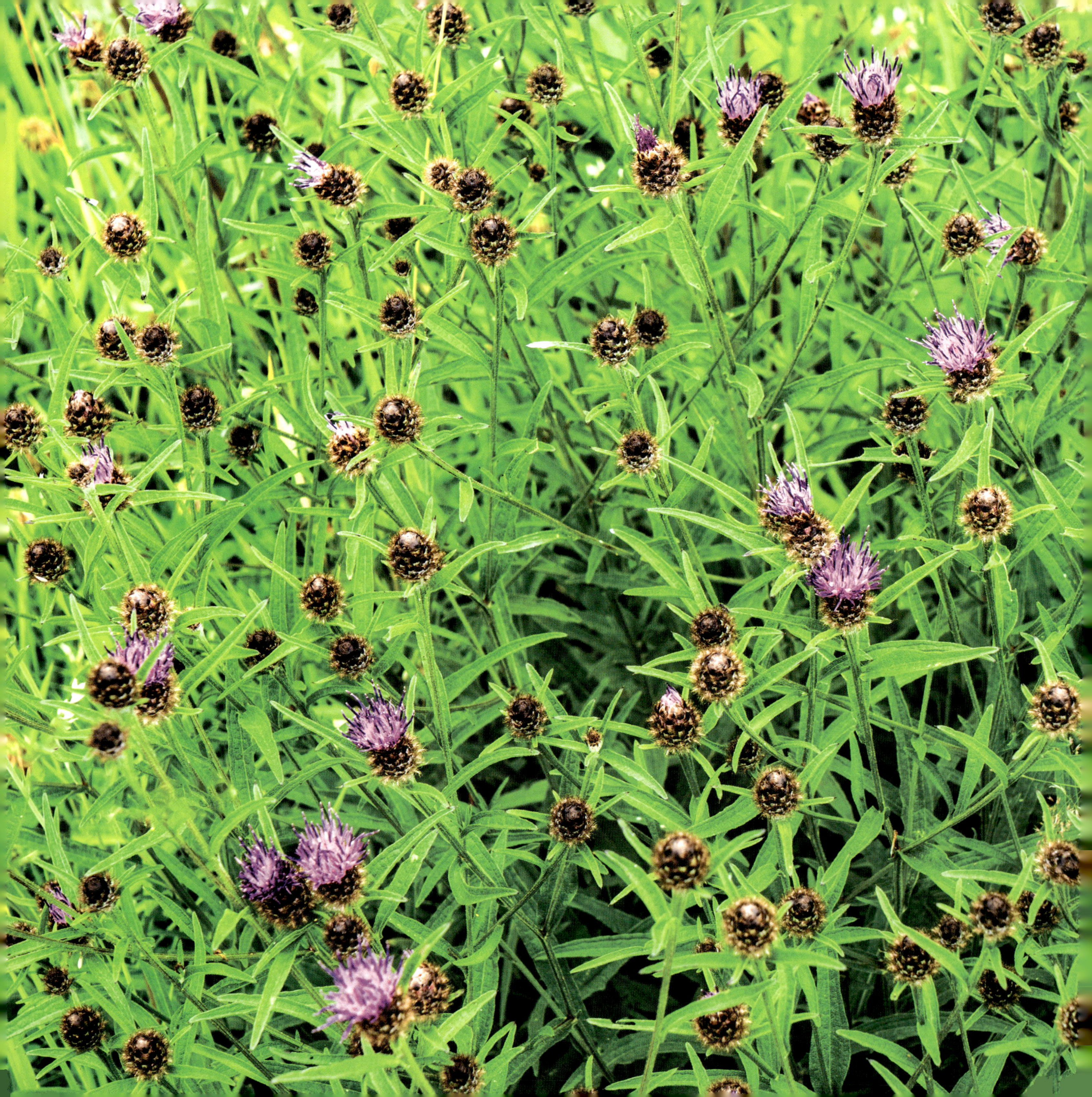

Greater Knapweed
Y Bengaled Fawr
Centaurea scabiosa

Greater knapweed grows in abundance on limestone cliffs, and the dramatically sculpted bays and headlands around Stack Rocks, on the Castlemartin Peninsula, are an ideal place to see it.

I can only feel enthusiasm for this flower, and I am not really sure why. Perhaps it is because it is an exaggerated and even more beautiful version of the common knapweed that I have always been so fond of.

The flower-heads are similar to knapweed in colour, being a vivid blend of pink and purple, but are much larger. Some of the florets around the edge of the composite head are longer than others, giving a slightly ragged appearance to the flower. The larger florets are sterile, and their entire purpose is to attract pollinators. It is only the smaller, neater florets at the centre that are fertile.

There is little folklore associated with this plant, probably because people did not differentiate between the species, and almost everything claimed of knapweed is also attributed to greater knapweed. The only specific reference I have found for greater knapweed associates it with the Celtic Goddess Brigid, and suggests that it has protective powers.

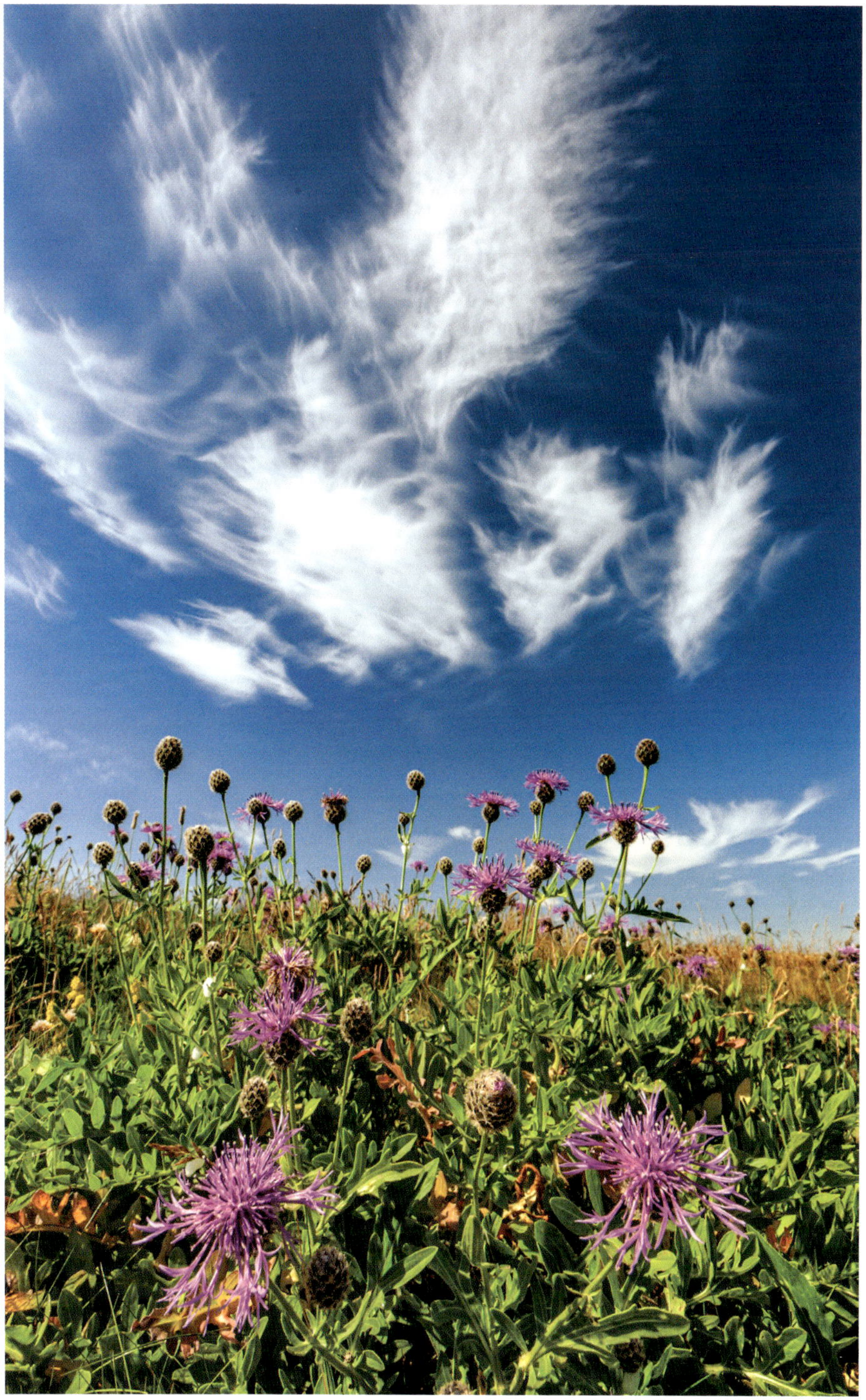

Right and next page:
Greater Knapweed
Y Bengaled Fawr
Centaurea scabiosa

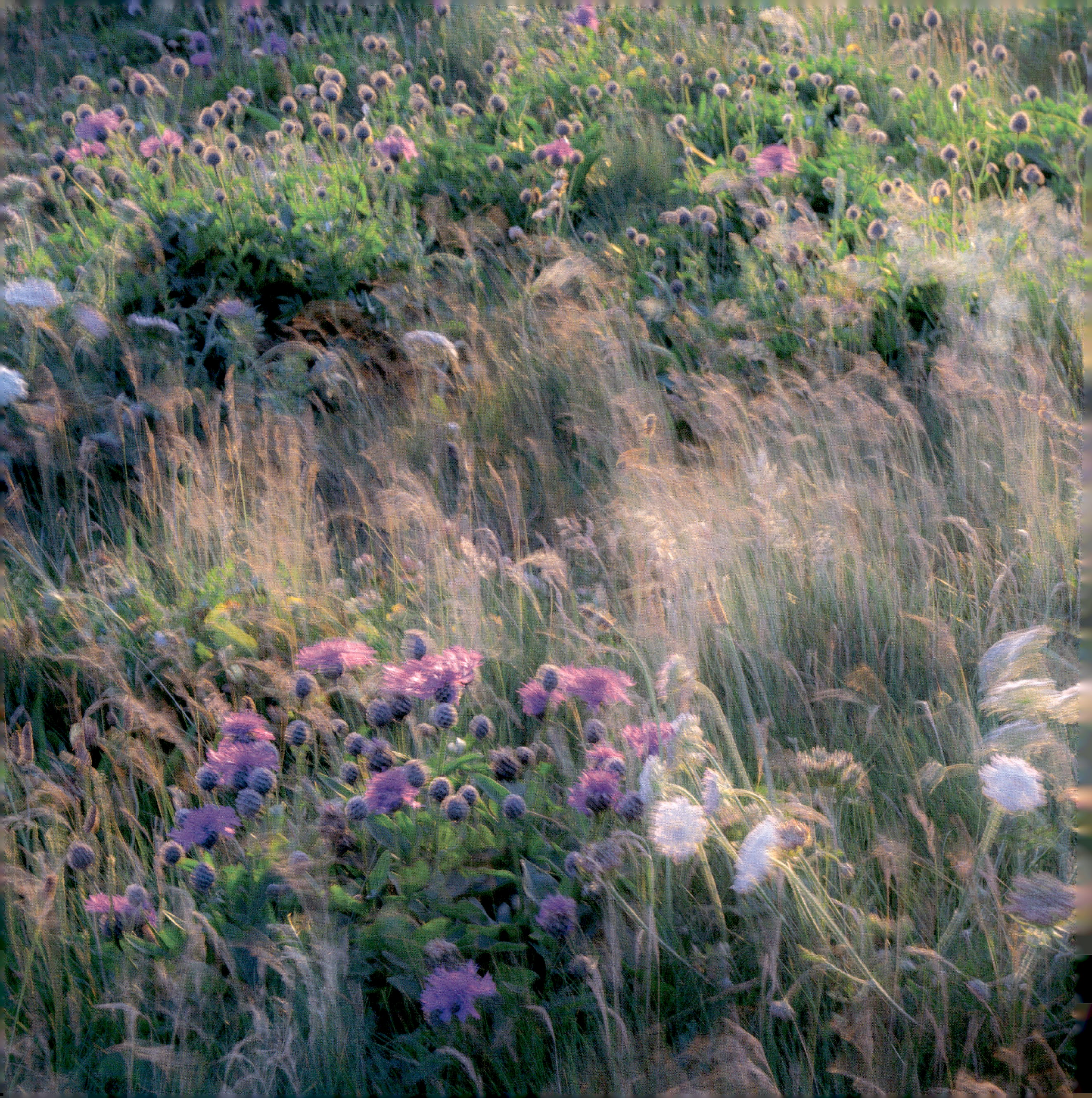

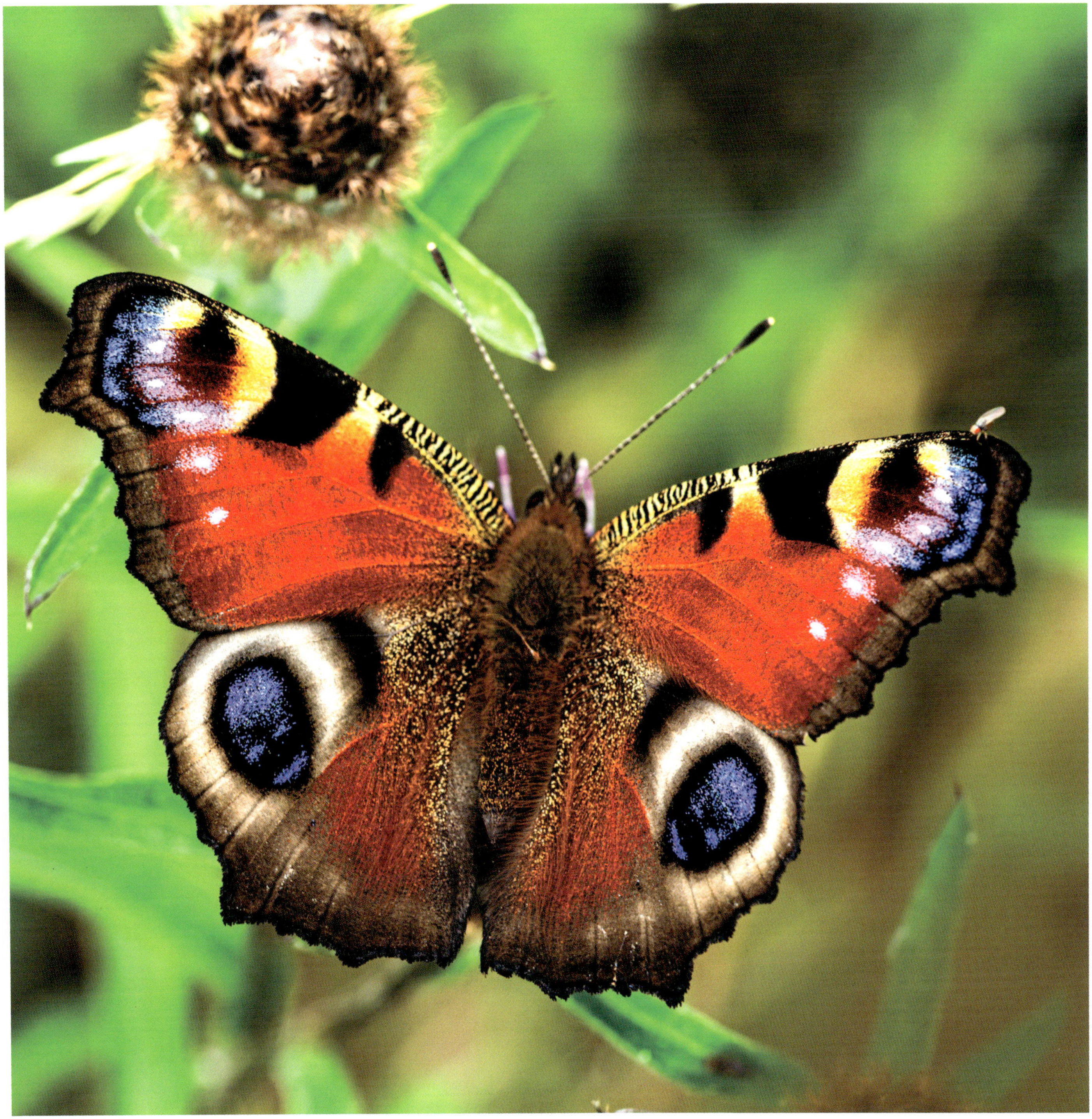

Peacock butterfly Mantell Paun *Aglais io*

Thistles Ysgall

Thistles are often regarded as agricultural weeds, and grouped together with docks and nettles as targets for herbicide control. A traditional farming practice was to scythe thistles before they produced seed. These 'problem' species are often associated with enriched areas or over-fertilised ground.

Although thistles are not highly regarded, they are actually attractive plants. They are also important for butterflies and other pollinators, and they provide a vital source of winter food for birds. Finches plucking the masses of fluffy thistle seeds make a beautiful image. With the spines removed, thistles were an important food for humans. The hearts of the flower heads were treated like artichokes, which are also members of the thistle family.

Marsh Thistle
Ysgallen y Gors
Cirsium palustre

Marsh thistle can grow to 1.5 m tall or more. The typical dark purple thistle heads are loosely clustered at the top of viciously spiny, winged stems, and the lobed leaves are also very spiny. Occasionally, you may find a plant with white flowers. As their name implies, they are most often found growing in damp or marshy places.

They are rated in the top ten of the most nectar-producing plants in the UK, so it is no coincidence that in the butterfly photographs of the small pearl-bordered fritillary and the marsh fritillary, both are resting on a marsh thistle.

Spear Thistle
Marchysgallen
Cirsium vulgare

Spear thistles, armoured with fearsome spines, exemplify everything that a thistle should be: tall, powerful, threatening and regal. The book I treasured most as a child was *The Ladybird Book of British Birds*. I was completely captivated by an illustration of a beautiful male goldfinch on a spear thistle, surrounded by white down, almost aware of his own magnificence compared to the dowdy immature bird sitting just below.

Spear thistles are not uncommon and they favour disturbed ground. You will find them at the edges of fields (particularly cultivated ones), roadside verges and on waste ground. This is the classic thistle, the Scottish national emblem, which first appeared as a royal symbol on coins minted in 1474.

Creeping Thistle
Ysgallen y Maes
Cirsium arvense

Creeping thistle is the most common species of thistle. They will appear almost anywhere, including grasslands, disturbed ground, roadsides and around the coast. The plants are tall and bushy, and, in place of the usual dark purple flowers, they have masses of delicate pale pink or violet heads.

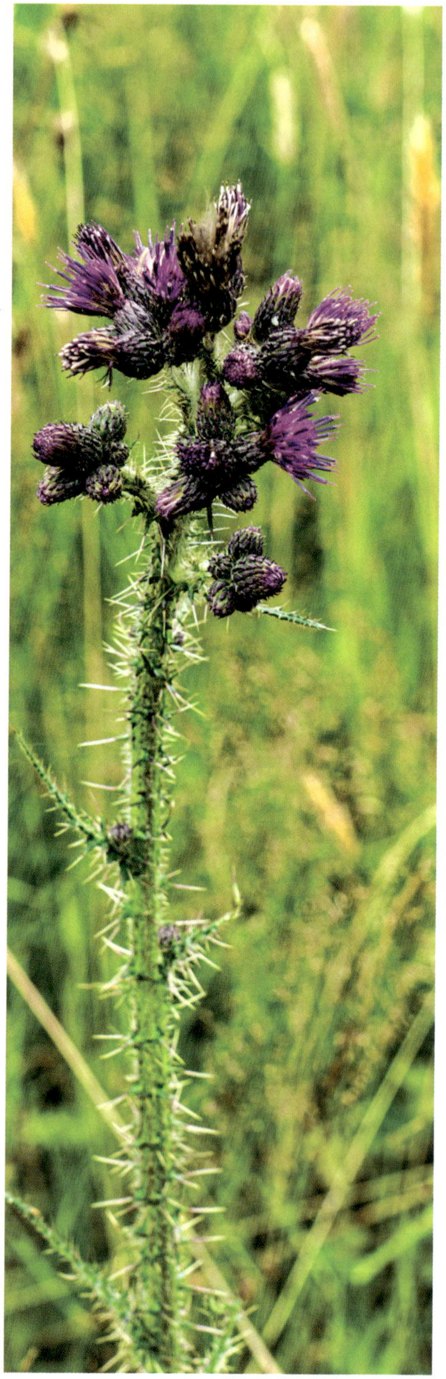

Marsh Thistle
Ysgallen y Gors
Cirsium palustre

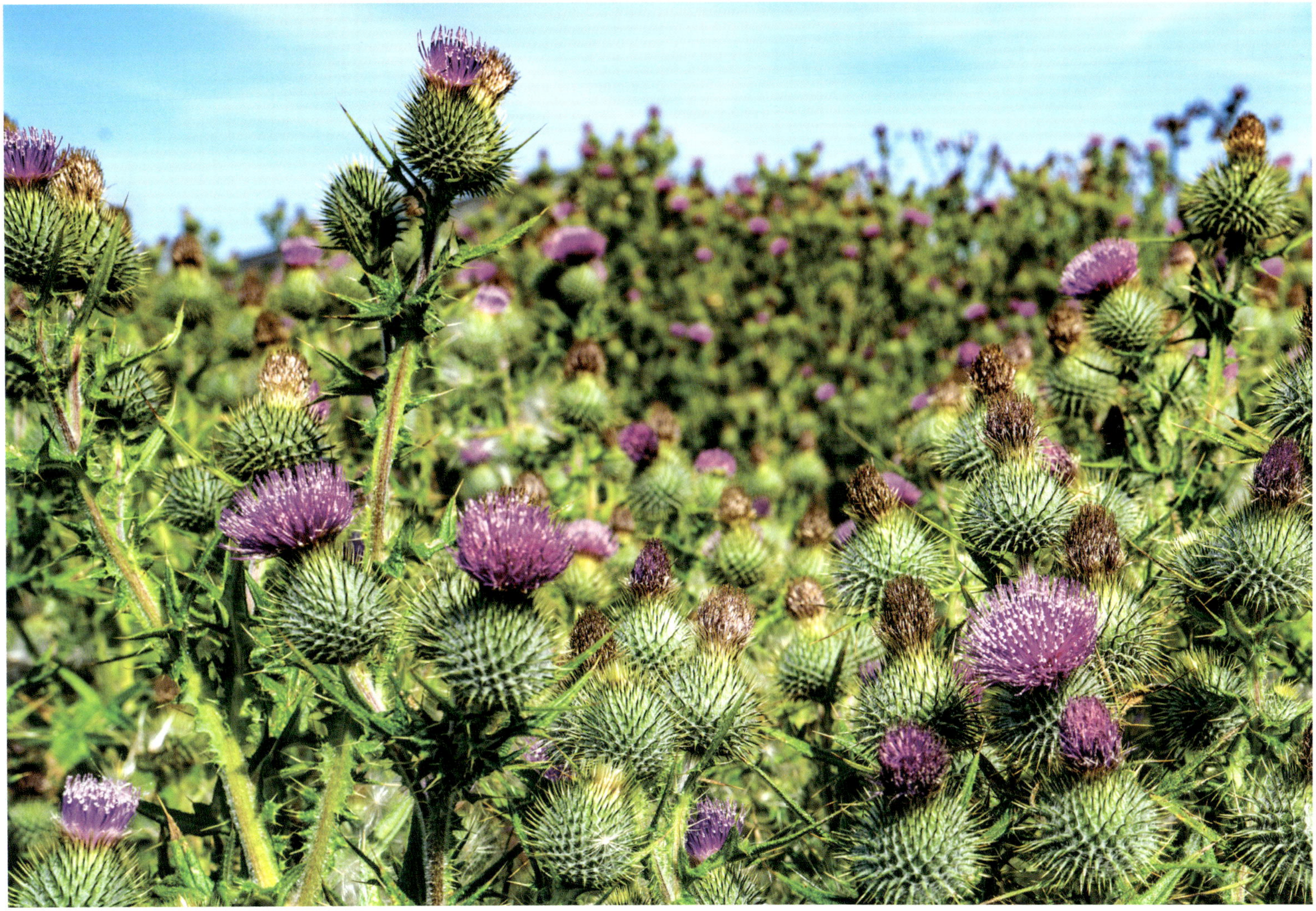

Spear Thistle Marchysgallen *Cirsium vulgare*

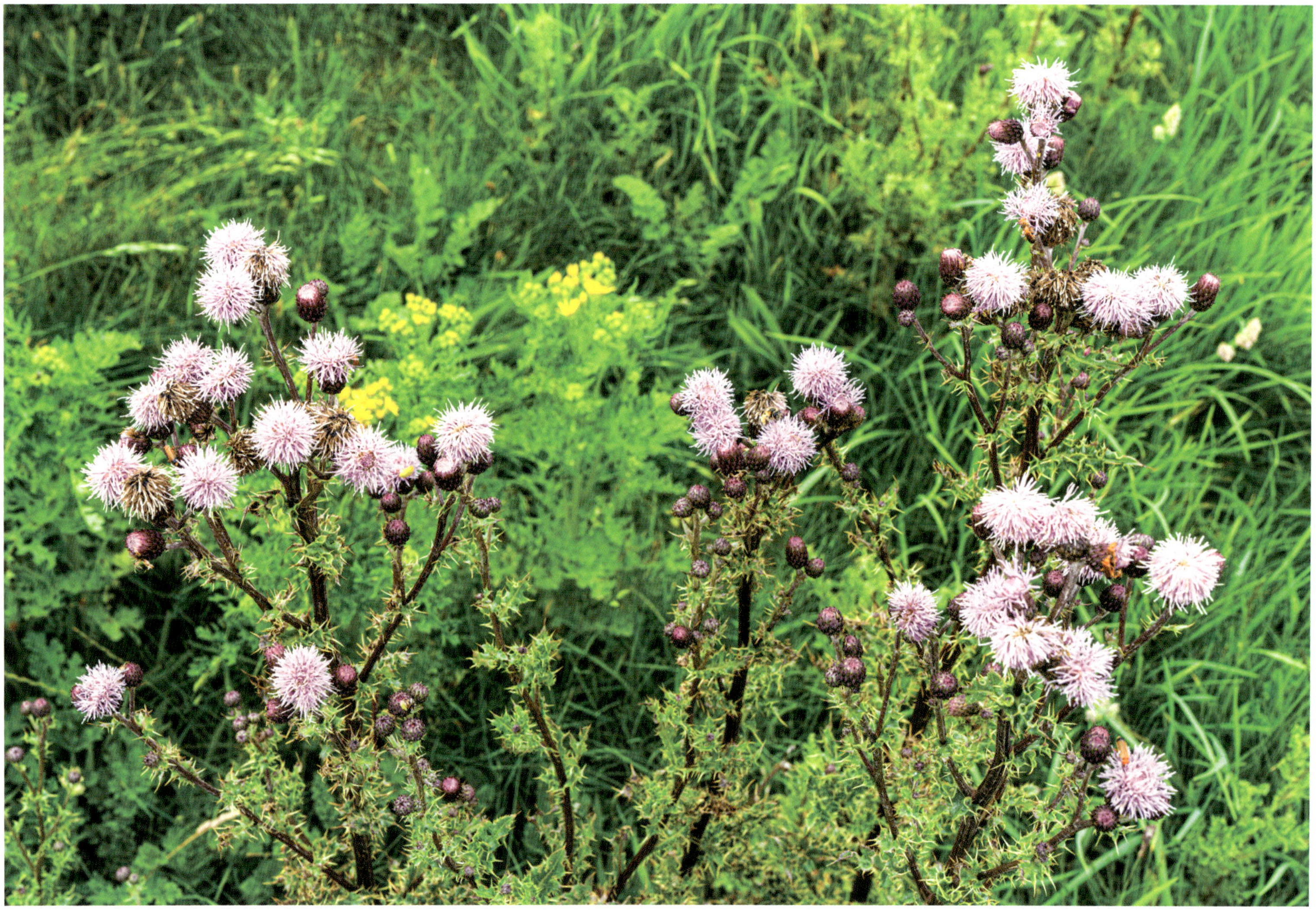

Creeping Thistle Ysgallen y Maes *Cirsium arvense*

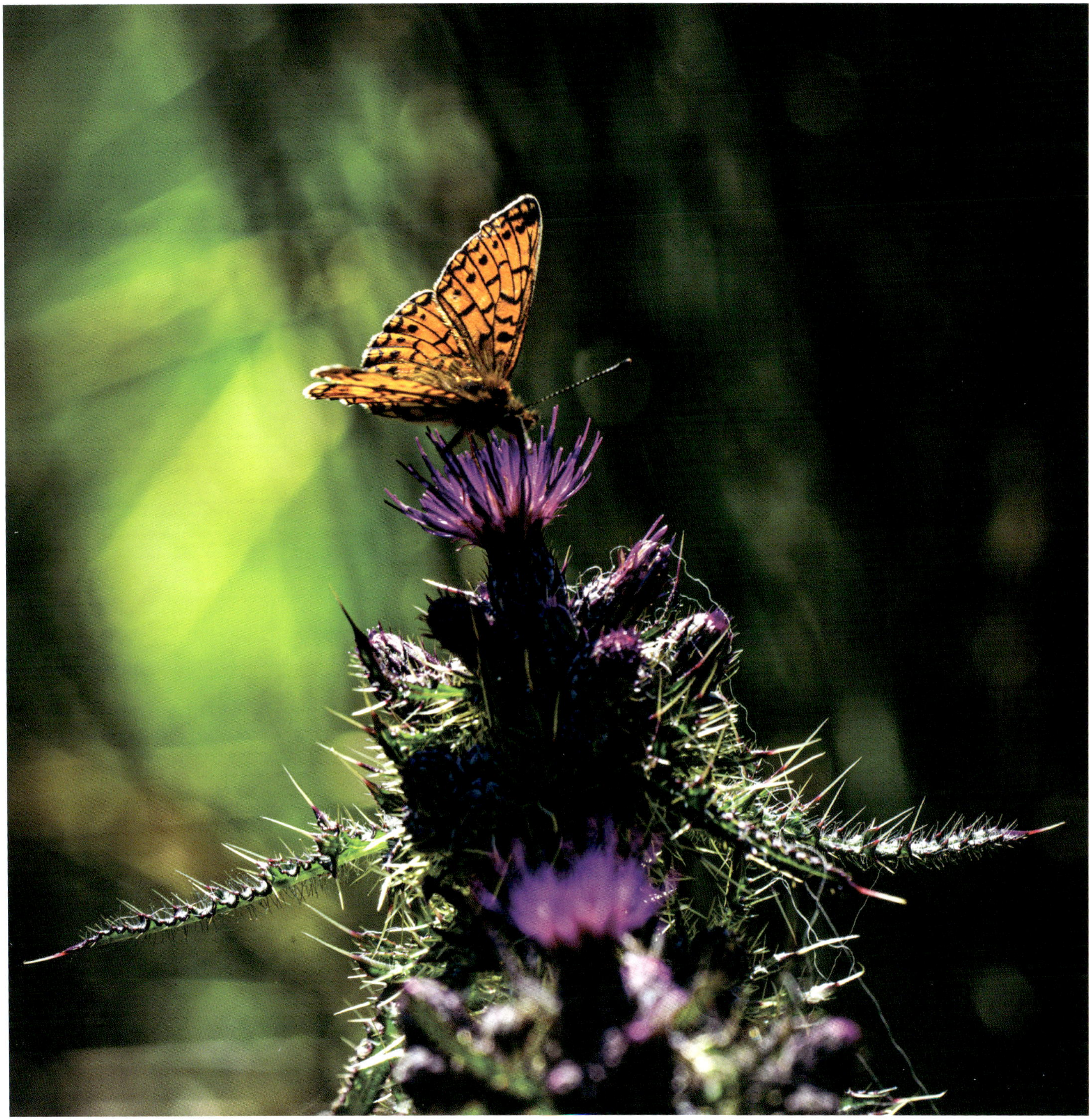

Small Pearl-bordered Fritillary butterfly Britheg Berlog Fach *Boloria selene*

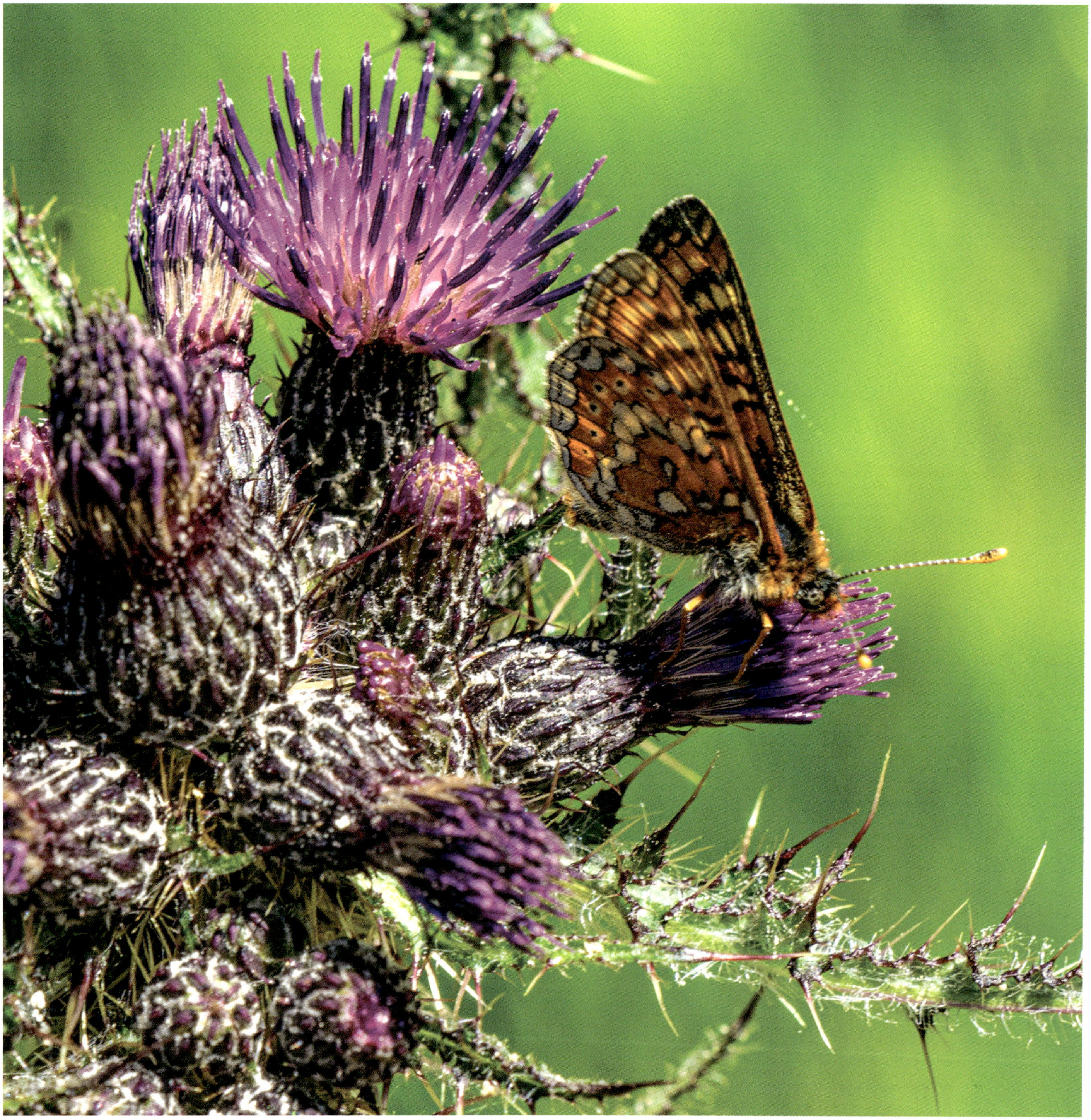

Marsh Fritillary butterfly Britheg y Gors *Euphydryas aurinia*

Dandelions and Dandelion-like Flowers Dant y Llew a Blodau Tebyg

This is another group of flowers which are members of the daisy family, grouped together because they all look like the common dandelion, a species that most people will be familiar with. While it may be easy to recognise common dandelions, the remainder of this large group can be difficult to identify with any confidence. I have only included some of the most recognisable species.

Dandelion
Dant y Llew
Taraxacum officinale

Dandelions are both loved and hated with equal passion. They can be an intrusive, pernicious weed, especially if you long for a perfect lawn, but they are also frequently celebrated in poems, especially children's verses. As a child, I was warned never to pick dandelions because if I did, I would be sure to wet the bed. This is a common folk-belief which has given rise to some vulgar names for the dandelion, including wet-the-bed, tiddle-beds and piss-a-bed. A frequently used Welsh name is *blodyn piso'r gwely* (piss-the-bed flower). The reason for these names is that dandelions are a powerful diuretic. Dandelion sap was also used as a cure for warts.

Cat's-ear
Melynydd
Hypochaeris radicata

Cat's-ear is another species that frequently finds its way into lawns, to the despair of fastidious gardeners. The long, lobed leaves grow in a rosette at the base of the plant. The forked flower stems are not always erect, and in exposed clifftop locations, they tend to sprawl in a tangle. Yellow flower-heads mature into balls of fluffy seed heads, similar to but much smaller than dandelion clocks. The common name refers to the shape and texture of the leaves, with their dusting of fine hairs. All parts of the plant can be eaten, and the root can be dried and ground as a coffee substitute.

Fox-and-cubs
Clust-y-llygoden Euraid
Pilosella aurantiaca

Fox-and-cubs has vibrant and unusual orange-coloured flowers, quite different to the yellows of the other flowers in this group. I am not convinced, but it is claimed that these flowers bear a resemblance to a fox's ear and cub's paws. It has an interesting collection of alternative names, including devil's paintbrush, grim-the-collier and grimy coalminer. The stems and leaves have black hairs which just might evoke an image of a collier fresh from the pit. This is a protected species in many European countries.

Mouse-ear Hawkweed
Clust y Llygoden
Pilosella officinarum

Mouse-ear hawkweed has delicate lemon-yellow flowers with just the slightest tinge of red on their outer florets, and, yes, the rosettes of spoon-shaped downy leaves at the base of the flower stem really do look like mouse ears. This is a flower that flourishes in a well-grazed, lime-rich sward. The photograph is taken in the sand dunes overlooking Bosherston Lily Ponds. The dunes and grazed clifftops along this south Pembrokeshire limestone coast are the perfect habitat for this species.

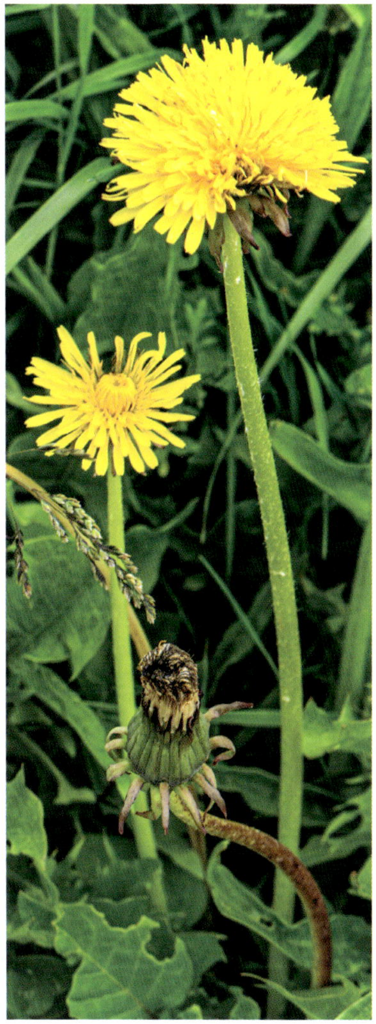

Dandelion
Dant y Llew
Taraxacum officinale

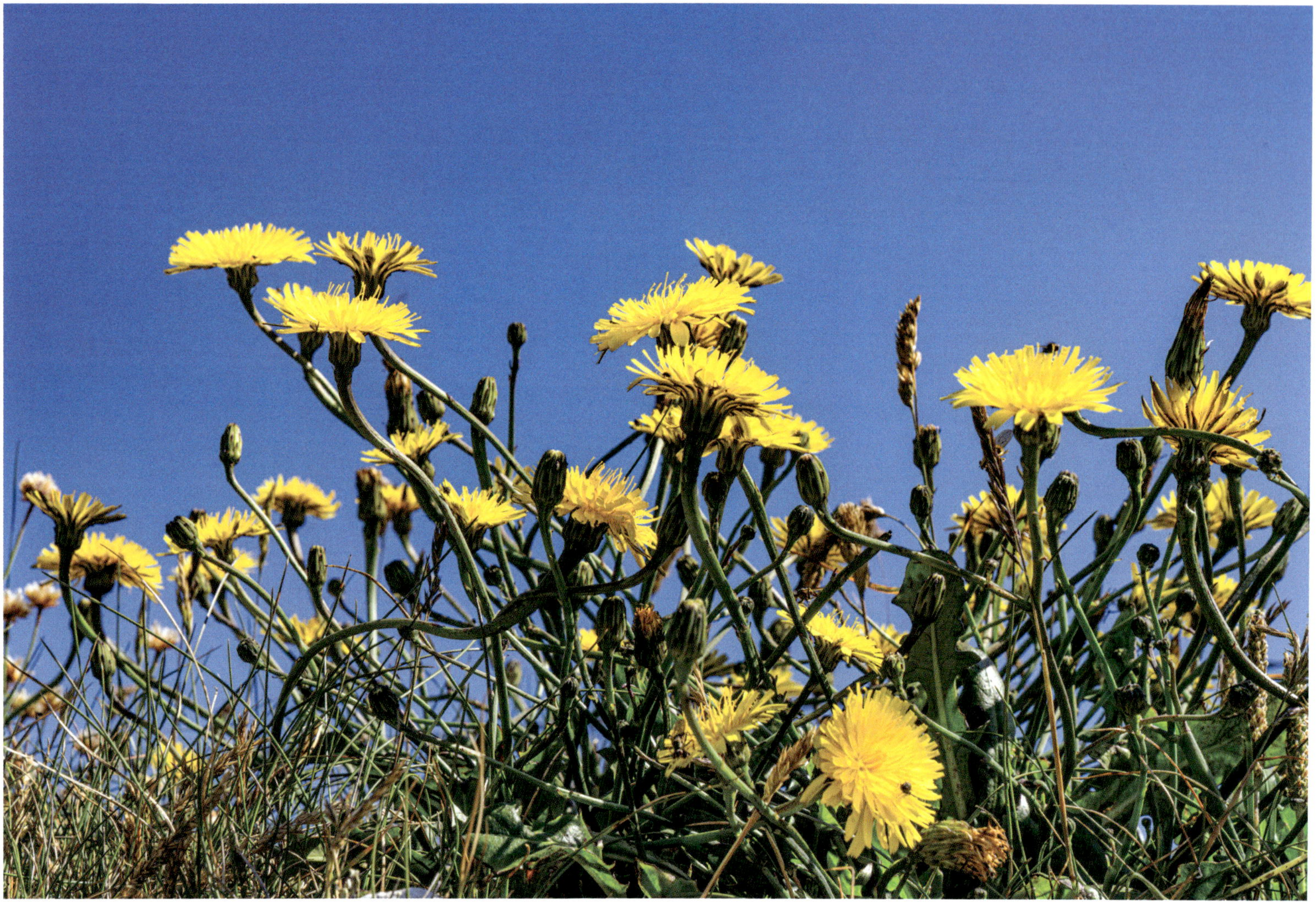

Cat's-ear Melynydd *Hypochaeris radicata*

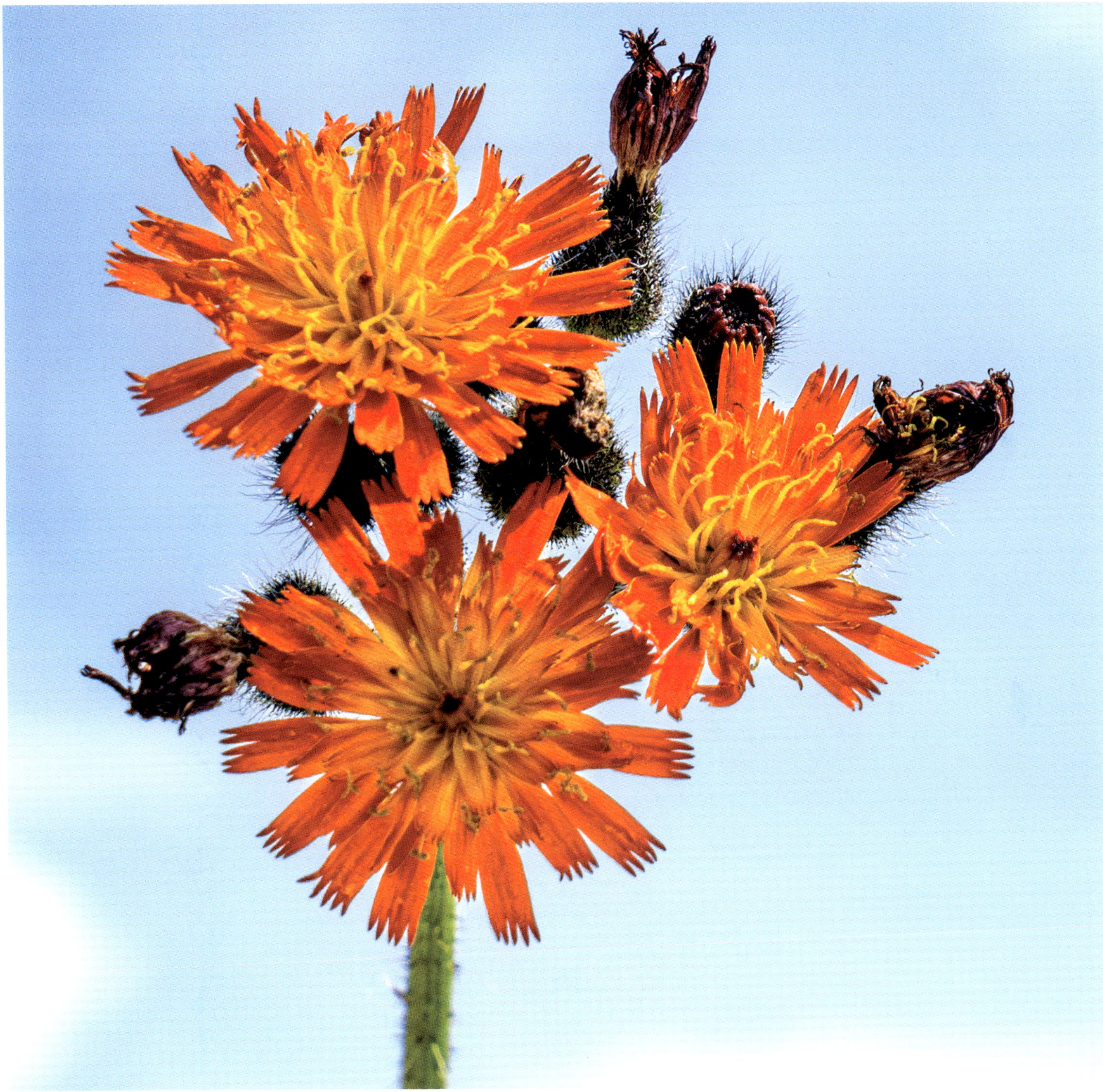

Fox-and-cubs Clust-y-llygoden Euraid *Pilosella aurantiaca*

Broad Haven

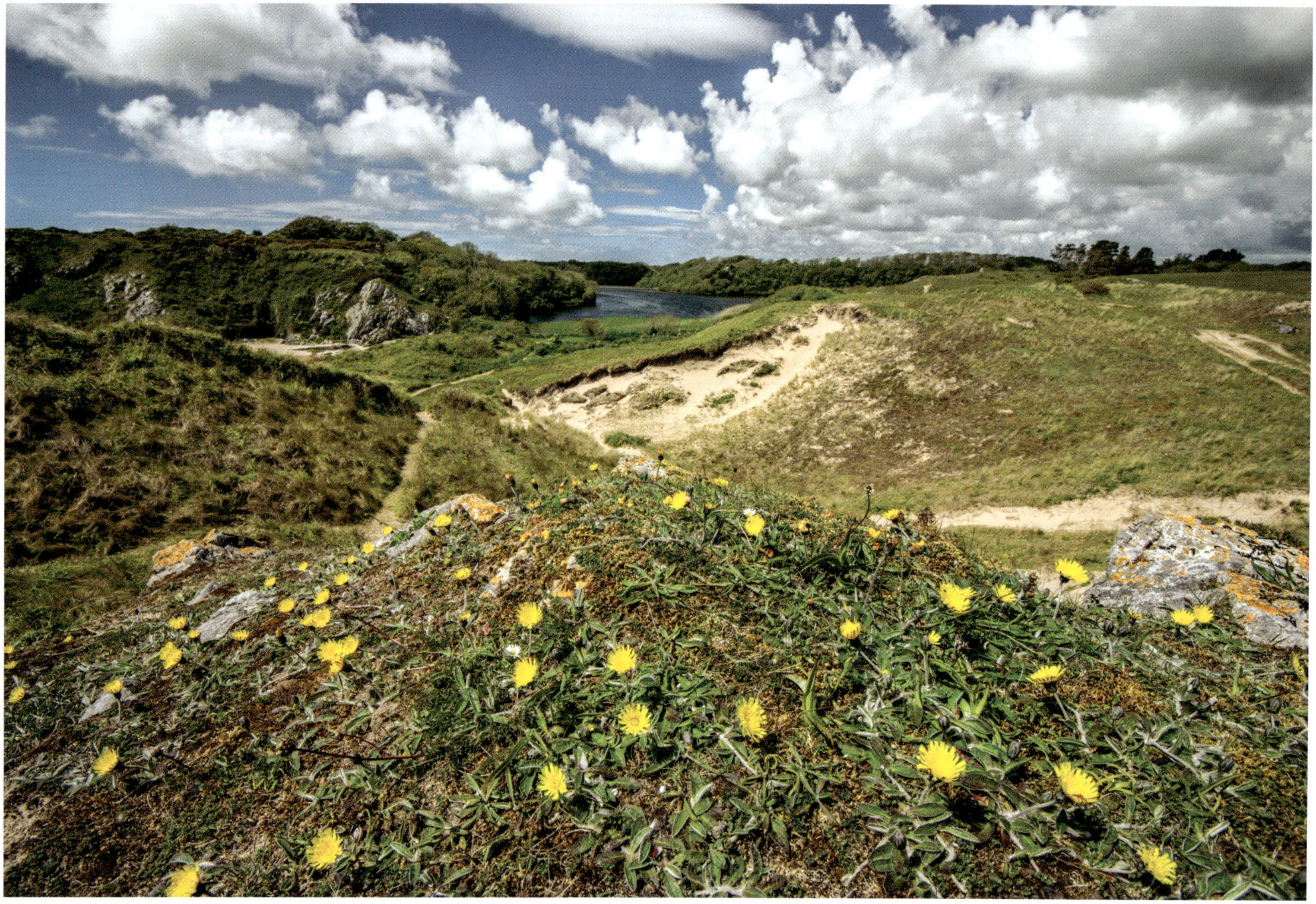

Mouse-ear Hawkweed Clust y Llygoden *Pilosella officinarum*

Asparagus Family Teulu'r Merllys

Some of us with longer memories may find the family name asparagus confusing, because earlier classification systems treated bluebells and spring squill as members of the lily family.

Bluebell
Clychau'r Gog
Hyacinthoides non-scripta

Bluebells are, without doubt, one of the highlights of early springtime, especially when they grow in the open on the Welsh sea cliffs and offshore islands. Almost nothing can compete with the vast swathes of shimmering blue which cover the greater part of Skomer Island in May and June. There, blue seas, blue skies and bluebells fill the view in a clash of colours that somehow manage to complement each other perfectly. They are beautiful flowers, with an unmistakable sweet fragrance that is both bold and delicate, becoming almost intoxicating on warm, still spring evenings. The key to understanding bluebells on Skomer's treeless cliffs is to appreciate their relationship with bracken. For most of their range in Britain, bluebells are regarded as a spring-flowering woodland species, which exploits the available light before the tree canopy begins to develop and close. When bracken becomes dominant on the island, it also provides a canopy, which does not close until late spring. This has much the same impact as the canopy in a bluebell wood.

The bluebell's scientific name is *Hyacinthoides non-scripta*. In Greek mythology, Hyacinthus, a handsome Spartan prince, was loved by Apollo and Zephyrus (the god of the west wind). One day, Hyacinthus was throwing the discus with Apollo when Zephyrus, jealous of his rival Apollo, deliberately blew the discus off course to strike Hyacinthus on the head. As Hyacinthus lay dying, a hyacinth flower sprang from his spilled blood, and Apollo inscribed the letters AI AI (Woe Woe), as an exclamation of his grief, on the petals. Botanists who first named the bluebell gave it the name *non-scripta* to distinguish it from other hyacinths, *non-scripta* meaning 'unlettered'.

Bluebells feature frequently in British and European folklore and myth. The bulbs are extremely toxic, and this toxicity may be part of the reason. The most common myth is that bluebells were said to ring when fairies were summoned to a gathering, but if humans heard the sound, they would fall under the fairy enchantment and die soon after. For much of my younger life I used the name *Endymion non-scriptus* for bluebells: it was only relatively recently changed to *Hyacinthoides*. My main reason for mentioning this is because it provides an opportunity to make the connection with John Keats' epic poem *Endymion*. The opening lines could easily have been written about bluebells:

> A thing of beauty is a joy for ever:
> Its loveliness increases; it will never
> Pass into nothingness; but still will keep
> A bower quiet for us, and a sleep
> Full of sweet dreams, and health, and quiet breathing.
> Therefore, on every morrow, are we wreathing
> A flowery band to bind us to the earth.

Whenever I think of the bluebells of west Wales, I am immediately reminded of R Williams Parry, one of our most celebrated and beloved Welsh poets, who won the Eisteddfod Chair for his poem '*Yr Haf*' (The Summer) in 1910. He is especially remembered for his poignant poem *Clychau'r Gog* (Bluebells), which beautifully captures the fleeting nature of flowers and, by extension, life itself. Parry's reflection echoes the sentiment found in Shelley's 'The Flower That Smiles Today', which I referenced in the introduction to this book. (The English translation of '*Clychau'r Gog*' is by Joseph P Clancy.)

Clychau'r Gog
R Williams Parry

Dyfod pan ddêl y gwcw,
Myned pan êl y maent,
Y gwyllt atgofus bersawr,
Yr hen lesmeiriol baent.
Cyrraedd, ac yna ffarwelio,
Ffarwelio. Och! na pharhaent

Bluebells
R Williams Parry

They come when the cuckoo comes
When she goes, they go too
The wild nostalgic scent,
The old enchanting hue.
Arriving, then bidding goodbye,
Ah, but their days are few

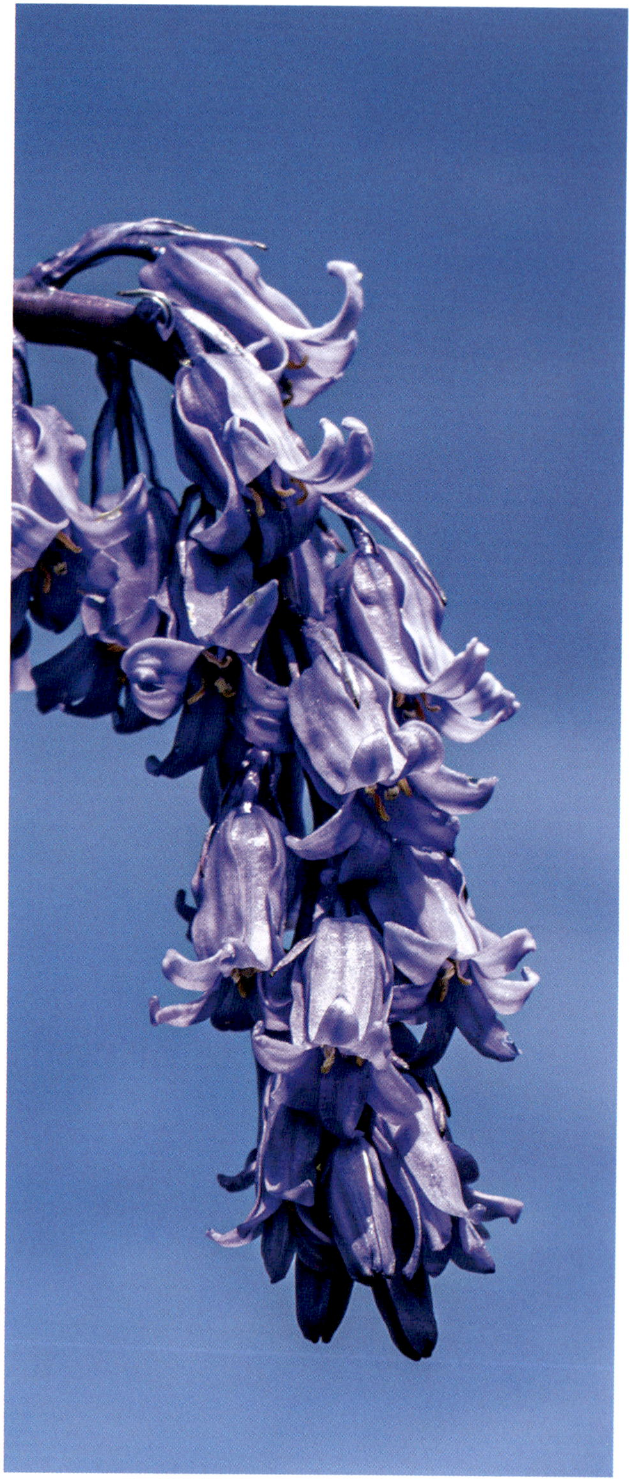

Right and next page:
Bluebell
Clychau'r Gog
Hyacinthoides non-scripta

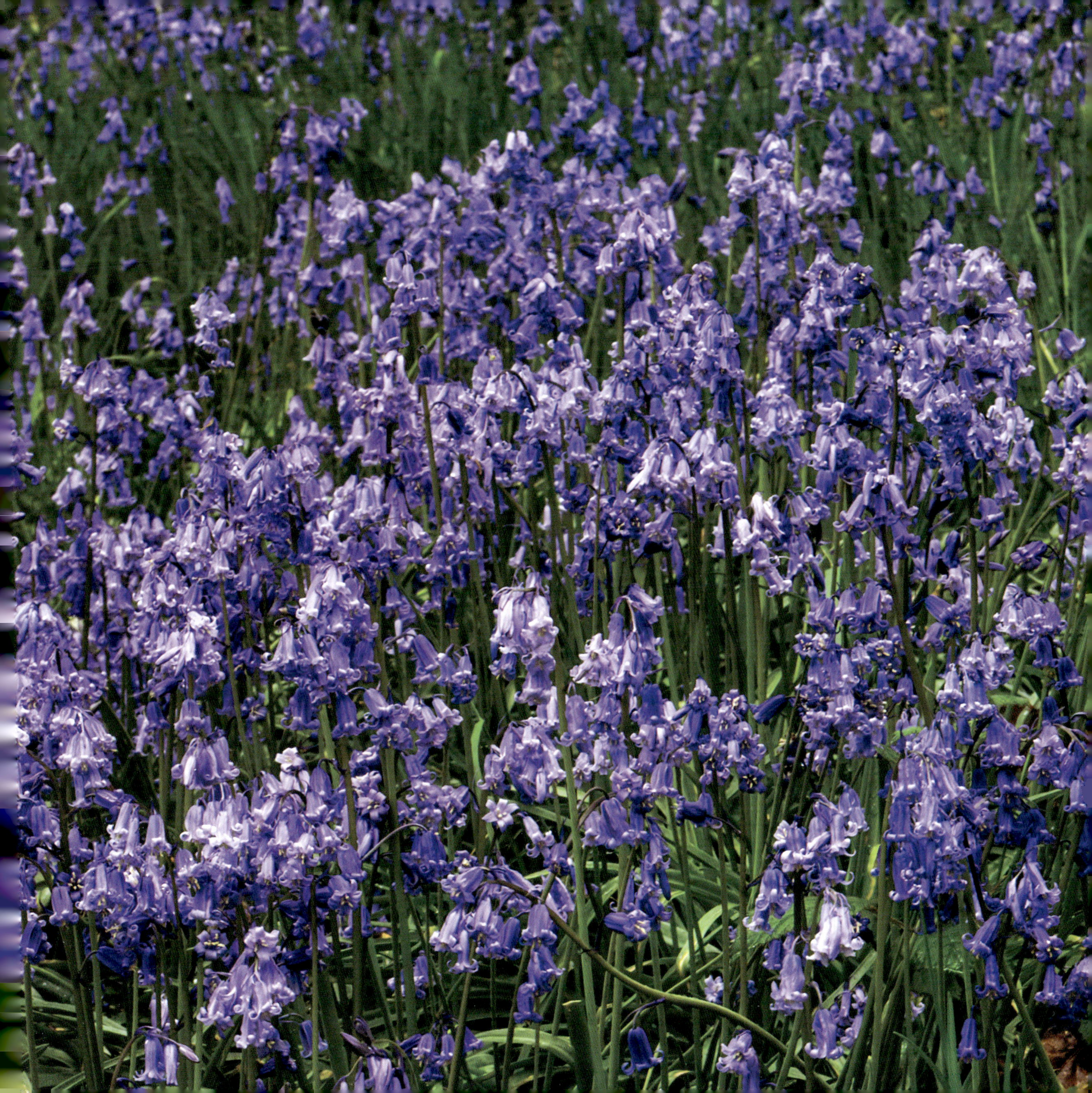

Skomer with Ynys Dewi (Ramsey) in the distance

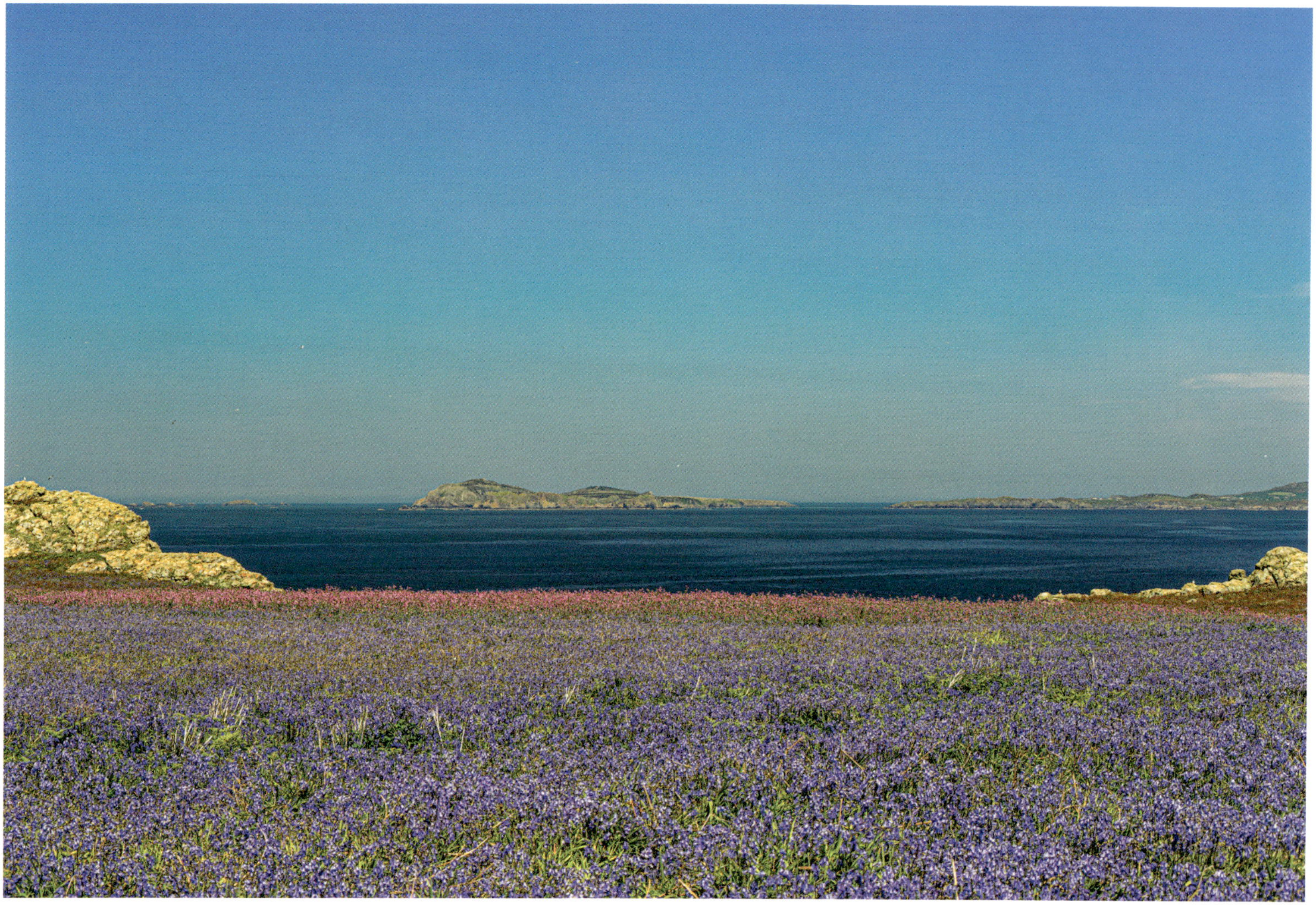

Bluebell Clychau'r Gog *Hyacinthoides non-scripta*

North Haven, Skomer, 1980

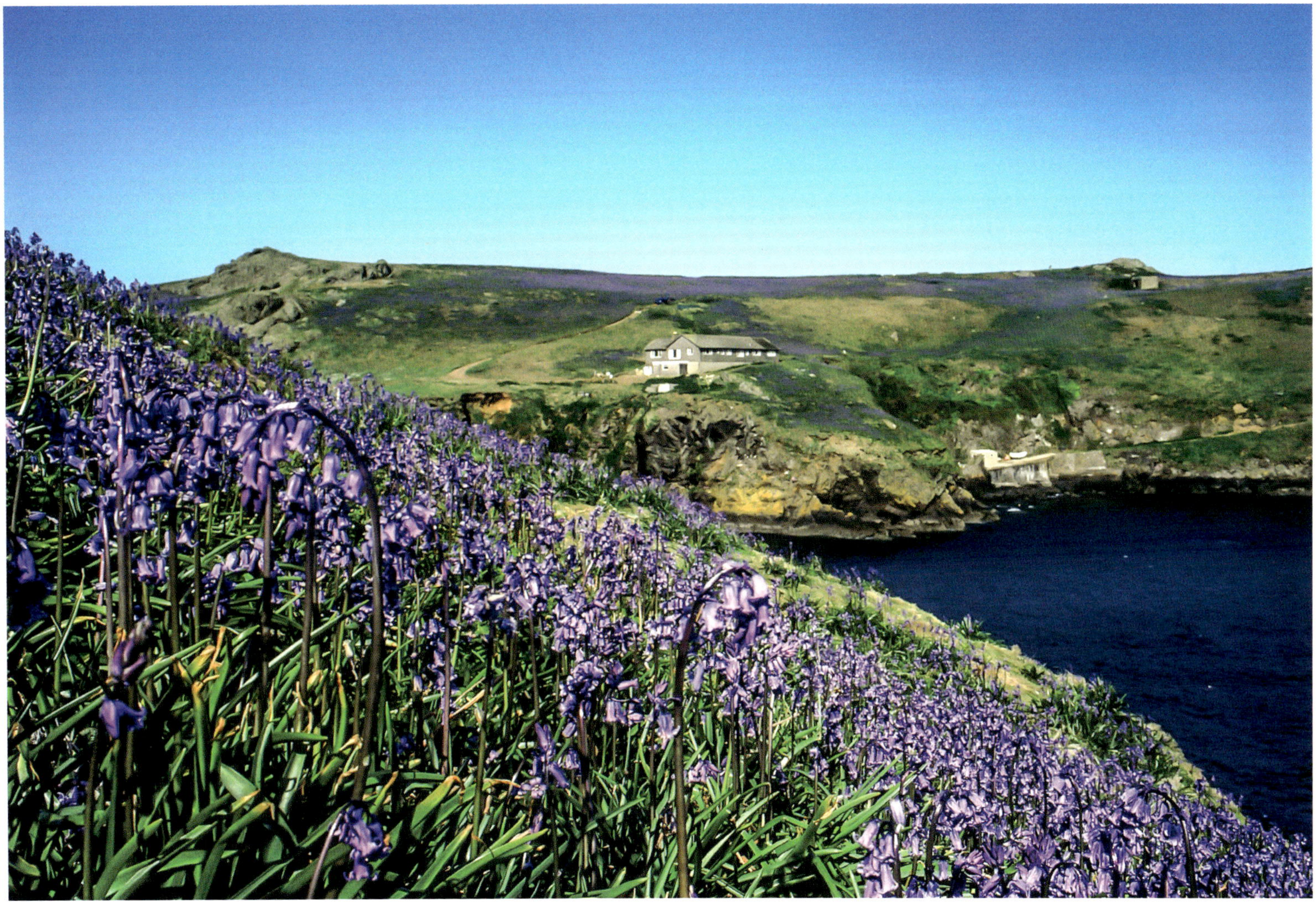

Bluebell Clychau'r Gog *Hyacinthoides non-scripta*

Skomer

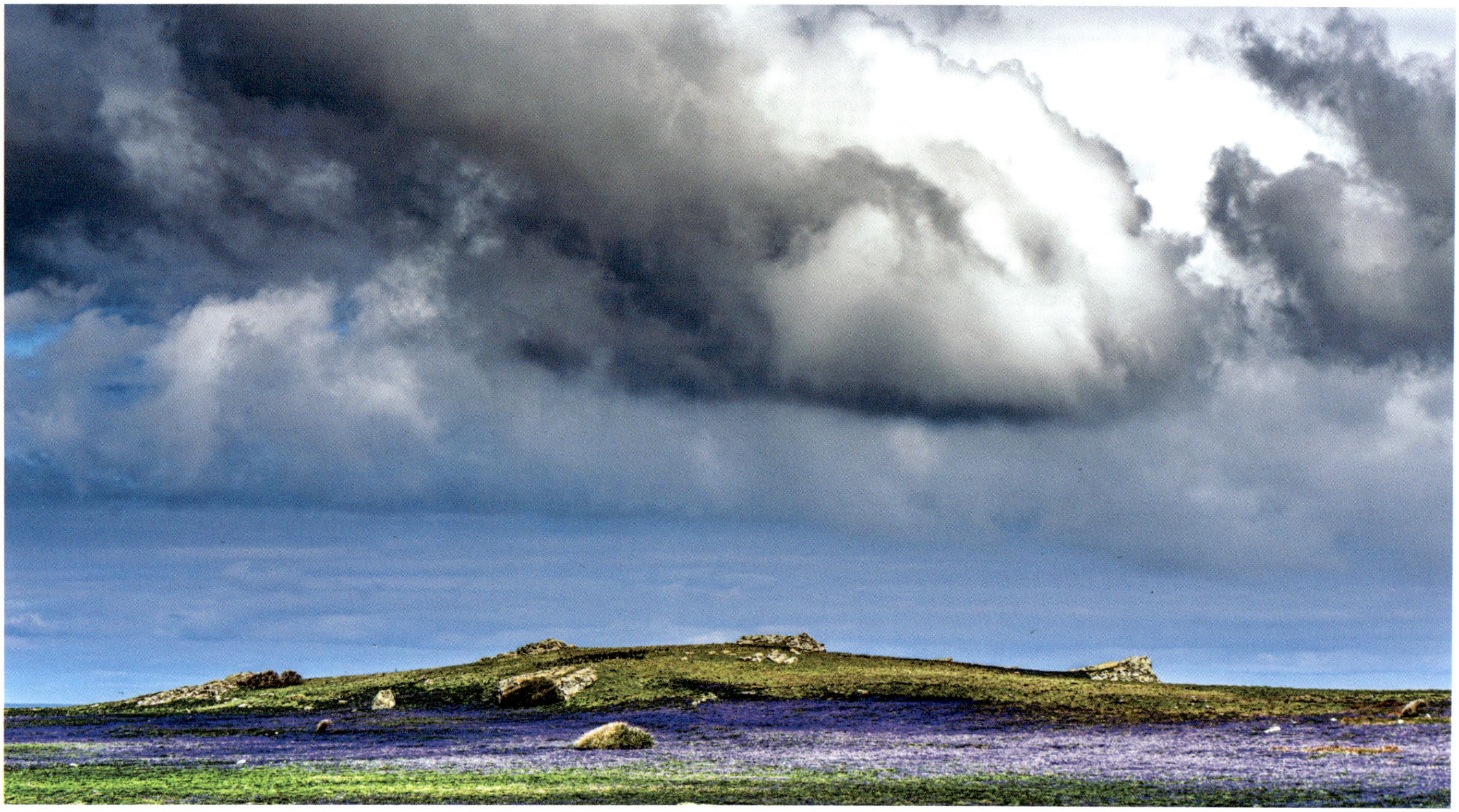

Bluebell Clychau'r Gog *Hyacinthoides non-scripta*

Spring Squill
Seren y Gwanwyn
Scilla verna

Spring squill has a Welsh name which means 'star of springtime'. The small star-shaped violet-blue flowers grow in a cluster on a short stem, but sadly, unlike bluebells, they have no scent. They are usually sprinkled sparsely through the sward, but there are a few places – such as Stackpole Head – where some years the squill appears in vast carpets, so dense that they can almost challenge the best of the bluebell cliffs. Regrettably, these delightful plants are in decline, and their distribution is now more or less limited to the west coasts of Britain and parts of the east coast of Ireland.

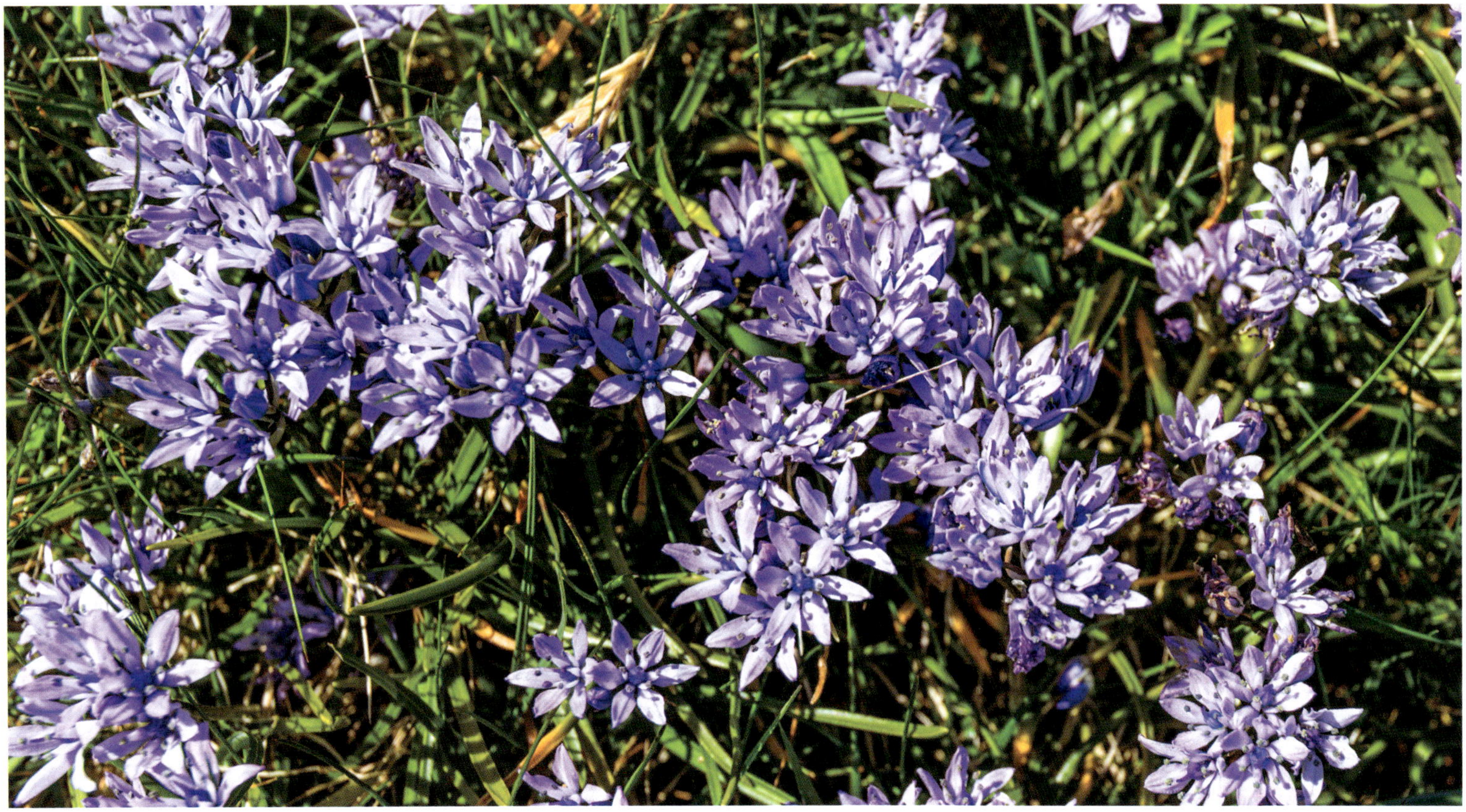

Spring Squill Seren y Gwanwyn *Scilla verna*

Saddle Point, Broad Haven

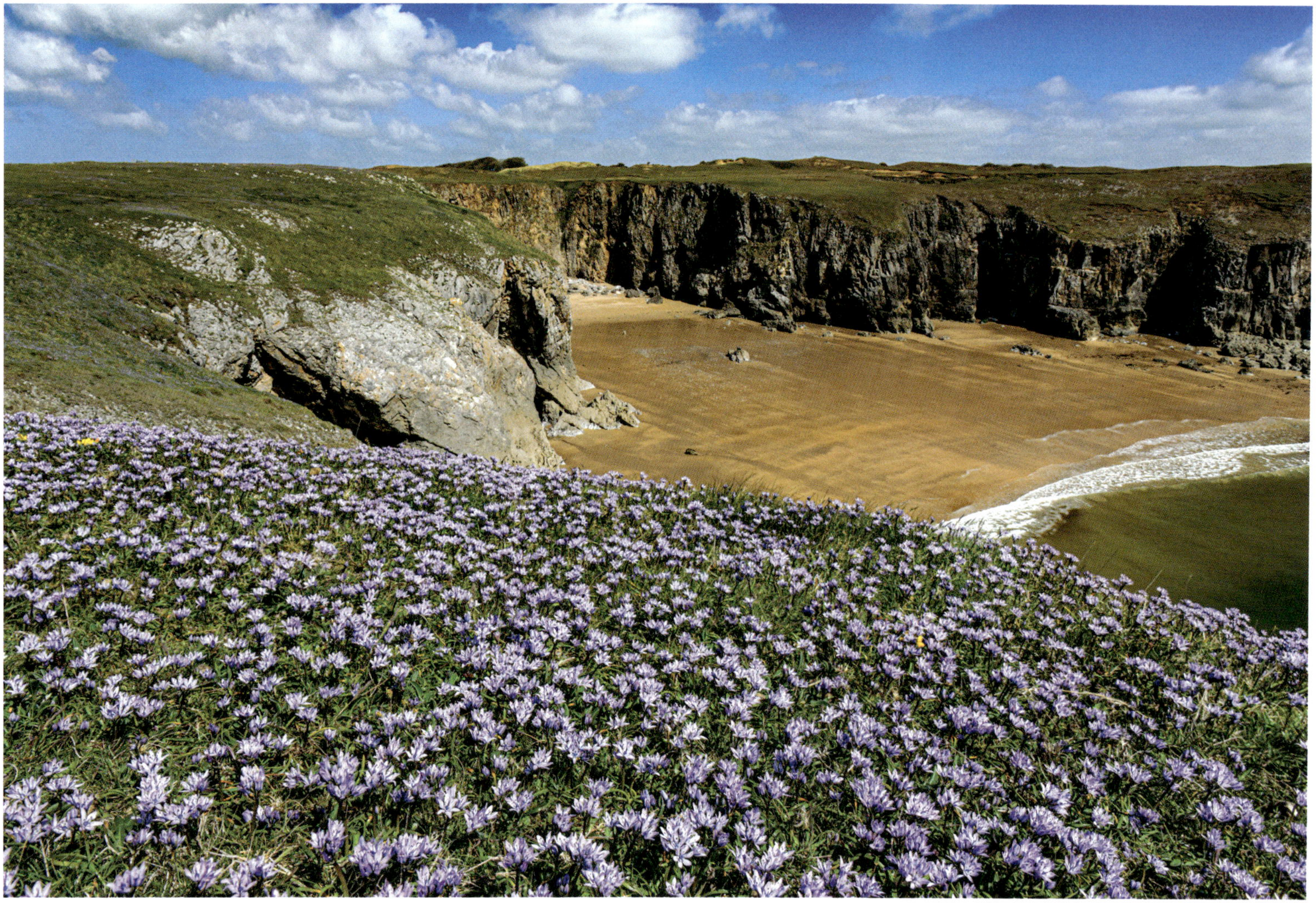

Spring Squill Seren y Gwanwyn *Scilla verna*

Ramsons Craf y Geifr

Ramsons
Craf y Geifr
Allium ursinum

Ramsons, also known as wild garlic or bear's garlic, are the wild relatives of garlic and onions. I spent a long time considering the inclusion of this species, because although it is frequently encountered on the coast, I always tend to associate it more with damp, calcareous deciduous woodlands. I finally resolved my dilemma when I realised that my favourite location for wild garlic is the coastal woodlands and lake-sides at Bosherston Lily Ponds. A spring visit is a special experience. The verdant mass of lush garlic indicates the presence of hundreds of thousands, if not millions, of bulbs that must exist unseen below the woodland soil. The dense swarm of vegetation, with each flower stem bearing an umbel of white starry flowers surrounded by grey-green oval leaves, can completely dominate parts of the woodland. The pungent aroma becomes so thick and heavy that it is sometimes almost overwhelming, especially as the flowering season is drawing to a close. Wild garlic exploits much the same niche in woodlands as bluebells, completing their flowering season before the woodland floor is denied any useful light by the closing of the tree canopy. Garlic cannot grow in the permanent shade of a conifer forest.

The earliest evidence of people using wild garlic for food comes from a Stone Age settlement in Denmark. It continues to be popular today, frequently appearing on menus in some of the most sophisticated restaurants. It also features in just about every guide to foraging wild food that I have ever read. The origin of the less common name, bear's garlic, and its scientific name, *ursinum* (meaning 'bear'), is fascinating. It stems from the belief that brown bears ate wild garlic bulbs following their long winter hibernation. The garlic would remove the build-up of toxins and help the bears regain their strength. Wild garlic also possesses medicinal properties which we consider useful, and is used for treating cardiovascular, respiratory and digestive ailments.

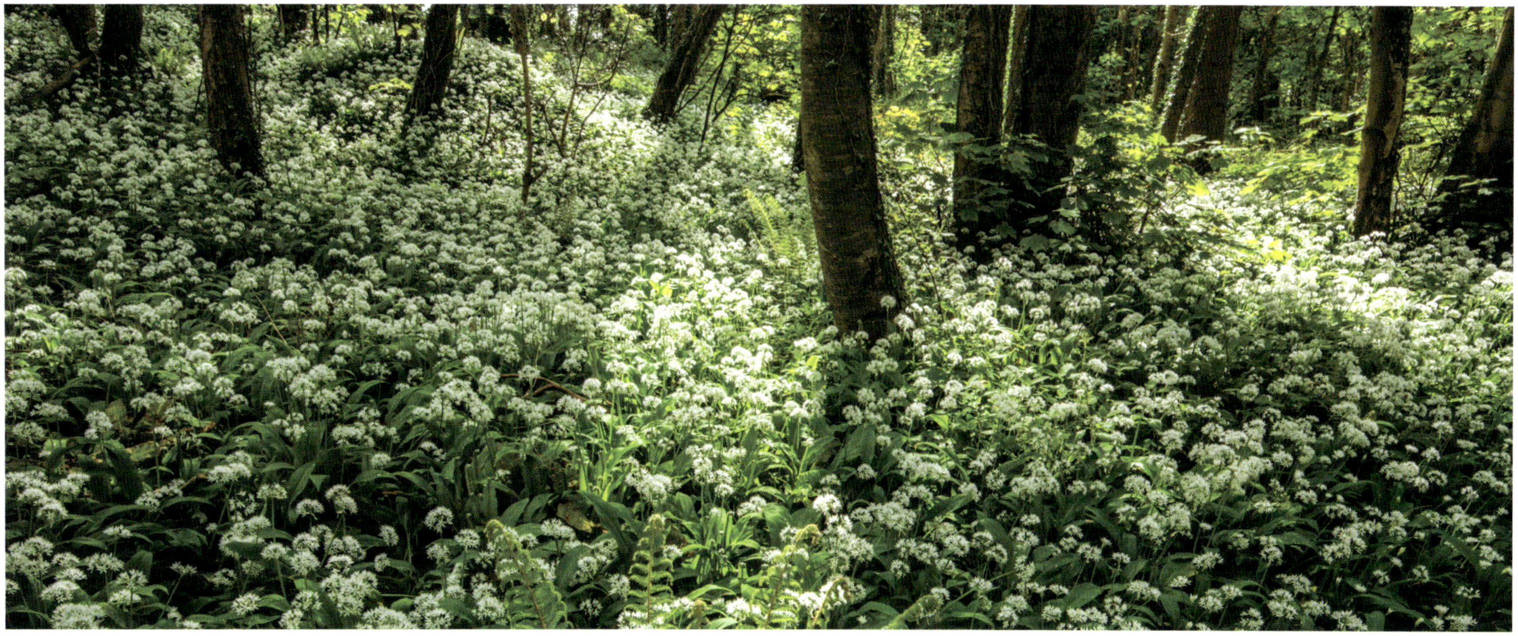

Ramsons Craf y Geifr *Allium ursinum*

Lodge Park, Stackpole Estate

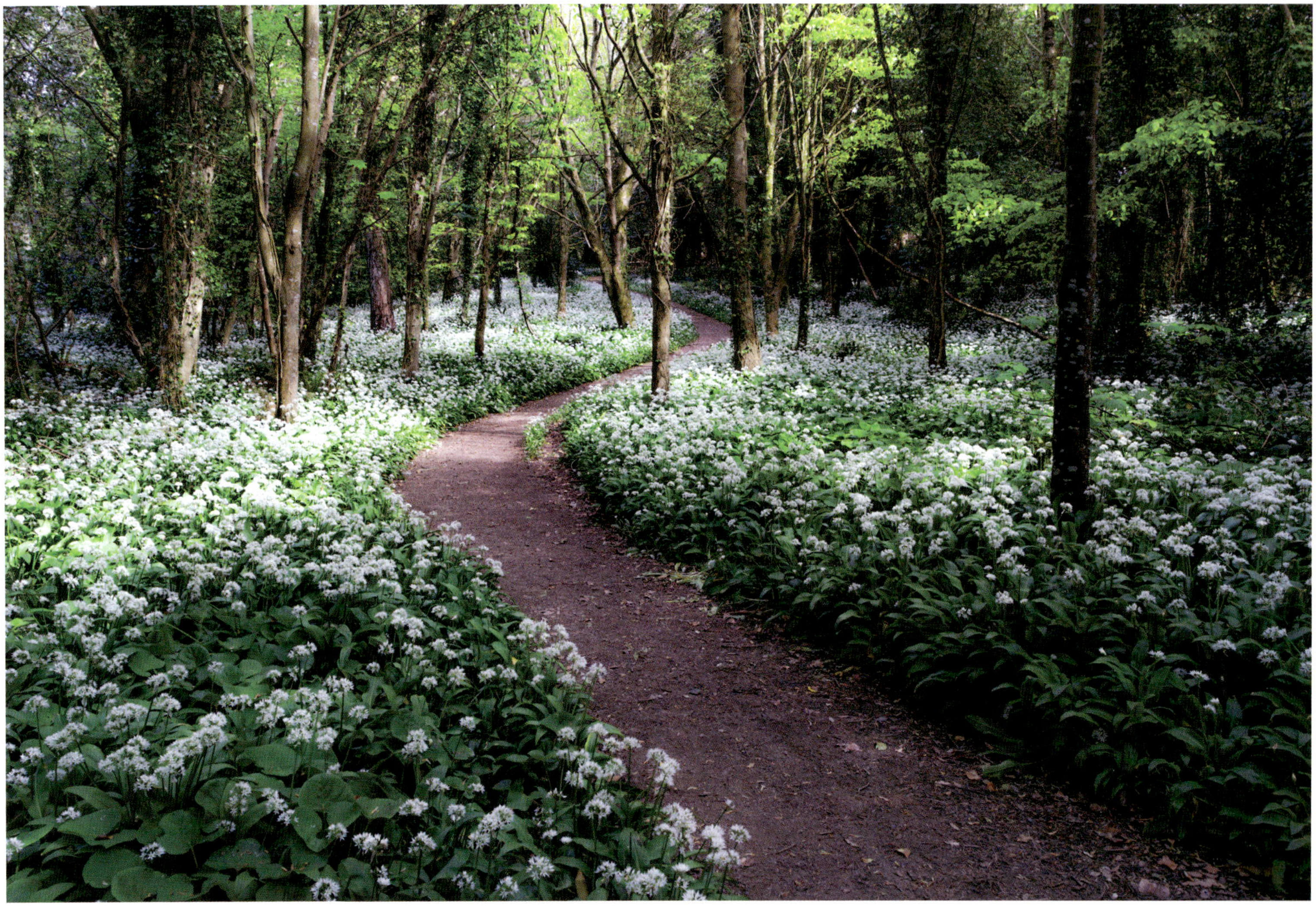

Ramsons Craf y Geifr *Allium ursinum*

Orchid Family Teulu'r Tegeirian

Globally, orchids are one of the largest families of flowering plants, and we have over 20 species in Wales. The coasts, and especially the sand dunes, are among the richest habitats for orchids. Occasionally, orchids can be locally abundant (there is, for example, always a springtime profusion of common spotted and pyramidal orchids on the dunes at Broad Haven, in south Pembrokeshire), but many species are rare and elusive. For good reasons, we give orchids an elevated status within our flora. They are widely admired for their delicate, exotic beauty and are said to possess mysterious or even magical qualities.

Charles Darwin, the father of evolutionary biology, was fascinated by orchids. In 1862 he published a book called *Fertilisation of Orchids*, writing in the closing chapter: 'In my examination of Orchids, hardly any fact has so much struck me as the endless diversity of structure, the prodigality of resources, for gaining the very same end, namely, the fertilisation of one flower by the pollen of another.' It is this 'diversity of structure' that makes for such a varied and visually exciting family – one which Darwin himself confessed 'interested me more than almost anything in my life'.

Orchids have tiny seeds – so small that, in the early stages of germination, they must rely on a relationship with mycorrhizal fungi. The fungal threads penetrate the orchid seed and provide it with all the necessary nutrients. The seeds germinate to produce a protocorm, a seedling stage almost unique to orchids. This grows root-like structures, which are also penetrated by fungal threads. Fungi continue to provide orchids with food until they are large enough to produce leaves and photosynthesize. This symbiotic relationship with fungi is maintained even when the orchids are fully grown, at which point the fungi receive their reward of sugar from the orchids.

I have chosen a selection of orchids to feature here, to include some of the most common ones along with a few rarer species.

Common Spotted-orchid
Tegeirian Brych
Dactylorhiza fuchsii

Common spotted-orchid is a member of the genus *Dactylorhiza*. The genus name has a Greek origin, meaning 'finger root'. This is because the roots have two to five flattened, finger-like tubers. Members of this genus are notoriously difficult to identify, as they are almost endlessly variable and they hybridise freely. Sometimes I think it best to just enjoy their beauty and variety, regardless of precisely who they are. You will find their tall, deep pink to white flowering spikes throughout the coastal zone, and quite frequently growing by the road alongside your route to the coast. Overleaf are two photographs of common spotted-orchids, illustrating the impressive and confusing variety within the species.

Pyramidal Orchid
Tegeirian Bera
Anacamptis pyramidalis

Pyramidal orchids are one of the few orchids that are increasing in number in Wales. You will find them all round the coast, but sand dunes and limestone cliffs are the best places. They can grow as tall as 60 cm and, generally, the flower heads sit above the surrounding vegetation, with the dense pyramid of small flowers clearly on display. The colours can be variable, including everything from darkish reds, through a variety of pinks, to the occasional white.

Green-winged Orchid
Tegeirian y Waun
Anacamptis morio

Green-winged orchids were once widespread, but now have a very restricted distribution. The best place to see these delicate blooms in profusion is the limestone cliff above St Govan's Chapel, in south Pembrokeshire. There is a spectacular and thriving colony which is fortunately protected by the National Park.

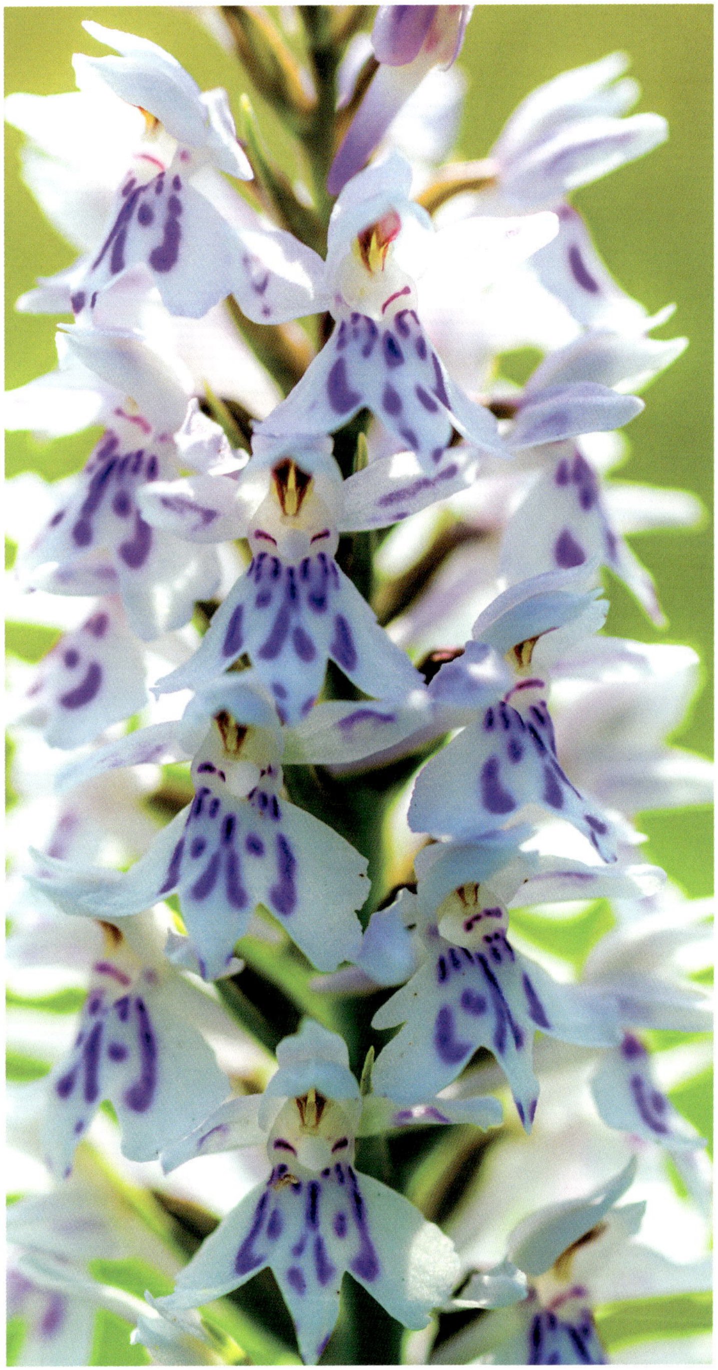

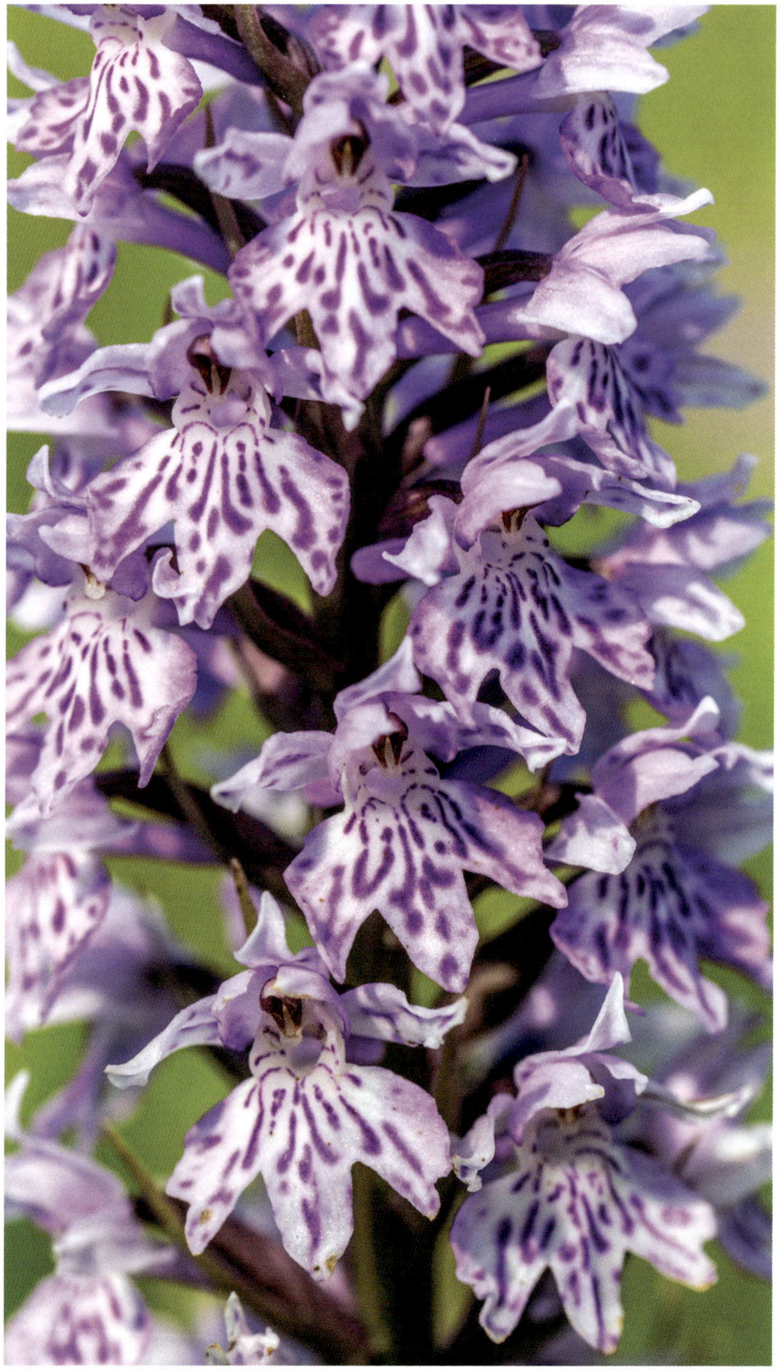

Common Spotted-orchid Tegeirian Brych *Dactylorhiza fuchsii*

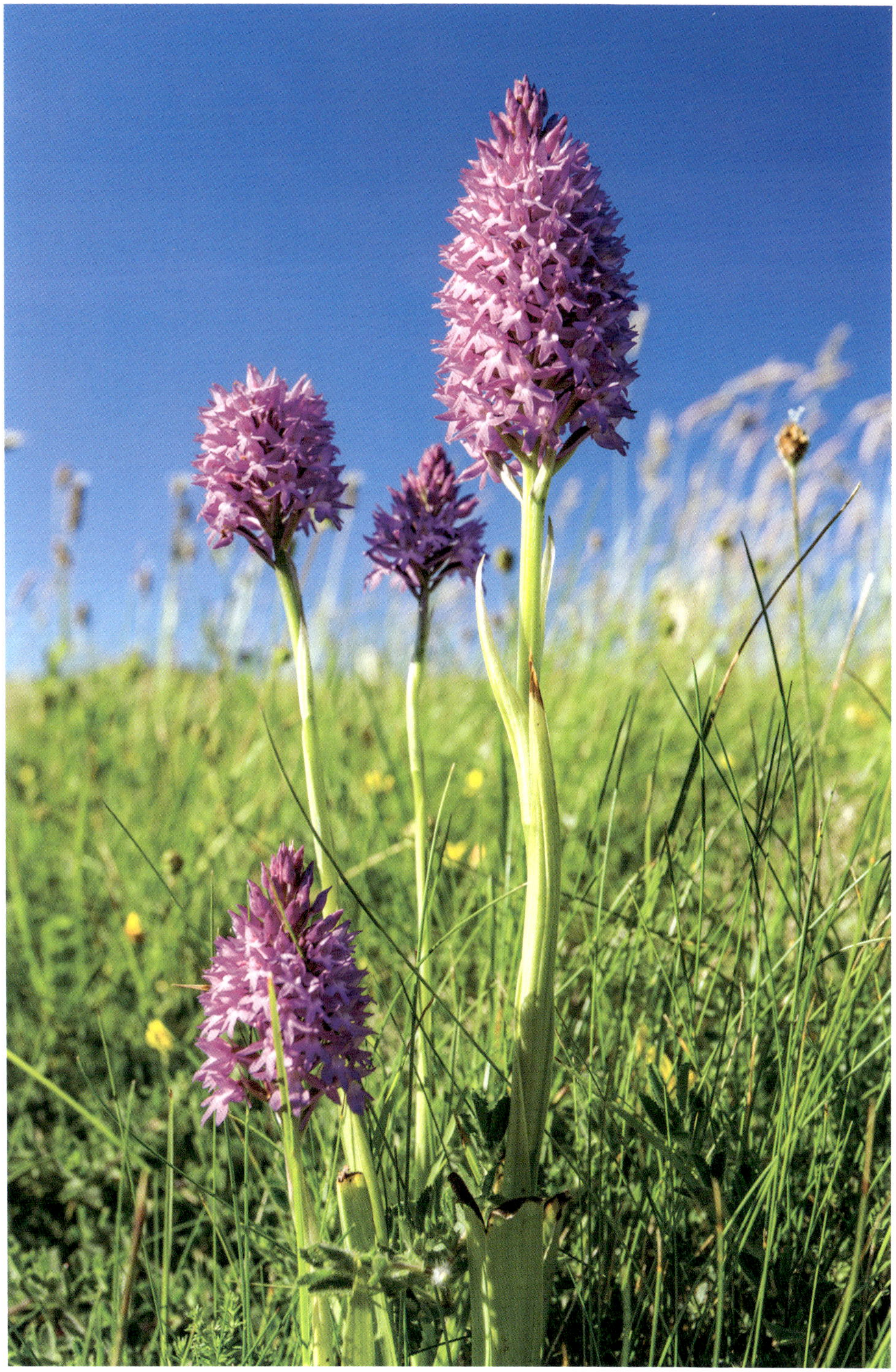

Pyramidal Orchid Tegeirian Bera *Anacamptis pyramidalis*

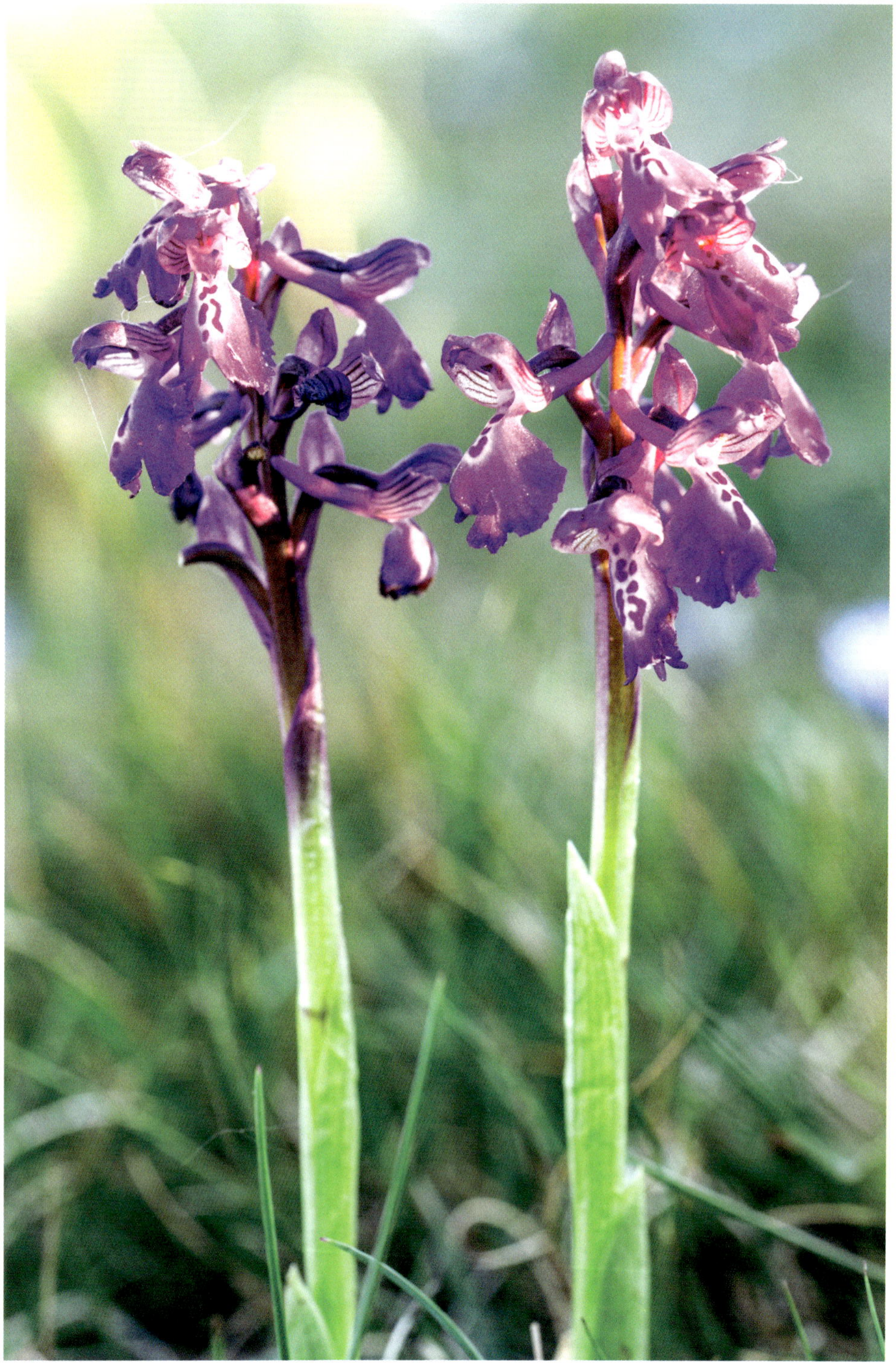

Green-winged Orchid Tegeirian y Waun *Anacamptis morio*

Common Twayblade
Caineirian
Neottia ovata

Common twayblades are widespread around the coast, but are easily overlooked because they lack any colour apart from shades of green, which blend subtly with the surrounding vegetation. The pair of broad (for an orchid) oval leaves at the base of the stem is very characteristic. I have included a close-up picture of the flowers, which are sometimes described as looking like a small person, although you might need a creative imagination to see it.

Greater Butterfly-orchid
Tegeirian Llydanwyrdd
Platanthera chlorantha

Greater butterfly-orchids are named because their open flower spikes, with spreading petals, can look like the wings of a flutter or kaleidoscope of white butterflies (two strikingly lovely collective nouns for a group of butterflies). I had never been truly convinced about this analogy until a friend told me to stand above the bloom, looking directly down on it – and, yes, I had to concede that I could see the butterflies. The Welsh name translates simply as 'broad green orchid', which doesn't seem to quite capture the essence of such a beautiful flower.

Marsh Helleborine
Caldrist y Gors
Epipactis palustris

Marsh helleborine bears beautifully delicate white and pink, or sometimes purple, flowers. Around coastal habitats, they favour damp sand-dune slacks, with Freshwater West being a good location. They can grow in dense clusters, blooming from late spring and early summer through to the beginning of autumn. Their name, helleborine, is something of a misnomer: true helleborines, known for their toxicity, are a very different plant genus. Marsh helleborines are said to represent beauty, grace and resilience.

Bee Orchid
Tegeirian y Wenynen
Ophrys apifera

Bee orchids must be one of my all-time favourites. They manage to mimic a female bumblebee so successfully that the males attracted to mate with them end up pollinating the flowers. Sadly, the bee species that the orchids attract do not live in the UK and so here the orchids are self-pollinating. They are a small but surprisingly sturdy species, and I have learned that the best places to look for them are in disturbed ground, including areas in stable sand dunes which have been trampled by cattle. The upright stem bears a loose cluster of up to 12 unmistakably bee-like flowers, with pink sepals to mimic the wings, and furry brown lips with yellow markings for the body. The scientific name, *ophrys*, is derived from the Greek word for eyebrow (apparently because women in ancient Rome used the flowers to darken their eyebrows), and *apifera* means 'bee-bringing', for obvious reasons.

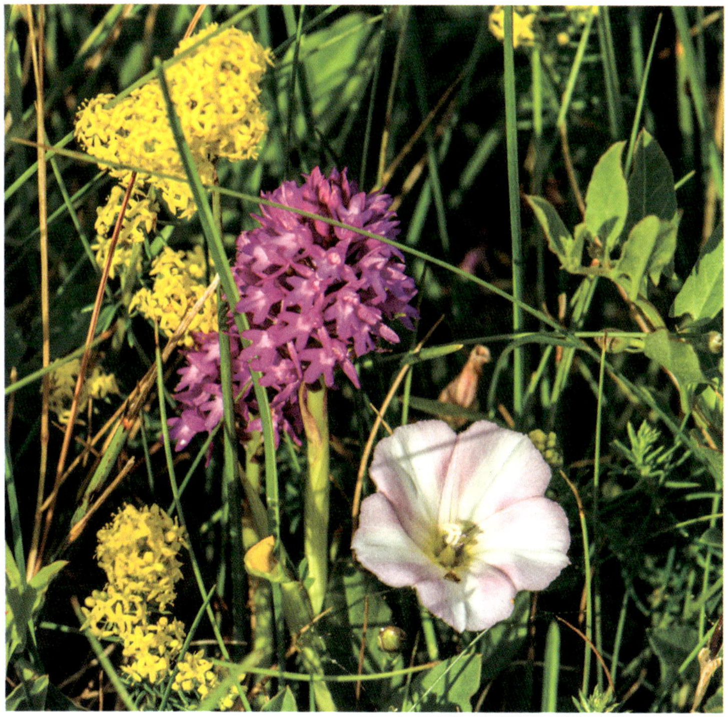

Pyramidal Orchid Tegeirian Bera *Anacamptis pyramidalis*

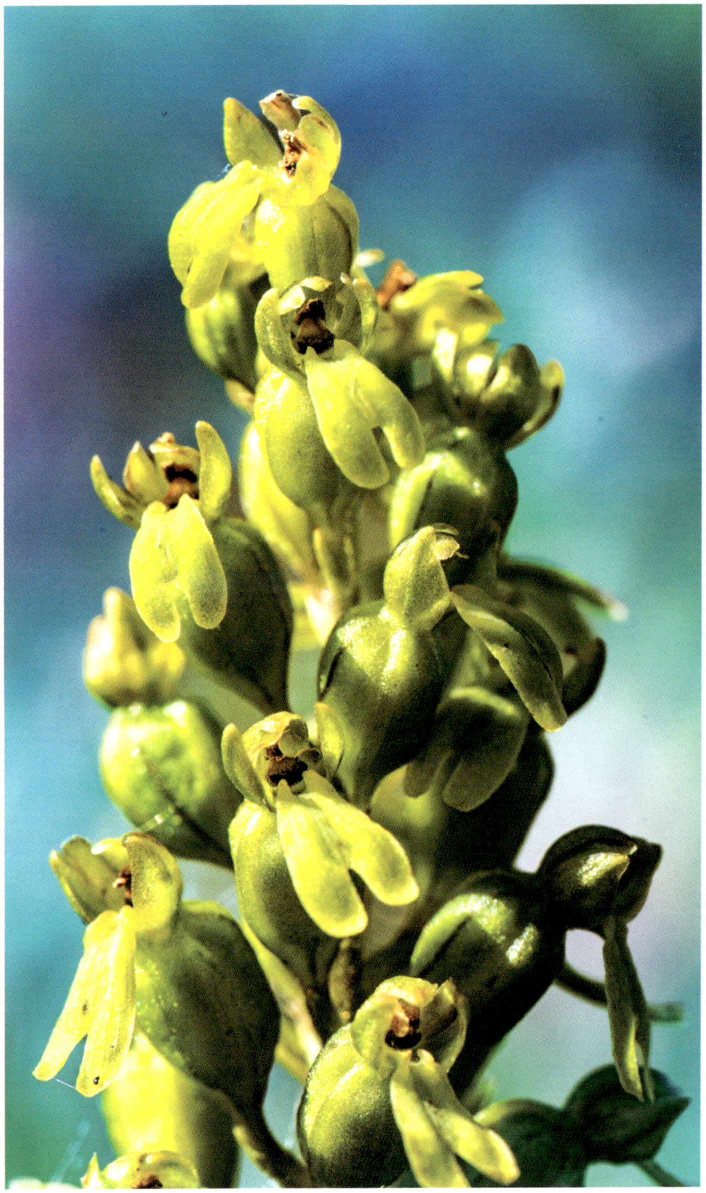

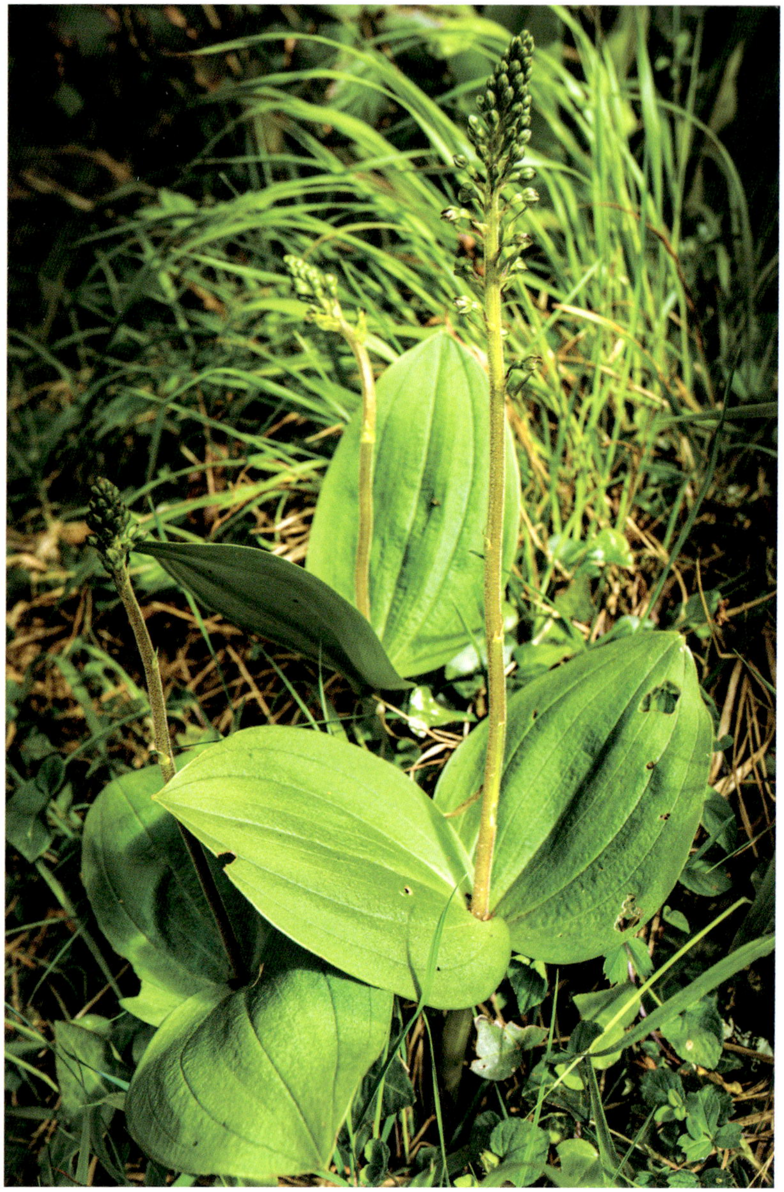

Common Twayblade Caineirian *Neottia ovata*

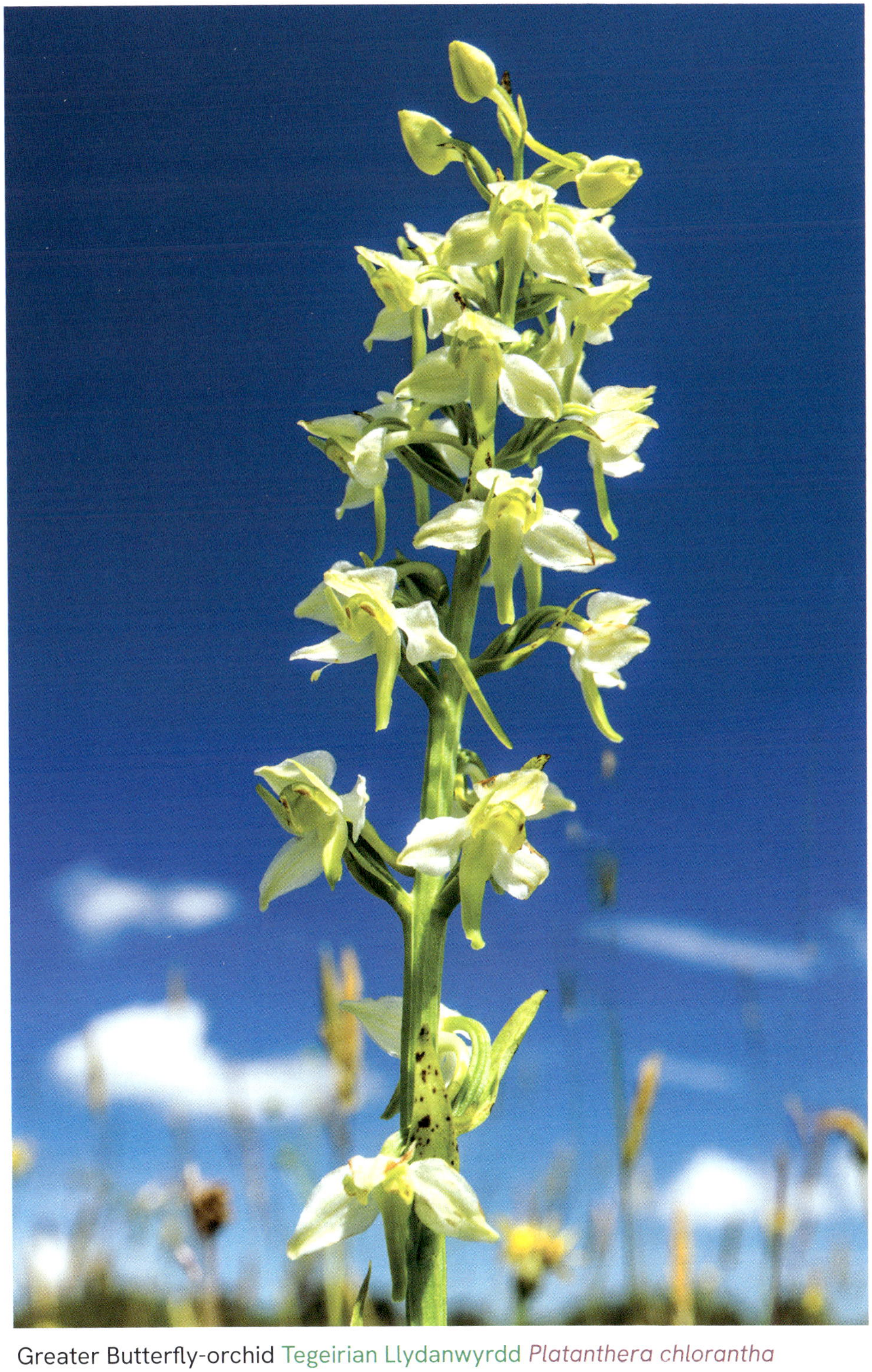

Greater Butterfly-orchid Tegeirian Llydanwyrdd *Platanthera chlorantha*

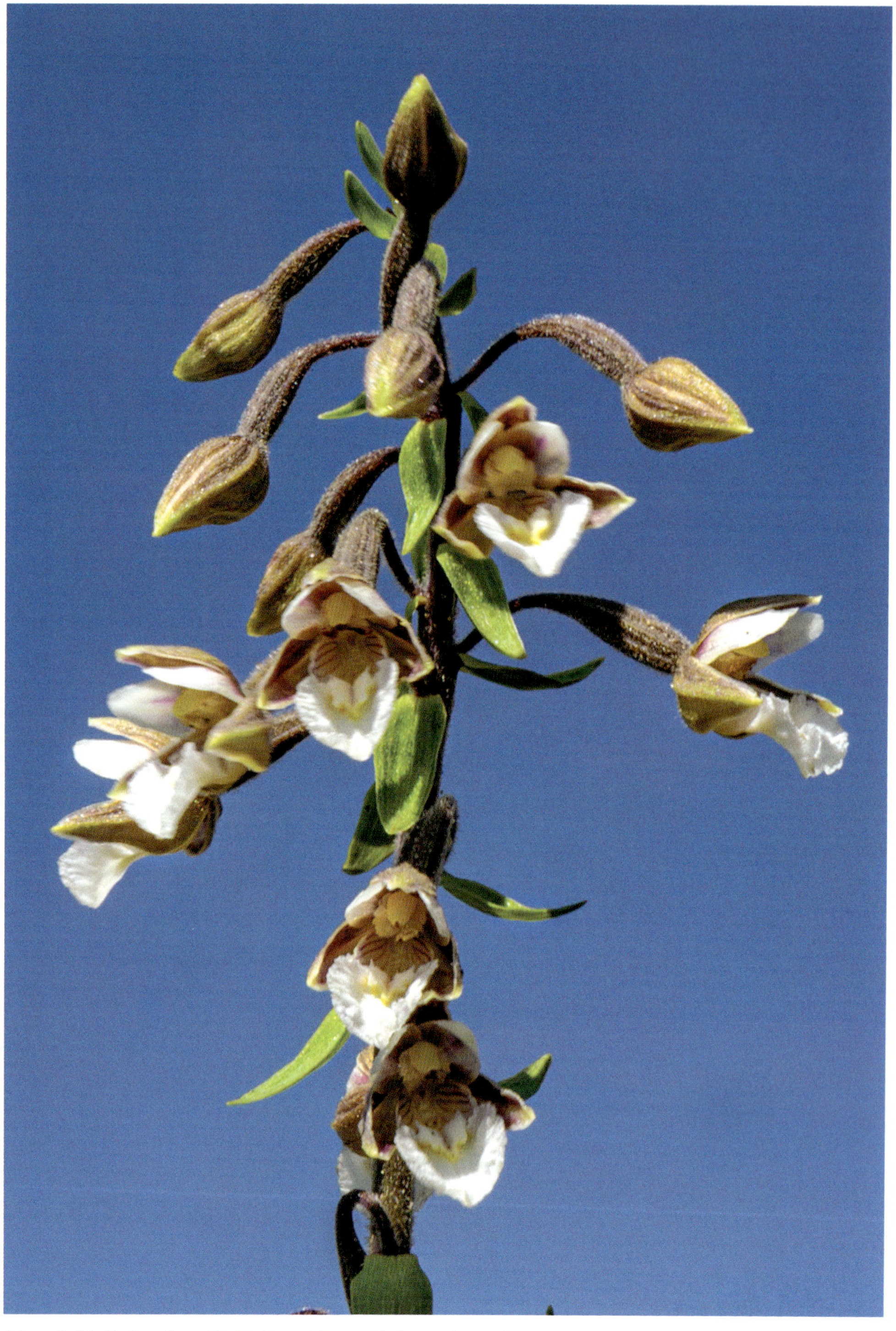

Marsh Helleborine Caldrist y Gors *Epipactis palustris*

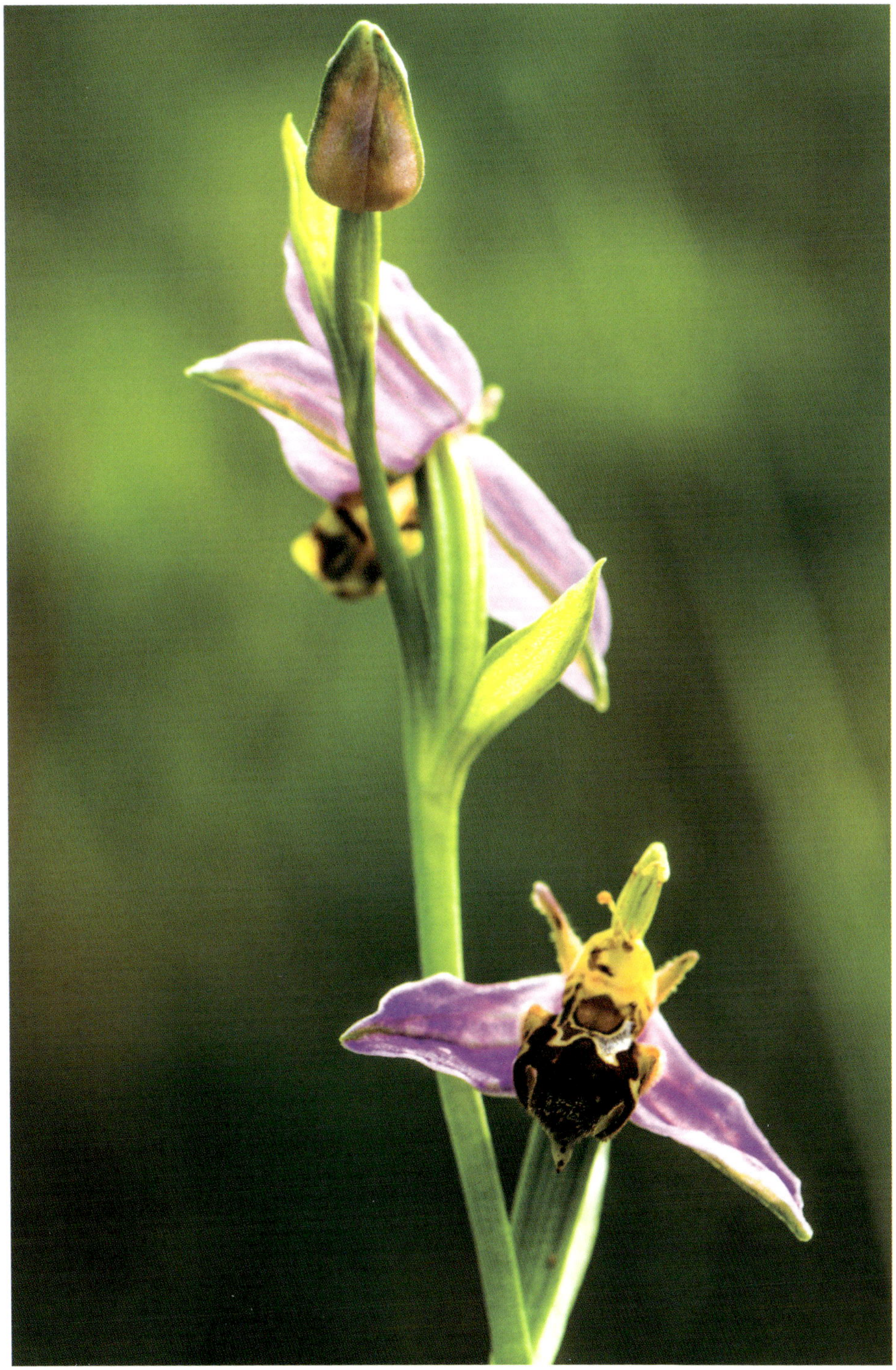

Bee Orchid Tegeirian y Wenynen *Ophrys apifera*

Acknowledgements

I could never have imagined that it would fall to me to write this, but, sadly, Mike died very suddenly and unexpectedly just a few months before the planned publication date. The manuscript was complete, and Mike was so excited about taking it through its final stages that there was never any question of it not going ahead without him.

If I'd had to summarise Mike in a single word, it would have been 'Skomer'. The island where he spent ten years as warden shaped him into the person he became, and I know he would have described it as the highlight of his life. But looking back over these words and pictures from a new perspective, I see a whole life here, crammed with the places he adored, which truly encompasses his vibrant personality. This book was actually created over decades, and only a tiny fragment of his experiences made it as far as this final selection. With the exception of a few lucky shots, every picture was probably years in the making. He searched determinedly for the right flower in the perfect setting, with the light falling exactly as it should. Even if he had walked miles, a single tarnished petal or a boring sky might mean that the photograph was abandoned, perhaps for another whole year. He gradually learnt that flowering seasons can be cruelly brief.

Though he travelled the world for his conservation work, I realise more clearly than ever, now, that his heart never left Wales. Every page shines with the certainty that this was the place he loved and cared passionately about: its people, its landscapes, its language and traditions.

The final honing of Mike's finished work, to make it everything he had hoped for, has been an extraordinary collaboration by some wonderful people. Carolyn Hodges, his editor, worked tirelessly, with an almost supernatural eye for detail, and held the whole thing together with dedication, professionalism and kindness. She had got to know Mike well when they worked on his book about Skomer, and I believe that no-one could have put more love and care into this. John Rodwell, a dear and long-standing friend of Mike's, has provided invaluable support throughout this process, and it has been a privilege to have the guidance of such an eminent botanist. Goronwy Wynne kindly helped with aspects of botany from a Welsh-language perspective, and I know how delighted Mike would have been by this contribution from an expert whose work he so admired. Sincere thanks go to Talat Chaudhri for his absolutely meticulous input and the generosity with which he has given his time to advise on details of Welsh vocabulary and grammar. Our designer Richard Huw Pritchard, who also worked with Mike on his Skomer book, has been patient and perceptive in trying to bring Mike's vision to fruition, and has ultimately produced something beautiful that all of us involved can feel proud of. I would like to express my gratitude to everyone at Y Lolfa who has worked so hard to see this book through to completion.

I did not want this to turn into a list of names, because that would inevitably mean leaving so many out. There are simply too many people who have inspired Mike throughout his life, but, now that I have started, it seems almost impossible not to add just a few of those whose enduring friendship has helped to develop his thoughts over decades: Lizzie Wilberforce, David Wheeler, Doug Oliver, Chris Perrins, Paul Culyer, Stephen Evans, Bob Haycock, Clive Faulkner, Mike Howe, Denis Bellamy, Tom Hellawell, James Perrins, Roger Bray and Ian Tillotson. I know this list barely grazes the surface of those people Mike would have liked to remember. He always recognised how much he gained from the variety of people and fresh perspectives he encountered: the schoolteacher who first took him on nature walks, aged four; the uncle who imparted a farmer's knowledge of the land and its deeper meanings; the countless friends and colleagues with such wide-ranging expertise; the students he taught, whose constant questioning kept his ideas alive. I hope anyone reading this and remembering Mike with fondness will feel included here.

Mike was a true enthusiast. Whatever he did, he did it with all his heart, and that could not apply to anything more than this book. His closeness to nature brought him profound happiness. I would love to think that these pages could persuade readers to glimpse the world, for a moment, through his eyes and be inspired by the beauty he found all around us. It may just bring an interlude of uplifting calm, but – as it was for Mike – it could be life-changing.

Rosanne Alexander
June 2026

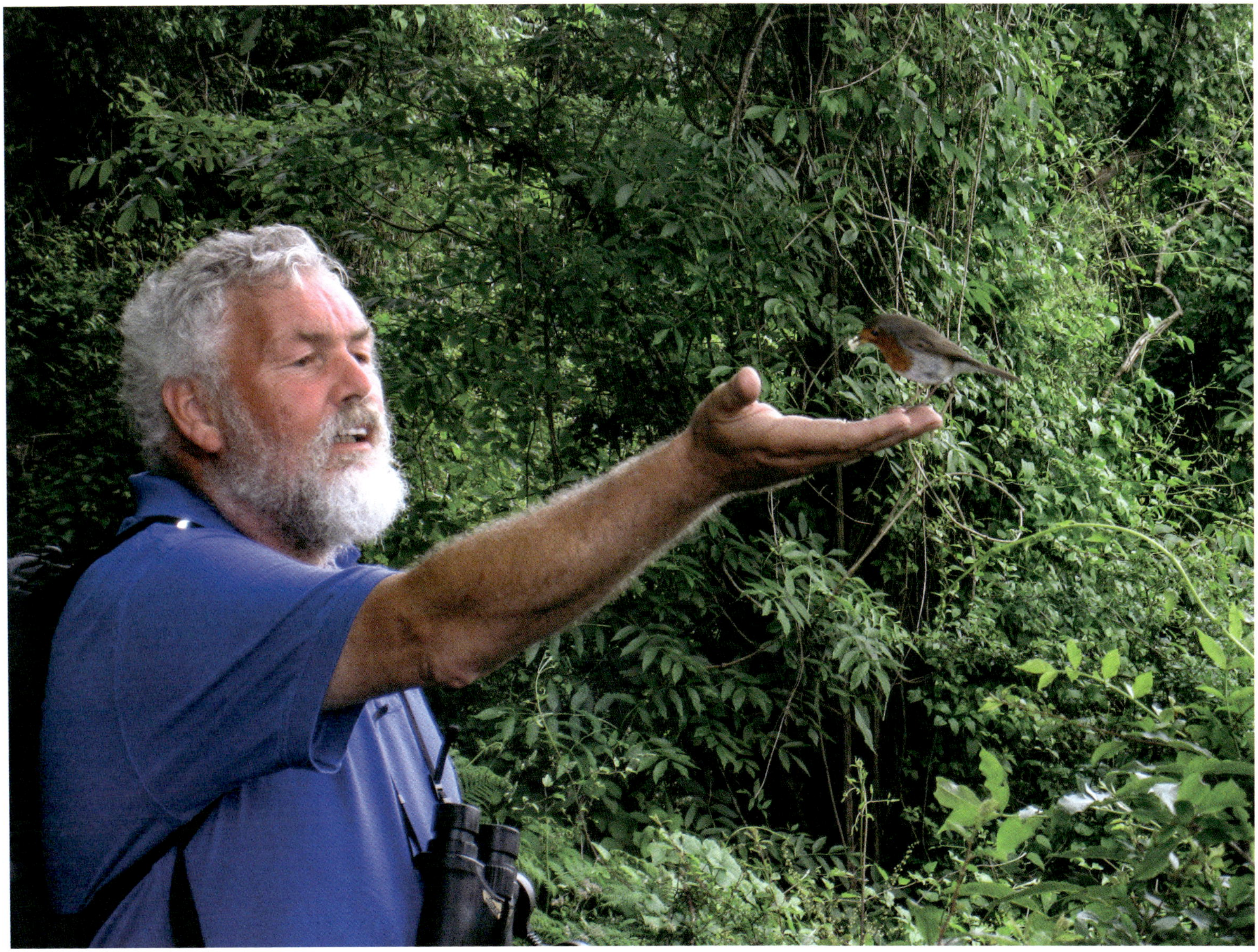

Mike Alexander

An excerpt from 'Lines Composed a Few Miles above Tintern Abbey, On Revisiting the Banks of the Wye during a Tour. July 13, 1798':

And I have felt
A presence that disturbs me with the joy
Of elevated thoughts; a sense sublime
Of something far more deeply interfused,
Whose dwelling is the light of setting suns,
And the round ocean and the living air,
And the blue sky, and in the mind of man:
A motion and a spirit, that impels
All thinking things, all objects of all thought,
And rolls through all things. Therefore am I still
A lover of the meadows and the woods,
And mountains; and of all that we behold
From this green earth; of all the mighty world
Of eye, and ear, – both what they half create,
And what perceive; well pleased to recognise
In nature and the language of the sense
The anchor of my purest thoughts, the nurse,
The guide, the guardian of my heart, and soul
Of all my moral being.

William Wordsworth

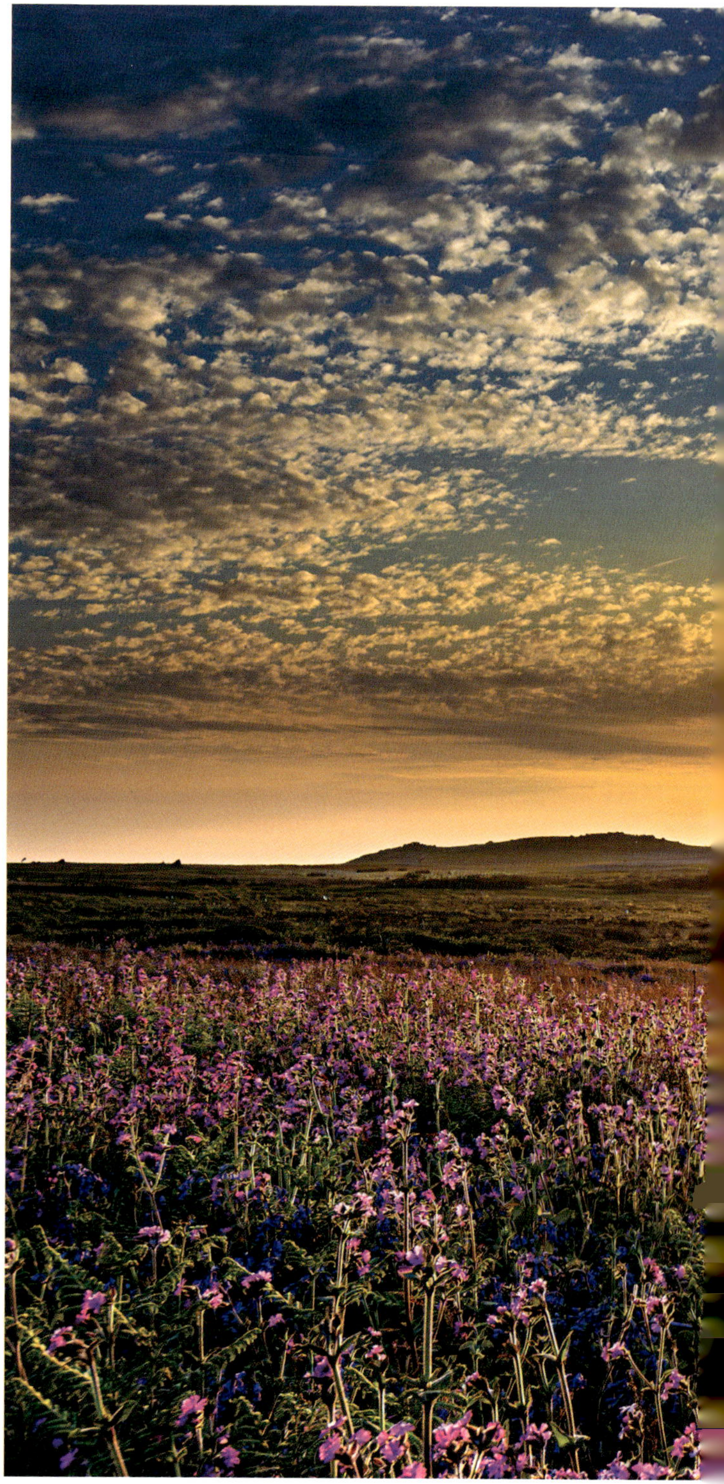

Bluebells and red campion on Skomer

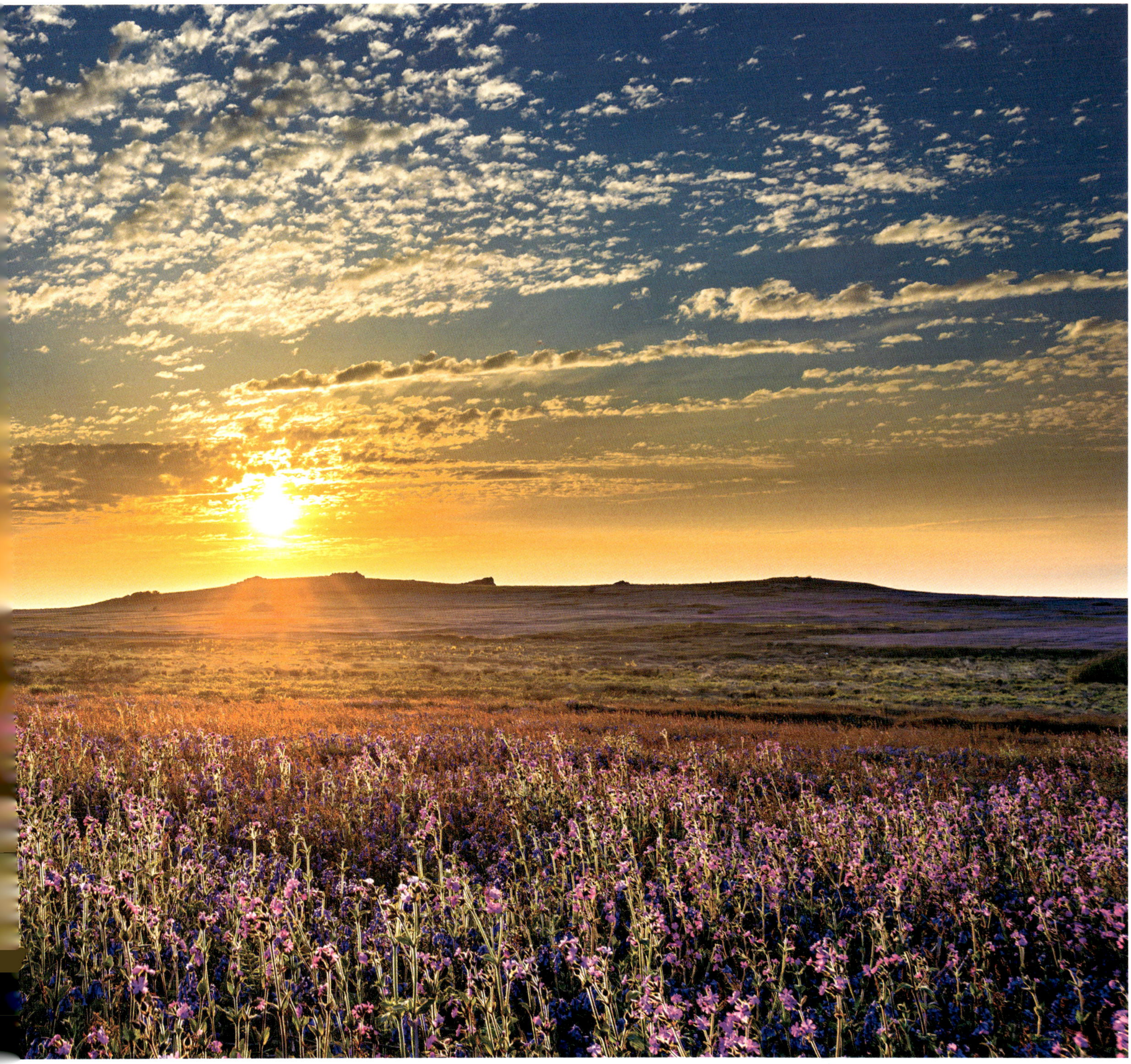

Glossary

agg./aggregate (after scientific name): group of closely related species treated, for simplicity, as a single collective species (see p.80)

basal leaves: leaves at the base of the stem

bloom: fine whitish coating on the surface of fruit or leaves

bract: a small, often leaf-like, structure, found at the base of some flowers where they meet the stem

calcareous (soil): rich in calcium carbonate, e.g. chalk, limestone or seashells

calyx: sepals forming the outer part of a flower

composite head: something appearing to be one flower but in fact made of multiple tiny flowers

cultivar: plant cultivated specifically to exhibit desired traits

cuticle: protective film covering leaves, shoots, etc

deciduous: shedding its leaves each autumn

fallow: land dug or ploughed but left unplanted to improve fertility

floret: small flower forming part of a larger flower-head

genus: group of similar plants including closely related species

germinate (of seed): start to grow

gland: capsule in a plant which produces and releases a substance

glaucous: bluish-green or bluish-grey

haw: fruit of the hawthorn

hemiparasitic: plants partly dependent on nourishment from host plant(s)

hip: fruit of the rose

husk: outer covering of seed

hybridise: two species reproducing to produce a new species

inflorescence: part of a plant made up of the flower-bearing stalks

leaflet: part of a multi-part leaf

legume: plants of the *Fabaceae* family (commonly known as the pea family)

linear leaves: long, narrow leaves with parallel sides

lobed leaves: leaves which are divided but not completely separated

perennial: plant living for more than two years

photosynthesise (of plants): produce food from light energy and chlorophyll

pinnate leaves: leaves with paired opposite leaflets

plant community: collection of different plants with a distinct and unique composition and structure, growing together (see fuller description on p.57)

prostrate: growing flat, close to the ground

relict: a previously widespread species or group, now occurring only in a few areas

rhizome: horizontal stem growing along or just under the ground, from which some plants grow

rosette: circular cluster of leaves at ground level at the base of a stem

scrub: vegetation dominated by low trees and bushes

sepal: outer part of a flower which protects the unopened bud

sessile (of flowers or leaves): growing directly from the stem with no stalk

slack: damp, low-lying area within a dune system which often supports rich vegetation

spur: slender, tubular, often nectar-producing projection, usually extending from the rear of a flower

ssp./subspecies (after scientific name): group within species with distinct physical or genetic differences

stamen: fine, delicate stalks growing in a flower's centre, which produce pollen

stand: distinct group of plants growing closely together

strandline: high tide line of seaweed, etc., which has been washed onto the beach

succulent: with thick, fleshy leaves or stems

sucker: strong shoot from the root, rhizome or stem base of a mature plant

sward: soil covered in grass and other herblike plants

taproot: the main long, thick root growing vertically downwards

trefoil: with compound leaves made up of three leaflets

tuber: short, thickened underground root or stem which stores nutrients

umbel: cluster of flowers with stalks of the same length springing from the same point, like an umbrella

variegated: edged or patterned with different colours

viscous (of liquid): thick and sticky

whorl: circular array of leaves of petals around the same point on the stem

winged: stem, seed pod, etc. with a raised 'wing' running along it

Sunset over the Llŷn Peninsula

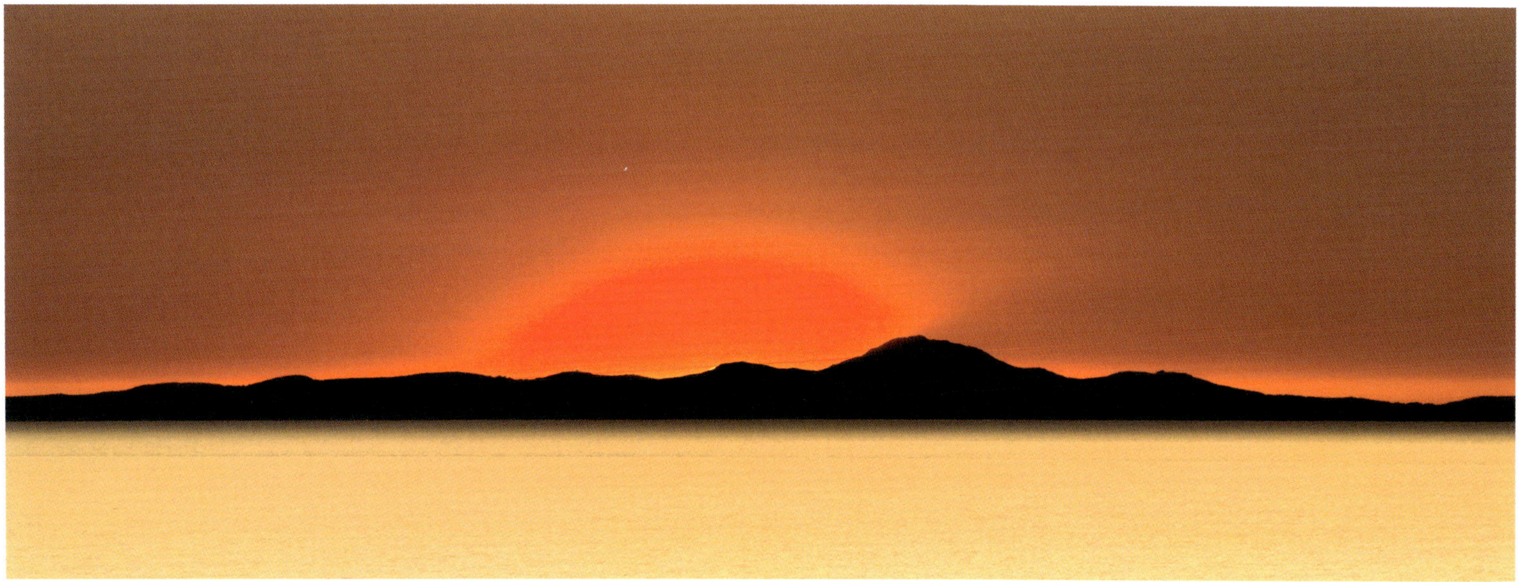

Index of Flowers Featured

NB Flower names have been standardised against the Botanical Society of the British Isles' *English Names of Wild Flowers* by J G Dony, S L Jury and F H Perring (2nd edition, 1986), and Cymdeithas Edward Llwyd's *Planhigion Blodeuol, Conwydd a Rhedyn* (first published in 2003).

Mike Alexander

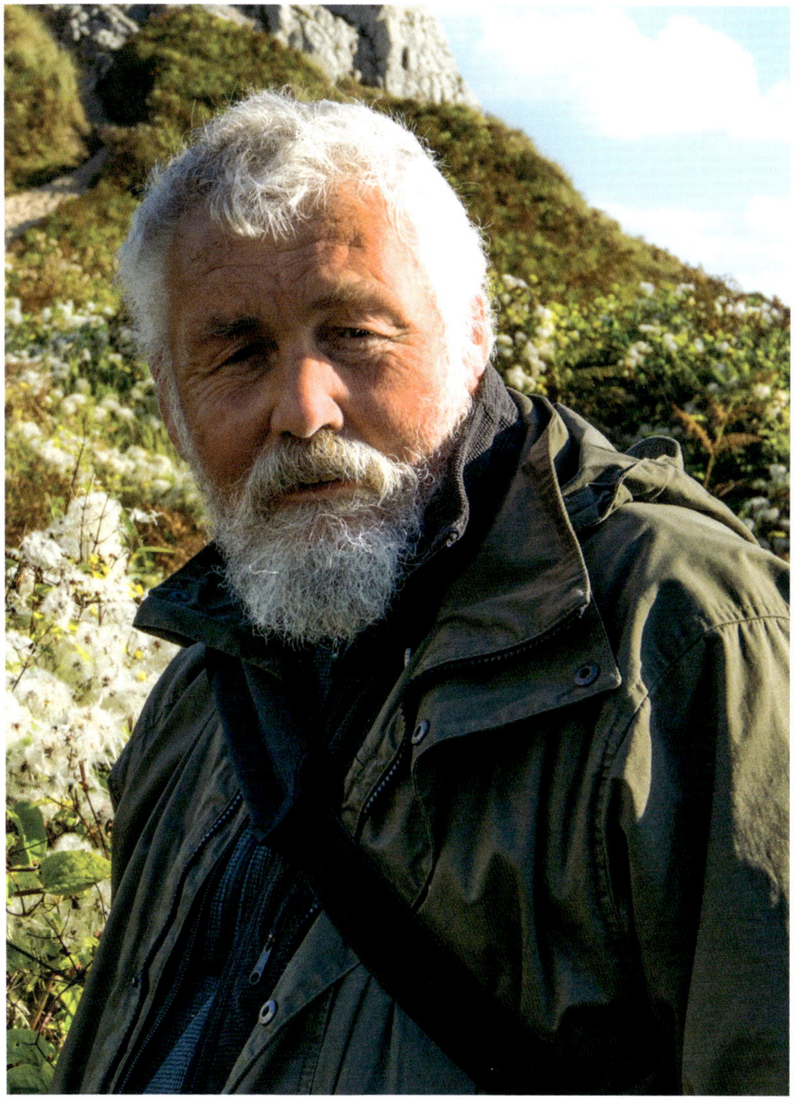

During the 1970s and 1980s, Mike Alexander spent ten years as Warden of Skomer, and he eventually became Chair of both the Wildlife Trust South and West Wales and the Islands Conservation Advisory Committee. He also worked for the Countryside Council for Wales, where his responsibilities included overseeing the management of all the National Nature Reserves in Wales, a position he held for over twenty years.

He was one of the founders, and later the Chair, of *Pori Natur a Threftadaeth* (PONT), an organisation established to build essential bridges between nature conservation and farmers in Wales.

For several decades, he was at the forefront of developing management planning for nature conservation, initially working with the main conservation organisations in Britain. Soon his work gained an international reputation and he became involved with countries as diverse as Costa Rica, Uganda, India, the Netherlands and Estonia. His book *Management Planning for Nature Conservation* (Springer, 2013) has become the standard international textbook on the subject and is now in its second edition.

He lectured at Bangor University, where he was involved in undergraduate and postgraduate teaching for almost thirty years, and at Birkbeck, University of London. He was elected a Fellow of both the Royal Society of Biology and the Chartered Institute of Ecology and Environmental Management.

He was also a very accomplished photographer, with his work appearing regularly in books and magazines such as *BBC Countryfile*.

Also by Mike Alexander:

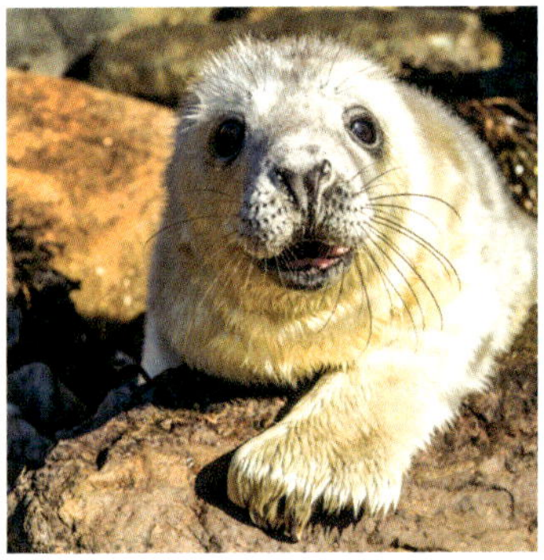

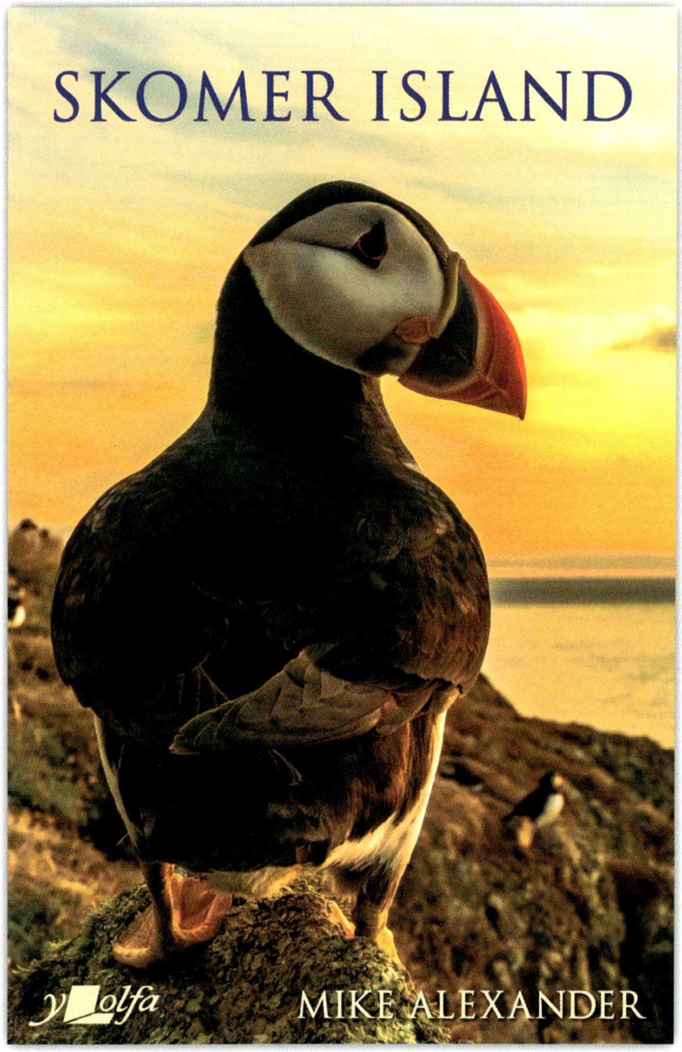

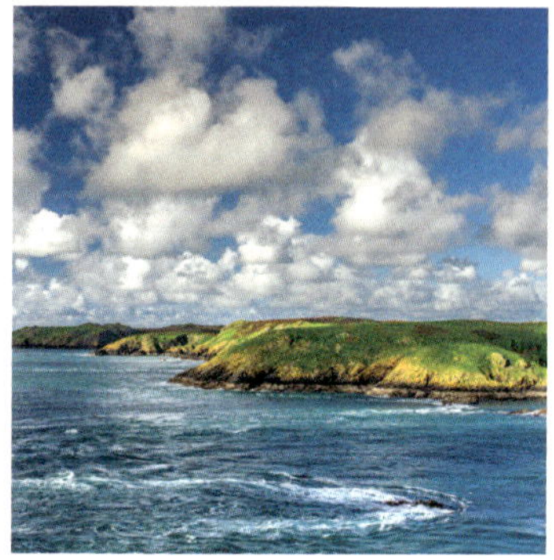

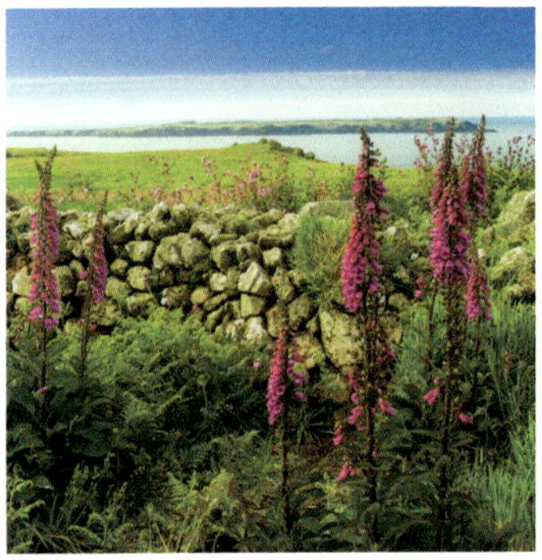

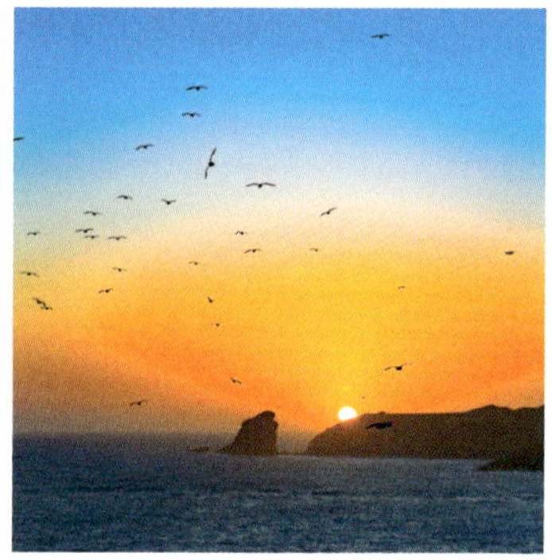

A detailed exploration of the history, landscape and wildlife of an incredibly special island, with hundreds of breathtaking colour photos. Forewords by Iolo Williams and Prof. Chris Perrins, FRS.

£35

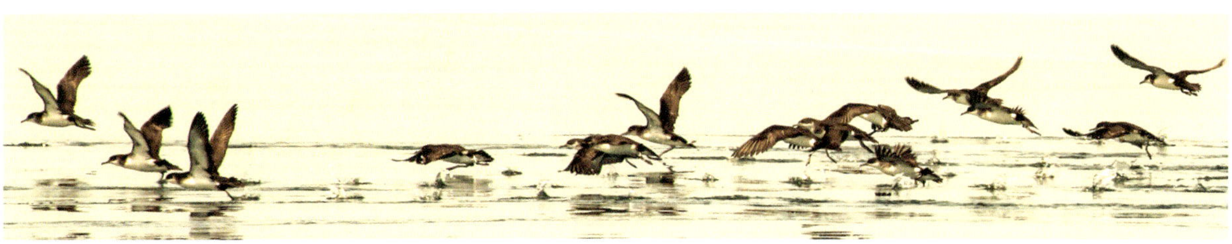